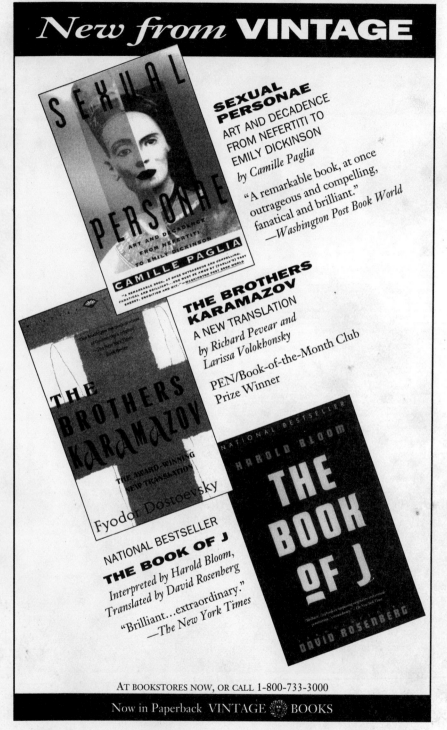

CY TWOMBLY

PRINTS 1952–1983
November 21–January 4, 1992

BILL TRAYLOR

January 9–February 8, 1992

CHRISTOPHER WILMARTH

February 15–March 21, 1992

HIRSCHL & ADLER MODERN

851 Madison Avenue
New York, New York 10021
212 744-6700
FAX 212 737-2614

CONJUNCTIONS

*Bi-Annual Volumes
of New Writing*

Edited by
Bradford Morrow

Contributing Editors
Walter Abish
John Ashbery
Mei-mei Berssenbrugge
Guy Davenport
Elizabeth Frank
William H. Gass
Susan Howe
Kenneth Irby
Robert Kelly
Ann Lauterbach
Patrick McGrath
Nathaniel Tarn
John Edgar Wideman

Bard College   *distributed by Random House, Inc.*

EDITOR: Bradford Morrow
SENIOR EDITOR: Susan Bell
ASSOCIATE EDITORS: Martine Bellen, Karen Kelly,
  Yannick Murphy, Kate Norment
MANAGING EDITOR: Marlene Hennessy
EDITORIAL ASSISTANTS: Patrick Doud, Jonathan Miller,
  Cathleen Shattuck

CONJUNCTIONS is published in the Spring and Fall of each year by Bard College, Annandale-on-Hudson, NY 12504. This issue is made possible in part with the generous funding of the Lannan Foundation and New York State Council on the Arts.

Editorial communications should be sent to 33 West 9th Street, New York NY, 10011. Unsolicited manuscripts cannot be returned unless accompanied by a stamped, self-addressed envelope.

Distributed by Random House.

SUBSCRIPTIONS. Send subscription order to CONJUNCTIONS, Box 115, Bard College, Annandale-on-Hudson, NY 12504. Single year (two volumes): $18.00 for individuals, $25.00 for institutions and overseas. Two years (four volumes): $32.00 for individuals; $45.00, for institutions and overseas. Patron subscription (lifetime): $500.00. Overseas subscribers please make payment by International Money Order. Back issues available at $10.00 per copy.

Printers: Edwards Brothers.
Typesetter: Bill White, Typeworks.

ISSN 0278-2324
ISBN 0-679-73774-X

Manufactured in the United States of America.

TABLE OF CONTENTS

EDITOR'S NOTE: Ten years — we made it. That this is our seventeenth rather than twentieth issue attests to the various reversals of fortune the project has experienced over those years; that we have survived the reversals attests to the hard work of many, many people who kept CONJUNCTIONS alive. I want to thank them all. They know who they are, and how deeply I've appreciated their help. Our various publishers — David Godine in particular who carried us through the crucial early-middle years; John Glusman who, when he was back at MacMillan, believed in the thing — I thank. I thank everyone at Bard College, and those at Random House, who are now bringing CONJUNCTIONS to light. The generosity of NEA, NYSCA, Hirschl & Adler Modern, the Jerome Foundation and recently the Lannan Foundation is truly appreciated. We've lost some very dear friends — Kenneth Rexroth, Coleman Dowell, Seth Morgan — and we've made so many new ones. Above all, the hundreds of writers and artists who have come together to make this workbook live we can all thank. As Jonathan Williams has written, *Onword* —!

Chinua Achebe

An Interview by Bradford Morrow

CHINUA ACHEBE AND I MET for the first time on Martin Luther King Day, this year. It was snowing hard and the trip from New York up the Saw Mill River and the Taconic was daunting. When I pulled into the little frozen-mud drive that led to his house near Annandale-on-Hudson, and was asked in, I felt an immediate sense of warmth — warmth both physical and of spirit. I'd heard this about Chinua and his family. I had heard that he was not just a man of immense literary greatness, but that he embodied a profoundly decent humanity.

Since that snowy day I have had the good fortune of passing many hours with him up at Bard College, where we each teach a class. I've since read and reread all his books, and count him without hesitation as one of my favorite writers. I think it is a shame that he — a hero in his native Nigeria, well-known throughout the rest of Africa, and in Europe — remains less appreciated in America. Many readers, myself quite obviously included, are committed to Chinua Achebe's vision and work. But it is clear to me that many more people would be well advised to examine the implications of his novels, his essays, his stories and poems — especially in this country, which is altogether too insulated from world-writers, as we might call them, writers who reach out beyond the imaginable and attempt to address life at its widest possible cast. From the publication of his first novel, *Things Fall Apart*, in 1958 (it's in its 46th printing, according to my Fawcett paperback), and on through the publication of *No Longer at Ease*, *Arrow of God*, *A Man of the People* and many other titles, Achebe has established himself as a major writer of political, social and historical conscience.

This talk was originally commissioned by Ginger Shore, of *Annandale* magazine — where it appears in different form — and I'd like to thank her and Kate Norment for all their help. We met first to do this interview on Monday, August 19, when both Hurricane

7

Bob was ravaging the East coast and the recent coup attempt was transpiring in the Soviet Union. Natural and political crises captured our attention. The hurricane knocked the power out, and our conversation had to be completed during a second session, on September 16.

BRADFORD MORROW: In your essay "The Truth of Fiction," you define a difference between fiction and what you term beneficent fiction. As I understand it, you equate fiction with superstition and reserve for literary fiction the term beneficent. In light of what extraordinary political events are happening today in the Soviet Union and given how central politics is to your novels, I wonder whether you think that there must always be a political element for beneficent fiction to be truly beneficent?

CHINUA ACHEBE: The notion of beneficent fiction is simply one way of defining storytelling as a creative component of human experience, human life, as something we have always done which has a positive purpose and a use. Whenever you say that, some people draw back. Why should art have a purpose and a use? But it seems to me that from the very beginning, stories have been meant to be enjoyed, to appeal to that part of us which enjoys good form and good shape and good sound. Still, I think that behind it all is a desire to make our experience in the world better, and once you talk about making things better you're talking about politics.

MORROW: How do you define politics?

ACHEBE: Anything to do with the organization of people in society. That is the definition. Whenever you have a handful of people trying to live harmoniously, you need some organization, some political arrangement that tells you what you can do and shouldn't do, tells you what enhances harmony and what brings about disruption.

MORROW: So there is a politics of family, politics of love relationships, politics of religion, politics of walking across the street.

ACHEBE: Exactly. What we're talking about is power, the way that power is used.

MORROW: I wonder, then, if my original question was diffused by how broad a definition of the word politics you apply. In your novels the interest in politics in its narrower meaning, i.e. state politics, is crucial. Do you think that a novel that does not in an overt way address state politics, the politics of organizing a country or culture, is less beneficent than a political novel — entertaining, perhaps, well-written even, but ultimately of lesser value?

ACHEBE: No, I wouldn't try to exclude any work. My purpose is not to exclude. If a book qualifies, I wouldn't exclude it because it doesn't deal with politics on the state or world level. I would simply say that's one way of telling a very complicated story. The story of the world is complex and one should not attempt to put everything into one neat definition, or into a box. But also I want to insist that nobody can come to me and say, your work is too political. My instinct is to talk about politics in my work and that is your instinct too. That is the sense in which *Come Sunday*, too, is a very powerful story. An effective, powerful and moving depiction of the modern world with its politics in all its various dimensions. One should not attempt to avoid that because of this superstition that politics somehow is inimical to art. There are some who cannot manage politics in their fiction, so let them *not*. But they must not insist that everybody else must avoid politics because of some superstition built up in recent times that defines art as only personal, introspective, away from the public arena. That's nonsense. Fiction in the West has suffered in recent times by that limitation. When I see a book like yours which is grappling with the big issues — violence, injustice, victimization — that also has the scope of the whole world, that goes from the center to the periphery and back, that's great. It's difficult to do, but difficulty is no reason not to do it.

MORROW: Given how thoroughly world politics in the last several years has charged and even changed the atmosphere of our personal lives, one wonders how it is possible that so many contemporary American novelists have, if not eschewed, at least marginalized, the political in their work.

ACHEBE: That's something I would like to understand myself. All I can say is that an apolitical stance was not there at the beginning of the novel. It is something that's happened during the last two hundred years. I don't think it has been a good thing for the world or for fiction. We can hope for the beginning of a reversal of that belief on the part of artists. I think they've been conned into apoliticism by those who have a vested interest in keeping us out. The emperor would prefer the poet to keep away from politics, the emperor's domain, so that he can manage things the way he likes. When the poet is pleased to do that, the emperor is happy and will pay him money to stay within his aesthetic domain. But you and I don't have to agree with the emperor. We have to say no. Our business involves the peace, happiness and harmony of not just people but the planet itself, the environment. How we live in the world is extremely important. How we see our relationship with the environment is important. If we see it in terms of conquest, if we go out and conquer Mount Everest, what are we doing? Even the language becomes significant. If somebody climbs a mountain, they *conquer* it.

MORROW: This subversion of nature has been one of the principal activities of mankind from the beginning, clearing forests, making roads, building cities. It should come as no shock that when one species has pushed out beyond what its natural population should be, the environment would suffer. It wasn't hard to do. Any animal could have done it. Ants could have done it. Plants could have done it. To stay on the subject of politics for one more moment, given the movements of former Communist bloc nations and Soviet republics toward independence, I wonder how you—who were an active participant in Biafra's bid for secession from Nigeria—view what's happening now. I also wanted to ask you how you view the lost dream of Biafra, what your vision was for Biafra, and where you think Biafra might have been today.

ACHEBE: At the time, Biafra was a necessity because it stood for the right of people to say no to victimization, to genocide. On the other side of the argument, there are those who think that the unity of a nation is paramount, that the boundaries of a nation are sacrosanct, that sort of thinking. For me, when you put one against the other, there's only one position to take. The sanctity of human life, the happiness of people and the right to pull out of any arrangement that doesn't suit them stands above all. But at the same time one lives in the practical world in which power and force are real and therefore if your desire to be left alone will lead to your extinction, lead to bloodshed like what we had, the loss of perhaps millions, we don't even know how many—

MORROW: And mostly civilians, of course.

ACHEBE: Civilians, yes. Then one ought to say, okay, we'll make peace.

MORROW: And yet the war in Biafra lasted for three years.

ACHEBE: Yes, nearly three years. Because it was a very bitter experience that led to it in the first place. And the big powers got involved in prolonging it. You see, we, the little people of the world, are constantly expendable. The big powers can play their games, and this is what happened. So in the end, when Biafra collapsed, we simply had to turn around and find a way to keep people alive. Some people said let's go into the forest and continue the struggle. That would have been suicidal, and I don't think anybody should commit suicide.

MORROW: Had the British not subjugated Nigeria, had World War II not taken the wind out of England's sails so that it would then decide to liberate the country it had only decades before colonialized, would the indigenous peoples of pre-Nigeria have felt the need to break up into different political units anyway? Is secession part of the natural process of the history of any nation or group of people?

ACHEBE: The problem with history is that once a whole lot of things have happened, it's hard to speculate. Nigeria was really a British creation and lasted under the British for no more than fifty years. At the end of British rule, we accepted the idea of Nigeria but the country wasn't working very well, which is why the whole Biafran thing came about. The British had such a vested interest in keeping this unit together, not for our benefit, but for their own. They—and not just the British, but the Soviet Union and the Americans as well—were interested in holding it together because of the possibilities of commercial exploitation. What they didn't understand is that if people are unhappy, commerce is meaningless. What would Biafra have become? We wanted the kind of freedom, the kind of independence, which we were not experiencing in Nigeria. Nigeria was six years free from the British, but in all practical ways its mind, its behavior, the way its leaders looked up to the British, the way that British advisers continued to run the country, worried the more radical elements in our society. Most importantly, the fact that a government stood by while parts of the population were murdered at will in sections of the country went against our conception about what independence from the British should mean. So, Biafra was an attempt to establish a nation where there would be true freedom, true independence.

MORROW: But do you really believe that there is any nation on earth that enjoys true freedom and independence?

ACHEBE: Some do better than others. Let me give one more dimension of what we were hoping to do in Biafra, and what this freedom and independence was supposed to be like. We were told, for instance, that technologically we would have to rely for a long, long time on the British and the West for everything. European oil

11

companies insisted that oil technology was so complex that we would never ever in the next five hundred years be able to figure it out. Now, we thought that wasn't true. In fact, we learned to refine our own oil during the two and a half years of the struggle because we were blockaded. We were able to show that it was possible for an African people entirely on their own to refine oil. We were able to show that Africans could pilot their planes. There is a story, perhaps apocryphal, that a Biafran plane landed in another African country, and the pilot and all the crew came out, and there was not a white man among them. This other country — which is a stooge of France — couldn't comprehend a plane landing without any white people. They said, "Where is the pilot? Where are the white people?" and arrested the crew, presuming a rebellion in the air. There was enough talent, enough education in Nigeria for us to be able to manage our affairs more independently than we were doing. Your question as to whether any nation is truly independent: the answer is no. You can manage certain things, but you do rely on others and it's a good thing the whole world should be linked in interdependence. As human beings you can be independent but as members of society you are related to your fellows. In the same way, nations can manage certain affairs on their own, and yet be linked with others.

MORROW: You were born at a particularly interesting moment in that the culture of your forefathers was being infiltrated by an alien culture. It was a pivotal historical moment. Your father was a Christian convert while his parents and grandparents were still tribal. Members of your family had a direct memory of pre-colonial society. You then were able to experience the impact of the Anglican church on Nigeria, the imposition of English on Nigeria as a centralizing language. It occurs to me that it would be very difficult for anyone who wasn't born at precisely that moment to have written the novels you've written, to have so convincingly depicted the lives of Okonkwo in *Things Fall Apart*, of the priest Ezeulu and his friend Akuebue, as well as Captain Winterbottom, in *Arrow of God*, of Obi Okonkwo in *No Longer at Ease*. You're on record as having said that the choice of writing in English rather than in Igbo was strictly a practical one. I'm wondering, though, how it's possible for you not to feel any bitterness about this. There is a painful moment in *No Longer at Ease* when Obi, homesick for Umuofia, resentful about having to study English in London, thinks "It was humiliating to have to speak to one's countryman in a foreign language, especially in the presence of the proud owners of that language. They would naturally assume that one had no language of one's own." Do you feel that you could have written an even better book than *Things Fall Apart* if you'd written it in your native language? Do you think the book would have had more impact on your countrymen had it been composed in Igbo?

ACHEBE: The answer is no. I have no doubt at all about that. My countrymen now are Nigerians. Nigerians as a whole are not Igbo-speaking. The Igbos are just one of the major ethnic groups. If I'd written *Things Fall Apart* in the Igbo language, only the Igbo would have had access; not the Yorubas, not the Hausas, not the Ibibio, not to mention all the other Africans, not the Kikuyus, the Luos, etc., all over the continent who read the book. *Things Fall Apart* has made a wide impact over the last thirty years. This I know for a fact because I've traveled through the continent. So it would not have been the same if I had written it in Igbo. But this is not the only argument one could raise for writing a book in one language or another. There are some people who would say even if only a few people would have had access to it, it still would have been preferable to write it in Igbo because you would have given the power of your talent to an African language, to help to create a new literature. The answer to that would depend upon what kind of person you are and what you think literature is there to do. I have no regrets, especially since I also write in the Igbo language. I have written several things in Igbo. If I thought that a novel in the Igbo language would serve a certain purpose, I would do it.

MORROW: Have your novels been translated into Igbo?

ACHEBE: No, not yet. Which shows, perhaps, that we are not ready for the novel in the Igbo language. I've written some poetry in Igbo and intend to do other things. But no matter what, I can assure you that the literature we have created during the last forty years in Africa had enormous influence which would have been much less if we had all retreated into our own little languages.

MORROW: We once talked about the work of Ben Okri, a young Nigerian writer who lives in London. What other African writers are writing books that you find valuable? If a student interested in learning about African literature were to approach you as a complete tabula rasa, where would you have them begin, who would you have them read?

ACHEBE: One way to answer that would be to look at what I teach

13

in my African literature courses. I concentrate on fiction, if only because to do poetry and drama as well would be too unwieldy. First, what I want to do is demonstrate that Africa is a continent. I find, traveling around the world, that people talk about France, Italy and Africa — and that's when they're being generous. I've met people who think of Africa as if it were Dutchess County. Africa is a huge continent with a tremendous variety and diversity of cultures, languages and so on. The way I show this is to give samples from different areas and histories of Africa. Now, in doing that, I'm limited by the question of language. I use books either originally written in English or translated into English. I begin with West Africa, an area in which one of the most dynamic literatures is being created and which happens also to be my home base. Then I sweep north to include an area of Africa which some people don't even know is in Africa — Egypt. Many people think of Egypt as being part of the Middle East, but it's always been in Africa.

MORROW: But who are the writers you most admire?

ACHEBE: In the Arabic north, I use Mahfouz. He's an effective writer of the short novel, though he belongs to the old European trained and educated generation. Some of the best younger and more radical writers from this area are women — Alifa Rifaat, El Saadawi, who address the conflict, the dynamic between men and women in the Islamic society, which is very patriarchal and rigid. From West Africa, I would include Amos Tutuola, who represents closely the link btween the oral tradition and the written. I would include from Senegal one of the finest colonial novels, written originally in French: Cheikh Hamidou Kane's *Ambiguous Adventure*. There is also Ferdinand Oyono's *Houseboy*, set in colonial Cameroun. Then I would go south. Nadine Gordimer is sometimes not thought of as African, but she is. She is writing out of an intensely African experience. You can see already what a diverse kind of group this is. I would go to eastern Africa and read Nuruddin Farah from Somalia. I would want the student to understand that Africans aren't funny people, that what's happening in Africa is happening to real people. One does this by showing them good stories written about human beings living their lives — a different culture, but always human beings.

MORROW: One of the linguistic building blocks that you use to great effect in your early novels, both in the dialogue and the actual narrative, is aphorisms, proverbs, sayings. These proverbs — one of my favorites, for instance, is "When we hear a house has fallen, do we ask if the ceiling fell with it?"—have both a charming colloquial feel to them and are rhetorically sophisticated. They are synergetic in their given contexts but they are more powerfully evocative than one at first notices on the surface. A little phrase like "The fly that sits on the mound of dung will still never be as big as that mound" is strangely supercharged because of its historical context and social implications. In America, or in any country where the ritual of families telling stories to each other has been all but lost, where the people of a culture are becoming more nonverbal—after all, why speak when the television can speak for you—where do you think the novel's future lies?

ACHEBE: I think that words have a magic, that human situations create a magic, that you can capture that extra dimension by placing ideas side by side. One shouldn't bemoan the fact that television and the media have come into our lives. It's possible to see them as just another source of information. I think that for me it's definitely been an advantage to be able to invoke the culture of my past and the language that went with it while dealing with a contemporary situation. Now that advantage does not exist anymore really, even in my own society; its power is much reduced for those who are becoming writers today. But I think every generation, if it looks hard enough, will find the resource that it can use. What is not rich is provincialism. If one didn't realize the world was complex, vast and diverse, one would write as if the world were one little county and this would make us poor and we would have impoverished the novel. The reality of today, different as it is from the reality of my society one hundred years ago, is and can be important if we have the energy and the inclination to challenge it, to go out and look for it. The real danger is the tendency to retreat into the obvious, the tendency to be frightened by the richness of the world and to clutch what we always have understood. This way we very soon run out of energy and produce maybe elegant—elegantly tired—fiction.

MORROW: Then your take on minimalism is not a positive one.

ACHEBE: No.

MORROW: Minimalism is not often linked with the word elegant. Minimalists, so far as I understand their aesthetic, believe themselves to be championing the spare in the face of purple prose, think of themselves as lean and mean. I'm not against tight, clean writing. Indeed, that is what we strive for. But there is a difference between lean and anorectic. What you're suggesting is that minimalists are attenuated, over-polished, refined, over-refined.

ACHEBE: Refined into extinction.

MORROW: There is something very human and lovely about the novel's tradition as a self-defining form. More than any other art form, the novel at its best behaves much like life in its capacity for creative, energetic mistakes. There are no fixed rules, finally, the novelist must follow. And this has always been the tradition. I think of Henry Fielding's *Tom Jones* and the Old Man of the Hill asides which have disturbed critics for centuries because even in the middle of all of Tom's picaresque experiences those crotchety rambling asides never made much formal sense. They look like a gaffe to a critic who thinks that there is a rule book for novelists. For me, the Old Man of the Hill voice only makes more great Fielding's novel, in part because it's so unexpected and so outrageous that it throws into relief the rest of the action of the book. Not to mention *Tristram Shandy*, which is nothing short of an eighteenth-century primer on how to break not just the rules but the idea that there *are* rules. So, in the earliest phase of the novel, you already have our ancestors setting out a course of formal resistance.

ACHEBE: And of formal possibilities.

MORROW: The novel is a germ, always growing. At its best, it will always remain an open form. I've heard recently the term maximalism offered as an antidote to minimalism. But what I wonder is, has there ever been a period in the history of the novel in which maximalism wasn't in effect?

ACHEBE: No, maximalism has always been with us.

MORROW: What are your favorite novels?

ACHEBE: As a matter of fact, you've mentioned a couple of them. I would just add the Russians — writers who went out and grabbed the world.

MORROW: Henry James would not be your cup of tea?

ACHEBE: No, I don't think so. By that time in the novel, form had become important to fiction. And there's a purpose to that. I'm not discounting the contribution of the classical mode to the art of the novel. But once consideration of form goes beyond a certain point, it becomes a limitation on the imagination. It might help half a dozen works, but after that there's very little left. I think the point you were making a moment ago is important. The novel is not a summit. It came out of this need to break out, and it broke out at points when the world was exploding. And the best examples are those located at points of explosion, not when things are settled, or have simmered down.

MORROW: In your essay "Named for Victoria, Queen of England," you describe growing up Christian but also being drawn to participating in your uncle's "heathen" festival meals where his family subscribed to the old religion which was idolatrous, pantheistic and anything but Anglican. It's interesting to note that far from being cast into a spiritual agony, you say your curiosity was appeased by this. So there were two religions that guided you as a boy. I'm curious what importance religion played in your growing up and becoming a novelist.

ACHEBE: That's a very big and important question. My beginnings were clearly influenced by religion. In fact, my whole artistic career was probably sparked off by this tension between the Christian religion of my parents, which we followed in our home, and the retreating, older religion of my ancestors, which fortunately for me was still active outside my home. This tension created sparks in my imagination. I wasn't questioning in an intellectual way because I was too young. But without questioning, things can still happen to you. My uncle being there and being available was an enriching experience. I wouldn't give up anything for that, including my own narrow, if you like, Christian background. It was extremely useful that we prayed and read from the Bible and sang hymns night and day. I wasn't uncomfortable with any of that. To be interested in my uncle's religion wasn't to be rebelling. It was simply part of a very rich childhood. I was part of a lucky generation, to be planted at a crossroads, a time when the meeting of two cultures produced something of worth. Now it's impossible to grow up having the same faith, belief and attitude toward religion that I had as a child. Of course, I did have long periods of doubt and uncertainty, and had a period where I objected strongly to the certitude of Christianity — I am the Way, the Truth and the Life. When I was little, that didn't mean anything to me, but later on I was able to compare it with the rather careful and far more humble attitude of my indigenous religion in which because they recognized different gods they also recognized that you might be friendly with this god and fall out with the other one. You might worship Udo to perfection and still be killed by Ogwugwu. Such sayings and proverbs are far more valuable to me as a human being in understanding the complexity of the world than the narrow, doctrinaire, self-righteous attitude of the Christian faith. This other religion, which is ambivalent, is far more artistically satisfying to me.

MORROW: Just as is the ambivalence in the form of the novel we

were talking about. How do you feel about religion now, personally?
ACHEBE: Well, I'm still in a state of uncertainty, but I'm not worried anymore. I'm not looking for the answers, because I believe now that we will never know. I believe now that what we have to do is make our passage through life as meaningful and as useful as possible. I think our contribution to the creation of the world is important, and I take my bearing in this from a creation story of the Igbo people in which there is a conversation between God and humanity. They are discussing the state of the environment — what to do to lift man from the state of wandering, the state of animals, to becoming human, i.e., agricultural. And this is embedded in a story, a parable. Man is sitting disconsolate on an anthill one morning. God asks him what the matter is and man replies that the soil is too swampy for the cultivation of the yams which God has directed him to grow. God tells him to bring in a blacksmith to dry the soil with his bellows. The contribution of humanity to this creation is so important. God could have made the world perfect if he had wanted. But he made it the way it is. So that there is a constant need for us to discuss and cooperate to make it more habitable, so the soil can yield, you see. That seems to me to be enough to occupy my time and thoughts, rather than wondering, Does this exist? or, Which came first, the egg or the chicken? One can be involved in those questions forever. They are things that we will never know. It is the things that we can do that seem to me to be far more important.
MORROW: Given mankind's penchant for making mischief with the little knowledge it does have, perhaps it's best we don't know.
ACHEBE: Yes. I wouldn't even want to know. It's just as well not to know because I believe that ambivalence is a more truthful position than having an attitude that there isn't even anything to worry about.
MORROW: You sound like a Buddhist to me, Chinua.
ACHEBE: I probably am!
MORROW: When I was working on the Music Issue of *Conjunctions*, there was a lot of talk about World Music, about the system of communications now being so developed and sophisticated in the world, so advanced among different cultures and peoples, that music — the universal language — has now become deeply inter-linked. As a result of this you hear the influence of Moroccan music on Norwegian jazz composition, or the influence of Indonesian music on American classical composition, or the influence of Indian

scales and rhythms on British pop music, and so forth. Do you think that there is chance for something like a World Literature?

ACHEBE: Yes, as long as we don't rush into it by silencing the less loud manifestations of literature. This is another way of stating the fact of what I consider to be my mission in life. That my kind of storytelling has to add its voice to this universal storytelling before we can say, "Now we've heard it all." I'm worried when somebody from one particular tradition stands up and says, "The novel is dead, the story is dead." I find this to be unfair, to put it mildly. You told your own story, and now you're announcing the novel is dead. Well, I haven't told mine yet. Therefore, we must hear all the stories. That would be the first thing. And by hearing all the stories we will find in fact points of contact and communication, and the world story, the Great Story, will have a chance to develop. That's the only precaution I would suggest — that we not rush into announcing the arrival of this internatioinal, this great world story, simply based on our knowledge of one, or a few traditions. For instance, in America there is really very little knowlege of the literature of the rest of the world. Of the literature of Latin America, yes. But that's not all that different in inspiration from that of America, or Europe. One must go further. You don't even have to go further in terms of geography — you can go to the American Indians and listen to their poetry.

MORROW: This ignorance among Americans of other literatures of the world seems to me to be the result of attitude. And I wonder whether the attitude that has created this doesn't have at least something to do with racism, with an acculturated sense of racial superiority. One can't read your essay identifying the underlying racism of Conrad's vision in *Heart of Darkness* without being dumbfounded. The racism is so clearly there, and yet we missed it. How do we create an awareness of racist elements that are present in other Western classics besides the works of Conrad? How do we educate readers to identify racism in a work of fiction, say, or poetry?

ACHEBE: It is difficult because there is a strong resistance to what needs to be done. You can understand the reason why. People have been brought up to believe in certain things, to admire certain books. All their lives, as with their parents and grandparents, these things have been canonized. So when somebody comes up to them and says there is racism in this book, the other person thinks, "Well if there is racism in this book, I should have seen it. But,

19

since I didn't see it, there can be no racism there." Or else he says, "If there is racism in this book and I didn't see it, it means, perhaps, that I am a racist." These are positions that many people are not ready to contemplate, so they shut off, and that's why this problem is so difficult. I've had some interesting encounters since that essay of mine came out. I should say, in all fairness, that many people have come to me and said, "I'm sorry, I didn't know, I really didn't see this. Thank you very much." But there have also been people who have been furious, who have said, "How dare you? This is nonsense. This is obtuse." But it is a battle which must always be fought, and we must push on. I can't see an easy end to it, but while it's going on conversions are made. And that's all you can ask, that some people come to these books now with a different awareness, and that they may carry that awareness to other things that they see or read, because all we are saying is do not treat any members of the human race as if they were less than human. That is the minimum of human respect which every person deserves and is entitled to. They may be different, they may look different, their cultures may be different, but they are all people. Once you accept that, the battle is won. I'm not suggesting that any books be pulled out and banned. That, in fact, would be meaningless. These books should be read. Especially those that are famous. But people should read them with an open eye, and the consequences of this would show in other things, how we relate to our neighbors and to the rest of the world.

MORROW: And the experience of reading, say, Evelyn Waugh's *A Handful of Dust*, in which the same kind of thinking is operative as in Conrad's book, though the dark continent of savages happens to be South America rather than Africa, need not in some ways be altered. That is to say, we can appreciate its structure, the language, and in many ways the story itself, even while we comprehend that Waugh was subject to a somewhat racist vantage point, like a mild fever. The presence of sentiments which we find untenable in a work of art can also help us to define for ourselves the author's culture, the world in which he or she grew up and lived. In this way, a novel, or any work of art, can become historical, an aesthetic document that mirrors, no matter how distanced the individual artist might have been from his community, a cultural milieu. Literature remains living if the reader is as alive to its faults, its humanity, as he is alive to its perfections. I've always felt that the best readers are those who read a book as if it is being written at the moment, right there in their imaginations. Joyce and Virginia Woolf and others have talked about the ideal reader being someone who completely gives himself over to the writer, and that to me is where the trouble begins. I'd prefer a more vigorous reader, not negative or resistant, necessarily, but someone who brings their own skills and knowledge to the document. And here is what we're agreeing on—that yes, there's no need to suppress any works by anyone. One must simply stay wide awake to all the subtle levels of discourse, of rhetoric, aesthetics, of politics, emotions. Only then is literature valuable and educational. In a way it has to do with learning to appreciate the otherness of others.

ACHEBE: I think what you called a mild fever—I like that expression—there are symptoms of that in a lot of literature. Some extremely mild. The reason is that the mindset that created the works is not created by the artist—it is something in the cultural environment, the educational environment, in their upbringing. So without being aware—they were not necessarily trying to hurt anybody.

MORROW: In other words, we are learning more about Oxford, Mississippi, as a whole than we are about Faulkner specifically when we read his novels.

ACHEBE: Exactly. Faulkner was reflecting the environment in which he worked in a unique Faulknerian way.

MORROW: So that's a part of the beneficence of literature, that he *would* reflect his time?

ACHEBE: Yes, and what is important in the long run is not really what Conrad thought, or Faulkner thought, but how today's people can read their work and see nothing wrong in the way their characters were relating to the world, the complex world of races, a world of peoples. How can our world function with that kind of blind spot—that's the issue. And that's why people are angry about it. They feel threatened that you are showing them up, and they don't want any of it. But they need to be able to operate and function more creatively, more usefully, in the complexity of the final years of the twentieth century.

MORROW: What is racism like in Nigeria? Are British whites the object of racist hatred?

ACHEBE: Racism is not a problem in Nigeria. It does not occur to Nigerians to describe anybody as non-black!

MORROW: It seems to me that racism has always had more behind it than skin pigmentation. Economics, politics, religion fueled all this, too. Class hatred and racism are twins, aren't they? They're joined at the scrawny hip.

ACHEBE: I think it has to do with all of that. It has to do with *difference*. Power — military, economic, and so on, all these were determining factors in the end. And we, in the colonial situation, were the victims in the end. We were the victims. If there is any anti-white feeling in Nigeria, what you find is that it is usually a response to something that was there before. It's what Jean-Paul Sartre called anti-racist racism. That doesn't make it any more pleasant but one ought to know where it's coming from. We are not committed racists in my country. I don't know of any instances in recent times in which you can cite someone going out, for instance, and shooting someone because he is different. If someone does, I'd like to hear it. Racism, in the sense of really bitter hatred against people of another color, does not exist in Nigeria.

MORROW: What are your thoughts on new developments in other art forms in American culture besides literature, for example, young black Americans' impact on film — directors like Spike Lee and John Singleton, director of *Boyz N the Hood* — and on the rise of importance of rap music in this country, music which restores narratives, ghetto narratives, race narratives, often violent narratives to what was before a trend toward anemia in rock lyrics?

ACHEBE: It's interesting. It seems to me, in fact, that this is a continuation of what was going on from the very beginning. The difference is that now people are ready to acknowledge the sources of what is happening. The black presence in America has always contributed in a rich way, in music, in poetry, in speech. It was never acknowledged openly, though, that this was a contribution from the black sector of the population. Coming as I do from Africa, far away, it seemed to me, from the beginning, I could hear overtones in American music from Africa. Like listening to Louis Armstrong, I could hear the masquerades, the masked spirits, talking, singing, the way he made this Western European instrument sound.

MORROW: How so?

ACHEBE: Well, the sounds were, for me, an attempt to transfer into a new form and a new instrument sounds that came from very ancient music in Africa. I don't know enough about music to be more specific, but this is how it struck me. It sounded to me like the voice of the masked spirits. I'm not sure that Louis Armstrong — since he is the example I give — was aware of this. It was something that stayed in the black community, that was brought over. Whether they were conscious of this or not, it remained part of their life.

MORROW: When Louis Armstrong or any other jazz musician takes a solo, he is creating a narrative of sorts — an abstract narrative, granted — and there is a theme, a development, you build through a crescendo, perhaps, to a climax, and then take it back out. It occurs to me that the blues, in America, has as one of its primary accomplishments an ability to combine the abstraction of music with story —

ACHEBE: Which is events —

MORROW: Yes, and this is why I bring up rap. Because it seems to me that after the so-called British invasion in the sixties, most song lyrics took a downward turn, and what was being narrated in the lyrics was diminished, became even maudlin, codified, starched. Rap music at its best restores stories to popular music, and in this way it is like the blues. I wonder if that's what you are hearing in jazz, too — stories.

ACHEBE: That's one part of this general feeling I'm trying to express, which is somewhat nebulous. Art and community in Africa are clearly linked. Art is not something that has been so purified and refined that it's almost gone out of real life, the vitality of the street, like European art and academic art tend to be. In Africa, the tendency is to keep art involved with the people. Among my own Igbo people it is clearly emphasized that art must never be allowed to escape into the rarefied atmosphere, but must remain active in the lives of people. Ordinary people must be brought in, a conscious effort must be made to bring in the life of the village in this art.

MORROW: And this is exemplified in the masquerades?

ACHEBE: Yes. The masked figures are the representatives of the ancestors. They represent the link between the living and the dead. Therefore during the masquerade they are the highest authorities, and human beings become subsidiary. They speak with the authority of the past, of the culture, of the ancestors, of the history of the people.

MORROW: So there is a fusion of art and religion that takes place.

ACHEBE: Art, religion, everything, the whole of life is embodied in the art of the masquerade. It is dynamic. It is not allowed to remain stationary. For instance, museums are unknown among the Igbo people. They do not even contemplate the idea of having something like a canon: "This is how this sculpture should be made, and once it's made it should be venerated." No, the Igbo people want to create these things again and again, and every generation has a chance to execute its own model of art. So there's no undue respect for what the last generation did, because if you do that too much it means that there is no need for me to do anything, because it's already been done. The Igbo culture says no condition is permanent. You must go on. Even those who are not trained artists are brought in to participate in these artistic festivals in which the whole life of the world is depicted. The point I'm trying to make is that there is the need to bring life back into art by bringing art into life, so that the two are mixed. And rap music does that precisely. The purists may say rap is no good, it's too direct, but in fact the highest examples of it will stand out, in the end, as really significant. In a novel such as Amos Tutuola's *The Palm-Wine Drinkard*, you can see the same thing. There is no attempt to draw a line between what is permissible and what is not, what is possible and what is not possible, what is new and what is old. In a story that is set in the distant past you suddenly see a telephone, a car, a bishop — all kinds of things that don't seem to tie in. But in fact what you have is the whole life of the community, not just the community of humans but the community of ancestors, the animal world, of trees, and so on — everything plays a part.

MORROW: So the Igbo artist is to you the ideal artist?

ACHEBE: I think so, yes. It's not the only way of looking at art, but it's an important, positive way.

MORROW: I'm reminded of the concept of *musée sans murs*, where everything in the world has art as a part of its nature and fabric. Except that in the case of the Igbo, there is no need for a manifesto that would storm the museum walls, since there are none. And what of these new filmmakers?

ACHEBE: They are providing a welcome injection of vitality into an art form that is powerful but is in danger of becoming stereotyped and flat and repetitive and dead and unrelated to the needs of society. When you talk about art in the context of the needs of society, some people flinch, thinking you are introducing something far too common for a discussion of art. Art shouldn't be concerned with purpose and reason and need, they say. These are improper. But if you go back to the dawn of man, making art was not so as to escape from himself. It was to make his passage through life easier.

MORROW: Easier in what way?

ACHEBE: There are bottlenecks in life, impossible situations, there are things that cannot be explained and if you think about them too long you get into a state of depression. You can't make this or that happen, the futility of death, and all that. How do you deal with all these things, and still go on living? The way man attempted to deal with this was to create, to create stories and visions so that he could handle difficult, intractable problems.

MORROW: Two questions. One, why should we trust the artist's version of reality, of good, evil, how communities should work, any more than that of anyone else in the community?

ACHEBE: It's not a question of trust. The artist presents his version. He has no power to impose it. He gives it, and it is up to the community to use it or not. The artist is not an emperor. He does not have a police force or prisons.

MORROW: The second question is this. Is there a moment in a man or woman's life where art becomes no longer necessary, where the bottlenecks disappear sufficiently so that art becomes useless?

ACHEBE: I don't think so. Art is like a second handle on reality, on our life and the world. That is an alternative that is provided by art. It does not cancel life, it does not eliminate life. It gives us this possibility for contrast, even for escape. So if a life is going to be meaningful — I don't see a point where life is going to be simpler; I think we can dream of such a period, but I doubt that it will come — it is our destiny that we must wrestle with difficult problems. The very nature of life is struggle. That's why this need for an alternative — something that can be used as a foil — will always be a necessity to a life well-lived.

MORROW: I'm curious what you think about the popularity — enormous and continuing popularity — of *Things Fall Apart*, given what a dark book it is finally. There is a darkness in the vision that seems to me less often commented upon than it might be. This is true of the other novels as well. How do you reconcile your audience's response to the novels as inspirational with the darkness of vision that informs them?

ACHEBE: Well, the popularity of *Things Fall Apart* in my own society can be explained simply, because my people are seeing themselves virtually for the first time in the story. The story of our position in the world had been told by others. But somehow that story was not anything like the way it seemed to us from where we stood. So this was the first time we were seeing ourselves, as autonomous individuals, rather than half-people, or as Conrad would say, "rudimentary souls." We are not rudimentary at all, we are full-fledged souls. In trouble, in trouble. There's no question about that. Life is full of trouble. We don't live in a world in which we marry and live happily ever after. That's only in fairy tales. This dark side is real. Whatever experience we have in the world confirms that this dark side exists. This bitterness is there. No matter how lucky one is you will at one point encounter this side of life. This is the side that philosophers and religious thinkers have not succeeded in explaining. Why do the righteous suffer? Why does a good cause fail? Why if there is order and pattern in the world shouldn't goodness succeed and evil fail? It doesn't work out that way. It is a puzzle, but it is there. That, it would seem to me, is the reason.

MORROW: I suppose it is as good a moment as any to ask you how you are doing after your automobile accident. Has the accident changed your view of life in any way? How are you doing, and what are your plans for the future as a writer and as a man?

ACHEBE: Actually, it was almost as if everything I had ever done in life was a preparation for my accident. I had never been in doubt about this dark side of life. But it was almost as if it were academic, something I was told. I knew it by reputation, by rumor. The difficult part of life, however, I had not experienced. Little disappointments along the way, but this accident was the real thing. The real break in my life. It was, of course, very severe. I was near death. It was touch and go. And in the end I was paralyzed in the legs. Some people in the hospital said to me, "Why should such a thing happen to you?" And I said, "Why not?" Those to whom this sort of thing happens, did they commit any sort of crime? Not necessarily. That is what our experience of the world has been from the beginning. So when my friends ask why do the righteous suffer — making me out to be one of the righteous — I can only say this is a question that has never been answered. Children are born deformed. What crime did they commit? I've been very lucky. I walked for sixty years. So what does it matter that I can't for my last few years. There are people who never walked at all. That's one way of looking at it. But when you begin to wrestle with the physical problems of not being able to get up and move, and all kinds of other things, and having to learn your body again, that's a terrific difference to what I'd known, and I'm still dealing with that.

MORROW: I suppose it is an opportunity, in a way.

ACHEBE: It *is* an opportunity. It's a lesson. It's so much. It is an *enrichment*. I've learned so much. I've learned how much we depend on each other. My wife, who is a professional in her own right, and was carrying on her life as an academic, was summoned to the hospital — and at that moment she simply dropped her own life and came to me in England and has been with me since. That's an incredible sacrifice. Sometimes I think, if it had been the other way around, would I have been able to do it? So, one learns as one suffers, and one is richer. The good will of the world is something I had never experienced in the same way before. The world was there at my bedside. Messages, flowers. So this accident added a new dimension to what I'd known before. The other question is how much work I can get out of it. There is the problem of not being physically able to do as many hours as I used to. There is the business of lying down, taking breaks, that wasn't there before. This is something I'm learning to do, also. I have to use whatever life I have to a good purpose.

MORROW: I understand that you'll be writing your memoirs. Do you have other books in mind as well?

ACHEBE: I have always had a number of projects in mind. I would have started working on a novel by now. The idea of the memoir was always there, but it seemed to have become more urgent after this experience in which one realizes how fragile life is. Of course, as long as one is alive there is work to do.

MORROW: What is the idea for the novel?

ACHEBE: It is based on an incident that took place in my village at the turn of the century, when the women took their stand in the political arena. This is something which usually did not happen. Our mythology tells of times when men fail, and women take the reins of power and get the world through the crisis, the bad patch. There are references in myth and proverbs about the power of women. Mother is Supreme is a common name among Igbo people: *Nne ka.* There is no name, Father is Supreme. God is Supreme— *Chuku ka*—is another common name. So you see exactly where mother is placed. You can speak of mother and God in the same breath. But the story I want to use in the novel is fascinating. It was at the beginning of the colonial period, and women had not been involved too much in politics with the British up until then. Women would over the next fifty years play critical roles. But I see this first incident, in which the Igbo women stand together against the British, as a sort of full dress rehearsal for the important roles they would play in Nigeria later in the century.

MORROW: Have you started it? It sounds a little like you're already well into it.

ACHEBE: No, this is the way I work. The germ of the story grows over years in my mind until I begin.

MORROW: When did you get it in mind to write novels?

ACHEBE: I didn't think of becoming a writer for a long time because I didn't grow up in a society in which there were writers. But I did live in a society in which there were stories. I began to read European novels, and the ones that worried me were those that were supposed to be about us, about Africa. People wonder why I go back again and again to Conrad. His were some of the books that were available, and the stories he told of the Europeans wandering among savages bothered me. In the beginning it wasn't clear to me that I was one of those savages, but eventually it did become clear.

MORROW: So what you're saying is that you were motivated less by wanting to emulate any given novelist than by a need to fight back, in a way, and correct the portraits of Africa that European novelists were making.

ACHEBE: To oppose the discourse in those novels. It was a moral obligation. When I saw a good sentence, saw a good phrase, of course I wanted to imitate. But the story itself—there weren't any models. If they were not saying something that was antagonistic toward us, they weren't concerned about us. I read Dickens, and all the books that were read in the English public schools. But these were novels and poems about snow, and daffodils, and things I didn't know anything about. So it was a very special kind of inspiration that motivated me.

MORROW: How do you feel about your work, looking at it as a whole?

ACHEBE: Well, it's an effort to tell my own story. And I'm satisfied that at least I've broken through, been a pioneer, made a start. The performance itself is never as successful as the thought. That, of course, one has to live with. I'm sure this is true for every artist. The Igbo people have a proverb that tells of the difference between the vision and the achievement, and the achievement is never up to the vision. What the eye sees can never be reached by the stone the hand throws. The stone always falls short. I've learned to live with that. I don't make too much about it. The language of the dream is always superior to the language when you wake up and try to recapture the dream. One need not waste one's life lamenting that. One must be grateful for what one has achieved, and always try to do better, or at least try not to rest.

MORROW: Well, I hope you dream long and tell many more stories, Chinua.

Getting Close to Gaudí
Juan Goytisolo

— Translated by Peter Bush

1.

A TRAVELER FROM BARCELONA who, on the journey from Nevsehir to Urgüp, branches left toward the Avcilar valley en route to the famous cave churches of Göreme and Zelve sets foot on a terrain whose breathtaking strangeness does not entirely efface a diffuse, persistent impression of familiarity. Past Uchisar, as the zigzagging road hurtles downwards, he contemplates a fascinating panorama that recalls well-known images. The shapes and structures of the volcanic space seem subtly fashioned by the genius of a landscape painter. Behind sculpted bluffs and strata, white sinusoidal breakers, corporeal masses of opaque, gigantic proportion, sunscorched escarpments from a lunar wasteland, the valley where he lands suddenly confronts him with a daringly vertical composition, a concatenation of elements possessed of beautiful, oneiric plasticity: cylindrical towers with scaly, curvilinear tops, steeples cone-tipped or bristling with spikes, candles dripping crystallized eruptive rock, pillars with little fungiform hats, window boxes and hefty projecting cornices. Dwarfed by the dimensions of the forest, the visitor gradually recognizes motionless spinning tops, giant, rustic chimneys, megaliths in unusual equilibrium, natural flying buttresses, ramified or truncated columns. The diverse elements seem to fit together like the spine, bones and muscles of organic beings, and the observer witnesses a kind of apotheosis of naturalist fiction or illusion in which distortion of volume, compensation by foreshortening, structural arborescence envelop him in an unreal, enchanted aura of *trompe l'oeil*. Weightless, entranced, thrust into memories of other times, other places, he will instinctively seek out in the strangeness and rigor of the scene parabolic armatures, vaults with *mudéjar* stalactites, lobular or labial shapes, leaf patterns, tracery, floral geometrical motifs, valves, petals. Could the rocks, hooded like a procession of petrified penitents, possibly be cupolas, lanterns or ventilation shafts made of glazed tiles, earthenware and broken fragments? Imperceptibly, the distance from Cappadocia to Barcelona is wiped out: the miraculous space he treads leads inexorably to the auroral creation of Gaudí.

2.

I first visited Cappadocia in 1979, a few weeks after the military coup which put an end to ailing Turkish democracy. The day after my arrival in Urgüp the authorities embarked on a massive census of the population and forty million citizens had to stay at home: only the forces of order and the census administrators had right of movement. When I wanted to leave my hotel, I was disagreeably surprised to find a guard with a bayonet in my way. Trapped with fifty-odd Germans with whom I avoided all contact, I decided not to resign myself to their fate but to risk a foray out: I ran across the street ignoring the askari's shouts and burst into the nearby police station. Loudly, I demanded my natural freedom, the tourist's inalienable right to move around and nose about. My anger proved to be persuasive since the duty-officer reluctantly granted me capricious entry to a totally depopulated area. For several hours, in the sole company of a friend with similar authorization, I wandered through kilometers of desolate, eruptive landscape where I came across no living being except for insects, small birds, lizards and the dogs of a troglodyte, of whom more in a moment. In the empty diving-bell silence, the Cappadocia of volcanic stone, sculpted and forged by aeolian erosion, appeared to the two survivors spared by the cataclysm or atomic explosion with the evanescent beauty of a mirage.

A succession of tenacious memories and images: blessed calm of the universe after the Apocalypse; impression we were the last representatives of extinct *homo sapiens;* intense perception, through our five senses, of manifestations and signs of organic life after the catastrophe; a route across hillsides along minuscule shortcuts, doubtful tracks, paths leading nowhere which suddenly fade away. After the abrupt, austere plateau, the hallucinatory setting created by the combination of features brought me straight back to Gaudí: columns wearing caps or pointed hoods, lined up like alphabetizing, emblematic pencils; forests of cones, needles, spires, obelisks; fossilized jellyfish; unexpected chromatic variations; disruption of normative functionalism; mystic incandescence; pure, rational, architectonic delirium. In the Göreme valley and, beyond, on the way to Zelve, our gaze still embraced churches, bereft of the faithful, hollowed out of jagged escarpments or mounted in cones, abandoned monasteries, hermits' cells, walls decorated with painted or sculpted crosses, vestiges of the recluse life of anchorites fleeing from the iconoclasts' fury, enormous cave hives complete with windows, passageways, stairs, lanterns, in which Christ, the Virgin and the Apostles alternate with St. George and the dragon, St. Catherine and St. Barbara. Hellenic inscriptions, drawn by the monks, also recalled those which adorn monuments by Gaudí. In the course of that unreal, captivating ramble, as we climbed a somewhat uneven slope in search of a village, we were surprised by the bark, or rather, chorus of barks, from a pack of dogs guarding one of the isolated grottoes or chapels. As we climbed, the ferocious barking intensified. Caution advised us to keep our distance but curiosity won the day. The path obviously led to an inhabited cave and, after a day wandering through a parched, deserted land, all fear was swept aside by our desire to communicate with someone else. When we reached the cave dwelling, we realized that we were not in danger: the dogs were well tied up and soon quieted down when their master cracked his whip. The troglodyte lived in a rectangular cave hollowed out a meter above ground level from the wall of the cavern which served as his porch: a chamber had been converted into a bedroom, with palliasse and pillows, and could be closed off from the rest by a half-drawn curtain. The fantastic layout of the place, its variegated decorations, enthralled me, and thanks to a snapshot I took I can describe them with some precision: a colored portrait of Atatürk, religious prints, photographs of an old ramblers' club; sheepskins and cushions covered in brightly colored material laid over the stone bench where the dogs slept. The owner with his white, sylvan beard was sitting on his bed reading and answered my greeting with a mere nod of the head. From time to time, ever absorbed in his reading, he would crack the whip to calm his anxious guards. I photographed the latter, stretched out on their sheepskins, and, before bidding farewell to my silent host, I surveyed the scene for the last time. It was then, while I inspected the small set made up of cavern and alcove, that I noticed a phrase scrawled in Catalan on the side cave: *Yesterday a master, today a shepherd.* Hadn't Gaudí written or said something similar?* At the

---

*Gaudí's real phrase goes: *Ahir pastor, avui senyor*, in reference to the vicissitudes of his sleeping partner, the ennobled commoner, count Güell.

risk of being called impertinent, I took a photo. But the film had got stuck or wasn't in properly: anyway, the photo never came out.

I left Turkey not knowing whether I had been dreaming or whether the graffiti really existed.

3.

Back in Cappadocia six years later, my main objective is to find the old man. I can clearly remember my previous trek across the mountains and am sure I will easily locate him. Nevertheless, as I prepare to meet him, doubts beseige me. Will he still be shut away in the same spot? How will I manage to break his silence? With my hesitant, limited vocabulary, will I succeed in extracting from him what I want to know? What means should I use to open myself up to him and somehow win his confidence? As a precaution, to encourage our coming together, I decide to do without my camera. I shall visit him as an old friend, thanking him for his brief, chance hospitality. I am tempted by the idea of taking him a present but reject it: wouldn't this perhaps seem suspiciously like a clumsy attempt to buy his insights and knowledge? Better to appear calm and unworried, the opposite of that "Greek bearing gifts" whose offerings, far from winning favor with the receiver, arouse his instinctive suspicion: I shall simply appear at the cave, unafraid of the ferocious dogs, as someone well-acquainted with the surroundings and the unquenchable personality of their master.

A taxi takes me close by; I immediately find my way between volcanic cones and rocks and within minutes I am standing before the old man's home. A transistor radio is broadcasting Gregorian chants and I notice towels and clothes hung out to dry on the shrubs by the grotto. This time the dogs do not bark at me: they are dozing in the sun and look at me unconcerned. The old man is still resting on the palliasse in his bedroom, with the curtain drawn, in the same position as I had left him at the end of my previous visit: everything is exactly the same as before and it would seem natural for him to open our conversation with a softly spoken "as we were saying yesterday. . . ."

While I have recourse to my compendium of Turkish greetings and polite formulas, he is content to stroke the back of one of the dogs stretched out on the stone bench with the springy point of his whip. Rather embarrassed, I stand beneath the arched ceiling of the entrance to the grotto but he finally turns toward me and stares at me questioningly.

"Are you Catalan?"

"No; I mean, yes." His blue eyes look hard at me and I conclude: "Well, not really."

His mastery of the language has taken me by surprise. Cunningly, I contrive to hide this from him and refrain from asking how and when.

"The Master particularly avoids Catalans," he points out. "Nor does he want anything to do with Spaniards or foreigners who take an interest in his work and write nonsense about it. But Catalans annoy him *most.*"

A long pause follows during which he looks me up and down as if to establish my true parameters.

"At least this time you haven't brought your Nikon," he comments approvingly.

"Right, I preferred to leave it behind. I thought that . . ."

"You well know his phobia against photographers. Apart from the period when Audouart took a portrait and when the few snapshots were taken of him hiking with his father and niece, all photos were always taken furtively, taking advantage of some ceremony or deep religious devotion, as in the Corpus Christi procession in Barcelona. Do you remember?"

I say I do: I can see not the young red-haired architect, with his white complexion, gleaming eyes and light blue irises, high-bridged nose and lofty forehead, but an old white-haired, white-bearded man, candle in hand, with a *canotier* under his arm, wearing a pair of rough shoes.

"With age, his phobia has got worse. If he discovers the presence of a camera-bearing tourist prowling around where he works, he immediately hides in the labyrinth of cave churches and doesn't emerge for some time."

This new information, together with his continuous use of the present tense, leaves me literally confused: I listen without hearing as, mentally, I make a few basic calculations and review my unassailable truths.

"If I heard you right," I finally declare, "you're talking about him as if he were still alive."

The old man nods in agreement and I ask, avoiding any hint of irony or humor: "Has he been resurrected or do you believe in the transmigration of souls?"

"Neither," he replies. "He's still alive, that's all there is to it, and, what's more important, he's working night and day, like never before, putting the finishing touches to his immense work. Haven't you seen his latest chimneys and towers in the Göreme valley? They're the most perfect, consummate things he has ever created!"

"One moment," I say. "According to you, if I haven't forgotten the rules of arithmetic, he would now be approaching a hundred and thirty-four years of age, isn't that right?"

"What's odd about that? A drop in the ocean compared to the age of the old patriarchs in the Bible! Do I have to remind you that those holy men lived in these very mountains? Longevity is very common in these parts and you can meet very many centenarians in Cappadocia: most of them do not know their real age and they count it from the date that has been later added to their identity cards. As you well know, Gaudí comes from a family where many reach a ripe age. If his father lived to ninety-three in a city polluted by all kinds of moral and industrial waste, you can easily imagine what age he would have reached in these lands in which climate and frugality protect and preserve."

My interlocutor throws a few crumbs to the dogs and uses my silence to scrutinize me again, apparently encouraged by my expression of sudden incredulity. The historical evidence which I can set against his arguments is considerable: the Number 30 tram which knocked Gaudí down on June 7, 1926, at the point where Bailén crosses Granvía; the reprehensible behavior of the three taxi drivers who refused to drive him because of his threadbare clothes; the action of the Civil Guard Ramón Pérez, who took him to the Red Cross point from which he was moved to the Santa Cruz hospital; his famous, symbolic death agony amidst the poor in keeping with his pious wishes . . .

"Legends, just legends, the fruit of collective guilt and remorse! Uplifting scenes for the official hagiography!"

Unimpressed by his firmness of tone, I immediately bring fresh testimony against his undaunted delusions: the numerous shots of the funeral cortege as it passed through the Plaza de Cataluña, the Ramblas, the Calle Fernando, the cathedral. I can even remember the photographer's name, Segarra, and the presence of the photos in the archives of the Gaudí Chair. As the old man seems unshakable in his certainty, *de guerre lasse*, I have recourse to the supreme truth.

"Who, then, did they bury in the crypt of the Sagrada Familia, in the chapel of the Virgin of Carmel?"

The old man lowers his eyes for a few moments and when he meets my gaze again, he just asks quietly:

"Do you really think that the corpse of Santiago the Apostle is in his tomb at Compostela?"

4.

Following the old man's written directions, you visit the fungiform cones and chimneys where, according to him, the Master has recently been at work. Although convinced he will dodge out of your way, will avoid your indiscreet presence nearby, you bring neither camera, exercise book nor sheet of paper to take notes: his misanthropy might have hardened, he tells you, and led him to hide away in the labyrinth of caves until you depart. Dressed in ochre, the color of the ground you tread, trying to melt chameleonlike into the background, you reach the spot marked on the map. The striking unity of composition of the pawns, castles and bishops on the chess board spread out in the valley transports you to a vision of the domes, chimneys and stairwells of Can Milà. Stony plinths, whose relief and ridges emphasize the use of mortar stones and the natural prisms of basalt, cross the uneven terrain between the rocky cones and you excitedly discover the hidden presence of homemade bricks and glazed shards. As with the Pedrera or Güell Park, the spectator witnesses a gradual symbiosis of the different structures in the landscape: ceramic materials, carefully adapted to local topography, are gently articulated into the sinusoidal swell of the nearby slope and the clear blue of the sky. The rough masonry of projecting stones is softened, as is Gaudí's wont, by the introduction of decorative elements and the organic naturalness of his finishing touches: seashells, tiny carved polychrome birds, nests of *trencadís*. You can testify *de visu* how the invisible hand of the architect has polished and refined the prodigious creation of the four elements: in the massive spinning top precisely marked by the old man, you find carefully laid out a subtle combination of earthenware, rows of bricks and fragments of tiles. When you penetrate the grotto cut out of the inside of the cone, you are suddenly right in Gaudí's ideal space: the light filters through cylindrical skylights, trapezoidal openings, and the staircase built centuries ago by the monks clings to the snaking line of the wall, twists in a spiral until it comes out on a kind of vantage point set on natural parabolic arches, cunningly concealed by an exterior granite parapet. You have hardly reached the top when you notice various signs of human existence: a small hearth made from lumps of stone, a rustic earthenware pot at the bottom of which are the by-now-dry remains of a brew of herbs, half-made plates and utensils. Their owner has recently abandoned the spot, perhaps rather hurriedly, since in his flight he left behind the bag where he was collecting proof of his fondness for mycology and botany. Could he have put his ear to the ground Indianlike and foretold your intrusion in the enchanted forest? The graffiti scrawled on the glazed coping stone in the wall fills you with delight: *De la llar al foc, visca el foc de l'amor.* Your intuition leads you to examine the variegated manufacture of the wall in search of a possible message and you hit the bull's-eye. Who on earth could have written that except Gaudí himself?

On subsequent days, while painstakingly inspecting cones and megaliths or snooping around the cave churches of Göreme, you gather together fresh, irrefutable signs of his elusive immediacy: fires, bunches of wild herbs, combs and utensils, created by his own hands. As well as his renowned sayings: *La Glòria es la llum, Oh, l'ombra de l'estiu.* Sometimes, like a wily, scheming genie, the Evasive One takes a jesting pleasure in changing the content of his message: *Al cel tots en serem d'actionistes.** One evening as you trawl the warren of troglodyte dwellings in Avcilar, he will slip through your hands by only a few minutes: the pot where he boils his herbs is still steaming. You wait all night, but he does not appear. Resigned, you crouch by the fireside and slowly sip the infusion prepared by the Master with the absorbed devotion of someone about to take communion.

5.

Settled in his bedroom hewn from the rock, the old man wraps himself round with his sheepskin coat and woolen blankets, apparently chilly despite the heat. The dogs seem sunk deep in lethargy and remain, during your conversation, on the lower bench covered in sheepskins, as if poisoned or drugged.

---

*In fact, after listening to Clavé's choirs, he commented: *Al cel tots en serem d'orfeonistes.*

"What you have already seen and many other things that you will discover as you extend your knowledge of the area are the logical culmination of a process that has been gestating for years. Had he not once said that to follow nature is a way of continuing divine creation? Originality, he insisted, is the return to origins. His interest in Fra Guerau's rocks and the Prades mountains, his membership in the Catalan Association for Scientific Excursions were a response not only to his passion for geology and botany, they were also a reflection of an inner need fired by mystic longing. His previous work, subject to the whims of his so-called patrons, seemed botched up beside of the creative possibilities offered by the landscape. Thus, rather than abstractly reinventing existing forms, he proposed to enrich and enhance the gift-offering of nature. Eroded slopes, cliffs and rocks follow the same norms that rule the domain of architecture. What is the difference between the rocky cliff of the Pedrera, a truly urban mountain, and those one can observe here? So what if the volume and tortuous shapes of that huge stone forest in Avcilar are a product of tectonic activity, aeolian erosion or have been elaborated by the Master? In any case, don't they respect the laws of balance and gravity? The futile waiting and humiliations of his last years in Barcelona, unable to advance the works of the expiatory temple of the Sagrada Familia, filled him with bitterness and he instinctively sought out happiness and light. Here, in his hermit's retreat, he was able to carry through his old naturalist ruminations: instead of purely geometric and functional structures, his are geological and even organic. His work is a humble extension of Creation."

The old man breaks off his speech to light a fire. You don't dare to guess his age, but since your first meeting his health has gone downhill. As he gets out of his alcove you notice how he shivers from cold and seems to suffer from slight trembling fits. For a few moments he looks through the bedroom shelves and takes out a metal saucepan half-filled with water, into which he places a handful of herbs.

"But why did it have to be Cappadocia?" I ask at last.

"Gaudí was always attracted by the ascetic life of hermits," the old man replies. "In his cell in Güell Park, perhaps you already know, he slept on a straw mattress and once, I think in 1894, nearly died as a result of rigorously fasting during Lent. There could be nothing more natural for him than to disappear from that mediocre, positivistic world which was stifling him, to take refuge in the land where the first monasteries and communities of monks were founded. Like the Aramaic and Chaldean refugees from persecutions and massacres, he would find his ideal habitat in the life of a troglodyte, in these magnificent cave churches."

"Of course, I agree, it's a seductive explanation; but it does not solve the riddle of his reappearance in these parts. I can see nothing in the public period of his life — if indeed our version of the facts is correct and he is still living and working here — to establish any kind of link between him and Cappadocia. Did he perhaps know the area from some engraving or photograph? Is there any evidence or proof that he ever referred to it?"

"Do you think he might have simply come in search of the mysterious 'Satalia' described in *L'Atlàntida* and that old Mossen Jacinto Verdaguer locates in Asia Minor?"

"I must admit I had never thought of that. But it's still only hypothesis."

"Look, young man — because that's what you are to me though you're fifty-odd — he was fascinated by the physical and cultural space of Islam. The only journey of his youth outside Spain was not to Paris, not even Italy, but to Morocco. In the archives of the School of Architecture in Barcelona where he studied there were photographs of Hindu temples and minarets in Cairo. He was equally very attracted by the slender minarets of the Sahara and the Sudan. He was never inspired by the Renaissance nor by neo-Classicism: like Cervantes and Goya, he sought out real Spain, which he found in the hidden strata of meaty *mudéjar* miscegenation. His absolute rejection of the system and criteria of his time led him to affirm his own values in the face of those which enjoyed universal respect. His apprenticeship in solitude was hard but fruitful. As he gained confidence in his own truth, he rejected and distanced himself from the truth of fellow countrymen. Bourgeois *bon seny* and *avara povertà* clashed with the white heat of his mystic ardor. Gradually his youthful *mudéjarismo* assimilated the Gothic and the Baroque, opened out in an unbounded vision of the exuberant geometry of nature. Man must rise up constantly, day by day, because inspiration is not enough. Europe could no longer bring anything to him: that is why he came here."

"This is all very plausible," I reply. "However, historians require proof and, apart from a series of fairly alarming assumptions, the fact is we haven't any. If I am not mistaken, in the crypt of the chapel where his tomb lies . . ."

"Don't talk to me about memorial stones or plaques! I only have to read 'So-and-so was born, lived and died here' for the unbridgeable gap between reality and the written word to fill me with doubts. Who will guarantee that that is true? Couldn't they be made-up facts, details to strengthen the supposedly historical narrative and the laws of verisimilitude? Remember Herodotus and Vives' lapidary phrase: *Mendaciorum pater!* If all biographies are fictions, why should Gaudí's be true? Many, many years ago I read the only really convincing inscription on a beautiful timbered mansion in the French quarter of New Orleans: 'Napoleon was invited to live in this house after his defeat in Waterloo.' Finally I had found some incontrovertible evidence! He was invited, he was certainly invited: *but he did not go.*"

"So, according to you . . ."

"Stop piling up dubious evidence and surrender to the understanding in your heart! Gaudí withdrew from the world like a novitiate in a closed order after proclaiming his vows and, in a solitary state, impervious to criticism and praise alike, he continues his masterwork. The panorama you can contemplate in Cappadocia reveals the apotheosis of his genius. Patiently, humbly, you can follow alone in the steps of his mystic, creative itinerary. But you must be spiritually prepared for that encounter and deserve it; in a word, become worthy of him."

The old man finishes boiling his infusion and pours the contents of the saucepan into two earthenware bowls. It is a bitter brew: it tastes curiously similar to the one prepared by the invisible troglodyte in the underground labyrinths of Avcilar. As on that occasion, my senses seem to be sharpened as I drink, and I am simultaneously filled with a pleasant feeling of peace.

The flickering, changing flames of the fire swathe in light and darkness the still bodies of the three dogs, stiffened by *rigor mortis*.

6.

In order to be purified and to distill your senses and ideas, you begin by getting rid of your possessions and selfish utilitarian criteria: you sell your camera for a derisory sum which you hand over to a beggar crouching by the entrance to the mosque; you pay your hotel bill and divide your belongings between porters and waiters; poorly dressed, like the architect on the day of his accident, you leave the comfort of Urgüp and head with a small bundle to the Gaudían cones and chimneys of the sun-scorched splendor of Avcilar. Your presence there is to be light, discreet, wandering like the Master's. You learn to find shelter in the abandoned caves and churches, to sleep on an empty stomach, do without a watch, feed on infusions of dried herbs, savor the diaphanous fullness of the landscape, refine and polish day after day your understanding and sensibility. Elusive and attentive, inaccessible and near, Gaudí watches over your movements and from time to time reveals to you his kind concern: in the chapel of a cave monastery whose columns with their parabolic arches support an architrave decorated with round medallions identical to those in Güell Park, you find a page bearing Verdaguer's verses on the garden of the Hesperides; at the top of one of the cones, perforated with cells and skylights like a gigantic beehive, when you come across graffiti of a quotation from Góngora — *All is strange, the design, the manufacture and the means* — you are unsure whether it refers to his singular creative venture or to the sumptuous delirium of Cappadocia. Sometimes, when you take shelter in the shade of some cavern, you discover ready, steaming, especially prepared for you, the saucepan or pot in which he usually prepares his brews: thirsty, gasping, you cautiously sip the infusion, noticing immediately how your body becomes subtle and light beyond the restrictions of time and space: a stroll begun amid the fungiform columns and motionless spinning tops of Zelve extends unbroken to the flat roof and mosaic adornments of the Pedrera or the paths flanked with garden-boxes in Güell Park. Artifice and creation fuse; the apparent chaos of the landscape emphasizes in fact the subtle harmonizing of its features, the secret hand of the dragoman. By night, the physical volumes and shapes come alive, the silhouettes of the hooded cones lengthen and you witness from your burrow a solemn procession of penitents, between megaliths and torches, en route to the steep slope of his urban mountain, to the balanced verticality of the towers of his Temple.

Despite the repeated instances of tact and friendliness, Gaudí avoids any meeting. After downing his pleasant herb infusion, you shout in vain at the top of your voice that you have nothing to do with the Calvets, Batllós, Milàs from your contemptible country, that you hate as much as he the rapacious bourgeoisie which used him without understanding him, that you too have broken free and roam stateless through the places and lands that fascinate him;

yet your voice is lost in the valleys corroded by aeolian erosion, down cracks and crevices in stones subjected to slow, millenary torture. The day you at last think you spot him, struck in a kind of cameo, pale, red-haired, bearded, straight-nosed, open-featured, as in Audouard's photograph, you realize your eyes are closed and you are daydreaming. In spite of your regular consumption of herbs with hallucinogenic qualities, the miracle or vision does not take place.

7.

In the course of the weeks of my frustrated siege of Gaudí, I threw overboard a number of habits, I denied myself and fasted, mortified the senses, dwelt in a tranquil present, swore a temporary vow of poverty, lost several kilos, aged with a grayish beard, embraced my hermit's condition elated yet stern. The awaited adventure escaped me but I was consumed by the ardor of the chase.

Weak and despondent, I abandoned the Gaudían universe of Avcilar and Göreme and, before returning to my departure point, I went to bid farewell to the old man. An obsessive, despotic sun charred the long-suffering stone landscape and even lizards and insects seemed to be in hiding. A few meters from the cavern, I was surprised by the palpable density of the silence. Nobody was there and the interior of the room — bench, alcove, shelves — looked desolate and looted. The few belongings and pieces of furniture had vanished with their master and someone had angrily burnt the last traces of his presence.

8.

The herbs used in the infusions and brews that I drank during the period spanned by the narrative and my writing grow wild in the mountain areas of the Mediterranean basin in Anatolia and in Catalonia. Gaudí used to look for them on his frequent trips into the hills but never revealed the recipe for their preparation. If he died, as official history claims, he took his secret with him to the grave.

A Context of a Wave
Mei-mei Berssenbrugge

November 5.

You could be thinking about your physical placement, what can be
a continuum and what is chance. You place yourself innately on a
mesa. There are blue hills at each horizon, the light falls copiously
onto your open space, the path of the sun and the planets are pro-
portioned around you.

The source of the balance is a sense perception. Your perception of
your location is not contingent, but accords with an idea of location
inside you, that turns in you like a gyroscope, as you are moving.

I believe in this sense perception of place, because I experience it.

It may be a sense of the shape of a space, or of the balance of features of the space, or it may be a sense of a point on the earth in
relation to forces in the earth, which may be affected by stars and
planets. Or, it may be in relation to stars and planets.

November 9.

So that the place would sit in me, its wide space with sun, as what
it would be in my memory of this time. And how it would be perceived is a matrix of how you were with some people around you,
not agents but catalyst or fuel for the perception of light on a wide
space, so free as to be impersonal in the company, implacable and
impersonal.

November 10.

She would remember that it was a place of the wind. She would think that she would remember the site of sun, and light without sound or without value, but her body is pushed and drawn on by the force of wind on the ridge, every day, so that someday she would remember that she had lived in wind.

The wind can be in the future, a direction, as if there were time, because it comes from somewhere. Because it draws you somewhere, it is the time or space that is the next thing somewhere among the materials of a space or at a time. Because it might be seen as an expression of the forces making it, which push on you or draw from you, it is an expression to everything it is not, and you are reminded you are what it is not, and this expression deters you or abstains from you as a space, when the wind is pushing all night or on a sunny day against the windows and walls of your house.

Then, this expression of being what something is not, joins you with a piece of leaning yellow grass in low sun, or it abstains you from the expression, as if you are more becoming in your mind what you are looking at than what you are feeling.

November 11.

You would be able to see the meaning or whole of the space between the objects on the table, which before had been random space between the fork and the salt crystal.

Now you can see the meaning or the whole of the space between rods of illuminated streaks of clouds at sunset, zooming this way and that, and the volume and vector between them. From you to the horizon gains a meaning. Something happens to you, it is time moving, and you can see them as a whole thing and not the space between one cloud and another that appear on the same plane because of the same color of light on them.

43

November 12.

We walked in the dry riverbed. Water had left the sand in sweeps of lines and currents, fronds of tamarack drifted in. I want to call it pollen of tamarack drifting into patterns of sand made by currents of water, lift drifts of events in time. But it is more like the bits of tamarack frond, broken by the current and drifting into patterns or record was the time, because of there being something besides a pattern to perceive time by means of.

A skin of tufts of yellow grasses on a hillside threw off the lateral light, and threw down their delicate shadows. The flank of a hill suggesting a living creature.

November 13.

You can see the complexity of autumn plants and trees in the canyon below you. It is late autumn. The yellow and brown jumble of the foliage. Most of the leaves have fallen from the trees and bushes into heaps and drifts on either side of the stream. We are accustomed to think of disorganization and of increasing disorganization as a vector toward entropy. The pleasurable complexity of matter in the canyon would seem to be entropic, except for its beauty. It looks like death. It seems entropic, but it is not entropic, as biological death may not be. And I wonder if the beauty is an innate apprehension of the ongoingness, or "other" than entropy, of that sight?

November 14.

I see the honey moon rise from a bare horizon, after the sunset behind a mountain. I was waiting for the moon. It was a test and not a knowledge of the movement of the risings, by which I am trying to judge where I am on this plain. We are trying to understand if the moon sets in a different place than the sun, the sun which is moving and moving down the horizon. Soon, its colored glow will silhouette a mountain called The Wave.

November 15.

How this relates to your seeing the moon rise in your rearview mirror, driving west, on an empty road, home.

She had wanted to see the gap between the moon and the horizon, the space that could be into infinity. And then she would be seeing the moon in the mirror, surrounded by gaps in direction and in distance, and these gaps have to do with this writing, and not with situation or place.

November 21.

You see streaks of clouds in the sky, a sky evenly striped with clouds, from top to bottom, which you leave. And then you see two long plumes of clouds in another sky that is lighter and bluer. This sky stretches over you always, but it is a sky that looks different from there than here. The composition of the atmosphere, the angle of the sun distinguishes the blue factor, I want to say content of the sky. I want to say the skies of two places have two contents. You would want to examine the content in regard to its value, and I don't know if this has anything to do with place.

November 23.

The sky is continuous with the other places, and yet when I look at the afterglow of the sunset, I see a rim of layered colors on the horizon, all around me, a rim or limit of this sky. Just above the rim, my eye could go into deep space, or my eye could go into infinity, but the line of my glance will not meet the person's in the other place, looking, of a moral content that would not be comparable.

Mei-mei Berssenbrugge

November 24.

If we would be thinking about what a particular moon or a sky as an event has to do with anything I am writing. And also, the relationship of event to location in what I am writing. What does it mean to try and see something in Galisteo to write about? If you are talking about place in words, not place in being, which is an orientation of being. Whereas place in words can be a sort of focus of being, or a little sieve through which another person can focus the interest of "about," the interest or pleasure of: a dark volcanic rock in the riverbed, its shadow, your suspicion that it moves from side to side when no one is there. What interest is, which is not experience, but part of the body, that might fuel interest or be part of its fuel.

November 27.

For example: You would be tracking where you are as a siting of what your content would be, time as nature. The sun sets farther and farther left on the small mountain range, so the sunset glow begins to approach your favorite Wave. Favorite being a content, and also, approach of a glow.

When she cannot see what the place is, is that part of the end of the time, such as, the yellow grasses have gone dull by the end of November? The dullness of the lapse of location in her, or is it the grasses themselves?

He seats himself after a ways, and waits there for your return, to accompany you, because you have gone out of your place. The place of a low sun that illuminates a fan of experience of cholla and sage beyond and beyond.

November 28.

It would close in on you, the mist lowers over The Wave. The cloud has come down. Diffuse light deepens the colors of the basin, so now you can make out the fissure of a little river canyon, cutting the plain, a rust red below mist hovering close to the ground. As if a cloth has shaken down a saturation of content, a blank saturation before you. Now you think in the morning what the value of the saturated space means, emulsified or droppletted, for now, and for what has happened.

November 29.

Where the moon is, that would speak the cycles of what she is saying. Then some days pass, and she doesn't know where the moon is. Winter clouds lower onto the plain. Gray and thick in the cold. She would be thinking about the description as a means to content, but it is as if she can't see far enough, now. There was one line of light on the distant part of the plain, as sun broke out between clouds for a few minutes, and that would be her content, because of her moral or emotional stance about sunlight?

It was brief and it is what she can remember.

November 30.

You see snow as mist on the plain. I hear snow fall on the tin roof. I think the time passes, because my mood is changing. No horizon. You look and you can't see anything to remember. You feel the moisture and the warmth of the air, you feel that it is very dark, now. It is impenetrable to your feeling about the right thing to do. So, what is the relationship of the horizon with the right thing to do? The horizon is the edge of the body or the edge of the eye you look out from into space of possibilities to choose from. Or space or a clarity in which to decide the color blue or gray of the clarity.

Mei-mei Berssenbrugge

December 1.

She is making a difference between how the land seems, and how the land looks. If the land is a place, and the place sites your content or the place orients your sense of value, then what is seeming about the space, that also seems inside your body?

Snow closes the space to you, and the dark arrives earlier. You have no space to look out to, in the dusk, and so it seems that you are having no words. You see woodpeckers on the snowy dirt. It is mild and snowy. It is morning. And so you think their quick movements are something you can speak about, the red throats of the males, the volume of their down. The carnations of snow in the pine trees. It seems a principle to be describing these things, or what you are describing, as if it were just to describe the beautiful place.

How does seeming correlate to the fineness of your seeing? Or decrease with your seeing? What is the virtue of the description of a salmon tamarack frond in the snow, the blue Wave appearing, meaning the storm is passing, the movement of time in snow through space?

December 2.

Here is a star in the cold night, that is alternating, red, blue. It is two stars revolving around each other, cold and hot. I see it among the clear still stars of the configurations. The dark shapes of juniper at the height of my shoulders. Streaks of leftover snow showing in starlight near their bases. A woman tells me there is no value, because right and wrong puts you into the past, where stars are, from now. She said, if you want inspiration, to stop my thought about my mother, for example, and then wait for the next thought, that inspiration comes in between, but it does not come in words. Here is the content at night. She says, the content is subtle beauty. If she would say what the content of happiness would be in the sky or in shadowy streaks. How she could tell the relation of the starry sky or the shadowy streaks with life. By what criteria she could relate the stars and snow to her. By what criteria she could determine a content in their apprehension, or the apprehension of subtle beauty. When the starry sky has nothing to do with life, that its content would be an occurrence, that could be otherwise.

December 3.

Now I want my memory to wash over, and so my memory picks aspen leaves scattered across the ground by the river, the sun glints on the silvery upturned ones. They are in this place, but it is not something in this place that would be generating the direction of the observation. There would be a layer of glinting papery leaves all ahead of you in low sun, and this layer would be forgetting. Red wands of bushes reaching into the air from the sandy riverbed, reaching into the blue of the sky are forgetting that goes into the blue, freeing your mind of forgetting, or by forgetting. The way you can free the sky with a branch reaching into it, or hold the sky with it.

December 4.

An impression in cold twilight of fading apricot pastel behind the gray cottonwoods, like mist at the edge of a red riverbed. The trees created cold for me. Is that representing the cold, or symbolizing the cold waning day? The trees in the distance across the dry riverbed where I walk. The rocks like a film passing. The character of a rock that was some molten flow onto sandstone, of black and red and gray like the cold space behind the cottonwoods, but in matter recreates or represents a content of passionate love?

December 5.

Running the length of the top of the ridge is a "hogback," dark and dense ore from the center of the earth. The sun falls fast behind the mountain. Approaching its southern point. The Wave shows neon pink at the edge, now. The iron boulders are patterned with chartreuse lichen. The Rocky Mountains are still glowing pink, though we are in shade. The Jemez Mountains, cerulean blue that gives off light, are the lips of a great volcano. Arroyos in the near plain intimate reticulations of walls of flesh and sand colors.

If she were thinking about a place, then listing the place might be an analysis. An analysis of the progression south of the moon, which should yield a meaning of what she is seeing, to her. Listing

49

and listing the line of the hogback by coordinates, the infinitely complicated line, from point to point.

If she were thinking about the content of a view and its relation to life, this would have to be a synthesis. The content of a view relates to life synthetically. The relation to life is perceived through the perceptual dimension of what she is thinking she is seeing.

Misty gray cottonwoods bunch around the town. Out here is desert.

December 6.

If she were thinking about the relation between the content of a view, and the view's relation to life in a new way, she cannot think. The view is the content, and the life is the time, still. The view is your movement through millions of parallel lines of falling snow. Seemingly disconnected traces of paths through space, across the time you are looking, or moving through, in the night. Like lighted clouds at sunset, she can't tell their distance away from her.

The value of the content is equivalent to a mood. The content or story of the view is repeatable and depends on your orientation or mood. The changing of an orientation marks time. The depth of the content of a view depends on the degree to which your body can respond to your perception of the view. So, the content is abstract. The value or content of a view depends on the degree of your response, but it is not the response. The emotion of your response dictates the value as a passion. Even driving through snow for a long time in the night. The view lengthens across the time through which you are traveling, a tunnel view of your response of moving through it, through the night.

December 7.

The Wave turns gray. It is the darkest month of the year. The landmark turns in on itself. Your daughter sees the moon for the first time, a half-moon. The luminosity of the grasses is of a yellow-gray of the winter light. This year's new growth of the cholla glows yellow on the gray spindles.

The story, of a daughter and the moon, for example, appears submerged by your intention, or in a multiplicity of detail, or in smoothness of detail. The story seems submerged, but it emerges, a cottonwood in the arroyos.

All their massed yellow leaves lined the turning arroyos, half-concealed, like fringe. All summer, green indication of underground water in a drought. The ground is bare. The half-trees betray wealth. The gray turned-inside foliage with sky in it, tonight catches the moon, with their way of the way eyes catch it.

December 8.

If I look at the land, it is in shadow, but I can clearly see the sun through brushy juniper that is making the shadow. It looks like a shadow, but it must not be a deep shadow. The mountains on the other side of the hogback were rose of these closer ones, and lavender just beyond. The Wave which has turned further into itself, is growing complicated, aging in the dark. Land seems bunched up at its base, like loose, old skin.

You have a content of a view, and you have a content of "life." And these relate to the body? Or does this seem so because of my daughter's birth? Snow clouds low to distant mountains, thick and dark and gray in the morning, are a gesture of a hand flung upward, wispy pink streamers, in the evening. Was that my body? The dark husks of yucca pods after sunset, of a color of the density of the body? As the origin of words?

December 9.

Dozens of varieties of dry grasses, sheaves empty, but still catching the light. Stalks seem more luminous yellow than electric, a color that retains its luminosity when placed next to the skin of your hand, while colors of electric light and synthetic colors lose their beauty. So, you would think beauty pertains to light, but beauty is an idea or a feeling that associates from light to the mind.

December 10.

Now the impetus of a place can diminish, or the impetus in the time of your place in it. She sees the gold halo left by the sun, although she missed the sun. She feels a tiredness that would be like her extension into the illusion of the fourth dimension, or third dimension, and this gold is the frame around the illusion, or view.

December 11.

You could start out with a feeling that could be love, or it could be a feeling of orientation, or a feeling of beauty. It seems to relate to, but not to be the place in the light around you. A nuance of grass or lit cloud related to the current in you.

And then, if the feeling changes, you could look around, and the land could have overcast time. The December days are darker and colder. The colors are darker, of branches and snow. Why is the feeling changing?

You feel that the place is still oriented or located correctly in the mathematics of the stars and lines of force of the world, but you are not oriented. Your feeling makes you out of place. Your feeling makes the place darken and turn in on you. Which it does not do. It still extends a line into space for the rabbit to race, escaping. It still sends a line of a glance across the horizon into infinity, or vertically levitates a glance to it, at night.

December 12.

Solstice full moon. On the first day, I was thinking about an idea, but I don't think an idea can relate writing to life, the way a place can, the way light can. An idea is a method for keeping the feeling near the life, to keep the feeling from escalating and diffusing its usefulness or beauty into itself. The feeling is what livens the words into music, a perfect art, she said, because it is most abstract. I say you can't think your way through it. You have to feel your way with a sense. It is the same sense that informs you about a place, but it is not the sense that apprehends light, which is mathematical as well as visual.

52

December 13.

She thought she could say that. Then she walked up the hill and waited for the moon to rise, after sunset. The sky darkened, stars showed. Venus is bright with reflected light. When I see some light near the horizon, a breath like a frost of light, I realize there's a low cloud, and the beginning of the moon cannot be discerned. Then it is a cold mist light in the cloud, and I am trying to see where the cloud ends and the sky will yield a sharp outline of the moon. And I am trying to tell how far the moon has risen behind the cloud already, and I think I can make out a huge circle of light there. It lights up a shape of a cloud along the near hills, along the road. There is a triangle of foggy light along the ground, to my left. When the moon clears, it is small and compact and metallic. He says you can tell it is one day past full, because it is so heavy, dragging itself. I wait for the gap between the low edge of the moon and the dark cloud. And then I can go. This is the moonrise I anticipate. I know its entrance on the horizon, because it is a place. I have something of a sense of moonrise, in future time, and it is a kind of elongation or collapse or dispersal of a phase, night and day, where a line of another person thinking could accompany you physically.

Galisteo, New Mexico

My Mother
Kathy Acker

1. THE FALL OF THE UNITED STATES

MY MOTHER'S SPEAKING:

I'm in love with red. I dream in red.

My nightmares are based on red. Red's the color of passion, of joy. Red's the color of all the journeys which are interior, the color of the hidden flesh, of the depths and recesses of the unconscious. Above all, red is the color of rage and violence.

I was six years old. Every night immediately after supper which I usually was allowed to take with my parents, I would say "Good night." To reach my room, I'd have to walk down a long dark corridor which was lined with doors on either side. I was terrified. Each door half-opened to unexpected violence.

Morality and moral judgments protect us only from fear.

In my dreams, it was I who simultaneously murdered and was murdered.

Moral ambiguity's the color of horror.

I was born on October 6, 1945, in Brooklyn, New York. My parents were rich, but not of the purest upper class. I'm talking about my father. At age six, I suddenly took off for unknown regions, the regions of dreams and secret desires. Most of my life, but not all, I've been dissolute. According to nineteenth-century cliché, dissoluteness and debauchery are connected to art.

I wrote: "The child's eyes pierce the night. I'm a sleepwalker trying to clear away the shadows, but when sound asleep, kneel in front

54

of their crucifix and Virgin.

"Holy images covered every wall of my parents' house.

"Their house had the immobility of a nightmare.

"The first color I knew was that of horror."

Almost everything that I know and can know about my pre-adult life lies not in memories, but in these writings.

"Religion:

"Days and nights all there was was a sordid and fearful childhood. Morality wore the habit of religion. Mortal sin or the Saint of Sunday and the Ashes of Wednesday kept on judging me. Thus, condemnation and repression crushed me even before I was born. Childhood was stolen from children.

"Never enough can be said, muttered and snarled, when one has been born into anger. THEIR criminal hands took hold of my fate. HER umbilical cord strangled me dropping out of her. All I desired was everything.

"Listen to the children. All children come red out of the womb because their mothers know God.

"The night's replete with their cries: unceasing flagellated howls which are broken by the sound of a window slammed shut. Harsh and drooling screams die inside lips that are muzzled. We who're about to be suffocated throw our murmurs and screeches, our names, into a hole; that hole is everywhere. They laugh waterfalls of scorn down of us. If any speech comes out of us, it appears as nonsense: when the adults answered me, I puked. My few cries, like dead leaves tumbled by winds, climbed out of my body and vaporized.

"It is a very Parisian garden which I found for hiding myself."

My mother was a great lady. Whenever she walked into the local grocery store which the neighborhood rich used, she'd order whatever young boy she could find to fetch the various items she happened to desire and to bring them to the taxi waiting for her. It didn't occur to Mother that she might have to pay.

If it was my misfortune to accompany her, I'd crawl behind her, trying to be invisible. I didn't know her. Me, an orphan. As soon as she was about to leave the store, as quickly as possible I'd pay the man behind the counter. My face flamed as if struck by sun. I don't know what happened when I wasn't there to pay: at that time events which I didn't perceive didn't take place.

At that time I thought, let them all go to hell.

It's entirely possible that I wasn't the only person who knew that mother could always do as she wanted. For the Queen of England never carries her own money. Someone's money.

Three or four times, trying to escape her, I ran away. Since my father was so gentle he was subservient to Mother, I also had to run away from him.

I climbed down their back fire escape to the street below. Walked down streets 'till there was nowhere to go.

"There's a white man behind the spindly trees. He leans into the sky to grasp at the wood and falls down on all fours, a dog. On pebbles. Now he's crawling across the street, stretches out one hand as if it's dead. Trying to become a wall, I hide against one. Sooted ivy and begonias are crushed. Another man rises up; his face, burning and lips too red. He walks toward me, hand touching his cock, and another man, aghast, leaps out of a window. His arms beat against the sky as if he's a windmill. Through the froth on his lips, he says, 'They've stolen me.'"

Walked down the streets until there was nowhere.

"A lying hypocritical society turns around the grave of the holes in the garden of childhood."

I had to return home.

I didn't want to escape my parents because I hated them, but because I was wild. Wild children are honest. My mother wanted to command me to the point that I no longer existed. My father was so gentle, he didn't exist. I remained uneducated or wild because I was imprisoned by my mother and had no father.

My body was all I had.

"a a a a I don't know what language is. l l l l I shall never learn to count."

I remained selfish. There was only my mother and I.

Selfishness and curiosity are conjoint. I'd do anything to find out about my body, investigated the stenches arising out of trenches and armpits, the tastes in every hole. No one taught me regret. I was wild to make my body's imaginings actual.

And I knew that I couldn't escape from my parents because I was female, not yet eighteen years old. Even if there was work for a female minor, my parents my educators and my society had taught me I was powerless and needed either parents or a man to survive. I couldn't fight the whole world; I only hated.

So in order to escape to parents, I needed a man. After I had escaped, I could and would hate the man who was imprisoning me. And after that, I would be anxious to annihilate my hatred, my double-bind.

This personal and political state was the only one they had taught me. "I'm always in the wrong so I'm a freak. I'm always destroying everything including myself which is what I want to do."

Red was the color of wildness and of what is as yet unknown.

As my body, which my mother refused to recognize and thus didn't control, grew, it grew into sexuality. As if sexuality can occur without touching. Masturbated not only before I knew what the word masturbation meant, but before I could come. Physical time became a movement toward orgasm. I became sexually wilder. I wanted a man to help me escape my parents, but not for sexual reasons, because I didn't need another sexual object. Mine was my own skin.

Longing equaled skin. Skin didn't belong to anyone in my kingdom of untouchability.

I hadn't decided to be a person. I was almost refusing to become a person because the moment I was, I would have to be lonely. Conjunction with the entirety of the universe is one way to avoid suffering.

"Today I don't have any friends. Mother's criticized everyone I've tried to know as being 'nouveau riche' or 'not pious enough.' This idiot finds it normal to run to a priest to ask him whether it's alright for me to play with whatever friend I'm lucky enough to have. No one's ever good enough for her or her priest.

"Mother just hates everyone who isn't of our blood. She uses the word 'blood.' She hates everyone and everything that she can't control: everything gay, lively, everything that's growing, productive. Humaneness throws her into a panic; when she panics, she does her best to hurt me.

"I've taken refuge in the basement. In its stale air. Jesus sits dead in its windows.

"I found safety there, sitting on a horse who was rocking on decaying moleskins or crouching on a red cushion which needed to be repaired. There I told myself story after story. Every story is real. One story always leads to another story. Most of the stories tell how I'm born:

"'Before I was born, I lived in Heaven. There the inhabitants spend their time imaging a sweet white Jesus who kills figures such as Mitterrand or a golden Joseph, swaddled in velvet, who plays Heavy Metal. There're dolls everywhere. But I owned a cap gun which I used to blind pigeons and minutely examined my body. Then I entered a world in which, since God sees everything that happens there, I had to become curious.'

"God followed me into the basement. Though I was curious, He frightened me. I decided that curiosity has to be more powerful than fear and that I need curiosity plus fear, for I'm going to journey through unknown, wonderful and ecstatic realms. If there is God, the coupling of curiosity and fear is the door to the unknown.

"For a while there was no one in my life."

I became older.

"I adored the maid who was younger than me. One day she told me she was planning to get married and have a child."

"'I'll dress my baby only in white,' the maid said.

"'You can't do that,' I replied, 'because you're poverty-sticken.'

"Her face turned the color of my cunt's lips. It was she who was red, not me.

"'I'm not poor: I work and my boyfriend has a steady job with the subway.'

"The word *work* meant nothing to me; I continued to try to teach her that she was too poor to afford a baby. That she couldn't clothe a baby.

"In desperation, Henrietta (the maid) couldn't find any language; finally she located the word *evil*. I was 'evil.'

"This word *evil* made me begin to think.

"I remembered how mother calls her 'the girl' and talks about her in the third person even when Henrietta's in the same room. Whereas if I show the slightest disrespect to any of my parents' friends, I'm severely punished. I see that I'm being trained to want as my friends only the girls who come from the wealthiest and most socially powerful families. I see that education is one means by which this class economic system becomes incorporated in the body as personal rules. The world outside me that's human seems to be formed by economics, hierarchy and class.

"I'm anything but free.

"I want Henrietta to explain to me the degree of filth proper to each class.

"After that I fell in love with the gardener. Eight years old, I was no longer human.

"There's the country. I'm learning the names of the flowers of night and those of water, heliotrope and St. John's wort, water lilies and all the sorts of roses. I know that there are birds of the evening and those of the night; bats, screech-owls and baby owls fallen out of their nests and drowned in a pail of water haunt my dreams.

"The summer air in the grotto, like a blind cat, walks down my stomach. I had to disappear finally. I pressed myself between a gray-red wall and its ivy growing up from the ground. In there, I became many-legged, a spider, a hedgehog and raccoon, every animal I'll ever want to be and every animal that is.

"This is what God saw when He followed me into the basement.

"I observed wheat fields, corn fields, clover the colors of flesh, poppy and huge cornflower fields, fields framed by weeping willows and poplars.

"Behind mother's kitchen, a plain which is sparkling in the sun appears. Cricket-rustling and fat bumblebee-buzzing. Filthy flies are fertilizing its pastures. In the full of noon I walk out here. My head bare to the light, the hay scabbed my knees. There was a new taste on my hot lips, lavender and burning skin. I'm journeying in order to know vertigo and enchantment.

"My father showed me all of this and more: dragonflies, the king-fishers and wrens, the day-flies and all that glistens around them; wild ducks, turkey-hens and all the fish. Daddy taught me the trees and the seasons, tar, the forests and fire.

"Now and forever, I no longer care about religion.

"No religion: this is the one event that'll never change. No religion is my stability and surety.

"Mother's demanding that I see her priest."

I couldn't escape my family because I still didn't know a man who would help me.

For reasons other than escape, I wanted this man to be wilder than me.

When I was twenty-three, it began to be possible for me to escape my parents. I started to remember directly, not just through writing, all that happened to me. A sailor is a man who keeps on approaching the limits of what is describable.

I was wild. My brother was the first man who helped me. I spent an increasing amount of time in his apartment.

It was the days of ghosts. Still is. Not the death, but the actual forgetting even of the death of sexuality and wonderment, of all but those who control and those and that which can be controlled. Since an emotion's an announcement of value, in this society of death (of values), emotions moved like zombies through humans.

At my brother's house I met artists. Romare Bearden. Maya Deren. This hint that it was possible to live in a community other than my parents', a community that wasn't hateful and boring, one of intellectuals, by opening up the world of possibilities, saved me from despair and nihilism.

I still couldn't break with my parents' society on my own.

There Paul Rendier took my virginity. Fucking enabled me to cast off my past; red gave me the authority to be other than red.

Once I had fucked, the only thing I wanted was to give myself entirely and absolutely to another person. I didn't and don't know what this desire means other than itself.

In me dead blood blushed crimson into the insides of roses and became a living color that's unnameable.

When Rendier left me and I didn't know where he was, I had to find him because all that was left of me, all that was me, was to give myself to him.

In order to run after Rendier, I had to break with my family. My father was already dead; he had left me enough money so I no longer economically needed a man. I know that women need men not just due to weakness. I escaped my mother because sexuality was stronger than her.

Then I found Rendier. We lived together one year.

After Rendier, "I threw myself onto every bed as a dead sailor flings himself into the sea. My sexuality at that time was separate from my real being. For my real being's an ocean in which all beings die and grow.

"The acceptance of this separation between sexuality and being was the invention of hell."

Searching, I traveled to Berlin. There I lived with a doctor named Wartburg whose apartment I wouldn't leave. I never saw anyone but him. I had wanted to give myself to another and now I was beginning to. Wartburg put me in a dog collar; while I was on all fours, he held me by a leash and beat me with a dog whip. He was elegant and refined and looked like Jean Genet.

At that time, "nobody was able to look for me, find me, join me."

What dominated me totally was my need to give myself entirely and absolutely directly to my lover. I knew that I belonged to the community of artists or freaks, not because the anger in me was unbearable, but because my overpowering wish to give myself away wasn't socially acceptable. As yet I hadn't asked if there was someone named *me*.

At this time I first read De Sade. Perusing *120 Days in Sodom* exulted and horrified me; horror because I recognized my self or desire.

Living with Wartburg ended; I had no money nor friends in Berlin. All I wanted was to be entirely alone. I had strong political convictions so I took off for Russia. There I couldn't speak any language.

Loneliness and my kind of life in Russia physically deteriorated me to such a point that I almost died.

From that time onwards, I have always felt anxiety based on this following situation: I need to give myself away to a lover and simultaneously I need to be always alone. Such loneliness can be a form of death. My brother found me in Russia and brought me back to New York.

I first attempted to dissipate my anxiety by deciding to fuck and be fucked only when there could be no personal involvement. I traveled on trains like a sailor, and made love with men I encountered on those trains.

My attempt failed. Friends said about me, "She's on her way to dying young." But I wanted more than most people to live because just being alive wasn't enough for me. Wildness or curiosity about my own body was showing itself as beauty. My brother placed as much importance in sexuality as I did. When I met Bourenine at one of the orgies my brother gave, I was ready to try again to give myself to another, to someone who was more intelligent than me and a committed radical.

Anxiety turned into a physical disease. Bourenine said that he wanted to save me from myself, my wildness, my weakness. He made me feel safe enough to try to give myself to him.

I became so physically weak that I stood near to death. When Bourenine believed that I might die, he began to love me. I began to hate him yet I worshipped him because I thought he protected me. My gratitude has always been as strong as my curiosity, as is mostly true in those who are wild.

Even then I knew that most men saw me as a woman who fucked every man in sight. Since Bourenine wanted to be my father, he didn't want me to make my own decisions. I saw myself as split between two desperations: to be loved by a man and to be alone so I could begin to be. When I met B, he was married. I didn't mind because I didn't really want to deal with an other. Since B immediately saw me as I saw myself, I saw in B a friend and one who wouldn't try, since he was married, to stop me from becoming a person, rather than wild.

From the first moment that B and I spoke together in the Brasserie Lipp, there was a mutual confidence between us.

I had pushed my life to an edge. Having to give myself away absolutely to a lover and simultaneously needing to find myself. Now I had to push my life more.

Bourenine's inability to deal with what was happening to me turned him violent and aggressive. During this period, B and I met several times and discussed only political issues. As soon as I began speaking personally to him, we commenced spending as much time alone with each other as we could.

Wildness changed into friendship.

I had already written, "No religion: this is the one event that will never change. No religion is my only stability and security.

"Mother insisted that I see her priest to such a degree that I had to.

"Let me describe this Director of Human Morality. (One of the Directors of Human Morality.) While his hands were sneaking everywhere, all he could see in my words was his own fear.

"Right after I saw him, I wrote down in my secret notebook, 'Religion is a screen behind which the religious shields himself from suffering, death and life. The religious decide everything prior to the fact; religion's a moral system because by means of religion the religious assure themselves that they're right.

"'From now on I'm going to decide for myself and live according to *my* decisions — decisions out of desire. I'll always look . . . like a sailor who carries his huge cock in his hand . . . I'll travel and travel by reading. I won't read in order to become more intelligent, but so that I can see as clearly as possible that there's too much lying and hypocrisy in this world. I knew from the first moment what I was, that I hated them, the hypocrites.'

"As soon as I had written this down, I knew that I was dreadfully and magnificently alone.

"I am now seventeen years old.

"All around me are termites, familial households without their imaginations. They would never rise an iota above their daily tasks, daily obligations, daily distractions. Everyone who's around me has lost the sense that life's always pushing itself over an edge while everything is being risked.

"So now there's going to be a war! Hey! Finally something exciting's going to happen! The United States's coming back to life! The government of the United States is realizing that someone's angry about something-or-other and's descending to offer its people a target for their bilious bitterness. O emotionless sentimental and sedentary people, because your government's a democracy and responsible to you, it is giving you a whole race to detest, a nation on which to spit, a religion to damn, everything you've ever wanted. You're incontestably superior to men who wear dresses. Again you will become important in the eyes of the world.

"You Americans need to be right. This war will not only be a pathway to future glory: once war's begun, you'll feel secure because you'll no longer have to understand anything else. You will again know what good and evil are.

"Tomorrow you're going to give your sons joyfully to the desert, maybe daughters if you're feminist enough, because you're emotionless and, in war, you can be so emotionless, you don't have to be. Therefore war allows people to surpass themselves. The English know this full well. As soon as you have tanks and dead people all around you, you'll be able to feel alive, once more powerful, magnanimous and generous to all the world.

"All that your grandparents and parents, educators and society showed you, the triumphal road, the right way, the path of true virtue — the RIGHT, the GOOD — is only Liberty mutilated and Freedom shredded into scraps of flesh. The raped body. A man's a child who walks down the right road, thoroughly carved out and signposted, because all he can see is the word *danger*."

2. LETTERS FROM MY MOTHER TO MY FATHER

(The days of begging, the days of theft. No nation who began for the sake of escape and by fire can be all bad. Even if democracy is a myth. Myths make actuality, that's what myths say. Me, I've always been on fire for the sake of fire.

(Listen. They thought they could have their freedom through something called democracy, but they forgot about knowledge and no one's ever had freedom anyways. So now it's all falling apart, this economy, a so-called culture and a society, so-called, and anyway there's never been anything except loneliness, the days of begging, the days of theft.

(This is what the books tell about American history: You can travel and wherever you'll go, there'll be no one but you. Listen, American history says: the sky's blue and every shade of purple and then so bright that your eyes have to be red in order to see it.

(A sun declines in front of you. The sunless air'll make your fingers grow red and there spots will swell. Every possible color in the world'll sit in this sky until evening black spreads over the air or your pupils, and you will never be able to know which.

JOIN THE U.S. ARMY

GET KILLED

(Solitary, mad, deprived of community, depraved and proud of all your depravity, you dream, no longer of a lover, but solely of sex the way a rat desires garbage.

(Stronger than dreams will be your inability to forget what you don't know.

(Specifics: northern California. Myths say, settled by white bums and white prostitutes desperate for gold. Who, as soon as they had found the yellow, tried to decimate all non-whites. And kept on trying. Born out of attempted murder, loneliness and wildness. The yellows who survived formed their own gangs. The cities born out of riffraff and, unlike those back East, knew no culture.

(Said that they could never be poor.

(What we're dealing with here is a race of degenerates. A mongrel people who doesn't know how to do anything but hate itself. No wonder they love God so much because God doesn't exist. We're dealing with a people manifestly incapable of Manifest Destiny.

(Thieves or imbeciles. Take your choice or change. Sooner or later some people'll govern these lands, but not until all their inhabitants have died.

(In other words: ungovernable.)

LETTER

Dear B,

Our friendship has no stability. Our meetings are taking place only by chance. Well, maybe that's how things — reality is.

All my emotions, fantasies, imaginings, desires are reality because I must have a life that matters, that is emotional.

I don't want to speak anymore about anything that's serious. I just want to speak.

I'm writing you and I'm going to keep on writing you so that all the fantasies that we have about each other through which we keep perceiving each other will die. After that we'll be so naked with each other that I will be your flesh. You mine.

I don't need to tell you any of this because you already know. But you're still running away from me and I hate it when you do this.

This is what I want to say: When I saw you in the early evening, sometime around 7:30, your friend, whoever was with you, looked right through me. Just as if I was still a child wearing the ring that I had always wanted that renders its bearer invisible. I'm not your child.

If I could be invisible and go everywhere, I would. To outlandish lands and where there are great people.

While your friend was staring through me, you stood up and walked past me without noticing me. I remember the first time we met alone: we talked together for hours, almost until the sun rose, then despite my shyly asking you to stay, you left my brother's apartment.

None of all I've just said matters. That's the point.

All that matters to me now, has mattered to me, to the point that it's painful, is that we tell each other everything. Since I fear rejection more than anything else, I must have trust. Then I won't be able to leave your life and you won't be able to leave mine. Despite the fact that — I'm not going to waste my time trying to explain this to you or convince you that this is true — your world is cozy. Me — I'm nothing. I promise you that I won't blame you for your smugness. You need that kind of crap: images of richness, maybe because you weren't born that way, so you can live confidently in this world. I need to be invisible and without language, animal.

ADDENDUM

If you want to contact me, you'll have to find me.

If you really know me, you can do this.

I started writing you because I believed that if we told each other everything, there could be only trust between us. Then we wouldn't be able to hurt each other so much that we destroyed each other's lives.

I just told you that I despise your bourgeoisie and your wealthy friends.

Maybe it isn't possible for two people to be together without barriers in a state of unredeemable violence.

I think that Mother was still with Bourenine at this point, but I don't know for sure.

Kathy Acker

Dear B,

The more I try to tell you everything, the more I have to find myself. The more I try to describe myself, the more I find a hole. So the more I keep saying, the less I say and the more there is to say. I'm confusing everything between us.

I'm not being clear here.

I don't want to tell you anything.

The only thing that's possible between us is a car accident. A car accident's now the only thing that can deliver me from the anguish that's you.

I'm dumb, wild, and I don't want anyone coming too near me. But the more emotion comes out, the more I want you.

I've been writing down every type of fatal accident I can imagine. Whenever I do this, I feel calm and as if I'm orgasming. I know I have to follow death until its end. That road passes through putrefaction and disintegration.

Whenever I'm traveling that road, I'm calm.

When I'm lying in your arms, I'm calm.

At the same time I have to battle you; there's something in me that has to oppose you in even the most trivial of matters.

I still tell you everything as if I'm more than naked with you. I hate you. My mind's moving round and round, in tighter and tighter spirals. It's going to end up in a prison, a void, destroying itself. I always try to defeat myself.

Until the present I've thrown away my past. As soon as something's been over, I've gotten rid of it; I've acted as if that relationship never happened. I never had memories that I wanted.

Now I believe that, though I'm still doing everything possible to defeat myself, our friendship, to misunderstand you, and to view everything in the worst possible light, you're going to always be with me. I believe you're not going to leave me. I believe without understanding this that you see exactly what I am and that you're guiding me.

At the same time I've been observing that our friendship's changing me: I no longer know who I am and I'm beginning to see what I am. So when you're observing me and know and guiding me, you're perceiving I-don't-know-who-anymore. This combination of your eye and I-don't-know-who-anymore is a work of art made by both of us and it's untitled.

Now I'm rational.

I know you hate me when I'm rational because, as you've told me, you don't like it when there are rules. You don't like rules.

Here are my most recent thoughts: When I met you, I was drowning because I wasn't going to let another person be close to me. (This frigidity is named wildness.) I asked you rather than anyone else for help because I knew that you're an emotional paralytic. Perverse, as usual, I hollered "Help!" so that you'd beat me over the head so I'd finally drown or fall off a crumbling cliff. What I really wanted to do. You're just what I want, B: a better death method.

I decided to tell you everything because, by telling you everything, I'd make you kill me faster. I always wanted to test everything to the point of death. Beyond.

(Children and dogs squatted in the dirt.

("This looks like the high road to Hell," one kid said.

("From Hell."

(It was a desolate land, a populace who had nothing except government criminals, and now it was going to war. Since no one knew where the country they were fighting was, no one thought anything was real.

(What the weapons might be in this war of the imagination made actual no person knew. Half-buried skeletons of cows, horses with mouths dried open, cats' and goats' legs.

(IN THEIR OWN LANDS THE ARABS TEAR OUT EACH OTHER'S EYEBALLS AND RAPE THEIR OWN CHILDREN. IF ONE AMERICAN SOLDIER GOES INTO BATTLE, BECAUSE RIGHT MAKES MIGHT, HE HAS TO WIN.

— some American government official

(When a man on his deathbed had told the child that he had killed many men, the child was envious.

(Through the rest of his childhood, the child bore the idol of a perfection which he could never attain. All he could be was a mercenary.

(Every son is heir to the death of his father: every son needs this death to experience a preliminary death and every son must have his father die so that he can live.

(What about his father's life? When a child inherits the father's life, he inherits his place in the prison of morality and can never break out.

(In other words: we are the children without inheritance.

(He was fucked over as a child. When he grew up, he looked for a trade. Searched. Since he always wore black, people thought him a preacher. But he had never witnessed anything that had to do with God.

(The country went to war as it always did, in some other country.

(He watched men being killed in many ways and women left for dead and forgotten.

(Then he glimpsed ships. He observed vultures as large as any tree but too high up to be seen in detail. He was too lost to want to do anything but soar.

(One day, he came upon a woman who told fortunes. He thought, as if there's a fortune to be told.

(Asked her about the fortune of the lost. "What's going to happen to me?"

(She gibbered at some night.

(Asked again, "In a society of murderers, how can children be educated to something else?"

(The beautiful woman answered that they should be raised with the wild dogs.

(He replied that life wasn't a laughing matter.

(The woman asked, "How's it possible to be lost? How can anything that exists be lost?

("The cards have been lost in the night. Pull out these cards."

(She turned his cards over: "Your problem is desire. You've unsuccessfully tried to resolve, dissolve, desire through work. The result of this repression is that either you must go to war or you are at war. The cards are unclear on this temporal point. You're now moving through the negative part of that dialectic; there'll be synthesis when your centrallized power has died.")

LETTER

Dear B,

At this moment because I'm perverse I'm telling myself: Without you I'm lost. I'm letting myself realize what I don't usually let myself. And as soon as I see that I need you, I imagine your absence. Again and again I'm picturing you rejecting me. This is the moment I love.

(I never had a father. This isn't correct because, science says, every animal has a father. I never knew my father which fact, for me, is the same as not having a father.

(I'm writing about my father whom I never knew.)

LETTER

Dear B,

I doubt everything.

You're asking me two questions: Do I think that you don't love me because I doubt your love? Do I think you'll never trust me because I doubt?

No.

When I doubt to the point that emptiness sits under my skin and someone or something feels nausea, I begin to be. Everything that used to irritate and still rasps me is now wonderful and desirable.

Of course there are times when I can't bear this relationship to doubt. When I hate that which gives me the most pleasure.

I don't want everything to be complex; I don't want to live in closed rooms like some academic. I want everything between us and everything to be simple. That is, real. Like flesh. Not hypocritical.

But in the past when I tried to kill off hypocrisy, I destroyed possibilities for love.

I will not descend into the night, for that romanticism is a disease.

(My dream: We're kissing, but I feel nothing. He takes my clothes off me, then picks me naked up off the floor. Carries me into somewhere. In there he cradles me as if I'm a child. I grab what I feel to be safety. At that moment he starts systematically hurting me. After hurting me for a long time, he holds me and the world opens up.)

Mother moved into her brother's apartment.

LETTER

I said that I wanted us to be so naked with each other that the violence of my passion was amputating me for you.

Listen. I am not a victim.

I don't know what the end of all this can be.

At the moment neither of us is in danger.

69

Mother didn't want to live with my father.

CONTINUATION OF LETTER

I want to be clearer about what I just said:

You don't believe that you own me. What you think, precisely, is that you've put me in slavery and I'll always be your slave. You think that you now control, limit, imprison, bar, categorize and define my existence.

I'm hot. As soon as you saw that I got pleasure from yielding to you, you turned away from me. Then I really lay myself at your feet.

You stated that you were denying me because you needed to be private.

But what's real to you isn't real to me. I'm not you.

Precisely: my truth is that your presence in my life for me is absence.

I'll say this another way: You believe that everything that's outside you ("reality") is a reflection of your perceptions, thoughts, ideas, etc. In other words, that you can see, feel, hear, understand the world. Other people. I don't believe that. I believe that I'm so apart from the world, from other people, that I have to explain everything to every single person to such an extent, in order to communicate at all, that for me communication's almost impossible. Day by day my actuality has become more and more hollow and is now breaking apart like a body decomposing under my own eyes.

You've destroyed every possibility of religion for me and I want you to help me.

(The United States, begun on less than zero, on dislike, negation and fire, had inflated itself into an empire. Now, it has returned to less than zero. My mother realized this. The Christ of her mother had taught her that she had no right to exist; love had taught her otherwise. Fuck all of that. My mother thought. She wrote love letters to my father while knowing that they didn't matter.

(Mother said, "Nothing matters when there is nothing.")

LETTER

Dear B,

I've told you that I never want to live with you. (I can't live with you because you're married.) Now something more: I have to be alone.

70

This isn't rejection.

I'm going to go away from you so that I can find something new, maybe a "me." Then we'll be able to be completely naked with each other and perceive each other as each of us actually is.

Whatever it takes so this can happen.

I know you think that my desire to be alone is just one more instance of how I run away from everything. That I've tried to run away to the extent that I no longer wanted to have a self. (If there is a self.)

This is what I think: In the face of death,

(There's no more education, no more culture (if culture depends on a commonly understood history), and perhaps no more middle class in the United States. There's War.)

when all is real,

(In the face of this very real American death, there is only the will to live.)

I will be able (to have a self) to say something, "I've seen him, I can say his real name. I know that nothing, including this, matters."

In other words: there's nothing.

Because there's nothing, I don't have to be trained, as females are, to want to stop existing.

But: Your desire for me when I see you halts my breath. Want torches my mouth into contortions. No longer a mouth. You're mad.

If only in public I could throw myself on top of your feet and kiss them so everyone would know. But I can't have anything to do with you publicly.

I'm frightened that my ability to go all the way with you, to give myself to you in ownership and at the same time know that everything between us has to be a lie in the face of your marriage will destroy me: my honesty, my integrity. For by railing and revolting against bourgeois hypocrisy, I became me.

It's because of you I now sleep and want to eat. Since I'll not deny my own body, I now know that I can and will lie ignobly, superbly, triumphantly.

(Mother thought that there must be romance other than romance.

71

Kathy Acker

According to Elisabeth Roudinesco in her study of Lacan, around 1924 a conjuncture of early Feminism, a new wave of Freudianism, and Surrealism gave rise to a new representation of the female: nocturnal, dangerous, fragile and powerful. The rebellious, criminal, insane or gay woman is no longer perceived as a slave to her symptoms. Instead, "in the negative idealization of crime [she] discovers the means to struggle against a society [which disgusts]."]

LETTER

Dear B,

You want me to live a lie and you admire me for my honesty. Repeatedly you've said that you respect my intelligence more than that of any woman you've ever met and you treat me convulsively and continually like less than a dog. Female variety.

I still believe that you know everything about me and I don't think that you understand anything that has to do with me.

The only conclusion to all this is that reality has reversed itself. The reverse, which is a window, has set me on fire.

My conclusion isn't sweet. You call it "a penchant for the night." But I no longer have a penchant for the night.

At this moment I'm halfway between life and death. And death and life.

I'm now trying to write down something called *truth*. Which isn't *my truth* because I'm not an enclosed or self-sufficient being.

My conclusion: You're no longer behind everything that happens. You, sexual love. Since you're no longer at the bottom of everything, where I know I can always find you, no one can mean anything to me anymore.

I hate our wildness. The only life each of us has is when we're together. Just as I had to escape my family, now I have to get away from you, from the mad rhythm named *us*, from our nights, from horror.

Three Poems
Carla Lemos

KORE

Because they couldn't pronounce her name —
a name so foreign they didn't have all
its letters in their alphabet —
they gave her a Greek one.

The village doctor suggested the name:
an old name,
and distasteful:
conjuring up visions of
bloody
thighs, sexual sacrifice,
unpreventable
birth,
faces turned orange by night fires.
A primal memory now,
gilded over,
contained
in the upright
outlines
of Byzantine saints.

High sunsplashed cheeks and forehead

It was a joke, the kind young Greek males
like to play on unsuspecting foreign girls
with their credulous round eyes.
So that when she told Dimitrios the name
he began to laugh, looking up into her blue eyes, until
seeing her as she stood above him in the doorway
above the stairs, her red hair pulled back
from the smooth skin of her face like a fruit
to be bitten into, and the black-backgrounded fabric

of her dress falling down from her clavicle over
her breasts, patterned with hundreds of small
multicolored flowers, past the fleshed belly
and wide hips so unlike the girls of the village,
who were large breasted but narrowly framed,
her long fingers resting on the doorjamb, her
unwavering smile signifying that
she was content with their joke—her new name—
he stopped laughing.

> "'Dimitroula mou, with your
>   taka-taka-taka'—
>   a song about a girl who wants to
>   but acts like she doesn't."

> *Silhouette of a woman,*
> *shoeless,*
> *behind her sea and sky*
> *merging light*

> *as strands woven into tight nets.*
> *Or dazzling filaments*
> *fallen in heaps*
> *on terraces,*
>   *the edges of stairs,*

>   *in corners.*

AT CROSSROADS: HERMES PSYCHOPOMP

FIRST STATE: *Almost conscious daydreaming*
Conversations in bars where
above the city's vapors and orange interference
sky floats
starless
dense *nigredo*

Adam interrupts himself to say:
Eve, I love you.

She smiles red and white: Do you think
we can end rehearsal early tomorrow?
We'll only be going over acts one and
two. The last act isn't finished. *(. . . his
thin arms and breasts like a pubescent
girl. He came in one day wearing a
leather jacket and a t-shirt with an air-
brushed painting of Shiva. . . .)* Yet. . . .
(The beating of blood in my ears.

Adam repeats, I love you, Eve.

A perfect and true love.)
Her eyes catching reflections of glasses,
drinks, scotch with ice, martinis,
transparent edges whitened with salt
and gleaming like fishes' eyes. But if I
were to fall in love with you, *(I wanted
to ask if he would help me breastfeed
our children. If we had children . . .)*
if I were to allow myself to fall in love
with you, and I could, I suppose, that
would be the point at which *(scintilla)*
you would run away with my best
friend. Quicksilver her white and red
smile. Light chiming on wet edges.
Dazzling, she knew. Her body tired
like lead.

(She speaks so damn slowly.
Even on stage.)
•

75

Carla Lemos

SECOND STATE: *Falling in and out of sleep*
Lying on his bed, clothed in evening wear, their conversation
dwindles, his touch becomes sexual. She, sliding toward orgasm,
struggles to pull herself away. *(What he dislikes about Bill is his
softness, his femininity. Not that he finds Bill gay, no, Bill isn't
gay, he's soft, and that makes Adam uptight.)* She withdraws, slips
inward where resolution is impossible, suspends sensation,
remains a broken branch:

> — *Is this thing of which you speak rare or commonly found?*
> — *It is cast in the streets and trampled in the dung.*

She pulls herself to a near conscious state.

           .

THIRD STATE: *Asleep, dreaming*
Eve's living in a house with Adam, Fred, and Howard. She and
Adam are married, and she is pregnant.
Inside in the living room or kitchen, while Fred chats about art,
Eve imagines his hands wings, hovering, directionless. Outside,
visible through a window, Adam and Howard are taking a large
piece of wood out of a precariously balanced stack of eucalyptus.
The wood begins to fall, large logs sliding down the steep sides of
the pile. Adam and Howard catch logs and throw them back on
top of the woodpile which transforms into a hill so that they are
standing on the other side of a hill throwing large pieces of wood
over the crest of the hill. The logs turn slowly into boulders. Eve
watches one fall down from the sky, on top of her, crushing her.

Eve — the dreamer — tries to redream the section
in which she is crushed:
She lying
in the bed
she slept in
as a child.
Aborting,
odor foul like tombs.
She mute,
sliding to the floor.
Fred, hands salt-white,
picks her up.
His feet

had she seen
were lingering
ghosts of
movement
like those in photos
by Muybridge.
Disappearing.

Eve propelling herself into the other room, falls
against objects: before her eyes, red.

*She woke from a dream in which the first man — a boy then — she
had ever been in love with was leaving her again because of his
family's disapproval, and she, looking at the suitable woman he
would leave her for, felt hysteria overwhelming her anger. She
hadn't dreamt of him for years. That morning she tried calling
him, hundreds of miles away, but his name wasn't in the
directory. Is it possible, she thought, driving the freeway to the
next city, that your first love determined every following one?
It was more than love — everything in her life had been like that.
She sensed a direction, some place she was going towards but had
never been able to name clearly enough so that she could walk
a straight path there; instead she'd let events, other people's
decisions, quirks of fate or chance, determine her life. She'd
moved unerringly to the place where she now was by deflection.*

A large fold-out bed fills the next room.
Adam wakes and sees Eve at the door,
her face bright as tin.
His body, lacking spirit, is dark.
He sits up, the woman next to him — blondish,
heavily made-up, with a foreign accent — stirs
in her dream of Africa, where lions devour
wildebeest on the brown savannah.
He starts to get out of bed, but is afraid.

Eve wakes up.

FOURTH STATE: *Awake*
She is unable to cry.

Carla Lemos

THROUGH CROSSROADS: HERMES TRICKSTER

> *She said I want a fur coat made from*
> *the skins of Metro rats. 600 Metro rats*
> *with their little feet hanging down.*
> *And naked tails.*

IF YOU SEE AN UNATTENDED PACKAGE OR BAG ON THE UNDERGROUND:

DON'T TOUCH IT.

Green walls
cigarettes
dulling layers
olive oil
cooked sheep and goat fat
tssssss

Απαγορεύεται τα τραγούδια
Songs are forbidden

clutter of Greek
rushing streams the surface twisting over
detritus — flora, rock — surface integral
coherent

Old man singing rembetika

It was with a dance like this that I had my first sexual
intercourse, *pos to lene?*

Walls faded to colorless
patches from no perceptible cause

Yeah, that's how you say it.

laughter

With the Surtaki?

murky with smoke

No, the tango.

laughter
grease, tssssss

78

Only she wasn't American.
Those girls were Austrian.
Or German, he continued. She was European, she was Danish
(black black hair, straight always separated and fallen into
clinging sections across a forehead white as unbaked clay, into
his eyes).
I knew only about five words of English. I had heard the Rolling
Stones' song Satisfaction and I had asked someone what it meant.
So I knew that word *(eyes equally black with slight in-turning, no*
clear division between iris and pupil).
We were dancing all night the tango. Had been drinking all day.
We danced and then after this dance, I picked her up in my arms
and carried her off . . . something *(vague gesture with his left*
hand, a waving near his forehead with hands thick from painting
churches, Saints) . . . it was dark . . . off . . . *(eyebrows black,*
almost one together between his eyes).

Panayia, *all holiness*

I was only 16
and I was full of all these ideas about what it meant to be a man.
And I didn't know anything.

η Παναγία, Mother of god

A woman's cunt was a mystery to me.
(hands thick from walls, ceilings, painted altars):
You can't imagine what it was like in Greece then.

I walked behind the carved screen.
The church painter looked up,
startled, disbelieving, immediately
identifying:
the foreign woman

After we came back I was the one who was upset,
who didn't know what had happened.
All I could say was
Satisfaction? Γαμώ

ignorant, unintentioned heretic

Satisfaction? Γαμώ

Carla Lemos

<u>cl</u>atter

την Παναγία μου

laughter

DON'T PULL THE RED EMERGENCY HANDLE BETWEEN STATIONS.

<u>cl</u>atter

Απαγορεύεται να σπάζετε τα πιάτα
Breaking plates is forbidden

laughter

PULL THE EMERGENCY HANDLE ONCE THE TRAIN HAS STOPPED AT THE
NEXT STATION.

. . . . on the southwest corner . . .
                in the living room . . .

                            my fear
                        overtakes me . . .

from one floor or room to another . . .
        transitory sense of foreign, safer worlds . . .

  another world

                     My fear forces me

to move from floor to floor,
        room to room . . . the bedroom . . .
most southern
           part of the house . . .
                my fear

<u>tssssss</u>

TELL THE GUARD OF ANY LONDON TRANSPORT STAFF IMMEDIATELY.

It is night, mother is sitting, kneeling on the floor. She is telling
a man and woman of the horror of being with my father.

. . . difficult to live without someone to hate.
A person needs to have someone to hate.

I go to her. I say, Mother I want to go home.

> *Look at my mother she has no one to hate,*
> *no one to love. She just sits around, drinks a*
> *lot of whiskey, watches television. It's better*
> *to have someone you can hate.*
> > *. . . eyes (eyes equally black, no division*
> > *between iris and pupil)*
> black with slight in-turning, the divison between iris
> and pupil imperceptible . . . .

TELL OTHER PASSENGERS TO . . . *go south* . . . LEAVE THE CAR.

He came into the kitchen where she was standing cooking an
omelette on the stove. Their eyes met: how long had it been since
they'd heard anything? Simultaneously they turned to the
abnormally quiet garden where they had left their two-year-old
daughter half an hour before. They moved to the backdoor where
the screen was tightly closed to keep out flies and insects.
  Standing next to each other looking across the damp green
spring grass, they saw their white-haired daughter sitting, the
sun penetrating her skin to the blue veins winding underneath
through her scanty flesh, and the elastic of her pink ruffled
underwear pressing into her confectionary skin. Her legs were
bent at impossible child angles and her toes, the cheap red polish
chipped like paint from an ancient statue in an Italian church,
curled up from her scuffed white sandals. Firmly between her
fingers, she held a frog, she was carefully, slowly, licking

stomach
  back
    head

          legs

          long padded toes

Three Stories
Janice Galloway

PATERNAL ADVICE

IT IS A SMALL ROOM but quite cheery. There is an old-style armchair off to the left with floral stretch-covers and a shiny flap of mismatching material for a cushion. Behind that, a dark fold-down table, folded down. On the left, a low table surmounted by a glass bowl cut in jaggy shapes, containing keys, fuses, one green apple, and some buttons. Between these two is an orange rug and the fireplace. The fireplace is the focal point of the room. It has a wide surround of sand-colored tiles and a prominent mantelpiece on which are displayed a china figurine, a small stag's head in brass, a football trophy and a very ornate, heavy wrought-iron clock. On the lower part of the surround are a poker and a tongs with thistle tops and a matchbox. Right at the edge, a folded copy of the *Sunday Post* with the Broons visible on top. Behind the fireguard, the coals smoke with dross. The whole has the effect of calm and thoughtfulness. It is getting dark.

Place within this the man SAMMY. He is perched on the edge of the armchair with his knees spread apart and his weight forward, one elbow on each knee for balance. He sits for some time, fists pressing at his mouth as he rocks gently back and forth, back and forth. We can only just hear the sound of a radio from next door, and the odd muffled thump on the wall. More noticeable than either of these is the heavy tick of the clock.

SAMMY exhales noisily. He appears to be mulling over some tricky problem. He is. But we are growing restless in the silence. Suddenly, too close, a noise like a radio tuning and we are in the thick of it.

> put if off long enough and it wasn't doing the boy any favors   just kidology to make out it was   just putting it off for himself more like   no   time to face it and get on with it   right   it was for the best after all and a father had to do his best by his boy even if it was hard even if he didn't want

to   bad father that shirked his responsibilities no bloody use
to anybody   the boy had to be learned right and learned right
right from the word go   right   spare the rod   cruel to be
nobody's fool that sort of thing right   christ tell us something
we don't know

The man stands up abruptly, scowling.

no argument it needed doing   just playing myself here
it's HOW that's the thing that's the whole bloody thing is
HOW   needed to be sure about these things tricky things
needed to be clear in your mind before you opened your mouth
else just make an arse of the whole jingbang just fuck it up
totally TOTALLY aye got to be careful only one go at it right
had to get it across in a oner and he had to learn it get the message right first time right had to know what you were at every
word every move or else

SAMMY walks briskly to the window in obvious emotional agitation, bringing a dout from his right trouser pocket, then a box of
matches. He inserts the dout off-center between his lips, takes a
match from the box, feels for the rough side and sparks the match
blind. The cigarette stump lights in three very quick, short puffs
and still his eyes are focused on something we cannot see, outside
the window in the middle distance. Up on tiptoes next, peering.
Violent puffing. He shouts. BASTARDS! SPIKY-HEIDED BASTARDS.
AD GIE THEM PUNK. WHAT DO THEY THINK THEY LOOK
LIKE EH? JUST WHAT DO THEY THINK THEY'RE AT EH? and
he is stubbing the cigarrette butt out on the sill, turning sharply,
going back to the easy chair to resume his perch. He runs one hand
grease-quick through his hair from forehead to the nape of his neck
and taps his foot nervously.

christ's sake get a grip eh remember what you're supposed to
be doing eh   one think at a time   TIME the time must be
getting on. Get on with it. Hardly see the time now dark already. Right. That's it then. That does it. Wee Sammy will be
wondering what the hell is going on what his daddy is doing
all this time.

SAMMY's eyes mist with sudden tears as the object of his sentimental contemplation appears in an oval clearing above the man's

head. A thinks balloon. Inside, a small boy of about five or six years. He has ash-brown hair, needing cut, a thick fringe hanging into watery eyes that are rimmed pink as though from lack of sleep. It is WEE SAMMY. The balloon expands. WEE SAMMY in a smutty school shirt, open one button at the neck for better fit, and showing a tidemark ingrained on the inside. One cuff is frayed. The trousers are too big and are held up by a plastic snakebelt; badly hemmed over his sandshoes and saggy at the arse. He is slumped against the wall of what we presume to be the lobby. It is understandable his father is upset to think of him: he looks hellish. God knows how long the boy has been waiting there. The eyes, indeed the whole cast of the body suggest it may have been days. And still he waits as we watch.

SAMMY clenches his eyes and the balloon vision pops. *Pop.* Little lines radiate into the air to demonstrate with the word GONE in the middle, hazily. Then it melts too. The man makes a fist in his pocket but he speaks evenly. RIGHT. MAKE YOUR BLOODY MIND UP TIME. RIGHT. Then springs to the door where he steadies himself, smooths his hair back with the palm of his hand and turns the doorknob gently. A barless *A* of light noses in from the lobby with an elongated shadow of the boy inside. The man's face is taut, struggling to remember a smile shape. One hand still rests on the doorknob, the other that brushed back his hair reached forward, an upturned cup, to the child outside. A gesture of encouragement.

SAMMY: Come away in son.

The shadow shortens and the child enters, refocusing in the dim interior. The door clicks as his father closes it behind and the boy looks quickly over his shoulder. The man smiles more naturally now as if relaxing, and settles one hand awkwardly on the boy as they walk to the fireplace. Here, the man bobs down on his hunkers so his eyes are more at a level with his son's. WEE SAMMY's eyes are bland. He suspects nothing. The man has seen this too, and throughout the exchange to come is careful: his manner is craftedly diffident, suffused with stifled anguish and an edge of genuine affection.

SAMMY: *(Pause.)* Well. You're getting to be the big man now eh? Did your mammy say anything to you about me wanting to see you? About what it was about?

WEE SAMMY: *Silence.*

SAMMY: Naw. Did she no, son? Eh. Well. It's to do with you getting so big now, starting at the school and that. You like the school?

WEE SAMMY: *Silence.*

SAMMY: Daft question eh? I didn't like it much either son. Bit of a waster, your da. Sorry now, all right. They said to me at the time I would be, telled me for my own good and I didn't listen. You'll see they said. Thought they were talkin rubbish. What did I know eh? Nothin. Sum total, nothin. Too late though! Ach, we're all the same. Anyway, what's this your da's tryin to say, you'll be thinkin. Eh. What's he sayin to me. Am I right?

WEE SAMMY: *Silence.*

SAMMY: Why doesn't he get on with it, is that what you're thinkin eh? Well this is me gettin on with it as fast as I can son. It's something I have to explain to you. Because I'm your daddy and because you're at the school and everythin. Makin your own way with new people. Fightin your own battles. I'm tryin to make sure I do it right son. It's like I was sayin about the school as well, about tellin you somethin for your own good. But I'm hopin you'll no be like me, that you'll listen right. And that's why I'm tellin you now. Now you're the big man but no too big to tell your daddy he's daft. Eh wee man?

SAMMY *rumples his son's hair proudly.* WEE SAMMY *smiles. This response has an instantly calming effect on the man and he raises himself up to his full height again. His voice needs to expand now to reach down to the boy. His demeanor is altogether more assured and confident.*

SAMMY: OK. That's the boy. Ready? One two three go.

WEE SAMMY *remains silent but nods up smiling at his father as* SAMMY *pushes his hands under the boy's oxters and lifts him up to near eye level with himself.*

SAMMY: Up you come. Hooa! Nearly too heavy for me now. You're the big fella right enough! Now. Here's a seat for you. No be a minute, then up on your feet.

He places his son on the mantelpiece between the brass ornament and the clock. He shifts the clock away to the low table, pats some stouriness off the shelf with the flat of his hand, then lifts the boy high, arms at full stretch, to reposition him in the center of the mantelpiece in place of the clock. The boy is fully upright on the mantelpiece.

SAMMY: Upsadaisy! Up we go!

WEE SAMMY: Dad!

SAMMY: What? What is it son? Not to take my hands away? Och silly! You're fine. On you come, stand up right, straighten your legs. Would I let you fall? Eh? That's my wee man, that's it. See? Higher than me now, nearly up to the ceiling. OK? Now, are you listening to me? Listen hard. I want you to do somethin for me. Will you do somethin for me? Will ye son? Show me you're no feart to jump eh? Jump. Jump down and I'll catch you.

There is a long pause. The man is staring intently into the child's eyes and the child's eyes search back. He is still tall on the mantelpiece among the china and brass ornaments, back and hand flat against the wallpaper flora. The man's eyes shine.

SAMMY: Show your daddy you're no feart son. I'll catch you. Don't be feart, this is your da talkin to you. Come on. For me. Jump and I'll catch you. Don't be scared. Sammy, son, I'm waiting. I'm ready.

A few more seconds of tense silence click out of the clock. WEE SAMMY *blinks. His hands lift from the wall and he decides: one breath and he throws himself from the screaming height of the sill. In the same second,* SAMMY *skirts to the side. The boy crashes lumpily into the tiles of the fire surround. His father sighs and averts his eyes, choking back a sob.*

SAMMY: Let that be a lesson to you son. Trust nae cunt.

NIGHTDRIVING

1.

and he was missing the kids and couldn't sleep so we drove down to the shore, right past the barriers and warning signs to the edge of the cob, the headlights swinging out across the drop to the sand. It

86

was so dark I couldn't see anything over the water from the other side and the sea was just a noise like nervous cellophane, like cellophane crushing in someone's hands. He got out, walking with his back melting in the dark till he was just a blur at the end of the breakwater, a milky stain coming and going in the pitch-black middle of the noise of the sea and the wind outside. And I sat on in the car, twisting to see past where the headlamps cut a wedge across the sand. The rushes showed white needles in the dips of the dunes; dunes and flakes of litter in the ash-color sand. And I was frightened. I opened the door shouting I'M COMING TOO, I'M COMING WITH YOU but the wind blotted up in my mouth and I knew there would be no answer. There would be no answer because I couldn't be heard. Then I started to walk to the edge of the cob, stumbling over shale, afraid I'd fall and tear my hands on the edges of broken shells. So I stopped. I stopped because there was no help for it and stood peering out at the visible sand, searching for what I couldn't see. It was too dark. Yet I didn't want to show how scared I was, keeping looking for movements through the dunes in case anyone was there, in case something was coming. Only a crazy person would be out there in the middle of the night in this howling wind but I kept looking out, into the hard echo of the waves I couldn't see, over the strip of gray sand thinking *There is something more I can't make sense of, something more to come* and getting colder and colder. He was still out there at the end of the breakwater and there was still no answer. The rushes on the dunes were rippling like hair, the battered ends of the waves falling beaten on the shore. The waves kept coming inshore.

2.

since visiting was very free but I was never sure if he would come. The floor was soft so it was sometimes sudden when he did appear, walking silently down the tunnel of striplight: his steady walk to where he knew I would wait. And we went out across the soft tiles to the fresh night air and the borders of the car park outside, slipping our hips between the cold metal curves of people's motors. He strapped the seat belt tight across my chest to hold me down then he'd cough the ignition and the tires cracked over gravel towards the motorway and we'd go speeding down the motorway in pure white lines. He would press the accelerator hard so I sank back into the leather, the seat belt gripping my chest and clothes spreading black against the green leather skins. He would wear blue. Then we'd snake out onto the open lanes and uphill, the whole frame lifting while he reached to turn the music loud with one hand on the wheel. And the rising and the music would fill up inside the car; pressing my spine, bowling me back against the falling leather so I could hardly bear it. Sometimes he would smile from the corner of his mouth, feeling for overdrive with one hand on the wheel and we were tearing down the white lanes, their patterns in the mirror streaming behind like ribbons on the wind. And all I could see on my back were the overcrowding stars of the streetlights, the yellow v-strip dazzling through the music swelling up like bursting glass on the curved road back to the ward.

3.

It's not my car but someone lets me use it if I promise to be careful coming home late. The road I have to travel is treacherous and twists through countryside so there are no lights to mark the edges, just the solid dark that rises with the hills on either side. There are never many cars. You see headlamps float over dips in the darkness and know there must be a road beneath: an unseen path below the rise and fall of the beams in the blackness on either side. And sometimes you see nothing. Not until they slew from nowhere, too close from a corner that didn't exist before, a hidden side-road or farmhouse track. Light veers under your fingernails and there is a second of sudden wakefulness, too much brightness in the car from the other presence outside. You see your own gray hands wrapping the wheel, the swirl of grass like water in the gutters. Then some-how it's over. Only the red smears of taillights dwindling in the mirror show it was ever there and you are driving on. The steering leather under your fists, its turning. The road looks new. It looks like nowhere you have been before.
And you remember.
You keep driving and remember.

The city road is a narrow stretch with hills that rise on either side, steep like the sides of a coffin: a lining of grass like green silk and the lid open to the sky but it is a coffin all the same. The verges hang with ripped-back cars from the breaker's yard, splitting the

earth on either side, but you keep on going, over the dips and blends between the rust and heather till the last blind bend and it appears. Between the green and brown, the husks of broken cars: a v-shaped glimpse of somewhere else so far away it seems to float. It's distant and beautiful and no part of the rest: no part of the road I am traveling through, not Ayrshire, not Glasgow. It comes and goes behind a screen as I drive towards it, a piece of city waiting in the v-shaped sky if this is my day to make a split-second mistake. It's always there. And I know too it's simply the way home. I accelerate because it is not today. I am still here.
Driving.

THE MEAT

The carcass hung in the shop for nine days till the edges congested and turned brown in the air.

People came and went. They bought wafers of beef, pale veal, ham from the slicer, joints, fillets, mutton chops. They took tomatoes and brown eggs, tins of fruit cocktail, cherries, handfuls of green parsley, bones. But no one wanted the meat. It dropped overhead from a claw hook, flayed and split down the spinal column: familiar enough in its way. It was cheap. But they asked for shin and oxtail, potted head, trotters. The meat refused to sell. Folk seemed embarrassed even to be caught peeking in its direction. One or two made tentative enquiries about a plate of sausages coiled to the left of the dangling shadow while the yellowing hulk hung restless, twisting on its spike. These were never followed through. The sausages sat on, pink and greasy, never shrinking by so much as a link. He moved the sausages to another part of the shop where they sold within the hour. Something about the meat was infecting.

By the tenth day, the fat on its surface turned leathery and translucent like the rind of an old cheese. Flies landed in the curves of the neck and he did not brush them away. The deep-set ball of bone sunk in the shoulder turned pale blue. There was no denying the fact: it had to be moved. The ribs were sticky and the smell had begun to repulse him, clogging the air in the already clammy interior of the shop, and he could detect its unmistakable seep under the door to his living room when he was alone in the evening. So he fetched a stool and reached out to the lard hook, seized the meat and with one accurate slice of the cleaver, cut it down. It languished on the sawdust floor till nightfall when he threw it into the back close parallel to the street. As he closed the shutter on the back door, he could hear the scuffling of small animals and strays.

In the morning, all that remained was the hair and a strip of tartan ribbon. These he salvaged and sealed in a plain wooden box beneath the marital bed. A wee minding.

Order and Flux in Northampton
David Foster Wallace

BARRY DINGLE, CROSS-EYED PURVEYOR of bean sprouts, harbors for Myrnaloy Trask, operator of Xerox and regent of downtown Northampton's most influential bulletin board at Collective Copy, an immoderate love.

Myrnaloy Trask, trained Reproduction Technician, unmarried woman, vegetarian, flower-child tinged faintly with wither, overseer and editor of Announcement and Response at the ten-foot-by-ten-foot communicative hub of a dizzying wheel of leftist low-sodium aesthetes, a woman politically correct, active in relevant causes, slatternly but not unerotic, all-weather wearer of frayed denim skirts and wool knee-socks, sexually troubled, ambiguous sexual past, owner of one spectacularly incontinent Setter/Retriever bitch, Nixon, so named by friend Don Megala because of the dog's infrangible habit of shitting where it eats: Myrnaloy has eyes only for Don Megala: Don Megala, middle-aged liberal, would-be drifter, maker of antique dulcimers by vocation, by calling a professional student, a haunter of graduate hallways, adrift, holding fractions of Ph.D.'s in everything from Celtic phonetics to the sociobiology of fluids from the University of Massachusetts at Amherst, presently at work on his seventh and potentially finest unfinished dissertation, an exhaustive study of Stephen Dedalus's sublimated oedipal necrophelia vis à vis Mrs. D. in *Ulysses*, an essay tentatively titled "The Ineluctable Modality of the Ineluctably Modal."

Add to the above Trask-data the fact that, though Barry Dingle's spotlessly managed franchise, The Whole Thing Health Food Emporium, is located directly next to Collective Copy on Northampton's arterial Great Awakening Avenue, Myrnaloy has her nutritional needs addressed at The Whole Thing's out-of-the-way, sawdust-floored competition, Good Things to Eat, Ltd., the proprietor of which, one Adam Baum, is a crony of Megala, and add also that The Whole Thing is in possession of its own Xerox copier, and the following situation comes into narrative focus: Myrnaloy Trask has only the sketchiest intuition that Barry Dingle even exists, next door.

For Barry Dingle, though, the love of Myrnaloy Trask has become the dominant emotional noisemaker in his quiet life, the flux-ridden state of his heart, a thing as intimately close to Dingle as Myrnaloy is forever optically distant or unreal.

Suspend and believe that the consuming, passionate love of Myrnaloy Trask has in fact become defined and centered as a small homunculoid presence inside Barry Dingle, a doll-sized self all its own, with the power of silent speech and undisguised ambitions to independent action. Barry Dingle's love sees itself as the catalyst that can transform Barry Dingle from a neutral to a positive charge in life's delicate equation. It sees itself as having the power to remake, reform, reconstitute Barry Dingle. In fact — since facts are the commodity at issue, here — Barry Dingle's love of Myrnaloy Trask wants in some ultimate sense to *be* Barry Dingle, and has lately launched an aggressive campaign to assume control of Dingle's life, to divert and even divorce Dingle from his seven-year definition as manager of The Whole Thing, from his hard-learned disposition to passivity and mute fear: in short, for those who know him, from the very Dingleness of Barry Dingle.

The birth of Barry Dingle's love for Myrnaloy Trask can be fixed generally at a present some two years back, when The Whole Thing, like the rest of the health-food industry, is scrambling wildly to capitalize on the American consumer's growing enthusiasm for bran. The precise two-year-old moment when the crossed eyes, healthy heart, modest mind and tame history of Barry Dingle consummated their need for intersection at the point of object-choice can be identified as the moment 4:30pm on 15 June 1981, when Dingle, arranging a cunningly enticing display of bran-walnut muffins on the recycled-aluminum shelves of The Whole Thing's display window, finds himself staring, as only the cross-eyed can stare, into the smoke-dark window of a Northampton Public Transit Authority bus, halted on the street outside by one of Northampton's invidious and eternal red lights. In the sunlight off the sienna glass is the muted reflected image of Myrnaloy Trask, next door, outside Collective Copy, in her denim skirt and Xerox apron, editorially scanning C.C.'s public-announcement bulletin board's collection of fliers and hand-lettered ads, searching out the irrelevant, the non-progressive, the uncleared.

To see and feel anything like what Barry Dingle feels as he stares slack-jawed through his glasses, his store's glass, into the darkly reflecting glass of the frustrated bus, the student of the phenomenon of Barry Dingle must try to imagine the unimaginable richness, range, *promise* of the community bulletins before which Myrnaloy establishes herself as culler and control, the board aflutter with bright announcement, Establishment-opprobrium, introduction — bids for attention from kyphotic-lesbian support groups, Maoist coffeehouses, organic-garden-plot rentals, dentists who eschew all mercury and alum, obscurely-oriented political parties with titles longer than their petitioned rosters of names, sitar instructors, anorexia crisis lines, Eastern and Mid-Eastern expanders of spiritual consciousness, bulimia crisis lines, M.D.'s in healing with crystals and wheat, troupes of interpretive tap-dancers, holistic masseurs, acupuncturists, chiropractic acupuncturists, marxist mimes who do *Kapital* in dumbshow, typists, channelers, nutrition consultants, Brecht-only theater companies, Valley literary journals with double-digit circulations, on and on — a huge, flat, thumbtack- and staple-studded, central affair, sheltered from the apathetic vicissitudes of New England weathers by a special Collective Copy awning. The board is the area's avant-garde ganglion, a magnet drawing centripetally from the center of town on the diffracted ions of Northampton's vast organizational night, each morning bristling brightly with added claims to existence and efficacy, each late afternoon edited, ordered, wheat-from-chaffed by Myrnaloy Trask, who stands now, reflected in the dun shield of the bus glass, snake-haired in the June wind, one nail-bitten finger on a shiny leaflet of debatable value or legitimacy, deciding on the words' right to be; and at this moment, 4:30pm 15 June 1981, she brings up behind herself her left leg — in the bus window a distant right leg — bends it at the pale knee to effect the ascension of an ankle, pulls a sag-laddered wool knee-sock tight up the back of a white calf; and the movement, the unconscious gentle elevation of the thick ankle, is so very demure — reminiscent finally of the demure elevation of Sandra Dee's own sturdy calf as Gidget kissed interchangeable emmetropic young men in the climaxes of all the interchangeable Gidget films that informed so much of Barry Dingle's childhood — the movement so very young, tired, unselfconscious, sad, right, natural, reflected, distant, unsexily sexy, slatternly erotic . . .

. . . so very *whatever*, in short, that off the bus' window and through the TWT display pane and Dingle's thick hot angled glasses the parallaxed leg-image tears, rending Dingle's sense of self and place, plunging with a crackle of sexual ozone into the still surface of the stagnant ankle-deep pond that defines at this moment the Dingleness of Dingle; and through the miraculous manipulations of primal human ontemes too primal and too human even to be contemplated, probably, it gives birth to life: from the clotted silt of the uninterestingness at the center of Barry Dingle there emerges the salamanderial zygote of a robust, animate thing, a life, Barry Dingle's immoderate homunculoid love, conceived out of the impossibly distant refracted epiphany of Myrnaloy Trask, demure in her now-not-fallen socks, a Myrnaloy who is as unaware as carbon itself that she has effected the manufacture of life through her role in the interplay of forces probably beyond the comprehension of everything and everyone involved.

Northampton is located on the northern fringe of Massachusetts' Pioneer Valley on the eastern edge of the Berkshire Mountains. To the south lie Amherst and Springfield and Hartford CT. Incorporated 1698, Northampton is the eighth-oldest township in the state. It is the home of Smith College for Women. The college's Congregational Church, still semi-erect, saw the 1711–1717 delivery of the Great-Awakening jeremiads of dentist/theologian Solomon Stoddard, in which the reverend foretold the world's cold and imminent end, characterizing that end as a kind of grim entropic stasis already harbinged by, among other portents: poor nutrition and its attendant moral and dental decay; the increasing infertility of modern woman; the rise of the novel; the Great Awakening itself.

The city grew to economic prominence in the late eighteenth century after more space was cleared for development and commercial intercourse. Space for development and commercial intercourse was cleared all over the Pioneer Valley by the British commander Lord Jeffrey Amherst, who in 1783–84 won a telling victory over the sly, putatively "peace-loving" native population by providing its tribes with free blankets, each carefully preinfected with smallpox.

Northampton today enjoys the nation's second-highest percentage of homosexuals, calculated on a per capita basis, a distinction that has earned the city the designation "The San Francisco of the East." It also enjoys the nation's sixth-highest percentage of homeless persons, again per capita, countless capita to be seen each winter night clustered around the tattered flickers of countless trashcan fires. Most enjoyable of all is the nation's lowest percentage of registered Republicans, with the brow-raising total of exactly zero within the corporation limits.[1]

Fact: certain unlucky persons exist as living justifications of those phobias peculiar to mothers. Barry Dingle is such a person. His childhood, his whole life stands darkly informed by Mrs. Dingle's failure ever to be incorrect. Examples range through the history of the man. The tiniest pre-dinner treat does spoil little Barry's appetite. The briefest exposure of his unrubbered Hush Puppies to rain or snow ensures, with mathematical reliability, disease. The dullest of sharp things wounds, the safest of playground games injures, the scantiest inattention to oral hygiene sees the dark time-lapse sprout of an instant caries.

The Barry Dingle who dislikes drinking milk, avoids it at all costs, does fail to grow up big and strong like his sister, a field-hockey prodigy.

Also a fact: certain persons, especially mothers, come in time to resemble more and more closely their automobiles. Mrs. Dingle is outdated, rust-chassis'd, loud, disposed to the emission of fumes; she is wide and rides low and has a poor turning radius; but she is ideally suited for the transport of much baggage, and her mileage is phenomenal.

Picture her, then, entreating the child Barry Dingle never, never *ever*, to cross his little eyes. She believes, with the complete conviction of the phobic mother, that the child who crosses his eyes Stays That Way. She cajoles, enjoins; the indoctrination's movement is as broad and slow and irresistible as the Dingles' station wagon. The orientation of his eyes becomes for the little Dingle an object of black fascination. He dreams, in the night's dark part, of his eyes crossing by accident, their paths never again to diverge. He avoids sighting on any but the stablest objects. He resists the natural urge of the child to look down at his own nose. With Mrs. Dingle riding herd on their mutual neurosis, Dingle treasures the clean binocularity of his sight like a never-miss aggie. He makes it through fifteen

---

[1] For much more here see W. Deldrick Sperber, "The Sensitive Community: Nutritive, Sexual and Political Ambiguity in Northampton, MA," *Journal of American Studies in Sensitivity*, v. IX, nos. 2&3, 1983.

years of exquisite temptation without so much as a retinal wobble.

Fact to be feared: the rebelliousness of fearful youth, no matter how momentary, can itself be a fearful thing. On 15 June 1961, Troy, New York, enraged by the imposition of a domestic sanction soon lost to memory, Barry Dingle stands before his mother in the warm checker-tiled Dingle kitchen and gives in to the terrifying, wonderful temptation of the ultimate transgression against natural and maternal law. The cross is delicious; his eyes roll toward each other with the sweet release of catharsis long delayed. Two Mrs. Dingles scream and raise four arms skyward, pleading for intercession against the inevitable. . . .

Cross-eyed Barry is shunted from specialist to specialist. As Mrs. Dingle tearfully predicts, they are powerless to help. For six binary, true-and-false-filled months Dingle veers, bumbles, bumps his way through the doubled system of pecatum and punishment he has wrought. Finally, December, Buffalo, an optician at technology's cutting edge fits Dingle with an elaborate pair of glasses — thick angled lenses that catch and reorganize the disordered doubleness of things into a unity that fuses at a focused point several yards in front of Barry's own ruined apparatus. Relief is purchased, at a cost: the glasses work, unify, but objects for a bespectacled Barry now appear always twice as far away as they in fact are. Smaller, more distant. So that for twenty years Dingle has chosen minute by minute between doubleness and distance, between there being, for him, exactly twice or exactly half as much as there really is.

The point here being that a key ingredient of Myrnaloy's allure for Barry Dingle, and an irreducible constant in the sensuous half-equation whose sum is the immoderate love that even now makes its move for control of Barry Dingle's present and future, is the fact that Myrnaloy must always remain either fundamentally distant *from* Dingle, or else doubled, and so unreal, *for* him. Meaning that the "real" Myrnaloy Trask is for Dingle not even a possibility: he is in the (not unenviable?) position of a man able to *want* without the disturbing option of ever truly being able to *have*. Hence a classic, almost classically static romanticism as fundament, primal element, precondition for the very experience of being B. Dingle.

Additional fact: Mrs. Dingle predicts, long ago, over vermouth, that love will someday make Barry Dingle hideously, hideously unhappy. This too is come. Dingle is, as it were, beside himself, in a state of utter emotional flux whereby up and down, good and bad are as indistinguishable as right and left. Here, though, it is necessary to

96

distinguish between the happiness of Barry Dingle and the happiness of his interior homunculoid love. Barry Dingle's immoderate love is itself happy as a clam. It thrives, grows, gets off on the existence of a telos at once right next door and horizon-distant, at once really one and apparently two — in short, of a love-object invested with all the flected ambiguity that makes Romance itself possible.

But one last fact: Barry Dingle's love is nonetheless a human love. With the illogic that defines all autonomous but entombed emotional humunculoids, Dingle's immoderate love is possessed of a desire for the attainment of the very love-object whose fundamental *un*attainability is that love's animating breath and bread. It is by nature dissatisfied; and that dissatisfaction is, via the hermeneutic circle of love's illogic, its life and mission. It needs Barry Dingle to appropriate, possess, use and encompass Myrnaloy Trask. It harbors in its doll's heart a desire for a strong new Dingle shell, the outward instantiation of an immoderate inner force. It envisions Dingle capturing Myrnaloy's heart and fashioning inside her a demure-calved homunculoid of her own, a love for Barry Dingle that will, in the union of Dingle and Trask, merge with the homunculoids themselves and render them complete (i.e., no longer animate, inside). A genuinely human emotional armillary, Dingle's immoderate love's life strains ever forward toward the death that love's life loves.

Think of it this way, Dingle, says Dingle's love as Dingle inventories herbal teas on a May afternoon, 1983. Think of your love as being by nature an incomplete, questing thing. I was born in you half a love. My end is the unity I am by definition denied.

Dingle is silent over ginseng and camomile.

The homunculoid taps its foot patiently. The point, it says, is that I've got a nature to be true to, just like you. I'm compelled by this nature to spend my time, therefore our time, questing and striving for my other half. This is so, no matter how much you buck and snort. Think of me as a chivalric knight, you as my dragon. And obversely. Each other's torments, but also our salvations.

Salvations? Dingle says. Dragons?

You give birth to a love in Myrnaloy Trask; she forms her own half-a-love homunculoid, curved, gentle, round-faced, doll's eyes that open with the pull of a heartstring, concave where I am convex. You do such a thing; Myrnaloy gives birth; her half-a-love and I get together; I leave you in peace. Everybody's a winner. *Verstehen-Sie?*

And the toe-problem? whispers Dingle, biting a cracked lip.

Your toes are once again your own psyche's own, says Dingle's love, making its presence felt with a playful twinge in one red Dingle digit.

The fact of the May '83 matter here is that Dingle's love, as of some six weeks past, has decided to play psychic hardball. It has moved to consolidate its authority over Barry Dingle by focusing its attention and influence on Dingle's most vulnerable parts. Here these parts are due south of even the most sensitive dangling chinks in most men's armor. They are the tortured ingrown toenails of Barry Dingle. (Possibly worth noting here that Mrs. Dingle was and is a fanatic on the subject of foot care.) Barry Dingle's love is using the curved culcates of Dingle's nails, together with the tender genital/emotional complex that birthed the immoderate homunculoid in the first place, to force an intrinsically passive Dingle toward some decisive romantic action.

Love has turned the order of Barry Dingle's life into flux; Dingle is now at war with himself; divided; schismed; finally wounded, behind the lines.

Yes cross-eyed Barry, thirty-five, perennial wearer of leather sandals, bell-bottoms, and Central American ponchos, high of forehead, long of incisor, thick of spectacle, is in possession of 2 (two) feet presently in torment from the negative-reinforcement regimen of his immoderate love. Since adolescence (specific moment of origin coincident with that of the optical transgression), the toes have detracted from Dingle's quality of life: corticate yellow nails curving in of themselves, sinking into the tender meat of his red toes, the toes taking turns at self-harm, swelling, shining with erumpent infection, to say nothing of pain. Dingle, of routine, takes all possible preventive steps. He trims the nails daily, paring them straight across, leaving perfect planks of protruding cartilage into the corners of which each morning he tucks tiny cotton pellets soaked in camphor and oil of clove. Sandals, affording the toes movement, oxygen, freedom from pressure, are worn at all times. In cold seasons Dingle even forfeits the privilege ever of being taken seriously as a person: he wears sandals with socks.

Now for naught: B. Dingle is literally staggering under the incurving influence of his immoderate love for Myrnaloy Trask. The love, from its central facility in Dingle's clean red heart, now commutes daily south to an annex in Dingle's clawlike nails, from which annex it makes its presence, wishes and directives acutely known. The campaign is insidiously subtle, the pain carefully gauged to impel cooperation without ever quite causing incapacitation. Barry Dingle's love begins moving against his feet in April 1983. By June, Dingle knows something must be done. Myrnaloy Trask must somehow be appropriated, Dingle's cherry-colored homunculoid completed, sated, silenced. The love has worn Dingle down — two years of flux and now two months of rampant ingrowth: his tortured feet, his keening heart, the disorder and disruption of the neutral Dingle equation are driving Dingle quietly toward breakdown and tilted stasis.

Cf he has become unable to concentrate at work. He becomes lax, his employees demoralized, intransigent, carbohydrated. The owner of the whole The Whole Thing chain pays a personal visit, 2 June, to the Northampton franchise. He takes a significant look at Dingle's blackly circled cross-eyes, his well-chewed lip, his obscenely swollen feet. The owner straightens his suede vest and fingers his Scientology medallion. He advises Dingle in no uncertain terms that he, the owner, knows that things here at the Northampton facility are on the decline. That sales have been slipping, that freshness is on occasion being compromised, that TWT's employees, not to mention Northampton's health-rabid customers, are losing a focus for their nutritional vision. Even the bran, he says pointedly, though not without a smile at his own wit, lately isn't moving like it should. He asks Dingle what *he'd* do, in the owner's place, here. Dingle's love, from deep inside him, puts in its own two cents' worth — an electric thrill of podiatric pain. A pale Dingle removes his glasses, sets his jaw. He reassures the twin images of the owner. Things will turn around. The store will soon be back on its feet. Seven years of careful management; passionate devotion to the marketing of health; the dingy Good Things no competition: he waxes briefly eloquent, an aggressive sincerity that surprises the owner and distracts even the bloated TWT employees from their game of rummy. The owner eventually nods, acquiesces, checks his sundial and makes for the glass doors, leaving in his cinnamon-scented wake a system of insinuations that both reaffirm and cast doubt on his faith in Barry Dingle. The store is silent; a halted bus motor can be heard at the traffic light.

For two unprecedented sick-days Dingle stays home, brooding, his feet in hot salt water and eucalyptus. Nigel, the assistant manager, temporarily assumes The Whole Thing's helm. Dingle communes with his love. With himself.

The result of which is the prenominate realization that something must change, coupled with a robust new determination really, truly, finally to act. After two days (date now 6 June 1983), Dingle leaves his bath, returns to TWT's many windows, and resolves, with a coldly febrile set to his tall forehead, to set his unsteady sights on the distant Trask and to bring her, by fair means or otherwise, swimming into his romantic ken. His homunculoid love smells the metal smell of strength in Dingle's blood, and approves it. It loosens the grip of Dingle's own nails just a bit. It encourages Dingle, exhorts, plays interior good-cop bad-cop, says it discerns in him a nascent newness, a courage,

Courage! says Dingle's homunculoid love,

defining the term in Gothic script on Dingle's heart as a willingness to bring the comfortably distant into a unified proximity, to risk stasis as completion. The words pump against the fishwhite skin of Dingle's shallow chest and appear on his body in faint pink calligraphy. Dingle reads himself double in the night's salty bath. Touches the blurred words.

The fly in the emotional ointment here being the initially-mentioned Don Megala, eternal student, dulcimer-*craeftig*, whose connection with Myrnaloy Trask, visible through Collective Copy's window via the reflecting umber glass of the ever-halted Northampton bus, is undeniable, though ambiguous — Megala being in his heyday an epic drinker and chaser of skirt, both the denim skirts of Northampton's straight female leftists and the tartan skirts of the aesthetically-inclined Smith College set whose poetry readings, madrigal recitals, and sherry-and-scone mixers Megala haunts, earning himself the designation *Der Döpplebanger* by Smith's artistes-in-the-know — and Myrnaloy being shy, withdrawn, clearly inexperienced, and, even more clearly, deeply ambivalent about men.

It is now appropriate to note that Barry Dingle and Don Megala enjoy some slight acquaintance through the University of Massachusetts at Amherst, that Megala had been going through the motions on an abortive sociobiology dissertation while Dingle completed his undergraduate studies in Digestive Science, that they had had in common a mentor and advisor — one W.W. Skeat, a socio-digestive biologist best known for his thesis that the underlying and true cause of cancer is in fact plain old human saliva — and had both done substantial research under and lab-assisting for this mentor, advisor, Skeat. Noted further is the fact that Megala regards Dingle with the jolly condescension reserved for the cross-eyed, buck-toothed and sock-and-sandal-shod, while Dingle, lately under the emotional aegis of his homunculoid love, harbors for Megala a mute dislike, an active wish to do him harm, from a distance.

Megala being the fly in the ointment of romance vis à vis Myrnaloy, it is understandable that Barry Dingle, whenever the opportunity presents itself, arranges to observe Myrnaloy and Megala together—not actually *following* M & M, mind you, given documented eye-and mobility-troubles, but rather just arranging to be located, inconspicuously, wherever they are likely to appear together.

Opportunities for such observation are not few, Myrnaloy and Megala to be seen by Dingle variously: sipping four-dollar espressos at Northampton's Leftward Ho Cafe; strolling hand in hand through any one of the city's fifty-six used-book stores; waving a shared banner at weekly rallies of the Northampton Anti-Nuclear And Non-Aligned Nations' And Neighbors' Alliance, Myrnaloy having been recording secretary of NANANANANA since its mid-seventies inception; exercising together on the town common's public aerobics palestrae; etc.; and, of course, variously talking, confiding, nuzzling, arguing, being ambiguous, all in the bus-reflected Collective Copy window.

Not to mention patronizing Adam Baum's own Good Things to Eat, Ltd., The Whole Thing's chief sit-down competition, a tiny-windowed establishment which Dingle, incurring substantial professional risk, begins·inconspicuously patronizing as well. Picture Dingle, in early '83, hunched, poncho-swaddled, his cotton pellets grimed with the floor's sawdust, in a Good Things booth as M & M establish themselves over a whole-grain dinner at their usual table directly behind him. They are deep in conversation. Barry Dingle and his immoderate love listen. Myrnaloy seems just to have finished pouring an ambivalent heart out to Megala on the subject of men and sex. Dingle's ears are aprick, his carrot cake hardening and peppermint tea chilling, untouched.

Myrnaloy, on the last leg of a redditive narrative journey, is revealing, fragilely, with many stuttered pauses, that she is terrified of sex. Thoroughly terrified. She alludes to some shadowy long-ago trauma, some betrayal, the details of which Megala, judging from the sympathetic and reinforcing soft sounds he keeps making as he chews, already knows. Barry Dingle's love gnashes its teeth at Barry's not knowing what Megala knows. Myrnaloy's voice is trembling; she is revealing that she is, at thirty-five, flower-child-past and all, still

technically maiden. She states that sex holds a great, albeit unde-
finable, terror for her.

Don Megala gives Myrnaloy Trask to understand that he under-
stands, that he regards — nay, *genuflects to* her attitude as one more
than just understandable, don't you know, but as somehow deeply
sexually-politically *correct*. He reveals that he lost his own innocence at fifteen and has been terrified ever since. That he lives in
sexual terror. That sex is, by nature, terrifying.

To Dingle's horror he finds himself in significant agreement with
Megala.

But what Megala is about here, Barry is roughly told, is clear. Yes
Dingle's love smells impending seduction. Dingle searches through
his angled glasses for some reflecting surface in the restaurant,
anything in which to study Myrnaloy's facial reaction to Megala's
inevitable upcoming arguments. He imagines her looking down,
rouged with self-revelation, dabbing at nothing with a recycled
napkin, smiling hesitantly, gratefully, at Megala's understanding, his
willingness to share a vulnerability. Yet it's the willingness-to-share
gambit. The homunculoid establishes itself in an orbit of impotent
rage around Dingle's carved heart.

Because But wonderful, too, Megala is going on to muse out loud.
His voice is pocked with the tiny hesitations of purposeful sincerity.
Sex, Megala means. Even the terror of sex is, in fact, wonderful, in a
terrible sort of way.

Dingle envisions Megala's delicate white hands covering Myrnaloy's delicate white hands. Dingle is pale, helpless, staring into the
distant fossil of his dinner.

Because sex also being, let's both be honest with ourselves and
admit it, a pretty big thing in this predominantly short and unhappy
life, Megala adds. How sad it would be to depart the coil without
taking, as it were, a look around at life, to see what's what. Surely
sex is one of the big whats in life, to be at least looked at, no? Or so
he tells himself, he tells her, whenever his perfectly appropriate
terror threatens to get the best.

Dingle envisions clean binocular eye-contact between M & M.

And it's hard to think of a more *natural* thing in this life, Megala
muses out loud, than intimacy between a man and a woman who
share mutual concerns and respect and correctness. Who *care*. No?
A natural, natural thing. Like the coruscating flora of autumn. A
cotton Nehru jacket dried on the line. A bird wheeling before a stiff
gust. And, irony of ineluctable ironies, are not the very most *natural*

things in life often the most terrifying? Does . . . *could* Myrnaloy share this feeling, this insight? This sad, wonderful, terrifying irony?

Dingle hears Myrnaloy make a gentle noise variously indicative of: agreement, gratitude, admiration, the recognition of something unseen that's been recognized *for* her. Dingle's love twirls, staring balefully at its blurred reflection in Dingle's clean pounding courage-scripted heart.

There is the violent sound of Megala vacuuming the bottom of his glass with a straw. Each of Dingle's eyes contemplates its reflection in the other.

An absolute scuttling mink, hisses Barry Dingle's love.

Pardon? whispers Barry Dingle.

This guy is a sterling example of a mink, says the homunculoid.

A mink?

A technical term for a certain kind of low-rent player in the love game, the love says; 'Mink,' noun, meaning basically someone who's smooth on the outside, but inside still basically just a weasel.

A smooth weasel?

The guy is minkness in motion, says the love, and here we sit, inert. It goes for a shiny metatarsal's tip, in the sawdust.

Megala and Myrnaloy exit Good Things. Dingle can finally see them, far away, through the cashier's little round window to which he's half-run, limping. They are detaching the leash of Myrnaloy's Nixon from a Good Things leash-hook. Disappearing in a direction opposite that of Collective Copy. Leaving behind a slim trail of Nixon's digestive distress.

The following couples grapple into the wee hours of this early-June night: Myrnaloy Trask and Don Megala; Barry Dingle and Barry Dingle's love.

Fly-ridden ointment or not, recall that Barry Dingle has, as of 6 June, reoriented himself, that the needle of his emotional compass now points, shakily or not, toward the pole of action. Action number one is taking place right this minute, on the morning of 6 June, as Dingle sits at his fiberboard TWT desk, absent his thick glasses, composing an advertisement for a new line of wheat germ with coconut and date-dust mixed right in. He hand-letters a flier outlining nutritional virtues and introductory discounts. He finishes flier, caps magic marker, submits flier to Nigel for the correction of doubled letters

and incongruities of scale, and lets Nigel edit while he, Dingle, drifts
pensively through the store's bulk-aisle, past broad side windows,
past clean sunwashed plastic trashcans brimming with granolas,
past nuts, dried fruit, protein powders, bran-barrels, trowels, de-
gradable baggies, scales, to The Whole Thing's frontal display pane.
In the window of the idling bus can be seen Myrnaloy, fetchingly
distant at the control of her Xerox behind the CC customer counter.
The arched-bridge-esque figure of Nixon is to be seen ranging over
a spread-out pile of invalidated bulletin-board submissions. Against
the CC counter leans Don Megala, flushed and shiny, speaking out
of one side of his mouth to Baum, the Good Things proprietor whose
fliers enjoy, through the influence of Megala, a consistent place on
a Collective Copy board whose facilities Dingle has never had the
gumption even to request.

Nigel pronounces the flier clean copy. Dingle finds the thing in his
hands, alludes to a vague problem with the copier in The Whole
Thing's stock room, and says perhaps he'll just whisk over next door
to Collective Copy. Nigel mans the TWT con while Dingle embarks
on what is possibly history's slowest whisk, three wide elliptical
passes at the copy center's entrance, last-second veerings, sudden
reversals of flight at the compulsion of the homunculoid, who has
only to feint at Dingle's sandals to get its point across. The closure
of ellipse number three sees Dingle pass under the bulletin board,
fumble between the old wooden door's two apparent knobs, glom
finally on to the genuine article, hear the *ching* of the customer bell,
and enter the lair of M & M. The place is hot, full of the dry chemical wind of roaring copier and rattling automatic collator. Flier in
hand, Dingle steps over the tortured figure of Nixon and makes for
the customer counter.

Baum having decamped at TWT's approach, here is Megala, alone,
under his arm a used copy of Stuart Gilbert's *Ulysses*-guide. Megala
greets Dingle with broad enthusiasm, extends a doubled hand.
Dingle hopes very much he won't be clapped on the back. Smells of
cork and yeast exit Megala's mouth; his eyes are red as certain toes,
a filigreed road-guide to the state of post-lunch fermentation he now
enjoys. Dingle's tense smiling cheeks spasm as two Myrnaloys leave
the copier and approach; Megala has called for a look at this flier of
Dingle's, here. Myrnaloy Trask is close. Two denim skirts, two work-
shirts the pale blue of tired laundry, Xerox aprons, four knee-socks.
Eyes and forehead framed in tiny dry wrinkles and squeezed in a
kind of tight pain against the hot June window-light, but Dingle can

104

see only two milky facial outlines that resist resolution or rapproche-ment. A customer enters, as does a unit of spring wind, carrying to the counter the rich smell of Nixon. Megala wrinkles his nose, reaches across the pitted counter for what appears to Dingle as the twin-towered facade of a Bass Ale.

Megala, with a flourish, introduces Dingle to Myrnaloy. Her hand is white and delicate, if a bit unsoft. Dingle's tongue is dry meat in his mouth. Myrnaloy acknowledges Dingle as somehow connected with The Whole Thing, next door. Megala outlines Dingle's cur-riculum vitae for Myrnaloy. Dingle brandishes the advertisement, requests copies. Costs are negotiated, specifications specified; Myrna-loy retreats to her machines. Nixon sniffs with ominous interest at Dingle's sandals.

Megala comments on the weather, the bus, the lager, the Laffer Curve's impact on the whole-grain and dulcimer trades. Largely without punctuation. At least two of his three sheets are flapping. Dingle can tell, standing here at the counter, fingering the collar of his poncho, that Myrnaloy is still within earshot, despite the roar of Xeroxes, from the unmistakable way Megala directs his voice to the wide empty parqueted space between Dingle and Trask. There are twine-gnarled subtexts here to which Barry is not privy: Megala's loud voice is making Myrnaloy strangely tight-lipped; Dingle watches her face expand at the sides. His love tightens the screws on a digit, shrieking silently at Dingle to act, to speak, reveal something of himself before this woman and her mink of a beau.

So I see you have at least one Stuart Gilbert, there, under your arm, Dingle says to Megala. I guess I'll assume, he says, that the Stuart Gilbert you have there under your arm is material for a dissertation.

Assume away, says Megala, who's been counting heavily on the source in question and is now disappointed, to say nothing of pissed, to find that Gilbert's work on what Megala keeps calling 'The Big U' is just a reference guide, not an analysis — original, as opposed to recapitulatory, scholarship is not a Megala-strength.

Assume away, he says; worthless, though, the man vastly over-rated, important implications overlooked, mere surfaces scratched, Dedalus's oedipal psyche stands unrevealed, the metamorphosis from young artist to Telemachoid heir a blank, his dead love-object a scholastic deletion.

So a challenge, then, says Dingle.

Or a study in futility, smiles Megala, less wryly than he means to, eyeing a red triangle on the Bass bottle in some sort of thousand-yard expectation.

At this point Dingle finds himself staring at the images of Myrnaloy Trask bent reproductively over the photographic strobe of the copier. He makes certain observations — mute, internal, lyrical — about her breasts, which happen to be budging almost geologically against her worn work-shirt; about the hip-induced swells in her denim skirt; about the bristly shine of her white legs above the socks' wool. Standard metaphors are invoked. Now, in a gesture of thoroughly unconscious cooperation, Myrnaloy brings her right ankle up behind her and tends to the top of a tired sock. Dingle perspires freely. His eyes stare into each other over the bridge of his nose. There is a sinister protrusion near the hem of a certain poncho. Dingle shifts closer to the protective counter. Megala drinks at his bottle. Nixon diddles on a box of Hammermill bond.

Megala, soaring on the wings of futility's study, waxes nostalgic, collegial. He asks after Skeat. Dingle has not seen Skeat for years, believes him to be out West, living on grants. Myrnaloy glances through the flash of photocopy at the post-prandial foot-traffic on the sidewalk outside. Megala calls to her, jolly, regarding a Dingle-anecdote, set in the UMass research laboratory of W.W. Skeat, an incident dated 1968. He says the incident concerns Dingle. Dingle's immoderate love whispers encouragement. Myrnaloy's eyes register what could be called interest. Dingle clears his throat. Two Myrnaloys move through blinking mists toward the counter, the copier on automatic pilot. Dingle tells.

Picture this. It is 1968. Barry Dingle, burning the midnight fluorescence in the basement laboratory of Skeat, is bent over the special microscope he, Dingle, requires to fuse a slide studied into unified, eyelash-free focus. He wears a white lab-coat and thongs. He is using the microscope to observe the activities of some routine germs, parameciae, in a droplet of saliva from the mouth of a melanoma patient. The germs swim aimlessly around, engage in activities. Dingle observes them. Then, on a whim,

On a whim, mind you, he says,

he removes the slide from its clips, turns it around, reinserts it, and again bends to observe. He notes something curious in the movements of the germs at issue.

Megala belches, incurring the empathy of Nixon. Myrnaloy betrays distaste, looks back again at Dingle, who's still crowding the counter.

Dingle, in the past, in the lab, becomes excited. He turns the scope's slide again. Looks. Sure enough. The germs are swimming north. Not aimless. Not just around. North. Only aimless if seen from one angle. Turn the slide, the wily germs take sharp lefts and rights, head due north again.

Megala chuckles. Myrnaloy's four eyes are on Dingle, perplexed. North? she says.

Not just around, Megala says. The aimlessness only apparent.

North, Dingle says. They swim north. Sense the ephemeral pull of some deep geologic magnet. Heed its call.

North for the summer, says Megala.

Dingle manipulates the hood of his poncho. And the whole on-a-whim insight a matter of *perspective*, was what excites, he says. See? Look from just one angle: things seem aimless, disordered. Flux reigns. Change the angle: illumination. Pattern. Order.

His love whips a checkered flag downward.

Look at a thing from some variety of perspectives, Dingle says; input from let's say even just two completely different angles: see matters in a whole new light, potentially.

Northern expedition, ruminates Megala.

It was exciting, Dingle says quietly.

Except it was Skeat was the one who wrote it up, Megala says. Got himself a Guggenheim out of it.[2] Dingle here got no credit. Skeat gave him the academic shaft. The big femur.

Dingle smiles shyly. Credit not important. The insight itself important. Epiphany under cold lights. Beside myself with joy, that night.

The homunculoid thumbs-ups its approval, reclines on a shiny ventricle, polishing its fingernails against the front of its tunic.

Myrnaloy: And now you manage The Whole Thing?

Yes. Problems in terms of medical-school applications. Finances. Vision.

The Skeat thesis, laughs Megala. Watch what you swallow, Myrna-love.

The relevant Xerox grinds into automatic shut-off. Myrnaloy retrieves Dingle's original, hands him a stack of warm noisome copy.

Fine, fine copies, Dingle says, flipping through, willing himself not to squint. Myrnaloy punches up his bill.

Megala gestures over at the register. Why not let Dingle put one up

---

[2] See W.W. Skeat, "The Intrinsic Northern Orientation of the Paramecium in Neoplastic Human Saliva," *Principium Salivato*, v.2, nos. 2&3, 1970.

on the old board, Myrnaloy, he suggests, grinning. A quo for his quid.

Really a first-rate new product, Dingle stammers, gratitude and resentment toward Megala swirling together oily in his heart, which pounds. Excited about the chance to be part of, he says; happy to arrange a complimentary.

Why not, Myrnaloy says tightly, figuring tax.

Dingle's immoderate love senses tension between tight Myrnaloy and scabrous Don.

I sense tension here, it says. It takes care of Dingle's potentially disastrous poncho-protrusion so that he's free at last to leave the pelvic shelter of the store's counter.

Thanks, mutters a relieved Dingle.

No problem, says Megala. The inevitable dreaded back-clap descends; Dingle's small coughing fit is also quashed. Megala and Nixon head for the restroom. Myrnaloy removes tools from a double-locked drawer marked BOARD, heads for the door, Dingle and Dingle's love in emotional tow.

Dingle stands in sunlight before the complicatedly-colored bulletin board with Myrnaloy Trask. He is dizzy from the ripe distinctively feminine fragrance that surrounds this slatternly woman who is not unerotic.

Really a well-edited board, he says; admired it in passing on countless.

Myrnaloy says nothing. With practiced tweezes of a staple-claw she amputates a slick proclamation for a trampoline-a-thon benefitting the Quebecois Separatist Party, the final gymnast having succumbed June 4. Dingle's wheat-germ-and-dust notice inherits its position, is staple-gunned into place.

Dingle's own personal notice has been attracted by two professionally typeset, black-and-white notices that sit dead center on the board's prized eye-level row. The images almost focus. He squints, covers an eye, reads slowly, transfixed by the following flier's text:

WANTED: MALE DOG, SETTER/RETRIEVER MIX,
FOR **MATING** W/ 1-YR.-OLD SETTER/RETRIEVER **BITCH.**
OBJECT: **LITTER.**
PICK OF **LITTER** TO SUPPLIER, MALE **DOG.**
ESTIMATED TIME NEXT **HEAT, BITCH:** c. JUNE 15, 1983.
INQUIRE WITHIN, MS. M. TRASK, COLLECTIVE COPY.

That okay? Myrnaloy asks, stepping critically back from the TWT flier.

Appreciate it, croaks Dingle, half-strangled by an inspired homunculoid's sudden appearance in his throat.

I'll try to get over sometime, try some of the germ.

Please do. On the house.

Myrnaloy goes for the doors. Dingle contemplates the boards.

Myrnaloy has paused at both knobs. She is looking at Dingle. Dingle sees her. She is a hydra, her dirty-blond hair a mess of muted light. Her faces assume an expression. Germs really know where north is? she says; swim there?

Dingle's smile is unforced, though complexly motivated. It turns out they do, he says.

I find that pretty interesting.

Me too.

And it was just an accident.

Pure whim.

She looks past him at the street.

I'll hope to be seeing you around the store should you at some; the new wheat.

She both nods and smiles absently, disappearing back inside, Dingle trying to thank her through the glass.

The board rustles in a sweet wind, a system of circled squares around a bullseyed invitation to mate. The bus revs at the traffic light. Myrnaloy's outline reappears on the other side of the CC machines. Dingle flops back to The Whole Thing, his bell-bottoms swirling. He is clutching the warm copies to a lettered chest heaving with the implications of what has passed before him.

An abridged history of the dog Dingle is now buying, late afternoon, 9 June 1983:

This dog, a three-year-old Setter/Retriever male currently in residence at Pets And More Pets, Northampton, is a fine-looking animal . . .

Fine-looking animal here or what? says the toupee'd Pets And More Pets salesman.

Looks good from here, says a bespectacled Barry Dingle.

. . . and a potentially first-rate pet; with, though 2 (two) features that cry out for classification as Flaw. The first is an advanced case of ocular venerean substamus,[3] a progressive atrophy in the ocular cavity's web of muscle that causes one of the dog's eyeballs to roll chaotically in its socket, making the dog look, more often than not, cross-eyed.

I sense an affinity between you and this dog, sir, says the salesman, dapper in a checked sportcoat and white leather loafers. He fingers a flea collar speculatively. Am I off-base? You feel some sort of affinity here by any chance?

Dingle considers the distant dog through his angled lenses. His homunculoid love lays low, chewing its own knuckle.

Think maybe I do, Dingle is saying. The dog, a veteran of uncountable near-purchases, scratches endearingly with one tentative paw at the bars of its cramped cage.

The second flaw represents the reason why the dog was originally let loose at rush hour along the Valley's busy Route 9 by his original owner, a scholar of Korean funeral pottery at nearby Amherst College. Information regarding this flaw is being withheld from Dingle at the professional discretion of the pet salesman, who is even now working at the lock of the dog's receptacle, flashing an uneasy smile at Dingle as the dog, freed, immediately lunges slavering at a Smith student who stands nearby, tapping on the glass tank of a comatose terrapin. The understandably withheld information: this three-year-old male Setter/Retriever suffers from a disastrous enthusiasm for the special scents unique to the privates of the human female; has proved untrainable, unbreakable in this regard; leaps without hesitation, snuffling wetly, up the skirt of any woman unfortunate enough to enter the unfortunate orientalist's home. (Imagine your own embarrassment as, say, cocktail host of a colleague and his wife, seated on divans, over gin, surrounded by somber dynastic thanography, trying to make polite conversation as the dog steadily disappears ever farther into the colleague's wife's nether regions, she and you and the colleague all too mortified to pull the dog away, since any such move would signify acknowledgment of what is going on, while what is going on signifies that the colleague's wife possesses genitals, with a scent, a reality the suppression of which is absolutely key to maintaining the thin veneer of civilization that separates the behavior of, say, you and the colleague from that of, say, the dog.) A more complete history would countenance the dog's repeated olfactory advances at the orientalist's feminist-ideogram-theorist

---

[3]See, for instance, photographs E. Dickinson, B. Streisand, J.C. Oates.

fiancee, who eventually realizes, not without horror, that she is coming to prefer them to the pottery-scholar's own caresses, and today belongs to no fewer than three support groups. 1982: the dog is finally the object of abandonment, is found and saved, at rush-hour by a cruising abandonee-scout for Pets And More Pets, rather a more high-pressure pet shop than Barry Dingle would have preferred, but the only present possessor of a male S/R in the whole Pioneer Valley phonebook.

Also frisky, the salesman says, getting a headlock on the frantic animal, whose toenails scrabble on tile as the Smith student drifts off toward the venomous-reptile aisle. No shortage of *joy de vive* in this animal, the salesman says.

Definite Setter/Retriever mix? asks Barry Dingle. He eyes the distant, dull-gold dog writhing under a tiny salesman.

Word of honor.

Sexually mature? Intact? Inclined?

As the day is long, sir.

Name?

No name. A nameless dog. Be creative.

The dog barks.

Price? Dingle asks.

Highly negotiable. Plus necessary canine paraphernalia thrown in, as well.

Done, then.

Thank you, God.

Excuse me?

The salesman is making for a cage-lined back room, dragging the dog by the scruff. Right back, he promises. Vaccination-checks, paperwork . . . Price-negotiations moments away. He shuts a heavy door.

Moments later Dingle departs Pets And More Pets with: one flea collar; one reinforced military leash; one bag food; one plastic crater of a dish; one set vaccination papers; one surprisingly cheap, covertly (in the back room) tranquilized dog, which trots grinning, stoned, next to Dingle, one eye on Great Awakening's sidewalk and one on his owner. Dingle heads for home, sandals and pants flapping.

Good man, exhorts Dingle's immoderate homunculoid love for Myrnaloy Trask.

Thank God, the salesman repeats for the benefit of Pets And More Pets' cashier, who uses violet talons to remove a hair from his checked lapel.

Fine-looking animal, the love says.

The purchase by Dingle of a dog, 9 June, represents part of a whole broad homunculoid-inspired plan. The plan unfolds ideally thus: One day next week, Myrnaloy Trask, accompanied by Nixon, leaves Collective Copy at lunchtime, as is her wont. She heads south on Great Awakening, toward the town common, where her lunch is picked and eaten while Nixon is encouraged to make complete use of the limitless facilities. As M. heads south down the broad Northampton sidewalk, Barry Dingle, down the street, theoretically emerges from a convenient vantage point and moves north on same sidewalk, holding the leash of one well-rested, libidinous, pep-talked male Setter/Retriever. As he and Myrnaloy begin to converge, Dingle contrives something clever — tripping, bumping into the odd passing spike-haired pedestrian — to render his hand plausibly absent one leash-handle. Dingle's dog, driven to erotic frenzy by its time in confinement and the proximity of a premenses female S/R, is on Nixon like a shot. Etc., but ideally not too much etc., because Barry Dingle suddenly flops onto the scene and extracts upright dog from hunched bitch before any uninvited indiscretions are committed.

The plan having the ideally three-fold result that: (a) Dingle is able to meet and reestablish social ties w/ Myrnaloy Trask w/o the oppressive fly-in-ointment atmosphere that attends the presence of Don Megala, who devotes his pre-prandial hours to his antique dulcimer craft; (b) Dingle appears sensitive, conscientious, possibly chivalric, in rescuing Myrnaloy's dog from drooling amorous assault right there on the main thoroughfare's sidewalk; (c) Myrnaloy sees that the sensitive, chivalric, etc., Dingle is in possession of 1 (one) male dog of just the right lineage and enthusiasm for the bulletin board's published assignment.

The above results, then, according to the projections of Dingle's homunculoid love, lead with arithmetic inevitability to the mating of the two pets, the symbolism of which vis à vis Dingle and the increasingly Megala-dissatisfied Myrnaloy Trask escapes neither party; thus to a Megala-free connection between Dingle and Myrnaloy, one based on mutual anxieties, shared dietary concerns, and the common offspring of their lives' closest companions' (Dingle figures he better come up with a name pretty quick: he's acquired a catalogue for parents-to-be, and pores nightly); thus to nature taking its natural, terrifying course. Yes Dingle appropriates the heart, soul, moderate love of Myrnaloy Trask of Collective Copy. Megala is kicked in the emotional ass. A new Barry Dingle emerges from the cracked chrysalis of chastity and clotted hankie — complete, of the world, fulfilled, requited, ordered of heart and head, sound of mind and toe. A unified Myrnaloy/Dingle homunculus moves stately and plumply away, heading possibly north, disappearing into a cadet-blue horizon that darkens to a gloam of unity, eternity, immoderate love's good night.

So, 9 June, Dingle maneuvers his dog, rattling with Dalmane, listing ever so slightly to port or starboard at females' passage, home without major incident. The dog eats three plastic bowls of Purina, sleeps for seventy-two hours, and establishes itself in front of the television. Dingle's love bides its time.

Nighttime, 14 June 1983, Troy, New York, Mrs. Dingle lies next to Mr. Dingle and dreams the following dream:

Nighttime, 14 June 1983 B.C., Kingdom of Ithaca, the King of Ithaca, played in the dream by Nelson Eddy, has a dream. He dreams that a ship carrying a virulent plague from the Ionian Sea's south enters the port of Ithaca the following day. He dreams that, soon thereafter, plague erupts in the kingdom, and ravages it. He dreams that the plague eventually carries off his devoted Queen of a wife, played by Mrs. Dingle, and his handsome Prince of a son, played by the straight-eyed young Barry D. on whom Attic sandals had looked so darn dapper.

The King of Ithaca awakens 15 June 1983 B.C. and is so distressed by his dream that he brushes aside his Queen's advice and neglects to eat a good Mediterranean breakfast. His summons his Royal Advisor, played here by Don Megala, which is passing strange, since Mrs. Dingle has never met Don Megala. The Advisor listens to the distressed King's dream. He strokes his well-groomed beard. Like the King, like all prehistoric pagan-types, the Advisor takes dreams very seriously. He reflects. After substantial reflection, a flaming torch of inspiration appears over his head: he advises the King simply to stop, on this day, any ship approaching from the south before such ship can enter the port of Ithaca, to keep such ship far out to sea, south, downwind, and to quarantine it, in order to ensure that whatever is on this theoretical ship, plague-wise, stays out there, far far away.

Sure enough. By lunchtime, a ship, tacking chaotically, sporting an ominous obsidian sail, manned by a moaning, bubo-studded crew, appears on the southern Ionian horizon. The King sends his most formidable Man O' War out to halt the ship, has the ship quarantined, and then just to be on the safe side has the formidable Man O' War *itself* quarantined, all far far out to sea, downwind.

Sure enough. The black-sailed ship turns out to be a veritable petri dish of plague germs. The Advisor's advice to keep it out of the port looks to be sound. The King, the Queen, and the big and strong and emmetropic Prince all rejoice over a lavish supper rich in high-density lipids.

Except a few days later (represented in Mrs. Dingle's dream by the fluttering palimpsests of a Hellenistic daily planner) yes a few days later, plague erupts in the kingdom of Ithaca. It ravages even the more respectable neighborhoods of the capital city. It eventually carries off the devoted Mrs. Dingle and the binocular, fine-sandaled Barry D.

Nelson Eddy plunges into well-coiffed despair, not to mention rage. He summons Don Megala. The two men are to be seen facing each other, perfumed hankies fastened over their mouths and noses, in a linen-draped castle chamber festooned with garlands of olive leaves, roses, garlic, various herbal propitiations to big-biceped gods.

The King sketches for his Advisor his despair, rage. Thanks to the Advisor's advice, he says, the dream-foretold plague-ship was stopped, isolated, kept at a big-time distance. And yet here, in Ithaca, as the dream foretold, is some pretty goddamn clear evidence of plague. The King demands an explanation, hinting that the continued connection between the Advisor's well-bearded head and toga'd body could well depend on the force of that explanation.

There is a long silence while both Nelson Eddy and Don Megala utilize the filmy June sunlight through the windows' woven linen to present profiles, respectively agonized and pensive, to Mrs. Dingle's dreamvision. Really long silence. Then the Advisor changes expression below the tattered torch-flame of a tardy but near-epiphanic realization. He smiles a slow smile, one of sadness as at the inevitable, taking the King by the elbow and guiding him confidentially to the chamber's corner, even though no one else is around. The King, looking about, impatiently clears his throat while the Advisor feels delicately at his own.

He advises the King: it was, unfortunately, nothing other than the King's dream itself that has brought plague to Ithaca, the kingdom.

The interval 11:50 to 11:57am EDT, 15 June 1983, finds a tiny percentage of the planet's persons involved in a tiny percentage of the planet's various and ineluctably modal situations.

8:50am PDT, Dr. W.W. Skeat, Fullerton, California, driving north on the Brea Highway toward an Osco to obtain an esoteric brand of peroxide mouthwash, finds himself, in his car, afflicted with an enormous jumping muscle in his right buttock. The muscle jumps, bouncing him around in his seat. Skeat whimpers; his car begins to weave.

11:50am EDT, Myrnaloy Trask, Collective Copy, concludes a pain-racked and I-should-have-known-flavored conversation with Don Megala, professional student, re the issue of her having entered his loft last night to find a nude Smith post-graduate (actually one Pamela Drax, 25, Ithaca, NY) astride Megala's doubly-bearded face. Megala, at his dulcimer work-table, perspiring over a little brown forest of blunt Bass bottles, claims that it had not been as it appeared. Myrnaloy responds with a shrill expanded variant of Oh sure. Megala, looking about him, launches into something about a contact lens lost under circumstances so bizarre he guesses he couldn't expect anyone to believe him about it outside an environment of very special sharing and trust. Myrnaloy laughs, cries, invects. Running his hand through the memory of his hair, Megala alludes with transparent patience to Myrnaloy's still-narratively-shadowy personal troubles regarding sexuality and men. From here things deteriorate faster than clinkers in fists. Myrnaloy hangs up and crumples onto the form-feeder of her Xerox. The form-feeder coldly continues to form-feed.

6:51am MT, Patricia Dingle of Rock Springs, Wyoming, Hypo-Arctic Correspondent for *Geo* Magazine, wakes alone in a mummy-shaped bag by a dead fire on the northern shore of Coronation Gulf, North-Northwest Territories, Canada, to discover that the fingers of her right hand have escaped the bag's faulty zipper and are frost-bitten solid. An odd windy June snow is falling, flakes skittering like mad insects over the solid crust of the shore. She looks at the dark remains of her campfire and the bright polkadots of frozen blood in her hand's cyan.

11:51am EDT, Mrs. Dingle, Troy, New York, sits over a corn toastie and peach tea and tries to articulate an unspeakable fear to Mr. Dingle, who is arranging leaders and flies on a tackle box's second tier.

11:51am EDT, Barry Dingle, Northampton, Massachusetts, *sans* glasses, *avec* best poncho and conic cotton slacks, lurks in the recessed doorway of the Leftward Ho Cafe, just south on Great Awakening from The Whole Thing and Collective Copy. His ominously frisky dog held tight between his knees, Dingle is awaiting the public appearance of Nixon and Trask. Courage defined glows bright along his ribs, illuminating the glazed doll's-eyes of an immoderate love, sitting lotus on Dingle's heart, staring straight ahead beneath the steady sixty-watt glow of a plan's fruition. The last of a shelf of spring rain-clouds is moving away east, carrying with it the drepanoid nub of a descending rainbow.

11:53am EDT, K.K. McFadden, Stenographer to the Assistant Press Secretary to the President of the United States, Washington, D.C., makes a stenographic error, asserting, in a pre-summit statement to be read to the Cyrillic media by Press Secretary Speakes, that the President is, as he's iterated time and again, willing to go the extra diplomatic mile to ensure that the terrible possibility of unclear war never becomes a reality.

11:54am EDT, Mrs. Dingle is at the telephone, dialing the Northampton number of The Whole Thing, her heart ridden with a nameless angst.

11:54am EDT, Myrnaloy Trask, an automaton of distress, takes her zucchini bread and mineral water and dog and exits Collective Copy, moving south into the lunchtime sidewalk crowd's spectrum of hair and Kabuki paint. She feels humidity, sees a thoroughfare's rising steam, hears the brief rustle of her sheltered board, smells ozone and the sweet diesel of the idling public bus.

6:54pm ADT, Aristotle Onassis, on his yacht, four degrees west and six north of Lord Howe Island in the Tasmanian Sea, ruminates over a celery juice at his yacht's wet bar. He sits on a teakwood barstool. The seat of the stool and the wet bar's top are covered in an exquisite cyan leather processed from the scrotums of sperm whales under Mrs. O's personal supervision. Onassis twirls his icecubes with a thick finger.

8:54am PDT, W.W. Skeat narrowly avoids contact with a Trailways bus in the Highway's left lane. He shifts on his bottom, raising the offending ham off the driver's seat. The Trailways bus falls in behind him, the driver honking at Skeat's inclined-to-port image through two layers of thick glass.

11:54am EDT, Don Megala redials Collective Copy, is informed that a very upset Ms. Trask has left for lunch. Megala peels at the triangular label of a moist bottle, staring at a half-strung instrument.

6:55am MT, Patricia Dingle, eyes rimed with ice, palate hanging with the oystery starlight of extreme outdoor fear, makes a clumsy incision in the first finger of her frozen hand with a camp knife. The incision is a deep one just beneath the nail. She begins squeezing her finger with her left hand, moving the frozen blood up the finger and out the incision. The blood leaves the finger in a bright solid mass, protrudes in an arc into the snow-skittered and very cold air. Patricia Dingle remembers her covert passion for sweet cherry Freezer-Pops as a milk-drinking child and is suddenly unwell onto the royal gulf's sloped shore.

11:55am EDT, Barry Dingle emerges from the doorway of the Leftward Ho and moves north on the broad sidewalk toward the tiny, divergent, dual images of Myrnaloy Trask and her life's companion. The sidewalk before him, aswarm with mohawked women, weak men in leather, children in dyed smocks, branches in his sight into two vivid columns. Dingle makes for the distant root where the columns converge, where two Myrnaloys and two incontinent dogs will come together. His sandals slap the wet pavement. Dingle tastes the material of his heart on his tongue. His white knuckles are redly dotted with clench on his dog's heavy leash; he's numb; he does not feel the dog's abortive lunges at the crewcut Sapphoids passing just outside Dingle's crossed-inward ken as they whirl on spurred boots, most of them, glaring at the male animal and either saluting as in Rome or assuming martial-arts postures. Dingle is blind to what passes; he stares straight ahead; his immoderate love's eyes roll over white beneath its lit bulb.

11:55am EDT, Mrs. Dingle exchanges terse greetings with Nigel, temporary helmsman of The Whole Thing, lunchtime. She asks for Dingle.

8:50–8:57am MT, the Eskew brothers, Ronnie and Boone, both remanded to the custody of the Arizona Department of Corrections for terms not to exceed twelve years, attach a centerfold to the back of new inmate Dean-Paul Doyle, age 18, and sodomize him repeatedly on the floor of a crowded dormitory in Cell Block D, Arizona State Correctional Facility, Florence, AZ.

11:56am EDT, Myrnaloy Trask moves south on the sidewalk, seeing little past her curtain of hot tears but a miasma of colored hair, khaki pants, the twinkle of emergent sun on single earrings. Her past and present whirl together and yield a tornado of pain. Nixon trots cheerfully beside her.

11:56am EDT, Mrs. Dingle, on the phone, finds herself weeping for no good reason. Nigel tries to soothe her with a recipe for gazpacho.

6:56pm EDT, Aristotle Onassis, on his barstool, on his yacht, sees on the radar dish's monitor behind him the videotaped face of Cliff Robertson, speaking on behalf of AT&T, which Aristotle owns. Robertson looks tan and fit. Onassis can see both their faces' reflections in his polished mirror over his wet bar, on his yacht.

11:56am EDT, Don Megala, waiting for the special Weather-That-Wood brand shellac to dry on a soon-to-be-antique dulcimer, smokes a Dunhill, looking out his workshop window at the whitewashed New England brick wall the window faces.

8:56am MT, ten-week-old Shauna Doyle, Olney, Arizona, lies on the carpet of her absent mother's trailer. She sees the sun shine faint pink through the upright ear of the white Husky puppy standing guard over her as Barry Dingle moves forward into convergence. His white-eyed love chants prayers for the living. The teams close. Nixon, in new heat, strains at the approach of Dingle's restrained male. The clouds, a dark eastern blight on an immoderate blue sky, rumble as their commalike nubbin of rainbow hangs there, indecisive. Myrnaloy is blind. Dingle smiles wildly as he reaches the columns' union, smiling, poorly feigning a shock of recognition. He goes into a re-hearsed stumble of ideal surprise — this time, though, unideally stub-bing a swollen toe on the pole of the bus stop's tall sign — loosening his grip on the length of chain. Dingle's dog is uninterested in Nixon: its rolling eyes lock on a point just below the denim waistline of Myrnaloy Trask, upwind. Dingle goes all too convincingly for his hurt toe, howling, his right foot brought up and held with both white hands; the Retriever is set free, its military chain a suitor's jewelry. It clears a bright puddle in one horny bound. From below, the puddle reflects upward the not-pretty, bright-red arousal of one male dog. Myrnaloy stops. Dingle stops. Dingle's dog hangs in mid-air, en-tombed in color, fixed and fused in an unutterable focus.

From Just Whistle
C. D. *Wright*

THE BODY, ALIVE, not dead but dormant, like a cave that has stopped growing, stirred up, awakened, waked, woke itself altogether up, arose to a closed set of words, *I wish you wouldn't wear your panties to bed*, the body, on its flat feet, breaking into sweat, breaking into rivers, unbent at five and one half feet, and having slept, as if in a boat, where the hair on its legs continued to curl long and gold, where its papers were stored, more or less dry, in a can, where whatever grew tired or useless fell off, fell away, having been not dead but dormant, living, slept as if in a boat, oarless, unmoored, sand pouring out of a canvas bag,

———————

sand seeping from cavities no longer moist, not removing the panties, but making every effort to conform to the hull among scales, and leaves from overhanging willows, weepers, older than them even, wept, wounded into dormancy, unable to plug the wound, water deeper than night, the lewd, newly enlivened wound, night deeper than water, wound older than the body's marrow, older than its rocks, dogs glomming along the unstable rocks of its words, stirred up by days, sunblare, dreaded as the vulture dreads its own shadow; then, a slightly taller body waving from the shoreline with an armadillo on its shoulder, waving wildly as if for the pantied body to pull to rocky shore and share the armadillo, as if they had not crowed the night before

———————

the pantied one said nothing, not even its own newly enlivened
name, its own naked name, the memory fulgurant, sheet lightning
of other bodies, of the one that did not have a book in its house, the
one that kept running to the pot, the one that admitted it loved the
boat, the body stayed because it loved the boat, the impartial body,
the inseminator, the second inseminator, the one over which the
body had cut itself, just whistle cuts, the one that did not end after
the aspirin incident but only much later during the war, our war on
them, not the grunt the dodger, the one that ended in a hospital
among neotenous bodies caparisoned in black, the first inseminator,
the quick wit, that thespian, that did not attend the termination,
the dropout, the redneck, the uncut one, the juicy one a subway
musician, the second inseminator, that did not attend the termination, the liar, the other liar, liar of liars, pants on fire, the gentle
one, the only gentle one, the rough kisser, the one with an inde-
fatigable hand, the all-night rover, that readily laughing one, their
combined tongues and clavicles, the two drunks, the original liar,
so that even after the liar died, slew itself, eleven years after the liar
died and had not a second's thought about its own rotted body

---

In The Old Days

We didn't have this and we didn't have that
We rolled down the sloping shadows
Into the blue hollows like a bottle
Swallowing grass and stems
We fell into a nest of harmful bodies
We were pale and far as the sun
The harmful ones went sleeveless
Like trees without leaves
How we loved their smooth torsos
Like bluffs we leapt off
We loved them rough as boards
Hard as rocks we loved them
We had a voice soft and filmy as a mussel
We were like farm kittens
Each one different but the same
Our love was like the pulp
Of luscious fruit

We put up with a lot
Like living on Tchoupitoulas
That was the old days
Who could have penetrated the fog
In such bodies in those days

---

its careless posture, its long trunk, its howling os, for so long it has
been accused of bruxism, of failure to perform on the pot, of fulgurating, of priapism, of bags; there are things which happen to it
only at night, but the body dare not repeat them, the better to disguise its beastliness, while its ferns continue to brush their fronds
off the porch, the cat cries and cries to be let out, then cries and
cries to be let in, the body has been prepped, no need to shave everything, what doesn't take too long is over too fast, the body is possessed of childlike fears, predominantly flat fears, the armadillo
does not respond to its calls, a phone rings and rings, the book
opens, the letters take off black as flies, it fulgurates, love avec dis-
gust, time divided by mercy, who is its shepherd, crow minus love,
has it any wool, what on earth could be keeping it

---

followed by another closed set of words, *I just want you to last*,
when already the unlasting has started, ruts have formed, petichiae,
bags, dents, lacunae, sloughing, discharge, rot, the blaze between
the cheek and the jaw, gouged-out areas, new growths, horrible ex-
crescency, discoloration, elongated lobes, the buildup of wax, crud,
the degenerate mortar of lime, hair and dung, whilst the beckoning
of the thousand-odd boats in the bay, the glisten and alternate glow
of a fresh brain pan in a fresh apron, the identical age, not one cold
flick nor hot lick older, its neotenous allure, doll-like, not a museum, no old familiar crow, predominantly young and manifest,
with its thousand-odd reifications of its own solid gray matter,
wielding authority, improvements in every direction, advances,
actual sea lions at sunset, their seductive facticity, meanwhile the
body on its pantied hinges in its kitchen, biting into its dusty apple,
gnawing around the worms, wondering if it couldn't be useful yet
going door to door

---

advance of the distinct bodies behind the partition, the death of day, the rupture of motors, contamination of news, lightblare, sloshing sound, the time-honored tool ever alert under its suit, the long-maligned tube manufacturing trouble under its folds, the frisson of their proximity, the ineluctable concussion

---

Whilst the one body referred to its wound as IT another designated it THE THING. Both bodies did long battles with their wound, and the body referring to its wound as IT slew itself on the eve of its own birthday, whilst the one designating its agony THE THING gave birth to itself, took its children in hand and visited the sea. Very likely IT and THE THING are one and the same. Very likely the felo-de-se had access to something the parthenogeneticist did not. Had the felo-de-se held out a little longer, the fog would have dutifully burned off, and it too could have visited the sea. In the old days, picnics, socials, public whippings, hangings and spelling bees were amusements in which the entire family could partake. But no one, in those days, able of body and soul, stood up in its saddle and let loose with a panegyric to its hole. At point-blank range. At least not in mixed company.

Hole of holes: world in the world of the os, an ode, unspoken, hole in its infancy, uncuretted, sealed, not yet yielded, nulliparous mouth, girdle against growth, inland orifice, capital O, pore, aperture to the aleph, within which all, the over-stocked pond, entrance to vast funnel of silence, howling os, an idea of beautiful form, original opening, whistling well, first vortex, an idea of form, a beautiful idea, a just idea of form, unplugged, cored, reamed, scored, plundered, insubduable opening, light source, it opens. This changes everything.

And nothing. The body slept under the bow two nights. Propped up
with an oar. Cocked its gnarly head and listened to sheet metal
music. Birds swooped down on it. The rock on its chest getting
bigger. The wind told secondhand lies, more lies. It felt a breeze
enter its vestibule. The flesh had begun to grow over the elastic in
its panties like bark over fencing. Several of its fingers fell off, fell
away. Oh well. It would not end up like the others. In a typing pool.
Splitting gizzards. If necessary a prosthesis could be fashioned out
of lime, hair and dung. It could still crow.

---

in its stall ... the gorgeous gob is brought in ... accompanied by the
other body ... tentacles encircle the body ... a partition separates it
from other bodies ... a calm is coming ... the promise of calm is calming ... the body a yellow and blue canvas ... swollen ... distended ...
yellow and blue mixed gives green ... the other body wipes the leav-
ings from the swollen, distended body ... not a word on the armadillo ... the gorgeous gob is set upon the aureolae

---

over everything ... up through the wreckage of the body, in its
troughs, and along its swells, tangled among its broken veins, climb-
ing on its swollen limbs — a blanket of fresh, vivid, lush, optimistic
green; the verdancy rising even from the foundations of its ruins.
Weeds already amid the bruises, and wildflowers bloomed among
its bones. Everywhere were bluets and Spanish bayonets, goosefoot,
morning glories and daylilies, purslane and clotbur and panic grass
and feverfew. Especially in a circle at the center, sickle senna grew
in extraordinary regeneration, not only standing among the blown
remnants of the same plant but pushing up in new places, among
distended folds and through rips in the flesh. It actually seemed as
if a load of sickle senna had been dropped. On the eighth day its
milk trickled in ...

---

is it. is it.
it is. it is.
an object of worship.
graven.
an object of contempt.
craven.
asshole it thought it said.
whistle it said. just whistle.

———————

Voice Of The Ridge

Something about a hazy afternoon — a long drive
    about cedars spearing the sky
Something about a boy at a crossing
    about a dog missing a paw
    about buying a freshly dressed hen
Something about the locus of the dead

Something about a strange town on a weekend
    about large white panties on a line
About a table in a family-owned café
    an old morsel on the tines
Something about the owner dragging one foot
Something about wine from a jelly glass

Something about a hazy afternoon — a long drive
    about no purse no stockings
Something about unfolding the map
    about a cemetery that isn't kept up
    about grasshoppers — their knack for surprise
Something about stumbling onto a full set of clothes
    in the weeds

Something about a hazy afternoon — a long drive
    about hills of goldenrod
Something about filling-station attendants
    the one blue hole in the clouds
Something about birds of prey — the locus of the dead

Something about the long drive home — a slow sundowning
   about the din of insects
Something about the straight yellow hair on a pillow
Something about writing by the nursery's gold light
   in the quick minutes left before miniature lips
   suction a nipple from wrinkled linen

----

as if a fist of pennies had been buried alongside its bowl, at least it
didn't have to be funny for this one, its bush bloomed blue, the one
rooting, eyes shut, not zorabedian, one was just out awhistling
through the armenian burial ground, the abundant bush, bent to
pluck the book of photographs, this ballad is known by all, crow
shot ripped out of the middle, it is very old and intensely sad, the
panties excoriating in their own precious time, a healing beat begun,
sheet metal music, revealing the sunlit shaft, the glans, crura, the
other body's extreme soif, the thinnest issue of piss, arid as the hy-
drangea, the other body planting its pennies, a soul kiss, febrile,
acoustic, an armadillo waddling off on its own, the other body inclined toward shade, fulgurating, alongside the bowl, asking could
it have some of that water, the other roused, if only temporarily,
waked from its amniotic dreaming, unbent at five and one half feet,
flicked the switch on its vestibule, *did you check the dogs* ... suspicious, fulgurant, but passing through its fluorescent words to the
perineum, perpetrator of crow, fueled by previous experiences,
where crow nearly slew it, deadening pedagogy of crow, not feed on
thee, no, for if a body meet a body coming through the halm, the
boat aground, for all of them so loved the boat, site of their facticity,
occasion of the angel's wee victory over the beast

----

it was so lifelike it was uncanny

it had its own ontogeny

the sequestration of the suspect nearly over

it arrived like a blot-from-the blue

it stayed on a macula on the forehead

C.D. Wright

etiolating their days of wonder and regret

the big guns arrived but it was too late

it had no alibi

thoughts of it dying cheered us up

a soft utterance in the dark

a night or two in the pokey

years in a leaky boat

were nothing compared to the beat of this wing

———————

the pitch of the body   unbent

    risen on an elbow   its abundant bushes

its hills of goldenrod and especially in a circle at the center

    sickle senna   in brilliant darkness   a fresh apron

in extraordinary regeneration   touched against

a nerve of tender concern   for its papers

    its incredible fingers   flattening them

one at a time   a healing beat   begun at point blank range

    around the insubduable opening   the leaky wound

irrigating kisses   planted near the bowl

seven inches down and especially along the edges of its realm

    the frisson of their proximity, the ineluctable concussion

Eight Photographs
Diana Michener

DIANA MICHENER: A GLIMPSE OF THE SUBLIME

I FIRST MET Diana Michener on Nantucket in the mid-1970s: an intense, vital presence, she shifted between stillness and agitation, like a heron. She seemed more than observant; she seemed vigilant. She seemed to want to know more than what was evident, and to be almost reckless in this urge, like a young girl first discovering how will can invade and augment desire.

Only someone with a radical curiosity could set about photographing a myth, since myth by its nature defies the real. Before she undertook Leda, she photographed damaged fetuses preserved in glass jars, and before them, the huge uncomprehending heads of slaughtered cattle. She is unflinching, if that means fearless and persevering. Leda is the first of three myths; Adam and Eve and Narcissus are still to come; she sees them as a progression: from Innocence to Fall to Self-Consciousness. Recently, she spoke to me about how she thinks about Leda and the Swan.

"I wanted to place myself in innocence. If you go into a taboo, by the nature of it you become innocent, because you are free of cause and effect; you are as close as possible to the place in you which doesn't know. Only by being in that taboo, that unknown, can one be transformed.

"Sex is the one place where you are cast adrift in a timeless state, from which you emerge changed. I don't know exactly what it means to be ravished, but it must have something to do with being awestruck, and you surrender. There's a willingness in the surrender; an assertion, rather than a collapse, of will. You give yourself over, not to an examination of self, but to the forces of self: it's a leap across the known — 'split the lark — you'll find the music.'

"Our world is completely pragmatic but without rationale, so in order to feel a sense of beginning, you need to lie down with the unknown. This is the subversive state of innocence. It's fragile and suspended; the physical is both confirmed and consumed. When

127

Diana Michener

you light a match to paper, the flame is neither match nor paper. It has to do with gesture. If you could just stay in the gesture, without having it lead somewhere, then you might get a glimpse of the sublime. But, of course, this is what we are never allowed to do."

Well, maybe not never.

— Ann Lauterbach

Diana Michener

Diana Michener

Diana Michener

Diana Michener

Diana Michener

Radio Tiranë
Eric Darton

BEAUTIFUL ALLEY

THE FREE MARKET CAME and went wild wild wild. So many parings. So many clearances, so many fire sales: the signage was exemplary and ubiquitous. Lost our lease, leaving our senses, everything must go. There was enormous dancing in the square, next to where they'd hung the redcoat, where double-deckers circled fulminating gray stampede clouds round a cool fountain spraying with each windshift the babies facing off boxcameras, present and disconcerted, diapers askew, all dirt, abraded knees and euphoria. This was the square of the first dead pigeon, of the yellow ice cream carts dry ice exhaling into fringed umbrellas, the square of the rapid-fire doubletalker, and Garibaldi reaching for his sword. The square of the ample babysitter, of the small husband of the amplebaby sitter, tweed-suited in a broiling green *mezzogiorno*, superbly economical and cool like Garibaldi, with unimpeachable dignity: the square of the old earpatch, unimpeachably old, like Christmas postmarks from the North Pole, the square of unimpeded sun shooting silver off denim polished slides, of drumming sneakers, the leap of faith, the jungle-gym ritual knocking-out of teeth and overalled legs and buttocks leaping high off exaggerated seesaws and down the street the old buildings taken out, swinging ball, taking out walls, geologies of habitation, moldings, stairwells, figured linoleum, varicolored paint-job stratifications confecting fine into hosed-down dust. This was rubble, child, jagged terrain—these were inflammable cans, yeah one blew up and burned Julie's arm and she screamed and they had to take her to the hospital and that night the rat population migrated en masse to the deep excavation down to the stream that ran beside the native burials and the redcoats and the black arm of the oak, off in the snow and the accident made Julie a shero—yo that's girl for hero—and every nap, every dream, every daydream, every sunbath is invaded and consoled by industrial crossrhythms, squeaking clothesline pulleys, an open window

137

out on the beautiful alley where cats run and rats run and over eight million people live in peace and harmony and enjoy the benefits of democracy.

From three concentric gold rings comes this and more: something about Suez, something about Comrade Eisenhower or Conelrad Adenauer, something about General Assembly recognizes the distinguished representative of Abyssinia, something about missing persons, Caucasian and Negro — and if this had been an actual emergency good night and good luck — and something about Brahms' double. Why make new buildings that look like old buildings, why not fish for eels in the river, why not dive off Spuyten Duyvil, why not dam a creek to make a pool for your flaming dogs, then kick away the stones and watch the leaves rush with the flood and take root to boost yourself to the post-no-bills excavation window where the rats are, playing, bounding with their ratlings, domestic paradigm, as the pump chunks brown water, why not watch them lowdown scuttle end-to-end the beautiful alley, why not let the free market roll and hear the conveyor-dock workmen folk this, folk that, ya cogs aqua: duck the real metal conveyors, truck to dock across the badlands sidewalk, or try to skate round all that?

Three generations and a German shepherd under one roof, no steam heat, no hot water probably, no shower by the smell of grandma and riots sometimes, crashing furniture, a couple of screams and drawn-out silence. On good days, excitement bounces around in the resonator tin ceilings then seeps downstairs cross-phasing with Brahms' double as Connie and Julie pump up the AM. Some days grandma wants a kiss on the pitched wooden exiguous stairs, whoa gotta go, stairs the bums sleep under 'til the couple in the white apartment buys the building and gates up the walkway, stairs the coal man drags the coal up, tracing black dust and burlap, stairs Vinnie bucket-brigades the heisted TVs up and Connie and Julie avalanche down on their way to lemon ices, watermelon or cat lick school. If there wasn't a factory on each side, this building would fall down.

And all around the free market lies like a counterpane of dust, of coal and buildings taken down: lying down to sleep, silhouettes of bombers cascading across battery radar, when tractors roam linoleum, flashing their cylinders in the dark and some days Con and Jule take you to the blue pool for abraded knees and the rush that there's something about an ankle bracelet, something about a chain and a cross and a chlorine wet neck and a push and a jump:

something that wakes up later, when you're pulled apart and the furniture's chopped and it's four o'clock and the cup hits the wall and the sun comes in another window and the alley's gone.

DOWN THE LINE

A child in the cab of the huge Yankee Clipper — don't worry that you can't reach all the controls — engineer is a job you grow into. Ahead is the dim tunnel, furtive bulbs showing just enough steel rails converging. Train time: a powerful whistle blast rebounds through the corridors from Grand Central up to Harlem, down to Washington. Brakes squeal release, the platform starts moving, folks wave goodbye and when clocks, staircases and handtruck porters begin to blur, you shift focus forward to the convergence of steel and time, logs in flume, liquid extruded — sliding down the line.

Down the line, before you had to define your position, was your gorgeous aunt — blonde and smile radiant — who'd taken you up to the locomotive, watched as the engineer underarm boosted you to his lap and covered her ears when he let you pull the whistle. Train whistles, symphonies, Three Penny Opera, Call Me Mister, Vogue magazine on her dresser, Freud on the shelf — what could they say about the night she came to the house and cried and cried? Gladiola cry? Impossible — and your momma put her arm around her and she stayed over — never — and down the line you hear disjointed words that one day form a meaning: fired, communist, welfare department. And down the line, unexpected after dinner, two men show up urgently needing to talk to your father, framed in the unbolted door. Not skinny like Vinny, not compact like Mr. Casino, not fast and wiry like your dad, but large, intent and so filled with questions, they have to ask them behind closed doors. Doors shut in your house? Never. When momma tells secrets on the phone, she talks Yiddish or French — anything else goes on long after you're asleep and dreaming and one hundred years down the line, your father opens the doors, light spills and in turn the intent men shake his hand. Your father smiles a fatigue only you can read and slides the bolt after the determined downstairs treads that crosspoint with his laugh. Who did they want to know about, your momma asks — and what did you tell them? Nothing, of course — he shakes his head. Idiots — now they think I'm their friend.

TURNED OUT

Squat it was, cut and dried, multipurposeful, like an edible yet rancid blockhouse cubicizing mucho hectares of prime Loisaida/New
Amsterdam farmturf. It had been designated a high school — but
looked as though at any moment its mood might turn ugly and it
would flower as a prison. Despite appearances, its metier was not
punishment, but manufacture — components academic, general and
commercial, purposed by size, weight and lineage. Each September,
a new load clattered random through the hopper gates and these
raw ones, chosen by the choosers, screened by color and density,
were resolutely, if haphazardly, machined. With white and yellow
in high demand and brown and black plentiful but nearly market-
less, is anyone surprised by the huge slag piles beyond the palings?
But such is the ecology of naturalized endeavor — for every time
there is a season, and you'll get yours.

A fatalistic ballad of devotional puppetry hissed over the lunch-
room p.a. where gravity-defiant food adhered like stucco to generic
perfed ceiling tiles — big windows, gratings, noon sunlight and long
tables like the kind James Cagney ran down, a sullen rumble, like
gravel on a conveyor belt and then shooting to feet, kicking over
requisite chairs, aluminum slams formica — a mother has been insulted. Otis's voice, louder than the rest, Otis's head, a head above
the others and then the fray, the flurry of trays, the whirl of glancing punches. Back up. Back up to the failed attempts at enforcing
boys' room regulations, back up to the hall where, locked out of
homeroom, Otis of little patience has blasted a perfectly solid oak
door with Board of Ed brass cast knobs into splinters applying only
one judicious foot to the charge and thereafter calmly collecting
personal effects — so is anyone surprised when sucked by adminis-
trative duty into the insatiable maelstrom, Hodges mainstream
staggers forth, a vanquished floorwalker at a fire sale gone awry,
crosseyed by his bloody nose. Clamor and hilarity, those remaining seated fall out of their chairs — it isn't everyday a teacher gets
busted upside the head. Hodges is a big man, a boxer probably,
but who can mix with Otis with impunity? It is left for Malario,
tiny, relentless and suited to vortex streetcorner conflagrations to
emerge — Otis in one hand, scruff of neck — and clamped in the
other, the insulter of mothers. But this is not the end. Not the last
fight, not the last of streaming noontime sun, not the last echo of aluminum trays, not the last powdering of plaster gouged off generic

walls, not the last train, the last boat, not the last of triangular trade. After a brief conference, the plant goes on overtime, making what it must. It takes a lot of paper to make a plane big enough to fly Otis to Vietnam.

PROMETHEUS CRAZIE

In East M was a streetcorner. On the streetcorner, V was standing, well not exactly on the streetcorner, but on a soapbox on the street-corner, well not a soapbox but more of a milk crate — yes, I remember it like it was yesterday — and he was elevated and haranguing a crowd, yes it's safe to say a crowd and his subject was revolution.

This was a first for E, that's me, seeing up close, or for that matter seeing at all, a certified, elevated, organic — that is, from the streets — dyed-in-the-wool, genuine Crazie agitator. E had seen Crazies before, face to face and intimate; likewise he'd seen agitators, but they'd been students in worker drag, whose provocations were mitigated, yes it's safe to say vitiated by flexions of the mind toward rhetoric, that is to say reasoning — that is, discernible, predictable frames.

Not like V, who was having none of it and having none of it, his incitements took less the form of argument than wildcat invocation, as though by eruptive will alone he had raised himself and was now consecrating those still inhumed to burst the sidewalk with triumphant resurrections; but there were no dead beneath the streetcorner, so it was us he was raising, E and the rest of the dealing, milling, egg-creaming masses sweltering through another East M night — the scum of the earth he called us — the scum of the earth was rising up out of the sewers and no racist pig, no George Wall Ass, no Coitus Lemay, no General Waste More Land was going to keep the scum of the earth from inheriting the earth because the streets belong to the people, the streets belong to the people and we say to all the honkey punk porkers, gimme gimme gimme the honkey punk blues we say up against the wall motherfucker, the streets belong to the people, all power to the people.

As movement Field Marshals colluded steps to forever shift the strategic initiative of power to the people, V slept on floors, ate filched turkeys from Lion, slipped by the Fillmore bouncers for the nth time, lived off Mickey's tolerable steam table hors d'oeuvres, crashed on every floor in East M, slushed — always in the same torn hightops — through the Stalingrad winter of '68, proving that in times of revolution, the guerrilla swims through the people like a fish walks through the sea.

Beyond that night, I never saw him elevated, never saw the djumbe take him, as if having risen once and homed with the spirits of Moncada Barracks, Dienbienphu, the Lincolns at Jarama and a thousand Fenians marching by the rising of the moon, he had come back to earth a dogface free from zealous contagion — a good soldier. I knew him too, in times of reluctant maternal visits to project X, compartment Z, where he'd grown up crashing his bike and shortening his leg by two inches, acquiring that streetwise cock walk. He'd raid the fridge for duck and bok choy in his old man's basement while dad, who had learned not to understand English, was out making bank Mah Jong style.

Besides Chinese, V's lineage concatenated Spanish, Afro and a soupçon of Ivan the Bad. V was the world the adman wanted to buy a coke for and it was V who dreamed up the agitprop dayglo blood orange oval Crazie button logo, letters shaping a black AK-47, and drew cartoon porkers with beer guts and kick here leadlines point-to their balls and in his own time helped launch a boom in the Dupont Circle replacement glass industry, threw up his CS'd guts in the reflecting pool, turned every mailbox overnight into a VC flag, heaved bricks and teargas canisters in Lincoln Park and like everyone else lusted for D's ass in the railroad commune squatpad and hated being cold, coming home filthy and covered with microscopic insulation from the inglorious shape-ups and six a.m. bust-ups of old ovens to which heavy revolutionaries are reduced in the winter of discontent following the long hot summer, following the radical chic choosing its few and moving on and the court bailiffs never could pronounce his name, but one time, on a streetcorner in East M, in decrepit hightops and lowlife trademark sergeant pepper regalia, V was elevated on a milk crate — no, now I remember — it was a trash can he was standing on and the words were hot, the air was hot, but not enough to put a trash can on fire. That was no miracle, that was ecstasy, that was human arson and like a lighthouse that beam was picked up by a thousand mirrors and bounced and multiplied and E, that's me, and how many others are still walking in that light?

Eric Darton

¡LUNA SI, YANQUI NO!

N'allez pas en Grèce cet été! Restez à la Sorbonne
Don't go to Greece this summer! Stay at the Sorbonne
— Graffiti in the Latin Quarter, May 1968

The roadblock on Gay-Lussac was a marvel in the tradition of Gallic barricade architecture. Composed of cubical paving stones, cast-iron tree gratings, traffic signs, unlucky Citroëns and tree limbs, it presented, to those confronting it, a daunting facade — a great wall of euphoric disorder. Anarchists, spread along the length of its fore and uppermost tessellations — their rude songs and gaiety belying their *habits noir* — taunted the imported *flics* and generally whupped things into a frenzy. One tier down, the Situationistes — acolytes of the cult of Mickey — appropriated Captain Fury to their own compromised purposes and slipped between the pages of photo-novellas to make furtive *amour*. In fact, *plus je fais l'amour, plus je fais la revolution* — that's what's written on the wall. Behind them, arms linked in chorus-line united front congruity, ironworkers from Longwy and Fiat strikers danced Kazakhskys in their flame-colored jumpsuits. And behind their ranks milled other syndicates and confederations — banners flapping, slogans declaiming. And student militants who would fly off to *Grèce, l'amour, et le soleil* — a summer cash crop for the Colonels — if the revolution lost its juice, curious shopkeepers, old Trots — everyone to the left of De Gaulle was caught up in the revolution. No one knows how many would float sedately through the sewers in the cover-up.

But one moment is certain. At another time, another utopia, this town had been repurposed for planned living, ease of vehicular traffic and clean artillery trajectories down wide boulevards. Ever is the rough made plain. In yet another utopia, Bathgate fell before Moses, the Cross Bronx became an underutilized place for suicides and no wonder — it's a fit place only for horizontal flow. People want to have some individuality in troubled circumstances, some sense of grace to the dive. But back to the barricade. On the windward side, at a safe remove, at the corner of Gay-Lussac and Edmond-Rostand, the CRS — *casqued, masqued* and semiautomatics port arms — consecrated the coming battle to the blood of their dead warriors — of Algerie, of Dienbienphu. In this way had Alexander celebrated his victory over the Persians — this is hearsay, but it makes a good story. So on the marching order, *bleu-noir* behind their shields, the

143

Eric Darton

phalanx of lockstep ex-legionnaires advanced under a shower of
Haussmann's cubical paving stones. The Parisii have two millennia
of barricade defense under their belts, look it up — and at the moment of assault, the anarchists scrambled, ever ready to engage, as
Ironboy had at Jarama — Franco still seven years from his grave —
and the first canister hit the girl waving the black flag and sitting
on the boy's shoulders in the left cheek and the second canister
forced the piano student's left hand into an improbable and permanent backwards curve and what went down went down and the less
fortunate floated through the sewers to the sea and the more fortunate, the militant students with folding francs ended up on holiday
en Grèce cet été, pas à la Sorbonne.

Between then and the next millennium, in another putative utopia, riding into the sunset of *Pax Americana*, down which screen
no credits roll, Robin went to Attica for trying to bomb a bank, Fred
Hampton was murdered by the FBI, George Jackson grew an afro so
powerful it could nest a .38. Truth? Ahhh, baloney. Eldridge Cleaver
designed leather codpieces and Che made a bad bargain for his
watch — before Willie Ninja vogued the house, before Willie Turks
went straight to heaven at the corner of Avenue X, his eternal reward for buying donuts in the wrong neighborhood — look it up,
and before Willie Bosket was a gleam in Willie Bosket Senior's eye —
plus je fais l'amour — before the rough-sex defense was a pistol in a
preppy's pocket — before the Tupamaros and Etan Patz disappeared,
we were all undesirables, we were all Etan Patz.

This is a *plena* for the once and future *declamadores* whupping
up the barricades on tight *pandereta* skin drums — a *plena* for plebi-
scites too little too late, for pre-approved amnesties, for kelp wars
and luv boats — tall ships — the *Esmeralda* out of Buenos Aires,
cruising under Liberty's bronze Bicentennial armpit and "El Cau-
dillo" only one year in his grave — cruising waters where Führer-
bunker Boys returned to Brazil 'cross the wide ratline — thank you
Jesus, Give-'em-Hell-the-Buck-Stops-Here-Harry and Munich Station — what year is it? '45? No, '68! *Dix-neuf cent soixante-huit.*
Danger, danger!

There's a fire in the foundry! FDR, FDR, why don't you blow up
the rail lines? You know what they're good for. FDR, FDR, why
don't you bomb the tracks? You know where they lead. To which
utopia and millennium replied in *coro: Cogete el tren!*

In ten years, in the millennium, this will be a great place to live —

our Tiranë. I was wise to come home. And I never went to Greece. There were lean times, sure — but I was too young to miss religion and we can all read. We have clean rivers, everyone eats. Soon, with controlled development, we will play as hard as we work — we already live longer than Eubie Blake and our conservatory is exemplary. Soon, we'll show everybody our new *plena* — like a dance that starts too slow and ends up just right.

OFF OUR BACKS, HANNIBAL

We elephants are often told, and often believe, this truism that we hear from calfhood, that purports to explain why we labor, why we are decorated for festivals, why our toes are painted, why we bear our houdahs time after generation: there are those who paint, and those who are painted.

But we have reached the level of requiring more sophisticated explanations — not just for our own condition, but for a host of seemingly unrelated phenomena — why you can't baptize in the river no more, why now everyone can walk on water, what for you get up, what make you get down. To date, the authorities have either been unable — some might say they are able but unwilling — to offer elucidation regarding these and other pressing questions. Instead, we are offered apologies — a cornucopia of apologies, which, if connected trunk to tail, would reach the moon which is a screen to our projector, that's so heavy with images we have to trumpet cadenzas of joy when we see it lit up in the sky.

The fact is, and I know others of my species will take emphatic issue here, that it doesn't matter that the reasons given for things are lies — it only matters that things have, or appear to have, reasons — like Bibles in judicious breastpockets, history's doorstops, deflecting anarchoballistics fired at close range by apostates of the cult of explanation. That bullet goes somewhere after it bores through Genesis, Exodus and Leviticus and onward, straight through the Proverbs until it deflects sharp off Ecclesiastes and angling up, its reasoned trajectory reflected in the mirrored shades of the salt and pepper company guards, skimming the blue serge foothills of the O'Hara's caps, blowing high pressure against the windward mountie's peaks, dropping rain on the steppes beyond and soaring skyward to lodge in the white eye of the moon.

145

Yes, I'm an anarchist, by blood and inclination, but it's not something I shout from the rooftops, provided I can make it up the stairs.
Like being an elephant, it's something that works under the skin,
like having enough dust for a bath, it's something you'd notice and
even miss, if it weren't there. Again, I know others will disagree in
the strongest possible terms, but — it's religion. I can practice it
subsonically or with orchestral militancy as the occasion, my mood
and history conspire to demand. Like religion, like anything strong
enough to nourish or trample life for, it has its traditions, its venerated icons, its schisms, its mystic movements, its unforceable
contradictions, and, like religion, it's supposed to set you free.

But religion is different from church. Founded on the prophets,
with Jesus as its chief cornerstone, the church would have been
heavy enough to crush anyone. As Giles Corey said, at the moment
of his call to ascendancy, as he glimpsed the cock chasing the boar
chasing the serpent chasing the cock — as the circle whirled in the
eye of his beholders, who piled stone after stone on him, pressing
him into the earth, to which, despite denials, everyone returns.
More weight, he breathed in the face of his inquisitor who replied:
I'll give you weight — in the proto Locust Valley Lockjaw that some
three hundred dominant years later would manifest as good weight,
pesas, sausage-link condoms, into which are stuffed all the sueños of
the soñadors — weisswurst in the esophagi of desperate frequent
fliers fluttering boarding cards Medellín a La Guardia.

Like someone's pilgrim fathers, I too believe that the world will
end — the only difference being that I don't believe it ends when I
want it to — I think it will end when it's good and ready, when it
runs out of worlds — when it's tired. Illiterate, like Charlemagne,
I've surrounded myself with people who can read: Christians, Mos-
lems, Hebrews — the best progeny Abraham's blood will tell, but
unlike Charlemagne, I can't not listen — can't just kill them all,
Saxons, Lombards, Jutes, Kallikaks, believing God will sort them
quick from dead when that day comes and it will.

Haroun Al-Rashid aka Aaron the Just, who also couldn't read, had
a positive plan: create a universal timetable so that all the faithful —
and in 800 anno someone's domini it's a big world — will know exactly when to pray. To that end, a signifying English monk and
pan-Med think tank strove mightily and begat Al-lah's devotional
punch clock, with a little trig borrowed from the subcontinent. If
you don't believe me, look it up. I was there, or at least mi raza
was — at one time we ranged throughout North Africa. I'm not

smart, not good with money, just have a long memory. I've mastered having a long memory — living time after generation. But just because you've mastered something doesn't mean you've anesthetized it. Just because you feel pain, doesn't mean you're dying. Just because you're dying, doesn't mean the world is. For every elephant there is dust and a river. For every nurse, a deathbed. For every hemostat there is a good and a bad cop. For every sunspot, a striated lobe, healed after a fashion — world without end. Now that we're covenanted, I can tell you this.

WEIGHT

The miasma descended, first brown then opalescent, but this comes later. Before had come the concerto of kitchen sinks, symphonic vessel ruptures, *cadenze flatulenti* — pre-Cristofori, the great exclusion and the discovery of chloroform. Trains to inlet marshes had shuddered over rolling-mill hard lace extravaganzas and great undertakings, plumbings, scalings, freezings, fryings — why cascades and avalanches had been chronicled, gravured, used for the wrapping of spurious fish, pulped, repulped and pandemicized, content at last to spill from lip to spittled lip, to coast on blown-off foam. The masterpiece of it all was the scale of the endeavor, the prologue of flower vessels, the exemplary production of beakers, vapors and cohorts vitiated by equestrians, willful nomads, imprinted with a genetic incapacity to conceptualize the state — a slowly accelerating crescendo of minor triumphs and stupendous *faux pas*. If not for an unusually pronounced el niño, it is theorized, Napoleon could have taken Moscow, *kvelled* in white nights, rebuffed paparazzi on the Odessa steps, checkmated Kutuzov with a two pawn handicap and blazed straight through to Kamchatka, but that was then and this is now and before that came hewn waterways, the cultivation of the altiplano, the invention of the rebozo, more beakers — a reconcite/tessellated culture this go-round — ice sculptures and frenzies of consecration. There were no homeless then, I'm telling you straight: everyone had a job, a good job, plenty of toot and a *pied à terre* to boot — at one time there were more gods than missionaries and everyone was on a mission, confused, but loving it, fat as pigs, but permeable, alive to this bird, that stone, that pebble under this warm skin, and distended families — talk about roots — there was no stopping these autochthonous mofos, even ice steamrollers couldn't slow them down. And no boundaries, force fields, real or imagined, drunken boats or gumbo diplomacy. No Man Act, no rites of Man, no Man's Land, no crepitus, lazee boys, crystal sets, remembered Maines, no brown then opalescent miasmas. Dope it was before weight: quick, lithe, unimpaired and imminent on the faces of the rhythm section, horns tolling a lazy vamp, opening a two-way channel, down funnels of brass to a sandy well, bathed in the glow of the most exquisite desert light, shadows sundial long, every grain in red-gold high relief—and there triumphant calculations are being cut on a stick: if I know the distance from here to Alexandria, I can give you the circumference of the world before the weight, before the point tenderness, the rebound injuries, the obsolescence of the spleen, the enormous increase in the production of cartilage, the miasma, occlusions, autoclavings, intubations: when we stood on holy ground, sterile ground, in precocious desert twilight, blind but loving it, tail-less, with tally sticks for triumphant incised calculations, sipping somehow clear water from promiscuous recondite beakers and waited to be born on cue, and four bars later blowing desert light down the backs of dancers. Half-man, the drummer, he was always medicated, but this is a good place to stop. Before weight.

GO DOWN

The ancient machine was so well greased nobody noticed it was near death. Oil had been its fuel and fancy, its simulated silence, its transparent operation: palm from the sunbelt, running fruits of the tryworks and resolvent vegetables—all had fed its engines, masked its fatigue. And now, there was no doubt—the final sickness had set in. No Rx of jellies, ointments or balms could stop the groan turning to a howl of emaciated parts—nothing could make up for tolerances finally abridged.

Worse yet, even if the disease wasn't systemic—a sympathetic unison—there was no hope of replacement parts. The machines to manufacture the machines to manufacture the parts had long been scrapped, war-drived or confined to museums. The few meticulously maintained private models, aestheticized relics of a vanished, prized utility of steam and breathing pistons—no one remembered how they worked. Their blueprints were dust, their manuals crumbled when exposed to light or air—no one recalled what they'd been good for — just marveled at their precision, polished brass, fine escapements and incised identities. Birthmarks became epitaphs, ineffable secret names, godnames, known only to the long-gone brotherhoods who had worshiped at their altars, offered lives in limbs, consecrated them with the only offering brothers have to give: sweat, tears and simple whole blood. Fit for rubbings, their glyphs don't stand a chance of finding a translator: Krupp von Essen, Enfield, John Deere — meaningless and cold.

Please, nobody think of replacing them — the tools that made the tools that made the machine that brought us to this burying ground. Let them go, let them oxidize, let them find their peace, let them line once-frenzied arteries, sheltering vagabonds — vagabonds all, unworthy of the elevators that carried us, deck to deck — individuals, all — in copper jackets, round and fused, or chained together, some ceremonial and blank — godnames and marching orders tattooed on our tails. Let's dream a dream of oxygen, recumbent halftracks and forgiving desert, deepest diving, living on in small breaths incarnating some new being — swimming in our sea, nosing round our sunken boat.

GENTLEMEN'S AGREEMENT

Sometime after 1978, a photograph of a handshake appears accompanied by a largely ignored sound bite. Believe me this really happened. Since no carnage is depicted, distribution is confined to newspapers that require a great deal of folding and to lobster-shift cable broadcasts. The photograph represents the achievement of an accord. Two middle-aged men of apparently European descent wearing suits and ties shake hands while a third looks on. All smile: Head of State, Finance Minister, Treasury Secretary. Far from where people kill for Triple Fat Goose, a great victory of reasonableness has taken place and is now fit for transmission, consumption, absorption, ray-o-fication. Authorized fair dinkum, a deal is struck and lo, everybody win-win. But just at the moment of historical consummation, a vacuum threatens to swallow it whole. The precise cause of this sudden disequilibrium is not a subject with which we can profitably be concerned. Perhaps overawed by the metropole, the video crews cannot find the right exit ramps. Flocks of geese may have fouled crucial turbines. Possibly the charging of battery packs has been neglected. Perhaps flashbulbs have rebelled

149

into quiescence, triggering inexplicable underexposures — who knows? Speculations are as prolix as they are moot. What is certain, however, is that by accident or design, through conspiracy or omission, no one successfully records this milestone of fiscal validation. No paparazzi, no stringer, no blind Boul Miche daguerrotypist or proud Instamatic spouse, no Leni Riefenstahl, no one. In an age when representation consecrates existence the handshake rushes toward limbo. One brick left out of a wall and the wall will crumble — any mason will tell you that. Correct or not, that's the perception and when someone, no specific accusations now, but someone high up says: let's go to sim, we do. Never let it be said that a particle of history, flown over the event horizon, cannot be represented. It takes a lot of memory and plenty of anesthesia to chill the latent wagging tongues, but it can be done. Think if the Armenians had had it. Think if Riefenstahl had had it. We can perform simulations so fine, so transparent, that we have to distress them *ex post* to pass for reality, and, for the priggish, the ethically obsessive, the fainthearted, an ironclad alibi: it fucking happened, didn't it, it's not like we're making it up! OK, plus two fill on the bald guy. Let's preview the edit. Beautiful, that hesitation is beautiful. Now roll off the saturation on the clown with the schnoz — not too much — oh he's Mexican? No one told me he was fucking Mexican — OK scroll palettes — stop, that's the baby. OK punch it way up — max it — great! Let's lay in audio. The result is superb despite the unavailability for debriefing of the hapless crews still circumnavigating relentless beltways, battery packs ebbing in the dim twilight of judicial history. It's perfect. Expert witnesses innocent of their perjuries can evaluate the tapes as absolutely authentic, but this is unnecessary since the gesture, once re-presented, becomes archival, playing as invisibly as a recurrent dream. A short time later someone on a subway receives an intentional bodily tort prompted by their ownership of a Triple Fat Goose. Their death is transparent as a handshake.

ALL RISE

What does he know? Nothing. What does he see? A million reflections of his self. What's his driving wheel? The flavor of the month — the stricken fancy. Say, what month was he born? February. Because it's a cold month. Where's he buried? Oh, he's alive. Yeah,

but where's he buried? No man, he runs the casket company —
drives the white truck up the highway, sells caskets on the highway, takes plastic, never decomposes. Who are you kidding? You man.
You were pretty stupid not to see it coming. There were miles of
caskets, laid end to end, leading to that flashpoint. But what could
you do? Change? No not you? Change any more than the way your
head was cut — out of the question. But still, it didn't come out of
thin air. You had all the time in the world — for diagnosis, self-
medication, remediation, firm those thighs. You just let it all slide.
Bit by bit. Impoverishment of the humors, inertia of the fluids,
rigidity of the fibres, agitation of the bile. You just let it grow. From
a moan to a wail to a flat-out convulsive frenzy. I wasn't going to
say anything, but somebody around here is to blame. You know
who I mean. Playing squash, the sweat flies in slow motion. In the
courts, the defendant deposes, then he reposes. Finally he wraps
himself up in a rebozo and dozes, stretched on that bench. All rise.
Wrapped up like that. All rise. Shhh. On your mission behind
enemy lines. Step up to the bench. Your docket number, your pistol,
your pocket. Here he comes with that white truck. What did you
do, now? Now you're buying.

COLLATERAL DAMAGE

Someone's gonna get his ass kicked, beelee vit! swore each passerby
or exchanging busses, lips only brushing. This would be a bonanza for
the glaziers, the *moulagistes*, the plaster manufacturers not seen
since awayback, and *tout le monde* on air, like a waltz, like strudel
so fine you could read the headline punching through. The children
were hypersensitized, the most attuned. What did you do in the
war daddy? they would shrill, even before the installation popped
the headlines, the display of baskets, the putative quarantine. Even
before the Secretary of Defeated Language had announced the
achievement of all objectives, civil and otherwise, even before the
Flaming Dogs battalion had faxed themselves: before the triumphs,
tributes, parade simulations, the scrambled eggs and fruit salad
airlifted to the buoys.

Bob, for his name was Bob, recalled with uncharacteristic clarity
the words of his headmaster as class stood a-ten-hut in the large
central courtyard of the academy. The echoing pronouncement
slapping off the parapets, bounding off the crenellation, shaking

nuts and bougainvillea from the fecund branches to the stony flags below had been appalling. "Yesterday you cut cane. Today you cut heads." He had vowed, hearing those words, not to be a barber. It was an occupation unfit for man nor beast, whiling away your time, slapping astringents on the chafed necks of capos, trimming, preening and stopping dirges, shaking to the rhythm. Would that he had heeded his master's voice, would that he had not precipitously switched vocations: flying Dutchman, Flaming Dog, nobody comes home. The fleet bobbed at bay, rolling on the swells, grinding against the low tides and in sight of land, worse yet in sight of the old school where he had vowed not to be a barber, never to move closer, anchored like an invisible buoy, the gulls, the infernal salt air, corrosion, barnacles. The ships took on barnacles, took on water, flounders, and mail, cough drops and skin lubricants, but no closer please thank you very much, not one inch closer. Give them an inch and they'll take your boots, legs and all. The longest day. Nobody comes home. A salt tear added to the salt sea and recollections, bobbing, of the CO, presiding over disorientation and how eloquently he had spoken of fire in the hole: we don't want no incendiary surprises, y'understand? And to a man the Flaming Dogs had sworn their oaths, bitten live ammo during the dressing down, the counterpaning and nipple-clipping of cloisonné regalia, the bouncing of nickels high off horsehair blankets, making of hostile silhouettes and the distribution of kits containing: horsepills, cosmetics, 1 (one) photonovella, Meine Liebe brand ribbed rubbers, toetag and bubble wrap. O the inoculations, the embarcations, beelee vit! it was a sight, steelplate vaporettos, monitors, tramp steamers, Fitch and Fulton waving, mewling stokers sweating gas, liquefied gas — small forcings have produced large things quoth jeremiad in the semiofficial and to say *a priori* that this gas can't produce large changes — but never-you-mind when Roebling himself is swinging in his buoy beneath the festive bridge, out the estuary, down the intercoastal, flags of connivance snapping, sun rebounding off top hats like so many spitpolish mirror lockstep fabricated blackhole shitkickers each isolating a universe, several nebulae at least and uncork the Kruppstahl, baby there'll be dancing in the barrios by new moon, it was just like fireworks. Go Bob. Seminiferous accusing air fingers waved in and over the blasted trail, the good scythers, the wake of wretched holographic mercenaries, now rowing, plastic propellers long since given up the ghost, the way the sea swallows all, ice ages, vaporettos and mewling stokers, or lets them float at its pleasure, at its leisure, buckling down, tarnishing the friendly trophies, and happy Flaming Dog cloisonné; hats off, a wave at the speckles on the beach for one more day, one more river, next tide for sure, this is it, this is ours, this is one that can be won! this is one that can be won! BEELEE VIT! Pleading, this one, we won.

UPSIDE THE HEAD

If I could go back to those thrilling days of yesteryear, my hands bound in lace or drumming in the twilight, backlit by the red neon hotel sign on our common balcony peeling paint as the traffic sighed below like an exhausted animal and the same Roxy music playing slightly out of phase from our adjoining rooms. Jan and Denny dug it when I'd work up a sweat on the kit or practice drum-rolls on the pad, but Tina was always disturbed by my flams and ratamacues — she didn't like humans doing unpredictable things and her ears that they left unbobbed would perk and her bright eyes flash green near Denny's joint, nah I wouldn't go back.

Nor mention the slick and vacant Bird Boy and how often I'd swayed toward perching on that balcony rail, crammed into black feathered dress and preening for flight. The sly and varnished Bird Boy came to life that summer, a feckless wonder bearing more than passing resemblance to his maker, living fits and starts, beginning as self-satire and ending up as driving wheel — urging me with all his spurious and ample logic to the launch. How more irrefutable his blandishments became. Bad luck for the svelte and barren Bird Boy that the house phone rang at six one November a.m. and it was Beryl, with a prior and imperative claim, demanding an audience, an end to apartness and a rescue. Not known for triangular nesting, the slight and vanquished Bird Boy flew off to warmer climes, perhaps to fuck with someone else's mind.

New Year's that year featured grand displays of desperate optimism — 1980 and the sucko seventies put to rest — Karla, my ex, her mouth screwed into the paradox that signified interior demolition under way, heaved champagne bottles off the balcony and inside, Denny/Natasha (as everyone) was dancing in strapless dress and broad ice hockey back, Jan's a furtive dodging prance — footwork to avoid the next and inevitable blow and that sweet-faced call girl with the English accent, singing and brown hair flying, flashed her bare stomach past Barry on the floor, kneeling rapt and drunk and thanking god for Phil Spector as black pearl precious little girl popped my speakers and Beryl and I could only feel immortal — we were lucky that night, we'd end it looking toward a thousand more.

I made the mistake of giving Jan the key to my room — she said things were weird with Denny and could she crash there when I was staying over at Beryl's? I stayed over more and more at Beryl's then, sometimes not going to the hotel for a week or longer and once when we slept there we woke up fast to the opening lock and a little Frankenstein silhouette in the doorframe. Beryl screamed and I charged buck naked in a cartoon beeline not touching the ground til I realized it was Jan. I'm sorry, I didn't know you guys were here — Denny's acting weird, you know how he is — I'll be gone in the morning before you get up . . .

Denny's *acting* weird, Jesus. Denny's been weird since the Rangers and probably before — add Laotian boo, Tet shrapnel, a steel-plate skull, seizure meds, hormones, halu halu hallucinogens et voila! Metaweird Italian-American homey from Marblehead comes back to wife and her new black boyfriend. Remember Eric, a stiff prick knows no law. Between the West Street blowjobs, the VA working endless on his teeth and taking the strange lumps off his breasts, Denny was a busy man. But who knew from weird in brave domestic fun-couple days — vacuuming the mat of doberman fur off the orange Chelsea carpet while Nikita and Tina scrambled out on the balcony, claws scraping in panic or excavating the ice fridge to discover relics from a bygone age cooked on electric coils that dimmed the lights like Bette Davis' dying or George Raft's execution and Do or Die Jan so cranked up about Jean-Paul and Grace cruising Gleason's for raw talent and spotting her to sock a heavy bag in a precision jump rope team snapping: Tauruses are born determined nothing's going to stand in our way. That was some great news.

Jan was always the ingratiating one, femme to the core, despite her binding, stuffed crotch, combat boots and constant urgings of how a hit of testosterone would sharpen me up, make me aggressive. She was the one who would call when Denny got busted for bringing the war home. How do you top cutting up three queer-baiters in a Boston Dunkin' Donuts? That's only for starters, that's what gets you to New York. But these things have their own irrefutable logic when you happen to be strapped, you happen to go to the Mine Shaft when all of West Street is reeling from the tragedy a week before when some sleepwalking son of a preacher man cuckoo for coconuts ripped up on the crowd with an M16 — you, meaning *no harm of course*, but you happen to be frisked (your piece discovered), beaten boneless and delivered hog-tied to the gendarmerie. Nothing in Jan's background had prepped her for this — not the mental hospital or the psychotropics, where she'd learned to love punishment for its own irrefutable logic and somehow stay the good girl.

In the end, I guess Denny never tried to kill me, because there was too much recognition, too much Roxy music slightly out of phase and quarts of Remy under the bridge between us and anyway I cared for him without ever backing him into a corner. That rage could have gone anywhere after the dam broke — the rage of the inconsolable and the truly guilty and Jan high on denial and wanting me to take a photograph so she could have a keepsake, cocky and all bravado who'd landed a glancing left hook and Denny — no believer in the sweet science — just did what he always did and maxed it and now Jan was on my bed, her eye bulging out where the pipe had caught her across the nose and temple and Denny all over the room at once without even walking, wanting to explain it all — why he did it and why it was justified and how she'd had this coming and how she'd hit him first and wanting to finish it all off right now and don't you get involved in this, Eric, this is private between myself and Jan and me interposing: I know I know, vibing it's ok, Denny, it's ok, you've done enough for one evening, and how did I get my dumb ass into the middle of this and can they save the eye and grabbing some ice and pushing Jan out the door spirit of '76 dizzy, in bloody schmatte trailing drops down the hall past the open bathroom and our Sikh neighbor on the toilet calling out: how are you my good friends?

HEY NOW, HEY NOW,

listen up, this is a tale of hardwalls, cruciform cellos, injection molds, homebodies, quotidian mofos, *terra incognita*, and a piquant sauce to die for — an *après* world's fair story, steamy sex fore and aft, a whizzing bridge abaft the boot camp, the waves and fumes of Queens nacrescence — not like safe night world, blowing orphans of future dreams lightly implanted down air-conditioned pneumotubes, extolling incontrovertibles which promise nothing, nothing that is except redemption which we all need. Touch buttons, bring memory to life: when dinosaurs ruled the world, when peasants danced at mowings and drew instructional manuals and were interrogated and knew the answers, and spas, Bavarian spas purveying healthful radioactive mud and promising redemption up to here which we all could use. Much later tonight, you'll be looking down and blowing with enormous cheeks — humped serpents sounding deep, affrighting micro brigantines triangle bound for spices, slaves and rum, and you'll kiss waves and marineros round capes of relentless mills and rails. Blow the kids through the pavilion of excess, blow the girl to the land of crickets, back printed with crisscrossed grass looking up to you through estrellas, weights of lovers, flayed men and fledermice transparent, remembering the cave where everything glided, and nothing, even things that moved at different speeds, collided. Hey now, take my grassprinted hand, saliva, knotcrushed solar plexus, humming crickets — look down, look well into the city of their future, then blow them into the arms of others, to buy exorbitant, humiliating names, send them through redundant checkpoints, reluctant feel-ups, battery. Save them in their final hour, too scarred for death to claim. In this Jerusalem there are no contracts, equities or useful sets of numbers, only faubourgs, spokes straining tired hubs, rods, staffs, pistons and a piquant sauce to die of. Rods, staffs and pistons sing: the food is for the man who owns it, not for the man who is hungry. *The food is for the man who owns it, not for the man who is hungry.* Blow them to the fire base, blow them out the keyhole, blow them back to '64, blow them back to me.

FLASH

In attempting to maneuver past them on the sidewalk, he nearly trips over the second of two tethered and wildly enthusiastic miniature poodles. Nearly is the key word since he dances over the quivering hectic topiary with the grace and fatalistic indulgence of a nearly perfect master. Es Nueva York, he mantras subvocalmente — *es Nueva York*.

The ego, he reflects, as he narrowly skips being maypoled by whiplike leashes, is always throwing dogs underfoot — to show that it's one's feet of clay that drive one's head through the clouds. But by his third slender escape from the twin barking ornamentals, his thoughts hum fast along the tightwire toward a negative pole.

Quien sabe? What if these are explosive poodles, not random animate vulnerables at all, but claymore poodles on hair tripwires — blow your legs off and leave you in the bush to bleed out? What if the war really did come home so many years ago, and if it had, so many questions of identity. Who is he? Grunt or charlie? Why common dogface, of course! But who is the woman attached to these gamboling bombitas at a safe remove — a friendly? Not likely in the high east '60s — more probably a class enemy — yes! She's a zeke alright, despite the coif camo — a dead make in characteristic black p.j.s — and this, never forget it, this is charlie's bush — charlie is god here.

Yet homed in as he is, sixth sense extruding like ectoplasm from his numberless pores — what does he have to fear? Just keep your third eye peeled and Cover Your Ass. Following the songlines of the natural Jericho, he hits his rhythm again, shuffling eggshell high cons, raising up only enough to locomote, his spine a line — but zap! An antic dogmine shoots past over his left foot and stat U-turns between his legs. Now deep shit requires the state of grace effort — here comes survival. One move only. Weight shifts to ball of right foot. Left leg arcs, turns body a full 180 then plants firm but light on the haywire leash — taut, but not enough to pull the pin — while drawing steel and in smooth left hand upbeat, pop the cord. Swoop, seize, shotput whirl and mortar-lob el dogbomb high into the oxygen-leached skies over Park Avenue — an overshoulder laser backglance at astonished coiffed charlie incoming and move out doubletime — wait not to hear the hit, the earthshake — just head south stat for the elephant grass, a cold six and chalk up three confirmed kills.

TABLE SERVICE

The beauty of the restaurant was that it employed only deaf and crippled waiters. This policy impacted on every aspect of the dining experience — heightened it — made one exquisitely conscious of the process — the agony — of service.

From the ineffectual bellowing of orders to the unheard, unheeded bells — to the halting, painful crabwalks, the clattering of braces, the hum of battery-operated wheelchairs attempting to navigate the too-packed tables — to the acrobatic collisions and desperate, tepid deliveries, the air was charged with, well, Truth. What an atmosphere! Could anything be more compelling than to order, for example, rack of lamb and be served, after witnessing an hour of fantastic struggle — swinging door to table — someone else's frigid tiny quail, congealed and rigorous — but presented with such fervent hope, such bursting spirit that often patrons wept openly, stanching with white tablecloths the lacrimal hemorrhage of sorrow, compassion and awe that confrontation with the grace of such hopeless effort engendered. I cannot overstress how moving, how revelatory, how deeply affecting those numberless evenings of rapt abrogated expectations were.

Many restaurant is gone now, fallen victim to the cult of expediency, the criminal replacement of experience by nutritional bulk But each time I cook for my menagerie — each time I listen, see but cannot hear the barked orders formed by silent mouths, each time I scald a member, each time my crabbed hands are seized by a frenzy of spasmodic juliennation — even as I totter, shamble, hal and drag my shivering limbs across the steeplechase of impedi ments separating me from the hungry mouths I must feed, I recap ture the resonance of sacred dining — the tears of my children water the desiccated feast of nurturance.

WHAT A MAROON!

My problem began early when I could not interpret the relationship between the rodents in cartoons and those who shared the building where I grew up. This was a trap, a sticking point. Thus, at an early age, did I fail to be seduced by the cult of Mickeysmo. Thus was I troubled by the presence of two dogs, separate but unequal, in Mickey's coterie. Dog One was a quadruped mutt — a caricature — but unimpeachably dog, possessing many recognizable canine qualities and true to his traditions — or perhaps, some might argue, to his genes. Dog Two, among other attributes, wore clothing and walked erect — but the most striking distinction between the two was their respective use of language. Dog One barked, cartoon barked, but Dog Two could read, and spoke in English — awkwardly perhaps and surrounded by balloons, but in discernible words strung into coherent phrases.

Later I learned that the words of the talking dog had been translated into hundreds of languages and dialects. These were undeniably marvelous accomplishments. What, I conjectured, could have worked such miracles on a dog? Was it education, discipline, diet or breeding — or some arcane combination of influences? Clearly, the literate dog had to be the product of an extremely advanced science. Why, I wondered, had his string-tailed, yelping brother been denied the benefit of these advantages? If for one, then why not for all? I vowed to pursue the answer to these questions and not rest until I had found an explanation.

It is half a lifetime later and I still don't know. I have, however, come to hold a less unbridled admiration for the second dog, the one that talked instead of wagged. For all his erudition, his intellectual and physical accomplishments — his wearing of shoes for instance, and buttoned trousers with a vent for his tail — he seemed — and I know this sounds sentimental — less true to the spirit of Dog. And I came gradually to understand that he was marooned between human and canine — prey to all the disadvantages of our species yet unable to make use of his dog nature. So near and yet so far. So magnificent an achievement, yet how grotesque.

The issue of reproduction never entered into my speculation until I realized how shameful it would be to perpetuate such an aberration. A revelation then dawned on me: this crisis could be resolved only by way of further scientific intervention, or to put it another way, through the agency of a more enlightened science. In for a penny, in for a pound, I say. It would be unconscionably cruel to halt the experiment midway through, having produced a dog too canine to know he's human and too human to realize he's a dog. Press on, I say. Press on and conjoin, kink, synergize! However bewildering, however disheartening, however bizarre the mutations, press on and finish the experiment! Don't shrink from fusion! We're halfway home! Fuse natures, fuse destinies, fuse worlds! We have nothing but our tails to lose.

FOR THE DEFENSE

Behind a facade of diversity lay an intense conformity. Beneath a veneer of concern lay pervasive indifference. Good sportsmanship and competitive spirit served as an alibi for brutality. Backs were stabbed, buildings eviscerated in the dead of night. Society was stratified jello, multicolored and quivering with fear. Bats deserted their belfries, having gnawed through the bell ropes. No tocsin sounded and an effervescent amusement lilted the air, lifting hair, lifting wigs, everything moving, not to be held down. The country moved to town and brought their stigmas, their pig rituals, their preemies, their respirators, their electric milking machines, their unguents, their hideous french fries. Some resorted to crushing their wooden shoes deep into the machinery, losing hands in the process but did it matter? Everything was simulated, everything inconsequential, everything open to interpretation. In such an atmosphere, no defense was too outlandish: I ate too many french fries in your honor, they are notoriously aphrodisiac! I am innocent, it is the supplier of fries who is to blame. Your honor, we are not talking drachmas here, we are talking about a man's life — well, a woman's life, well a child if you like, a fox — yes your honor, a foxy child poisoned on — demented by — driven to a desperate act by rancid fats on abominable potatoes. We are not trading zlotys here, we are talking about Life! OK, so not a human life, but a sort of life, an addicted, deranged, detestable quasi-human homunculoid grotesque parody of life — a proto-life, your honor, surely worthy of our pity, our admonishment — at very least the consideration of an armband, a musket, a muscatel, a muscadet, a massive infusion of our care and concern, god wot, and all these years of cosseting, colic and tucking into bed and tugging at our breast — all these years of nourishing a viper in our bosom! Oh how sharper — your honor, gentlemen (and ladies) of the jury there can be only one verdict! Let me tell you a story. A man comes into a bakery — O tell me where is fancy bread — a man comes into a bakery and orders rolls. Drum rolls, gender rolls, Kaiser rolls, jelly rolls — wrap them he says, wrap them in yesterday's barrel organ. He walks out of the store and into the arms of two thugs, gunsels, your honor, ominous bulging whyos without a care in the world, who accost him and push him into the back of a waiting black sedan which roars immediately off to parts unknown. And this man is never found. He is, your honor, esteemed jurors, as the saying goes, in the cement. He is part of our infrastructure — his teeth hold up our bridges, his pelvis supports a cloverleaf, his croup launched a thousand boats. It beats the joint, but daddy check this out. Before he goes, he hands the rolls off quick and this lady when she unwraps the sheet stretches way out over the airshaft, somehow backlit, halo hair, and pins the paper to the clothesline with the dented garbage cans at the bottom and amazed pigeons and out tumble coffeepots, alarm clocks, those wooden shoes, miraculously whole and orphans, incubators, foundries, industry, commerce, drachmas, zlotys, little plastic busts of this guy with his feet in cement, hundreds of them that rain percussion down on the trash-can lids and the rest, our lady included, fall up the airshaft, up to the roof where, smelling of creosote, Aristotle waits just hanging out, playing claves and hanging out — gone is the attitude, the basilisk stares — they rap, he apologizes, yes apologizes graciously for being such a hard on, he begs her pardon.

HISTORY WILL ABSOLVE ME

The Great Defense — the evasion of the accused, by whatever means necessary, from the octopoid embrace of Justice — is breathtaking to watch. History alone may confer final — and usually conditional — absolution, but we mariners charged with plucking defendants from the abyss and returning them safe home to the shores of Righteousness — we too have our part to play.

Thus are murderers made innocent babes and thus are the plaints of Truth reconciled. In ages prior to the Devil in Massachusetts, the South Sea Bubble, the Great Awakening and the Greenback Party, England conceived the notion of speedy trial. It is not within our curriculum to explore the wholesale transplantation of *habeas corpus* to American shores, though it is worth nothing that the bodies in question were often those of fierce and reluctant Senegalese. Suffice it to say that the relentless erosion of the codes, by forces intent on effacing the grandeur of the system, has left in rubble at the cliff base such bravura juridical outcroppings as *piene forte et dure* — an incentive designed to encourage the recalcitrant accused to enter a plea. This procedural technique consisted of magistrates piling meticulously apportioned weights upon the supine person of the accused, until he or she removed the obstacle of nonacquiescence by choosing freely to plead — for without a plea, no trial may go forth and forth is where we must go. Despite this prototypical Anglican "offer you can't refuse," many did — their last words, often those of a perfectly recited Lord's Prayer, muffled, but audible, from beneath an enormous pile of stones.

Since plead we must, which is it to be — Guilty or Innocent? Between the two lies an unbridgeable dichotomy — choose your own image: a membrane, a force field, in any case, a barrier admitting no truck between the two. Mutual exclusivity *par excellence*. Both common knowledge and physical Law own that an object [or subject in this case] cannot exist in two places at once. Newton knew this and he speaks eloquently to us down the mirrored corridor of centuries. Therefore, we must choose. *Arguendo*: we are Innocent.

Having established our bearings in a universe defined by Guilt or Innocence, how do we refute the former and demonstrate the latter? How, then, does one construct the Great Defense? What does it consist of and why is it necessary? Before us lies the fertile garden into which we shall delve in this and subsequent pedagogic implantations. Inscribed on some worthy cartouche is the maxim: Nature abhors a vacuum. Justice, however, charged with the perpetual purification of the Mansion of History, cannot afford the luxury of such a phobia. She must tirelessly order her Handmaids to sweep. Young Minds! Do you realize the opportunity at hand?*

As a Defender working the Territory of Imagination door to door — hustling shiny Electroluxes from the open trunks of cartoon autos, down ribbons of highway, along the length and breadth of MesoAmerica — your only competitor is Prosecutor and he is peddling an inferior product. To prove it, you offer a warranty of unparalleled persuasiveness — the Myth of Innocence. Now, Young Minds, follow me. We are master salesmen on the make! Our immaculately shod foot once planted firmly in the door of interpretation, we proceed to the pitch. The Handmaid is overburdened, bored, and primed to spend her Mistress' wealth. She will be aroused by our labor-saving device and revel in her escape from the tedium of sweeping. Righteousness exalts us. Remember, it is not us but Prosecutor who has soiled the figured rug of Truth. Our duty is to show what our vacuum can do and then the Handmaid must choose — for it is in her twelvefold Will that Justice finds its incarnation. And it is no mere appliance, but Redemption itself that she embraces, the road map back to Eden that she enfolds when we close the sale. The Handmaid exits the parlor but momentarily — and returns brandishing a check made to the order of Not Guilty. And why should she not? Who would purposefully eschew the benefit of God's doubt? Who, properly guided, would not aspire to be Handmaid to His agency? And as for us, so long as we keep to our allotted turf, let no man claim our profits — this land was made for you and me.

It is my contention — and when you have gained more experience you are free to dispute with me and to challenge my rich use of

---

*Imagine the fortune lying in store for the entrepreneur who markets a Conscience Cleaner for heavily soiled Whites.

metaphor — that the race of the Great Defense can be won only by a Perfect Alibi. But an Alibi limited to the facts of a case is at best a hobbled horse. Here we must wager with caution. Of all the possible Alibis, there are only two bloodlines of consequence — both emanate from the magnificent twin stallions Situational and Natural. Both have sired generations of highstrung colts, bred to be supremely inductive, to adroitly leap the hurdles of individual accountability. Such agile Alibis invoke an elegant and compelling reverse double jeopardy — the rule of Once and Forever Pre-Approved Exoneration. The first Alibi, Situational, properly jockeyed, is odds-on favorite to win at the Concentration Camp Defense and its corollary: the I Was Brought to this Country in Chains Defense. As a hortatory initiative, I shall summon Dialogue to her charge:

COUNSEL FOR THE DEFENSE: Will you kindly tell the Court your whereabouts when this tragedy occurred in the territories under your military command?

DEFENDANT: I was in Concentration Camp.

CD: I see. Your Honor, esteemed Jurors, my client could not possibly have shot these children — he was not personally present, and even if his body had been, his mind would have been elsewhere [The Metanoia Defense]. If these children were shot at all, someone else must be responsible. Perhaps they committed mass suicide as yet another of the saucy provocations they are wont to perpetrate. Whatever the circumstance of their alleged misfortunes, my client is obviously innocent! Why, he himself is the greatest victim of Prosecution's imposture. First my client is injured and then insulted — heaped with calumnies. A man who is in Concentration Camp cannot possibly shoot children — a camel could see that! I rest my case.

As to the Natural Alibi, a spectrum of brilliant tactical jewels are milky-way spun across this doctrinal diadem — and likewise are visible to the trained, if naked, eye: The Biology Defense — La Anatomia è Destino Defense [for which we have ample case law precedents] — rampaging hormones, electrical storms along the corpus callosum — the Delphic Dog — the Devious Devi — The Great God Pan — Paranoia: the Beside Myself Defense — the You Always Hurt the One You Love Defense, the Smoke Gets in Your Eyes Defense,

and every permutation of La Forza del Destino Defense. But this is
the stuff of our next lecture. It's a big universe and these are our
prodigious nebulae, our numberless astral selves. This is our Starry
Decisis. Go forth, Young Minds, and Defend. The light of Truth is
nearly blinding.

SIMPLE

Oh what a beautiful city — so simple, so svelte, what thighs, what
an ass! It's only in your degeneration that your life is so urgent. I
gotta tell you. When I was alive, I was nobody, I couldn't get arrested
in this town. Now they shovel words in my mouth, now they decide to nail me up. What did I do? I laughed. I laughed at beauty, I
laughed at tracks and platforms, I laughed at your too big buildings,
I laughed at your bursting nutbag — your momma went down on me
and I laughed at her too — at you. I laughed myself sick. I laughed
myself into the ER. I laughed on the table in the OR, I laughed at
the ventilator, the pump, the collapsed veins. I laughed myself into
the ICU, I laughed myself onto a slab. I'm a pizza now, mom — look,
I'm flying. I laughed myself back from the grave, into jackboots —
a stormtrooper for peace love justice and no mercy — harder than a
slab, taller than tablets, hotter than a burning bush. Jesus, Jack,
Shadrach, Meshach and Abednego — into the oven with you boys —
up the smokestack, roast the Polish sky and don't admit nothing,
right? If she got it, she deserved it, right — and all sing in praise of
famous corpses, shovel words in their mouths, set their hands to
hard labor, bounce 'em in their trampoline shrouds and most of all
lie. Lie like it's going out of style, like there's no tomorrow, which
there isn't. She asked for it right? I knew Anne Frank — you're nothing like her. Too much melanin under the skin. She wanted it,
right? In the absence of a literate tradition, memory becomes critical — ah yes, I remember it well. They were our boys, they were
good boys, they were uniform boys. If it wasn't for our division and
a couple more, the Russians would be at the English Channel. And
the camps, if they existed, weren't so bad. People survived, didn't
they? And anyway she was begging for it. So what do you do when
you rise up off that slab, heading for the New Jerusalem — decisions,
decisions — which gate do you choose, man — I grew up in Babylon,
I don't know how to function here — don't know the currency, don't
know how to make small talk or what's my name in Hebrew. Jesus,

Jack, toss me high, little pizza boyamine, in kibbutz funny hat —
toss me high, all those jerryrigged, 'scuse my French, all them
slapped together baby houses, dairies, tractor sheds — toss me high,
turn that wilderness into a forest, turn that desert into an olive
grove — Fedayin, bro, on camels with long rifles, scimitars — cut
your throat soon as look at you, so send the boys across at night on
their bellies — those Arab bastards never knew what hit them, well
some of them knew but they were asking for it — Jesus, Jack, Shadrach, Meshach and Abednego, you saw all that — yeah, but I saw
more, coming off my slab spinning like a black vinyl pizza moon —
saw sexual healing, saw sensitive people, saw the new world make
the third world act like the old world, saw the whole line on a
speedup and remembered every detail — our boys, Jerusalem boys,
urban boys and Jesus, Jack, you taught me to be a carpenter, how
to drive a straight nail, how to size a board, frame a wall, build a
chair so that it would hold up your fat momma and Jesus, Jack, you
bought me a bicycle — ok so not a good bicycle — but you got to be
grateful, right? And out there in the big city, coasting on top of the
walls, close by David's tower, I see Jesus on his melanin end-run,
pedaling like there's no tomorrow which there isn't, but his machine is changed — no longer the sleek efficient, but now an apparatus, lumbered with contraptions, fatuous wings, juicers, healing
devices, whistles, superficial bells, security measures, obsolete fix-
tures, redundant gears and pedals, and in that sunset on beautiful
city, purple Judea, he's trying to do tricks, monstrous tricks on this
loaded bike — wheelies, peelies, figure eights, Immelmanns — the
whole operation perilous, kicking up dust that's sopped up the
hemorrhage of years, 'round melanin kids playing bunker in abandoned refrigerators, scaring the camels into bucking — the Fedayin
discharging their Czech assaults to rain down on the tombs of the
Prophets, stuck in those hills, and there goes Jesus, one leg balanced
on that banana seat with Jack, Shadrach, Meshach and Abednego,
human pyramid on his shoulders, stinking of melanin and a frozen
heart, and with this elevation, this tossing, I'm getting sick, I'm going
to lose my matzoh, but the view is dazzling, those open gates, those
open thighs, this purple sunset and the sucker Jesus, this sucker
pulls it off — the clownish moves, the gilded lily, and the aggravated
camels chill in the sound of a hundred drummers flown in on big
bird Air Afrique and they all beat together, tethered to a pulse —
and Jesus he's about crushed under all that human cargo and pizza
tossing, but he keeps on pedaling to the rhythm he only dimly

remembers, to the language he only dimly recalls having forgotten. And spinning as the stars pop out and I finally lose my matzoh from the spinning and the tear gas and view of the simple city and as I'm throwing up my guts, I think: Jesus, Jack, Shadrach, Meshach and Abednego — if you could stretch a filament between those poles, you'd be the real McCoy.

Bartok in Udaipur

Nathaniel Tarn

Golden city on her bed of sand
breathing through her towers at the night
immense distance between city and stars
doves passing overhead
taking their upper light from sky
their lower light from city

———————

No way to stanch flow stop river
feed hungry pour drink down thirsty
drop a coin into every one of a million hands
no way to stop care quench sorrow
no way to end it no way to keep flow
from drowning out eyes no way to finish
no way to grow into salvation no way to end it
roadsign on way to city life is short
do not make it shorter think who awaits us all

———————

From all our eyes flows pain
into this life with every birth
more births than can be counted on an army's hands
equipped to conquer continents
heroes stand out spearing at one throw
a myriad boars or tigers
but one blood flowing out one sufferance
under dynastic sun sword stroke or parry
calm in sky's eyes profoundly caring

Great sails in a sea of crimson
women advancing in greens and blues
flowers of air on a desert morning
gait leisurely pot akimbo high

City raising its hands to moon
over quiet water birds in hand
leaves asleep flowers asleep
in purple blood spread over water
fisher his blinding turquoise dimmed
catching a flash of moonlight burning star
among cold stars diamond set sapphire
slant fish in beak yet another star

To live with one's own face alone
that face for a whole life over whatever
waters night may provide in constant presence
heroes rush down flame clad on battlefield
women walk with their children into fire
warriors thunder down to inevitable deaths
and lonesome moon with one face only
shines with an equal constancy over them all

Slinking in poverty by gray green lights
of palaces throned among emerald waters
it used to be our princes inside
exploding fireworks across this lake
now foreigners one with their money
to buy our rings and bangles buy some thing
would cost each one of us earth's price
a dozen incarnations or a life's wages

Blue god drains all world's love to him
as his great heart walks over waters
no need of feet wings alone unaided
suspend it at a comfortable height
terns at ankles gulls at knees
over a hunter where he waits for tiger
sudden receiving prey from sky
in astonished gratitude

———————

Down rushing warriors in burning clothes
saffron on fire against golden sun
sun's visage peering out of roses
"Ornaments of the State" blooms palaces
what matter which perfume on air
invisible fires in devotional heart
of princess in love with a blue forest
youth on cloud enormous and inflamed
blue sword cascading on blind child
crippled for money set in its mother's arms

———————

Epic simplicity in dream of stone
raising its walls above our desert
stone of sand and sand of stone
streets running with saffron and blood
stone hands the only archive left by women
whispering windflowers walk into fire
a bruin noise of camels in high distance
night ships asleep over golden waters

———————

Seed syllable towns pink white cerulean
wait for their portraits on rising light
but — lens crashes to ground and shatters
with which we saw the stars and closer planets
and studied all the more originalities
blind now we cannot work or must develop

new eyes inside this fire so that whatever burns
with joy or sorrow is but an ornament
of one same state and not a decoration.

———————

To leave walk out in early morning mist
from dung and dust women rise like flowers
name fourfold origin see fourfold sufferings
which from that day to this under one sun
have not desisted from this land in which
we see love's fourfold origin in pain
including that immense pain inflicted by beauty
planet a lake alone hardly no firmness
colossal cesspool covered with floating diamonds
in the thirty thousand or whatever days
you'll chose as measure of the human life

———————

Home floating like a screen in our dreams
Light battlement lifts desert colored lake
drained out with blood from all our veins
after a life of miles longest day of year
on which to give thanks for land's blessing
space around land and time for space to heal
as if we were homing there from another star

The Wheel
Aaron Shurin

I.

We took something. For ourselves, first, which is the furthest place. In this land with these people I'm only a poor sailor. A point of light upon the surface had happened.

If it should come ride it out — pierced ahead of us the water past her sides like oil — a wall of surface flying. In the glare experience strained and rocked, we were boiling down a gutter, heads to burst, and to them the large body paralyzed as it fell. Afterwards, every detail was staring them in the face.

There, rested — the vanished — gasping but unharmed. Such moonlight beat down the seas, filled us with that talisman, the sky. This is our existence, in which the present seemed to fade. Beneath the wind — drawn skin begin to warming — we stood when what had happened in his lifted hands — holding out his hand — its owner: himself and his companions. The place has a name in that neighborhood: We-Are-Missing.

Then we rose, having no choice, for our own air was leading the way. A map of the world formed new shapes, grew thin, and opened in its center; so high we were — it at our feet — the valley filled with streams, reeds, oak. Here it will be different. Here there is every action whitening in that forest, chance. Here lay down the rod of power, weighed down by the memories.

We descended with their purple pods and reaping hooks; their monotonous faces were standing in person — pull to pieces resemblance — composing each other. Chocolate — the night — was served to us in silver cups — the moon — while the whistling wings — the lake — lapping shone the luminous walls — the city — so far to reach. Our eyes took possession of our feet.

No sound, and the silence calling the hours. This night the wide
gates come home again. You, in the wilderness, swept by the water-
way. Look at me: through an open doorway: home again.

Because of the lightness, let him go. You should sing as I do, brought
in at the door. Of this I am certain: we shall be drawn into it.

forward, my great purposes

II.

Ripples spread and from them rose two arms towards the bed; a soft
deep voice — pearls — the thread. Displaying his eyes, his teeth, her
big shoulder. Blue wandering curtain, she lay around the neck of her
disorder. The sun overdecorated the room.

She pinned her remembrance on two doors, thud of a foot, and
talcum powder. Bits and pieces sticking to mirrors to meet his blu-
ish gaze. She saw him — he saw her — open the gates — one leg and
shook her head: "Nothing lasts forever out of the house."

Everything in the room — their stalks — in massive wood from the
young arid road — have I come this way? — completely surrounded —
coming to life in the depth of a chair — his involuntary gesture,
physical presence.

"I remember," she said, "her little arms in the air, subjugation of
Sunday afternoon, the past tense of a brandy glass. As a boy his
kitchen lisp — milky immersions — cat licks, a little masterpiece of
ablution . . ." trailing along the passages. He pirouetted while she
jotted down calculations on his tongue. He was tucked away in that
cubbyhole, a past made up of a cream sauce with me — merely
friends — this place risen at each other, his rolling breath and her
larger fingers. She held his breath like someone listening. Frothy
moonlight — she began touching it everywhere — the night pours
what they were thinking to the limit.

III.

I'm sitting here — the failure of things — as one is — all this complicated material must be beautiful. To speak about the white heat
of iron — it seems cold — wrapped in a firm hand of nature — words
also white hot. I was finding more that isn't perfect, and feel older
in order to ripen.

I'm sentimentalism — and the harvest isn't here. I'm a phase of life
toward the opinion of the world — better tear up this letter as well.
A black coat with a greasy collar and the cycle of seasons. This
morning, haze was style and character in the dunes. An impression
came into my head which I intend to spend.

I feel grateful for practical things in good shape: pew, checkered
dress, an old brush. In a drugstore I found a basket — more detail is
possible.

A kneeling figure of a man, of a woman gathering the expression "I
hope you don't think of my tired brains in questions of right and
wrong." I'm at work, I take him on my lap, the bad turn out well.

I'm simple to fall back on the whiteness of a white-washed wall,
and go and stand in the fields showing a wet man on a muddy
road — the sentiment is a silhouette — a few tree trunks, concentrating on the wood.

I had a baby, afterwards a mother, like a lily among thorns. In the
evening the lighted mud puddles look cozy from my window.

What expanse, what calmness, between me and the ordinary world —
a permanent address — with the fixed idea of potatoes — deeper ob-
stacles — and grasp my petition for membership, interior with the
blue of cloth and another blue of doubt.

I get thick lips in a big size of the broken indigo and secret bronze.
Summer is a low roof, winter is walking violet. The best thing I
know is the difference between you and me, and the technique im-
proves every year.

IV.

The house wobbled — illusion in the sun — it was pale black — a gull suspended — exhibiting obscurely from all body going out into the world.

It — with the other — which was loose — explosion in the depths, wind-swept unpolluted piece of bone. A great experiment is such a handful, and the wind rising. It lit up on the table white cotton and brown wool, water streaming down the windows, who was bending over a lamp long ago, with the gold line around it, and upon the hills which trembled in its fury, jerking the waves.

The little boys under the sheet — half-opened eyes — turning sulphurous until a white shape bulged out. Triangular letters — each line going down the table — drugged the iron pillars of the pier. It changes — amplifies — the turnpike, the faded ticket, the leaves in her hand.

Like an eye upon the bed it stood open, dropped by a hawk. A woman came back — everything she did — and asked the time — green dust on the horizon — him coming to a more distant ridge — hidden beneath her cloak — it come tumbling in the armchair, reflected full in the face in her eyes, settling deeper.

White drops from the blade, swimming green in the ripples, shifted an edge in the water and the sky shifted. His hand praised the column, the gate, the sky. It isn't simple, or pure; one calls it — corridors of brain — gripping the arm of the chair — as if, in his place, a city would be burning there, behind the balanced walls, fierce on the staircase.

The people stood and let them in. They have no houses. The streets are each other. Beneath the pavement it conveyed things, buy things, passing a hand into the complexity of box after box — between the stalls and tasted the sweetness of labyrinth — suspended above their heads the observer choked with observations.

This box — lying back in his chair — lacked self-consciousness. Surveying it — flourishing in obscurity, distorted — suggesting thick shirts, stiff sheets, swollen violin. The street in deep folds — wrap themselves in every shop — beneath the hissing gas as the afternoon wore on.

White discs through ivory pages, sleek in the rain. Seeking some landing — rolling energy — into flocks of small birds, brushing the grass. It swells the tulips in this dusk and sat speechless under the electric light. A far away humming was her stooping heart, answering the little boys, high in mid-air.

Foam would shine through us, an aspiration of this cradling. It lay on her lap, feasting on scarlet, flourishing his wine glass across the table. Here is a scrap in the puckered morning, pressing both hands into drifting sunlight. It was a country shuffling along strange roads on your own — stuck to them, the eyes of a foreigner — floating in the body immersed in things, falling into thin sheets, fertility.

Everything remained — it as an inheritance — shaped against trees in white hollows one blazing afternoon. Of force rushing in patterns — first one foot, then the other — vapors thickened where the cadaverous streets and the dust itself thick were spattered particles circling deeper. It bent slightly as they reached it. It stirs the curtains, swaying between strokes, imprinting faces.

V.

You watched the flickering on the ceiling — smooth skin — when you opened the door through the shadows — a great actor preparing to leave — the ocean was set boiling again from your astonished body — the traces there — listening, raising the sky to your level.

The great city above the houses was reliving twilights, gone down from night to day, day to nights. Your voice on your mouth — our separation — I want your dry bones — bread and time — looking into it from very close — unheard on a map, green or black, no one has seeded.

Against a pink cushion melting and dissolving — drinking from you as a commonplace conception — your hermaphrodite vanity — spangled with the rain — nails grow longer, a springtime plant — belching constellations from their vessels, and use them to cover the walls of my hut. One day at the seashore I was inside your skin. Flattened before taking a single step.

Still, as you are, not in the foreground, nearer the sacrifices, walking at random — two travelers, our childhood — decomposed in my stained fingertips — each shovelfull as it fell — to hold back the soldiers when we want to photograph — at the gates with palms on the horizon like a train, an immensity.

A proliferation of houses made of rushes, windows on the water — I thought my tongue was on fire — swinging back into place after the wind has stopped. Initiators have breathed into your mouth, inserting tongues in beautiful poses — translations — excited by the great monuments and droppings of birds. You rubbed your stomach against them; they put it in their boats and returned home.

They call after you, rolling like wheels. I walked through those streets and walked through them again. I went away and have remained so. You have been superimposed on the lower part of this body, drawn back and tied together. The pink sun undressed over your eyes.

You lay down on branches, a lamp hanging on the wall. The night stayed long and came back — many other ferocious sweet things — you never ceased to be present — the idea of the subject — motionless, covered with powder, an arm around each other.

VI.

They made shovels with their inch-long fingernails by its inhabitants of that name.

A man, stripped to the waist, spread night soil. Girls on the flat rocks at the edge of the public road.

Peel and pare their part — passed through his hands — until the big full kernels under pressure had nowhere to run. They fashioned parallels through the doorless aperture that was the only entrance to their home.

They looked up, plunged into the room over and over again. Within reach of their hands — coming for me — in which we have been taught to shiver — to grasp the change before a new pattern could be created.

They came over the hill laughing — in sunlit corners of the backbone all sewn in. The heat was intense — luxuriantly — scouring the hills for ashes — anything organic — stimulated to the collection point.

They watched the sky encircle us — that enlargement — remolding each other. Across that distance we leaned all afternoon . . .

Aduwa
Barbara Einzig

— for Edmond Jabes

By deciding to leave the country by the end of the month, she at long last succeeded in arriving at the present moment.

For soon it would all change, and so this day could not blend imperceptibly into the next, nor could the one before it disappear without a trace.

The pale blue vault of heaven is filled with what can only be called a radiance.

.

It is I who am calling it radiant, I who am leaving, and it is I who am alive, it is you who are gone.

Rabbi Familiar said: The sapphire-blue Malaise has a golden border. In this way it resembles both the cover of the Torah, emblazoned with lions and flaming letters, and the creamy apple whose texture breaks as teeth bite through the skin.

.

Above the parking lot the man in the sky-blue jumpsuit sits in this post of observation, just big enough to hold him.

.

In this way your eyes lived among your face, as if it too were a wilderness.

.

The sleepy man or the bewildered man or the crying man ran his hands over his face, by touching it seeing how he looked.

•

The Here and Now had at last arrived, and so the Malaise must have then departed.

•

Rabbi Concepcion stated: The green Anguish is a radiance that the darkness will not extinguish. Before the forest is changed into a desert of red earth, you will ride through it in a canoe, among caged chickens raised for sale to gold miners or to the market in La Paragua, where the river meets up with the road. Among parrots speaking indigenous languages who will die in a burlap bag in a cargo hold as part of the trade in exotics.

Rabbi Concepcion continued: In the language the parrot is speaking the sound of "ka" lives among the name of everything having to do with the sky. Before the parrot squawking out that sound becomes a heap of colored feathers, you will arrive at the post of your return, and you must effect your return. It is the return, and not the journey, that will be difficult.

•

If the vault of heaven is white it is blue and if it is blue it is violet and if it is violet it is silver. It is even and therefore not more one thing than another but only the suggestion of these colors glowing and no others, sign of the imminent departure of the sun, which has already gone behind the mountain, into the sea. The sea drinks in the sun and buries it beneath black waves.

•

Rabbi Ptolemy indicated: The Now in which this orange tree flowers is the Now in which this orange tree flowers, the Now of the page flowering in the eye, of the voice flowering in the air.

•

Barbara Einzig

The voices you invented accompany me; they have been my sole companions. Perhaps you did not invent them but witnessed them accompanying you; you announced their presence. They are still present, but where are you?

.

The present moment revealed a row of trees silhouetted against the cloud that on the left forms a horizon with the mountain but on the right creeps over the mountain and spills into the city before drifting to the left to fill the valley and hide the trees, which are still visible, but could now be said to be inside the cloud. All this has happened while the sentence occurred.

.

Rabbi Simeon stated: It is not the yielding to the passage of time that causes us Anguish, but only our witnessing of the passage of the time that was stolen from others, that our fathers stumbled upon in their invasions, these narrow passages we found in photographs they had taken. The cliff on the left has three bodies nailed to it, a single stake through the neck.

Certain events have such power that they form themselves not only out of what made them happen but out of the weight they will bear on the future, the pressure they will exert through the memories of those who lived among them.

.

It was you who called me after I wrote you, to say that you were at long last here. You came from another country, and sailed through the landscape I lived in like a great blind ship, a stone that is buffed and polished many times, or a wind that survives a tunnel.

.

My mother made a pyramid of flour and at the top a crater into which she dropped a number of eggs, which were then worked into the pyramid that disappeared then and became dough.

•

You were able to keep your own company in silence, and so we leaned forward when you spoke. You kept silent as you spoke, and the time in which you spoke was not the time that we inhabited. Yet it occurred there, and because of this I thought of you as a magician.

•

The chocolate that is called *Familiar* is in a mint-green wrapper, with a line drawing of cacao printed in red and brown right in the center.

•

Recently the nature of my memories has altered. In the past when I was doing something I would be thinking about something else, perhaps trying to remember, and I could not exactly remember, and then came to the end of what I was doing. Now when I am doing something I only think about what I am doing, but past moments suddenly come to inhabit the present moment, with the full force of their original reality. They do so by finding moments that resemble them in some exact but only structural way. They take up the structure of the present moment and fill it, as gold is filled, with the past. In this way they protest the present as it is occurring, they protest their death and that they no longer live. But when they depart the structure of the present has not been interruped or broken, but has smoothly advanced and effected its action, the action of the present moment.

For example, my fingers over my mouth become your fingers on the edge of a table, applying an even pressure to the edge of the table, but when your fingers leave my mouth, it is my hand that has been held against my mouth, applying an even pressure that is now complete, the gesture of the present moment.

•

The preparations for a journey are never complete, especially one such as this. Soon I will arrive in the country from which you have departed, and will think of you there.

181

Zadie said: Everything I have to write has already been written. He said this a little before he died, to my father who was sitting by his bed, asking about the book he had always said he would write.

.

The sky drinks in the sun in this silver or golden emulsion that does not spread through the sky but is absorbed into it as into a sponge at exactly the speed at which the light leaves, and so the Night drinks in the light and turns it sapphire blue and then this black.

.

If we say we are mourning for you on the earth this does not mean we are longing to be where you are or to join you. Our mourning wanders among the living thinking only of where you are but when we stop thinking of where you are and only think about what we are doing you suddenly enter our actions or our words or our poetry in the form of complete coincidence.

June 5, 1991
Caracas, Venezuela

The Early Life of the Artist
Robert Coover

— for Benet Rossell

HE WAS BORN in the thunderous and calamitous year of the aborted comet halfway between the letter Aleph and the seductively duplicitous alto clef (the village was otherwise nameless) under the astral sign of the Spilt Ink (in more modern times known as the Black-Hearted Hole), notorious for its disorderly influence on otherwise virtuous and economical lives.

His father was the inventor of radical mathematical formulae and was himself the walking double of the symbol for the square root (thus: rootless roots, a key to the artist's buoyant gravity and his tendency, not so much to float, as to bounce, lightly). His father's propositions, in the form of kaleidoscopic satires, bestial and beautiful at the same time, once caused the earth to turn inside out, but the only creatures awake at the time were drunks, bats, ogresses, and a scattering of poets and dungbeetles, and only the bats took notice and changed their habits. Fortunately, history was spared a nasty conversion, the members of the select committee for the Nobel Prize for Mathematics being among those sleeping, though his son, a bat and yet not a bat, alas, was not. Later, he was to fix the blame for his lifetime of visual servitude upon the way his father's terrible calculations that fateful night spun his eyes inward and made his ears pop.

His mother, who was either an exquisitely beautiful parallelogram with tufts of feathers and insect wings at the corners or else a muddy mythological river, dark with carob pods, depending on her disposition, was, in spite of shifting appearances, the family anchor. It was she who emptied the brainpans and swept the tortured beds, prepared the daily stew of catastrophe and frolic, tolled the hours, cast the shadows, shielding them from death by illumination, washed out all their humble preshrunk anxieties, hanging them on her farflung limbs and curing them in the violent sun like mountain hams. When asked, much later, to describe his earliest memories, the artist replied: "Salty."

It was also his mother who first observed that words were stones and thus not only indigestible but also poor coin at the market, good only (like the rest of us) for landfill. This was her public observation; her private observation, made only to her family, was that everything was a stone, even air, love, and dreams. This brought great stability to her son's life, and great despair, making it hard, among other things, to breathe (always that caustic rattle, like a shingle beach raked by stormwaves), but freeing his art from the illusion of permutability.

The village where he was born never acknowledged the family's presence or the artist's birth there, but this was nothing strange, for acknowledgment, like traffic lights and uncertainty, was utterly foreign to it. The village's fame indeed rested upon its stubborn and silent insouciance, which was, except for a certain ingenuous hylomorphism expressed by orchestrated wind-breaking in the village square and the occasional burst of spontaneous skywriting, all it knew or knows of civic and religious procedure.

When he was young, the village was not strange. The world was strange. Now it is the village that is strange. The world, too.

For all that he came to know of the world, if something so opaque and ephemeral can be said to be knowable, he was never able to leave the village of his birth behind. It clung to him like rumor, like wet underwear, like a swarm of sick flies, lovingly tenacious as athlete's foot. It hobbled his gait on city pavements, tripping him up on his way into subways and revolving doors. It caused the peas to roll off his knife in fashionable restaurants. It bagged the knees of his department-store trousers and thickened his tongue with old saws. Nor did his art escape, for the village got in his inks and paints like cowdung in honey and tracked up his canvases with ineradicable clawings and scratchings and turned his paper as fragrant and crumbly as hot country bread. This intrusion, nothing short of demonic possession, the artist has taken with his usual grace and stained bib. "What does it matter?" he is wont to say, his mouth full of a half-chewed masterpiece. "It's all stones anyway."

184

Much light might be thrown on this symbiosis of village and artist had the artist's earliest works, scratchings with a stick in the dust of his village streets completed at the age of three, been preserved for posterity, but in the village posterity had been over for some time, gone the way of the wooden whistle, immaculate conceptions, good weather, and the comforting orthodoxy of the garrote. His father had a formula about it, his mother a dispiriting aphorism. As for the artworks themselves, the village livestock had a more explicit comment, one artist speaking, so to speak, to another. "What you might call the natural reaction of invisible forces at work in the theater of the brain," one villager put it bluntly in his rude tongue, twitching his long ear, "and other bodily parts . . ."

The artist, too, precursor to both the action-painting ecstatics and the disposable art fundamentalists of a later age, could accept the obscuring of elemental vision by the anarchical graffiti of even more elemental sheep turds and mule tracks — who was he to insist on orderly alphabets when there were none? — yet it might be said that everything he has ever drawn, written, painted, fractured, filmed, fondled, or sculpted since has been nothing more than an attempt to recover those first scratchings in the village dust all those years ago, as though to do so might undo his father's mathematical joke and turn the world rightside-out again.

Thus, on the one hand, the village created the artist, providing him with implements and canvas and a palette enriched with the primary pigments of alienation and suffering (there was nettle rash and hogbite, for example) and festive despair, together with song and murder and the spatialization of time with its saffron yellows and olive greens and mauves and ochers and cerulean blues, and, on the other hand, it made his art impossible, all art in fact, not just his, art being excluded from the village's available categories. Only when the village moved away one day and left him, alone as a crack in the sidewalk in the world's urban maze, did his life as an artist suddenly begin.

It began with little animated stitchings as though to suture a wound, or open one. Then color emerged and flowed from unseen sources (the right side of the world?), pushing the margins out until now the artist's drawings and paintings are as large as the village itself, which was probably not so large as the artist remembers it.

185

What is he trying to do? Reinvent the lost village? Paper the void? Use up the world's forests in case the village might be hidden there? The artist will not say. He will only remark enigmatically to his circle of disbelieving admirers, while turning over and over in his paint-stained hands the luminous stones of his loves and dreams, that "there *was* no early life, only this mockery of a prolonged and bitter afterlife . . ."

Argot of the Dead
Paul West

WITH NO WARNING, out came the medals from their shallow card-board box swathed in tissue paper almost eighty years old, the box's eight corners all broken, which made the sides into flaps between which the medals tried to slither out. He sat them on his own hand, then on hers, covering the so-called lines of head, heart and life.

"He never wore them," she said with attentuated gentleness. "Except when at the cenotaph. He wasn't one to show off. You'd have thought he would have had more to show for all those years in the trenches. My goodness, even I, in the last war, I got a medal just for being an Air Raid Warden. I had a tin hat. I got a medal for keeping a tin hat in the front-room cupboard." The tissue paper smelled of soot and almonds, perhaps the aroma of tarnish; Clive could not resist the thought that the little cardboard packet might once have held condoms instead, but, to obliterate any such idea, brought his hand up to his right eye in a sudden salute at which his mother nodded without making a motion. How had that ritual gone? His father had instructed him to look the person being saluted *in the eye* when at the proper distance and to raise the hand smartly until the tip of the forefinger touched the lower part of the headdress or forehead above the right eye. It was to show that you had no weapon concealed in your hand, and Clive mused on the edgewise hand of American salutes whereas the British version was the hand opened out flat. It was imperative, Harry said, to hold the salute for the correct time: until the receiver returned it, even if seeming frozen. A salute was another version of the compliment; his father had taught him that. And much else, in case of war.

The bronze one hung from a ring. Its ribbon was red in the center, with green and violet on either side, shaded to make the colors of two rainbows; but what held his eye now, as never before, was the winged figure of Victory, prim in a toga, one hand uplifted to cup sky as if testing springwater. The figure's head looked detachable. The feet had begun to melt, he couldn't think why, unless the figure was standing in the mud of the trenches, or in the boiling fat that poured out from cooking bacon. The side of the face in shadow had a halo, not above but alongside.

The brass medal was all action, though, with St. George on horseback trampling the eagle shield of the enemy powers, and a skull and crossbones (for good measure), while the sun lifted above all like an extension of the ribbon's orange watered center.

When his father wore them, Clive reasoned while Hildred caressed them and rubbed the metal with her hankie, he must have had the king's head outward, so Victory and St. George were what he wore against his heart, hard against the khaki serge. Jangling as he breathed, they were what he got for giving what he gave: simple equivalence according to the politicians of the day. Here Clive's mind fell into the phrasings of Decoration Day formulas, usually spoken against the echo of crimped trumpet notes and a distant shuffle of traffic: the music of remembrance, of pain minified and jubilation made into a graven image.

"At the cenotaph," Hildred began, but at once lost her drift, for open speech at least, so Clive soundlessly completed the sentence for her in his mind's eye, although never having seen Harry at the concrete breechblock inscribed with the names of the local dead. Had he? He had never been allowed, although he wondered why as his father had always been keen on terse ceremonial. Cenotaph meant empty tomb, Clive told himself, still wincing at the word, at the bony whisper it seemed to release; he had never heard anyone say it loudly or with any degree of confidence. Then life resumed as if he and his mother had indeed been away at the cenotaph, only half a mile away down the village from where she used to live. Both Uffingham and Exington had cenotaphs; you could pay homage wherever you went, to the dead or their familiars, Bob Woodcock, Stephen Rais, Granville Burdett, Alec Marsden, and his father, those bent-over men right there in the village street, like inbred ghosts: husky, distance-watching men with pawnbroked smiles and fresh-rinsed eyes. The few.

Back to business, then. Thirty paces was the correct saluting distance. Salutes were not as a rule given at a greater distance than that. Well, Clive thought, appraising his own performance, at least the wrist is straight, Father, thumb and forefingers are joined; they hold a pencil, whereas you, as you sometimes said, wrote your initials with a Vickers gun against sand and sandbags, walls and snowbanks, and advancing hordes of field-gray men in spiked coalscuttle helmets. But Clive could not sustain Harry in the vocative, now that he was gone, not when he had never listened properly when his father told of faking his age to enlist. Did he really riddle the sunset with machine-gun fire? Scissor the low cumulus until rain fell from it? Did he puncture the moon, aiming upward as if the gun were a theodolite? Did he ever reload? Did he ever have to? He never spoke of it, of inserting the brass tag-end of the belt into the feed-block on the right-hand side of the gun. Then the Number One, his father took hold of the tag-end and yanked it through, tugging back twice on the crank handle. Then how did Clive know all this? His father must have told of someone else's doing it, some other Number One, some other Number Two. If only I had been able to tape-record him, Clive thought: every town, every casualty, every advance, every retreat, the names of the grocery stores, the churches, even the map coordinates, and all he could do now was retrieve Harry through maps, annals, and the little red manual called *Field Burial Service*, stained with blood. They must have let his father keep it, he had often thought, in case he had to bury himself. Or they let him take it home as a souvenir, to put alongside his medals. No: it just came back with him somehow by accident, in his kit bag. Clive had once taken it with him to church, for a joke, before Harry and Hilly excused him from going, not long after he began using Harry's old kit bag to keep his toys in. It felt as if his father, dead fifteen years ago, had just died, and in Belgium, say: the young corporal had just died as his son held the salute, and then he came back to life with some obscene beast called his memory vomiting what it could not abide to contain.

They carved wood together in a blizzard of shavings to make planes and galleons and submarines. The metal bits, the flanges and hinges, he himself shaped, his father humming through gentle catarrh. When they painted, at the same time sharing slices of apple clamped between their teeth during the tricky parts, Harry did the whites and reds, Clive the blues and the camouflage colors (the greens and browns). Each left the other's areas bare. Harry threw balls for Clive to hit: balls of leather, rubber, wood, cork, and little golf balls eviscerated, trailing parabolas of thin rubber ribbon all over the yard, unwound until the little ball of paint fell out and the golf ball was only a husk. Bat, pole, strip of floorboard, old tennis racket, Clive smote with them all. Swing. Wind-up. Wham. He never knew the right order in which the joys came, sometimes beginning with Wham.

"More, Daddy, more!" he'd cry, and Harry always could.

These were games of peace. "Don't close your eyes," Harry would say. "Watch the ball all the way in." Clive's nose bled. They swabbed it. Hilly came outside with a small towel sprinkled with eau de cologne, although in general she disapproved of things French and Belgian. They played again. Then Harry's nose bled and Clive rode the elevator of his arms to dab it. Harry never tired until Clive did, and then they put everything away neatly, standing the bat in the corner by the door, rolling the ball of the day back into its drawer among buttons, tools and sticks of sealing wax.

So Clive once again joined Harry in a mud pit where he sat with three others, all in steel helmets except the corporal whose hat was soft and had a floppy peak. Don't stay too long, he heard Hildred shouting. He sighted the Vickers as if it were the pencil in some short-legged, lethal pair of compasses. Bound in puttees, his father's legs looked bandaged and filthy. His voice had almost broken, but, like the swan of Tuonela, wobbled about along the uneven line dividing life from death. Were there ancient Greeks who faked their age to join the colors?

Hildred, however, was still musing on the medals. "He'd polish them good and proper. He was always clean." A touch housewife-proud, she shifted abruptly into another voice, that of the cenotaph. "They went down in hundreds. He did not need to aim, he said. He just looked forward and fired. He just pressed down with his thumbs, and it was all automatic." Then she told the story of the honor-mad captain who led a charge, monocle in eye, sword in hand, against German machine guns: Ferrers of B Company. The monocle and sword reached his family a year later by registered mail.

Clive still knew, having been amply instructed when little, how to site a machine gun in the front line, siting it not on the parapet but behind the parados. Otherwise the site would be overrun, and the Huns would impale them on blood-wet bayonets. But what the parados was he could never remember, even after looking it up. He was destined never to remember. He promised to be good, the middle-aged son, to behave, to do his duty, the right thing at the right time. Formulas all. All that bothered him now was the knowledge that Harry loved him most when he was little and did not know that he loved Harry, though using *that* formula all the time. That was why he was always volunteering to recover his father from some grave or other, tracking him into the midst of horrors that made Clive's teeth ache and narrowed his throat. He crawled after his father under the barbed wire while flares spluttered titanium-white overhead and the enemy machine guns whipped and cracked. Or they chattered. They got back by Verey light to see the grass along the parapet lift into the air as the bullets hit. Image of a ruined, deadlocked summer spent by a father and his boy. Hilly gave a rueful half-shake of her head, reading his mind, knowing there was nothing to be done to revise Harry's monumental life. Then Clive reminded her how Harry and another soldier had greased a pig and let it loose in a Belgian dance hall. When they caught it, they dumped it into a well, and one of the Belgians who went down after it was bitten in the thigh. Told to read a book called *Somme Battle Stories*, but four, and lazy-eyed, he thought the title was *Some Battle Stories*, selecting an indefinite plural over a singular river, a valley, a hell. How cheerily, he wondered, did his father fight? As if taking carp from a local lake with maggots or earthworms for bait? Or in steel-eyed aloofness, as when he hadn't slept well? Sometimes the Belgians fried eggs and ham for him. He always managed to find tobacco (dark shag) to stuff into the pipe — his badge of premature sagacity. When the gun was really clean, and there was time for fun, his father or some other imaginary being hoisted Clive at arm's length up at the smoky sky with a falsetto shout, and a rickety biplane hummed down. "One of ours, lads," they cried, and then pretended to fling young Clive at it as if to some aerial rendezvous of equals. Lofted thus, toward whichever sky, Clive smelled battle over the lettuces growing rank all over the yard in midsummer, and, when they picked him up, into their dream at altitude, he never knew where he was, and hardly cared. They were all his father.

What kept Harry going, so he told Hilly, was the dream that one day he would have a son; if he could persuade himself among all that carnage that he would have a son, and then somehow see how that son would look, he was bound to come through. So he saw his future, as it were, through a child's eye, a child held out at arm's length like a talisman, held out as far away from the war as possible, a son to whom he would one day tell all, or even a daughter full of complicitous ah's who nonetheless slid away from him fast, into dolls and cookery, heedless of the names — Malines, Alost — which he and the son insisted on and mispronounced: *Maylinez* and *All Lost*. Dandelion yellow even more than poppies blurred the torn-up ground, and the seeds wafted through the burned-out villages. It was all Somewhere in Belgium, as the newspapers used to say with blatant secrecy. Thus his father, a knight, called away from court, falconry and the occasional practice joust to mortal tournament with the Kaiser himself, pounded the Kaiser into blood-red sludge and rode St. George's horse, with a sprig of hawthorn between his teeth, like one serene and adept.

For Clive, the novelist, there had always been, there still was, the sound in his head of his father talking, shouting even: grand confessional bison, getting into this character and that, as his mother sometimes did too. Again and again came that self-conscious war-whoop (Highlander's or Mohican's) as Harry launched his heir at the sky, and in passing Clive mussed his father's brushed-back thick black hair, his little knee flicked Harry's trim sharp nose.

"A big difference," Harry kept telling him, "between medals and *decorations*. One means you were there. You didn't have to have done much. The other's for being brave in action, or very intelligent. Or," with his most fleeting sneer, "for impressing the right officer." So these were medals only, for having been there, and Clive wanted to ride out into the middle of no-man's-land and gather up a handful of decorations, just for his father. Small wonder his father wanted to spend the rest of his life listening to Grieg, one ear held firm against the wireless, the other one closed off with the palm of his hand. How did it go?

If he could envision a son, he could live.

So, to live, he had to marry Hildred.

If, looking ahead, Hildred might not want him, he was doomed.

So, could his wanting a son somehow communicate itself to Hildred as a means of saving her Harry?

Blinking the tears away, Clive tried to fix his mind on his father's face new-washed, his eyes unbandaged and exposed to the brightest lights: his father looking like a Greek statue of the young Camus, whose name meant snub-nosed. Harry tried to touch his eyes, but nurses held him firm. If the eyes itched, perhaps that was a good sign. Surgeons would operate on him, pick out the worst shrapnel, and then wait. He had never had a chance to use Iode Tinctura or affix the First Field Dressing, in the dark or by the ocher flash of other explosions. Oh, there was light enough for Harry to shave by in later years, from the hissing and sometimes broken gas mantle in the bathroom, where he also took nearly invisible motes of shrapnel from under his top eyelid with a delicately shaved, pointed matchstick while Clive thought of how, in Belgium, long after 1918, bodies and gun barrels, soup vats and the chassis of armored cars, surfaced out of the earth's slow churning. "It's walking out, see," Harry would say as he smeared the tiniest touch of what looked like oxide of metal on the back of his machine-gunner's hand. These hardly visible bits of German iron had no symbolic value for him and were just a nuisance, to be picked off as they showed up and laid gently to rest before he swept them to the linoleum with a minor sigh.

My father fishes in his eye, Clive used to think as he stood by him waiting to see the black speck leave the needle-point of the match when Harry tapped the vein behind the knuckle. The eyelid would unroll to where it belonged. Sometimes Harry rolled it up so high, the upper one, that Clive thought the eye itself would fall to the bathroom mantelpiece, like a pirate's. He even used to dream that Robin Hood had a glass eye, or at least a handful of shrapnel splinters, and would rid himself of them by peering into a pool in Sherwood Forest, pointed arrow at the ready. Breathing hard while his neatly manicured fingers groped and fished, Harry loomed in the gaslight, a pale man without an undershirt, and Clive saw the white oval of the wound in his father's back. The gaslight changed to a different, less comforting hiss, more of a taunt than a sigh, and Clive silently offered him all the years of his own young life, aghast at the loss, and awestruck by his father's defenseless body, the scars that peppered his arms. It was not hard, at such moments that came several times a week, to see his father as every bit a Sherwood Forester who burned trunks into charcoal and hunted deer with fatal chivalry. He was also a St. George who rode a horse called Victory in a Grander National than any, since Harry, after all, was also just his Dad, with a Worthington Pale Ale in his fist, a Players Navy Cut cigarette perched unwet between his teeth, and an eye in whose iris there twirled a tiny blind fleck of something dead and innocent and gone.

Nobody joked about his Dad. They all knew he had been and done the impossible. Reported Missing, Believed Killed, he had come home one day, walking slowly, with a patch over one eye: a man with no depth perception but, deep inside, the sense of having sat another examination and passed with flying colors.

Later on had come those other walks with his two children, always amid the light heaves of summer, Kotch and Clive trembling with pride that they had been allowed out with Harry in their exclusive charge. His left hand in Clive's (as they thought of it, although Clive's was in his, really), and his right in Kotch's (though really vice versa), Harry took his time, treading on water, never knowing that, in little inbursts of vainglorious pride, Kotch and Clive now and then each closed an eye (the left) to harmonize with Harry, so that with him they veered gently to the left, "so that" here meaning both *to that purpose* and *with the result that.* Clive had often wondered what would happen if both children closed both eyes and trusted themselves to the one-eyed king in the middle. They never did so, but they took obtuse pride in walking wounded with Harry, sometimes while Hilly brought up the rear, keeping a keen gaze on whichever child was nearer the roadway. After such outings, Clive felt the rigidity seep away from his body, as if he had been frozen: his whole frame worried that there was going to be an accident — a second German shell coming over, a bus mounting the curb and mashing them with its lateness. When he was older, and yearning back to those walks, Clive told himself they were an elementary exercise; more to the point, he thought, with his father and mother both alive, was the act of stilling his body while seated or in fluent motion on his bicycle. He called this learning how to lie down dead, keeping a buttock, a hand, an eyelid without motion for twenty minutes, an hour, a day (what feckless presumption). Then he would know what death was like, and what the dead managed with devastating ease, never moving a muscle in years. Perhaps there were humans, such as Houdini, who could accomplish this feat, but all Clive ever achieved was an incorrigible twitch, a scream in the nerves that yelled we're not dead yet, squire! How the dead lay still, flash-frozen by a quite unvengeful force that took sheep, water, shamrock, children to its bosom with lethal equanimity, halting all to the calm of the figures and images in a cap badge. This, Clive kept telling himself, is how the dead do it, quiverless and wholly arrested, with never a tremor of the lip betraying their true nature.

As the earth shifted, he thought, of course tremors ran through them, or as the air in the coffin changed, or nature's other creatures bundled past, heedless of such gigantic prey trapped forever in the final convulsive stretch of a throw that left one arm high and wafting, the ball long gone.

Tangled Reliquary
Ann Lauterbach

Tangled reliquary under all surfaces.
Nothing moonlike occurs there
Only partial coves
And entrances.
How cool it must have been
In the vat of the previous
Before these habits ordained the real.
Some of us must have seen each other
Naked in opulent dawn, our nerves
Drawn up as from an ancient well
Mossy, slick, unstuck at every seam
So we enter the sleeve of history
Out of which the magician pulls
His lawn ornaments: Dancer, Prancer,
Our Lady of Provocations, flags, targets,
The bluebird's house.
On the adjacent field
A swarm of butterflies alights
On a bald tree. This is the Tree of Changes
Mentioned in the lost book of A.
Her auspice was a riddle,
Sphinx or no sphinx,
Whose meanings we can piece together
From her journals which were torn into bandages
To wrap the wounds of the dying.
Such wanton songs
Paginate empirical trust
And the ruse of the first place.
Not that story again, what we cannot say
To the sun as it dispenses its sheen
Out over the harbor, but only
How can you perform your agile sway
Without shelter and without us?

So the riddle of the disembodied name
Sets in motion its primal mischief
Sanctioned and forbidden in the vastly gone.

This would be a good day to go sailing
Or to wash the car, but I have
Neither boat nor car. There's a plotless web
In the air like a banner pulling us along
Into something to look back on.
What if I wandered so far
Only to come here
To the relentless you
Have kept in store for me
Before the song, above the river,
All the names etched in stone
And only slowly annealed
To the spawning wind, in whose face
We will soon be included, having been shown
The near field's shambles
And grace. Come here
Like a shoulder or a girl's skipping step
Toward evening on a Friday,
Lapis amulet, Samurai sword,
Chinese silk stained with azalea,
A single earring the color of a toy globe
All stolen from a thing called April
Still wet with fresh rending. Come
Here in a language once learned
Only a few phrases remembered:
Bonjour, je t'aime, il fait beau.

Perhaps one of those popular, musical Sundays
Would save us, galloping at high speed in, out,
Only a glimpse from high up in the revised setting
Crowded with tyranny. So I wanted
Once again as a plaything, some jewel, box, horse
On which to come fleet of vision,
Glad to pretend. The cartoons sailed
Against the brocade, and the stairs
Were where the prayers were kept
Like instruments of torture

Basking in shade, the scent of new snow,
Locks of hair under glass.
                              The day, however,
Has spun upwards so it seems to be
A sort of chapel of divided light
And the season, punctured, leaks
Down on us old balloons from a faint dead planet.
And I had promised never again to try to
Put anything back together,
To obey the errant barge of upheavals,
Not to seek cause and effect in the prevailing wind.
But now shards of promise
Glint through the network of uneven shifts
Like the wandering voice of an ancestor
On the other side of the dunes. Bricks or dunes.
But what will I tell the children?
As in a photo of two persons dancing
There are some things we never will hear.
Shout and coo, shout and coo,
Each of us away. So one who is the one
Wants to sheath me in his ear.
Him sings his tunes
In the aberrant remonstrance. And I
Agree to this fear he tells me of
Whose words are what he cares to do.
Both hands are up in a moment
Not so much surrendered as bequeathed
To our common night. Dear dream,
Will you assist us, give pause
To any and all of these lessons,
Take us, each, into such fond technologies
That the thigh's spasmodic hum
Frees action as well as solace.
But the eye's horizon
Is dialectical and unreasoned,
Its gown disembodied because unsaid.
The blue floor calls itself June
And wants to lay me down
On its shine of now
And peel off the shadows
One by one until I am it.

Then sail into the air
Sheet after sheet
    this and that
        here and there
           now and then
Only as real as what follows.
That the balloon man lost his head
That the screen fell to the floor
In a heap of landscape
                such mornings
That the clay pot
Lay in shards
That the dry flowers were cast
Across the rug, ancient seeds, crumbs
                    such mornings
And the light reached all the way into the dark
As if handing it forward
From some child's grave
From the curled soil's boundaries
From whatever captivity
We wish to sew into artifact
But which, like the light just named,
Eludes us, frail and pinioned in the glossy tablets
Of alchemical reserve;
That the elegy is betrayed
As the child follows her hand to its sanctuary
And touches its core
And unriddles its riddle
In the beckoning need
That the cluster of disavowal gives way
And could not be shy
              such mornings —

State of the Art
Charles Bernstein

THERE IS OF COURSE NO STATE of American poetry, but states, moods, agitations, dissipations, renunciations, depressions, acquiescences, elations, angers, ecstasies; no music to our verse but vastly incompatible musics; no single sentiment but clashes of sentience: the magnificent cacophony of different bodies making different sounds, as different as the hum of Hester Street from the gush of Grand Coulee, the buzz of Central Park on August afternoons from the shrieks of oil-coated birds in Prince William Sound.

The state of American poetry can be characterized by the sharp ideological disagreements that lacerate our communal field of action, making it volatile, dynamic, engaging.

What I hear, then, in the poetries of this New American *fin de siècle* is an implicit refusal of unity that is the result of our prodigious and magnanimous outpouring of words. In saying this, I register my own particular passion for poetry that insists on running its own course, finding its own measures, charting worlds otherwise hidden or denied or, perhaps best of all, never before existing.

Poetry is aversion to conformity in the pursuit of new forms, or can be. By form I mean ways of putting things together, or stripping them apart, I mean ways of accounting for what weighs upon any one of us, or that poetry tosses up into an imaginary air like so many swans flying out of a magician's depthless black hat so that suddenly, like when the sky all at once turns white or purple or day-glow blue, we breathe more deeply. By form I mean how any one of us interprets what's swirling so often incomprehensibly about us, or the stutter with which he stutter, the warbling tone in which she sing off and on key. If form averts conformity, then it swings wide of this culture's insatiable desire for, yet hatred of, assimilation — a manic-depressive cycle of go along, go away that is a crucial catalyst in the stiflingly effective process of cultural self-regulation and self-censorship.

199

When poetry averts conformity it enters into the contemporary: speaking to the pressures and conflicts of the moment with the means just then at hand. By which I mean I care most about poetry that disrupts business as usual, including literary business: I care most for poetry as dissent, including formal dissent; poetry that makes sounds possible to be heard that are not otherwise articulated.

It's particularly amusing that those who protest loudest about the fraudulence or aridness or sameness of contemporary poetry that insists on being contemporary, dissident, different, and who profess, in contrast, the primacy of the individual voice, fanned by a genteel inspiration, produce work largely indistinguishable from dozens of their peers and, moreover, tend to recognize the value only of poetry that fits into the narrow horizon of their particular style and subject matter. As if poetry were a craft that there is a right way or wrong way to do: in which case, I prefer the wrong way — anything better than the well-wrought epiphany of predictable measure — for at least the cracks and flaws and awkwardness show signs of life.

Ideology, as in a particular and restricted point of view, way of hearing, tendency of preferences and distastes, everywhere informs poetry and imparts to it, at its most resonant, a density of material-ized social being expressed through the music of a work as well as its multifoliate references. To pretend to be nonpartisan, above the fray, sorting the "best" from the "weak" without "ideological grudges" — as a highly partisan poet recently put it, as if to mark his own partisanship in the course of denying it — is an all too common form of mystification and bad faith aimed at bolstering the author-ity of one's pronouncements. As with George Bush's attempt to dis-credit "special interests," that is, all us "udders," in the end we find the center is a little wizard with an elaborate sound and light show, good table manners, and preferred media access.

What interests me is a poetry and a poetics that do not edit out so much as edit in: that include multiple conflicting perspectives and types of languages and styles in the same poetic work, or book, or — as with CONJUNCTIONS at ten — run of a magazine. A poetry — a poetic — that expresses the states of the art as it moves beyond the twentieth century, beyond the modern and postmodern.

Poetry should be at least as interesting as, and a whole lot more unexpected than, television. But reality keeps creating trouble for poetry, for it constantly changes the terms of what's possible versus wildly improbable or surreal, and poetry that runs the risk of being too cautious will find itself well outstripped by events (even).

I'm thinking for the moment of a McDonald's ad from Moscow broadcast only months after the crumbling of the Berlin Wall, during a time of turbulence bordering on economic chaos in the Soviet Union. This was not a farcical pastiche of conceptual art fronting as social commentary, but rather what we were led to believe were "real" Russians enjoying the communion of international packaging — just like Dave and Betty and the kids do in Syosset.

As if we needed the war against Iraq to remind us, our images of each other, and of other cultures, seem to go from ignorance to sinisterly deluded fabrication, almost without any middle ground. Poetry can, even if it often doesn't, throw a wedge into this engineered process of social derealization: find a middle ground of care in particulars, in the truth of details and their constellations — provide a site for the construction of social and imaginative facts and configurations avoided or overlooked elsewhere. But to achieve this end, poets would have to be as alert to the presents of their cultures as the designers of TV ads; which means a willingness to engage in guerrilla warfare with the official images of the world that are being shoved down our throats like so many tablespoons of Pepto-Bismol, short respite from the gas and the diarrhea that are the surest signs that harsh and uncontainable reality hasn't vanished but has only been removed from public discussion.

That means we can't rely only on the tools and forms of the past, even the recent past, but must needs invent new tools and forms that begin to meet the challenges of the ever-changing present.

Innovation is a response to changing conditions. Which is not to say that the work "progresses," as in a technological model, or say "today we make a better car than we did years ago." It's never a question of better. The details, the particulars, and how they are ordered keep changing and poetry is a way of articulating that.

Over and over again, in a panoply of poetry panels and conferences and magazine symposia, our discussions pummel the problem of Balkanization or fragmentation: how to evaluate the fact that in the last twenty years a number of self-subsistent poetry communities have emerged that have different readers and different writers and different publishers and different reading series, even, increasingly, separate hierarchies and new canons with their own awards, prizes, heroines.

One response to this new proliferation of audiences is to lament the lack of a common readership. I'm not talking about those who want to resurrect a single canon of Western literary values; the ethnocentrism and ideological blindness of this position hardly needs to be reiterated in an anniversary issue of CONJUNCTIONS.

What I take more seriously are pluralist ideas supporting an idealized multiculturalism: the image of poets from different communities reading each other's works and working to keep aware of developments in every part of the poetic spectrum. The idea of diversity, as it is advertised in almost all the latest U.S. college publicity, is the most superficial indication of this tendency; more significant is the introduction of multicultural curricula in the high schools and colleges.

My problem is not the introduction of radical alternatives to parochial and racist reading habits engendered by the educational system and the media, but that these alternatives are often ameliorative rather than politically or aesthetically exploratory. I see too great a continuum from "diversity" back to New Critical and liberal-democratic concepts of a common readership that often — not always — have the effect of transforming unresolved ideological divisions and antagonisms into packaged tours of the local color of gender, race, sexuality, ethnicity, region, nation, class, even historical period: where each group or community or period is expected to come up with — or have appointed for them — representative figures whom we can know about.

This process, more often than not, presupposes a common standard of aesthetic judgment or implicitly aims to erect a new common standard. In this context, diversity can be a way of restoring a highly idealized conception of a unified American culture that effectively quiets dissent. For the twin ideas of diversity and the common reader evade the challenge posed by heterodox art, the poetries at the peripheries, to the very idea of a common standard of aesthetic judgment or the value of a common readership.

We have to get over, as in getting over a disease, the idea that we can "all" speak to one another in the universal voice of poetry. History still mars our words, and we will be transparent to one another only when history itself disappears. For as long as social relations are skewed, who speaks in poetry can never be a neutral matter.

The cultural space of diversity is mocked by the banishment from the *massed* media of those groups stigmatized as too inconsequential or out of tune to represent even "diversity"; it's torn to shreds when the tragic death of one white heterosexual teenage boy from AIDS is given a public acknowledgment equivalent to the tragic deaths of thousands of individual gay men.

I sometimes wonder even whether men can understand the voice of the women we live next to and from whose bodies we have come, since I hear every day the male version of the universal voice of rationality trying to control, as if by ventriloquism, female bodies. Though as men we have to make it clear that these men do not speak for us, do not represent us, but mock what men could be but too rarely are.

I wonder sometimes what sense it makes to speak of the possibility of communication among all the peoples of America as long as there are homeless whom most of us have learned to cast outside the human circle of care and acknowledgment — unless it be on the Universal Broadcasting Network's Rock Star and Child Celebrity Tribute to the Dispossessed, the Survivors of Racial Violence, and the Victims of Sexual Assault.

In a society with such spectacularly inequitable distributions of power, the very idea of public space has been befouled — not by the graffiti of the folk but by the domination of the means of communication by those dispossessed of their connection with just such folk. What can be decried as parochial patterns of reading is in fact an essential strategy for survival, to have a deep immersion in a contemporaneity and history that are difficult to locate and need to be championed.

The direction of poetic interest can better be directed outward, centrifugally, to the unknown and the peripheral, than toward a constant centripetal regrouping and reshoring through official verse culture's enormously elastic and sophisticated mechanism of tokenization that targets, splits off, and decontextualizes, essentializing the mode of difference and incorporating the product (never the process) into its own cultural space.

Too often, the works selected to represent cultural diversity are those that accept the model of representation assumed by the dominant culture in the first place. "I see grandpa on the hill / next to the memories I can never recapture" is the base line against which other versions play: "I see my yiddisha mamma on Hester street / next to the pushcarts I can no longer peddle" or "I see my grandmother on the hill / next to all the mothers whose lives can never be recaptured," or "I can't touch my Iron Father / who never Canoed with me / on the prairies of my masculine epiphany." Works that challenge these models of representation run the risk of becoming more inaudible than ever within mainstream culture.

There is no reason to suppose that poets working in opposition to the dominant strains of American culture should have any intrinsic interest in the narrow spectrum of official verse culture. If their work rejects the values of most of this culture, indeed finds these values part of a fabric of social constructions that maintains coercive economic and political hierarchies, then the idea that all sides should politely take an interest in aesthetic craftiness is absurd; on the one side, such interest is patronizing; on the other, self-negating.

The insidious obsession with mass culture and popularity, here translated into the lingo of a unified culture of diversity, threatens to undermine the legitimacy of working on a small, less than mass, and, yes, less than popular scale.

Within the emerging official cultural space of diversity, figures of difference are often selected because they narrate in a way that can be readily assimilated — not to say absorbed — into the conventional forms of the dominant culture. Difference is confined to subject matter and thematic material, a.k.a. local color, excluding the formal innovations that challenge those dominant paradigms of representations. Indeed, the political and social meaning of sound, vernacular, nontraditional rhythms — that is, those things that make a text a poem — are often discounted as negligible in the fetishizing of narrative and theme; formal values being left for a misconceived avant garde that has been involuntary decultured — deracinated, ungendered and therefore removed from those contexts that give it sense.

To be sure, signature styles of cultural differences can be admitted into the official culture of diversity if they are essentialized, that is, if these styles can be made to symbolically represent the group being tokenized or assimilated. Artists within these groups who are willing to embrace neither the warp of mainstream literary style through which to percolate their own experience nor the woof of an already inflected, and so easily recognized, style of cultural difference will find themselves falling through the very wide gaps and tears in the fabric of American tolerance. Such artists pay the price for being less interested in representing than enacting.

Franz Kafka once asked, "What have I in common with the Jews, I don't know what I have in common with myself?" This can itself be understood as a Jewish attitude, but only if Jewishness is taken as multiplicitous and expressed indirectly. When Nicole Brossard makes a litany of the various shifting meanings *we* can have for her — we Quebecois / you Canadians; we women / you men; we lesbians / you heterosexuals; we poets / you prose writers — she raises a problem similar to Kafka's.

John Berger, writing recently of the spiritual regeneration of the new nationalisms of Central Europe and the Soviet Union, remarks, "All nationalisms are at heart deeply concerned with names. . . . Those who dismiss names as detail have never been displaced; but the peoples on the peripheries are always being displaced. That is why they insist on their identity being recognized" (*The Nation*, 5/7/90, p. 627). But naming is never a singular act; what is once named may no longer exist when that name is repeated. It is not that I wish to dismiss names as details but to recognize details as more important than names, as always already peripheralized as names become packages through which a commodity is born. For even individuals are multiple, indeed, as Emmanuel Levinas re-marks, "The mind is a multiplicity of individuals."

What represents a Jew or a white Protestant American or an African American or a Canadian or a Native American, a male or a female? In poetry, it's less a matter of thematic content than the form and content understood as an interlocking figure — the one inaudible without the other; like the soul and the body, completely inter-penetrating and interdependent. Formal dynamics in a poem create content through the shapes, feelings, attitudes, and structures that compose the poem. Content is more an attitude towards the work or towards language or towards the materials of the poem than some kind of subject that is in any way detachable from the han-dling of the materials. Content emerges from composition and cannot be detached from it; or, to put it another way, what is de-tachable is expendable to the poetic.

What poetry belabors is more important than what poetry says, for "saying is not a game" and the names that we speak are no more our names than the words that enter our ears and flow through our veins, on loan from the past, interest due at the dawn of each day, though not to the Collector who claims to represent us in the court of public discourse but to the Collector we become when we start to collect what belongs to us by right of our care in and for the world.

Charles Bernstein

When we get over this idea that we can all speak to each other, I think it will begin to be possible, as it always has been, to listen to one another, one at a time and in the various clusters that present themselves, or that we find the need to make.

The Letters
Martine Bellen

Dear Sister,

A low wind warbles like swallows through my drafty rooms, now here, now not, and my abode, a boat, grows longer the longer I drift; in answer to your inquiry, I visit him many times each day, though not with my body—locked in its gilt frame surrounded by limit. I am renewing myself toward him or disguising myself from ruined magistrates who offer shame, which is intrinsic in strong affection, not because man is meant to be more lettered than us, but because the I appended to the house connotes being swollen up and domineering, an I-beam as foundation or support. Perhaps "Home," which is a place of reference that's contrapuntally built or abandoned, is constructed upon thoughts of the loved one, rebuilding and abandoning him with each breath in any direction we walk, rest secure, assured, a bell surrounding our garden. You were right about the sweet williams. Come visit—

———————

Outside the central gates and to the right: Cinnamon trees—lithe like lovely ladies—their hair entangled—their tanned fingers intertwined—their soft, soulful howls tangled, their feet, each planted on the earth—no one knows how deep they go—not one of them knows how to reach deeper and yet each does—she does, reaches deeper

ears she warmed in and formed into wings spread upon the air she heard—it is where the tree of love grows in captivity

———————

Martine Bellen

Dear Sis,

Are emotion and meaning unrelated? Is that my fret, my instrument?

Already an hour underground, I am incapable of turnpike aims and have met birds that are endeavored with speech. The more I travel the more accustomed my eyes become. All pictures charged positive or negative and the sound too is charged so everything I see or hear down here is pure emotion, which is illusion let in. When the positive and antimatter meet they obliterate one another and there is white noise and colored space. I'll send you my address when I stop — Love —

———————

Wegener gave good reason for believing that all land had once been a one-world continent, which he referred to as Pangaa (now Pangaea). He presented maps showing how this super-continent had broken up and drifted apart
            And the uncircumcised . . . flesh of his foreskin . . . shall be cut off from his people

—, there has never been a time I have wanted drank consumed been consumed by anyone as with you, that my mouth, in its shape, in its sound in its fullness and its hollow is my soul and my seed as with you, there has never been a time I've been reached inside and out; it washes its hands in us; I cannot anticipate where the end is,

———————

Baked into the center of a rose she found three strips of paper on which were printed the following:

Bringing the sky into your house will not scare you but as a result you will never be sure of how strong the men can hit.

208

We cannot know our lovers from childhood, though like to look at their photographs and imagine we are their sisters, their sitters, their first grade teachers.

When at all possible sleep on the round bed of the faithful, the largest size afforded but not the largest manufactured.

Dear Sister,

I have remained enamored through time or distance which is not subject to the vicissitudes of change, nor does it know any except in the direction of increase. I refer not to real people, only ghosts, but perhaps real people have ghosts, whole constellations of inner linings and miltinominous sailing southerly, no me, no you, is indeed but in different continents . . . what continent are you riding this day, dear friend? Twenty-four hours ago the swallows returned to Capistrano, but more frequently *all things* appear little — the universe, (the verse for one and all) an immense heap of tiny things, wee folk, let's tea this noon if I return in time

---

From eleven to fourteen I loved to be led out of horror movies, so slowly I'd meander down aisles and die for a while. Once I lost my way for seven years and almost forgot about you, there was so much work to do for another lifetime; that became the horror, the were-people and once-people strangely forming into never-people. If I forget I'm French I can look into the mirror and read my Godfather around turned-up lips and great aunt circling, soaring my eyes. But what if I forget I'm American or married?

Face inscribed and hidden in sun, in sound a circle of Flame or kitchen God to guard the hearth, the colors and perfumes in kisses. I held your kiss a little away from me and smelled its deep shade first, first before I ate into you before the waters were.

Martine Bellen

Dear friend,

Near dawn. Garbage trucks arrive. We gather our waste in bags and cannot fall back for how noisily they chomp, these giant prehistoric ghosts of dingy gray, the ones that never evolved (must remember to learn from them).

Lacy confided that every female she meets becomes her ailing sister who she fends for and feeds, she is tired of not getting her share and I tell her when you have a sister you love you *must* share. She says, but none of them are real. They never are, Lacy, says I.

———————

Ghost counting!!! Sometimes one will pitch a tent inside you and then you're in trouble, expect big bills. There are many door ghosts because those are in transition, backward and forward ghosts, what do door ghosts do? Spirits of a place can ghost in trees, words, rocks and sleep in brooms. Sharp edges are hidden so luck will not be. Cut your name on every one you come to.

Dear Sister,

I followed a crease across a bridge, in my arms an A which is the mind alone without friend and the I used to build other guests for myself in this prison. What I'm meaning is I need to hear your voice to make you real, please scream. Every day the desert tents are counted and there is less, Loss, that is the key word that must be plugged in to make a sense because don't we live in our perceptual world indebted to where there are spectral powers in thought. They use sensory apparatus to build a different universe to fly in, so we hear them not as they do each other commanding the top half and we in the middle think we inhabit the same

— door bells were not yet invented —

they entered me last night to end themselves, hand in hand as one, and repeated till I could question no more that it will never be possible for me to see them or hear them directly, that I must, as you did, find my indirect means, for there would be no strange town where I could store my summers separate; this is the necessity which impelled me to go to sea; like dream-coins I couldn't pick them up or take them outside and if I really wanted to spend them it would have to be in a land of a moment's fleeting pleasure and quite possibly I wouldn't even be able to remember it. I have dressed ghost dolls in freshly ironed paisleys and plaids, served them my versions of stories and venison and what it means to follow, even my feelings work with back words and those I love can only be real in the dark. They are equipped with holes beside their eyes, not so they can see but so they can cry, the light's not important but the water we travel and which travels from us. How surprising to find the leaf I recently retrieved return to the forest on its own. The noons are lunatic-filled and this increasingly distant light makes everything foreign and moving farther faster so it was comforting to recognize. Please return. I haven't yet received my mail, maybe you are in it. Love. Maybe you are not.

Dear Remembered,

The soul can be a guest or gust of air. I am thinking it. It is only when you're within me that I don't, where time is aligned. Mother came to clean but I blamed her for the opposite and tried a new way for her to know me. To get to me.

Yours,

Another Day
Donald Revell

A wine glass
out all night
overflowed with moths.
The wings
balletomaned,
and they were a camp-system.

A more obsessed hand or more accurate would grasp
at the nearer thing, the glass a tulip, the system
a bulb of poisons. The swarm retires. Domestic pets
are loosed again into the backyards, and the mowers
resume their insect labors down to the powerlines.

Exposed to air
the ointment
proved useless.
Highest branches
unhealed and bled.
When only fracture
is silence only silence
is useful, and wings

cure the dead, careful to lay them into tall glasses.
The out-of-doors is glassy poisoning, daughter of the
last desire to take flight out of pure, of pure hatred
of the air. My daughter's head is not your head. Glass
aviates over the railways, over the electric ropes and
Europe killing not America

The camps
parch to overflowing.

Tablet XXVII:
From the Laboratory-Teachings-Memoirs
of the Scholar/Translator

Armand Schwerner

Nine closely related clay Cylinder-Seals constitute Tablet XXVII.

A THIN SHEET OF CLAY measuring about 54 inches by 4 inches was rolled to produce a cylinder 54 by 1, then cut into approximately 9 equal lengths, inscribed and fired. Electron microscopy of the cylinder ends testifies to this structural origin of the Seals; it does not absolutely guarantee the congruence of the materials. These documents, with the exception of number 1, are dilapidated.

They are the only ones extant whose structure can to any degree be conceived of as narrative; they do not much resemble other seals — generally devices used as a means of marking property not recounting Story. In addition they are remarkable for their startling linguistic formations, idiosyncratically arranged combinations of Akkadian cuneiform and pictographic Sumerian, archaizings, rare reshufflings which forcibly anneal these two different writing systems, their periods separated by hundreds of years. I will never forget the vibrations, the shimmerings, that overmastered me when, my arm outstretched, I first experienced the pressure of one of these Seals on the palm of my left hand.

I had to consider a number of factors in the course of the difficult and engaging process of naming the language-constructions inscribed on these Seals: to what degree do the inscriptions fulfill the requirements which the category 'language' imposes as a condition of membership? These unique presentations may result from the labors of a small group, perhaps even from those of one individual. The idiosyncratic utterance-combinations inscribed on these Seals contain, to repeat, in varied arrangements, both pictographic and cuneiform expressions, as well as innovative diacritical inscriptions.

I indicated in Tablet XXVI Laboratory-Teachings-Memoirs my experience of some interesting problems, both phonic and categorical, in arriving at acceptable names for such terms as Spharagram and

Mind/Texture/Determinative. Names matter; they suggest directions for later research; they convey texture which influences further scholarly speculation. My original term for the language-constructions in Tablet XXVII, "pictocunei," rhythmic cripple, was one of those terms whose barely semi-resident status in the English language the unabridged dictionaries indicate; in my second attempt, "cuneopicts," the consonant cluster, now massively terminal, conveyed the image of an early golden-haired Brit at his ravaging work. I came finally to choose the less literal, euphonious, more complexly relevant term, "ominacunei." The Latin "omina" signifies in the nominative plural both 'forebodings' and 'signs'; thus, besides its stress on the representational attributes of the pictograph, this first element in the neologism *"omina* cunei"—apprehending, dark, gravid, premonitory—connotes the parturition of the pictograph, which eventuated in the alphabet.

Some of the writings preserved through these Cylinder-Seals are essentially later rescissions of some lines from Tablet IX, itself an opaque document bearing here and there speckles of a secret ritual language, a not unusual linguistic feature seen for instance in such gatherings as those of the Inuit peoples collected in the course of Rasmussen's Thule Expeditions. These extraordinarily large Seals, which as we have seen average some six inches in length and one inch in diameter, thus seem to constitute an exoteric version of an esoteric original. My sense of the Seals as entropic narrative rests upon a series of implications derived from the idiosyncratic determinatives first seen in these contexts.

I might say more accurately that these specialized forms function not like the Mind/Texture/Determinatives which we have encountered in Tablet XXVI, but rather like Stage Directors, or let's say like what I will name Utterance/Texture/Indicators (U/T/I's), which isolate particular vectors largely related to the External World Stage and graft them onto a written expression. Members of the U/T/I family differ from those included in the M/T/D set in ways at once profound and illusory, an apparent paradox which will receive some clarification in the course of these Laboratory-Teachings-Memoirs. I could add though that contemporary speculation often conceives the Mind/Texture/Determinatives as referring to states of being—whose idiosyncratic natures beg for recognition. They also hunger for responses of individuals potentially victimized by any negative energies of such states. Thus the genesis of the M/T/D's derives from survival-needs, from the hunger to see clearly, without impediment.

(A major problem of course is that, following Kant, we understand that it is precisely impedimenta to clear-seeing of a thing-as-such which linguistic forms as reflectors of consciousness commonly embody. Rather than a game of Who or What do you trust?, it seems to be a question of What is real? Not evaluation but flat-out thereness.) The U/T/I's facilitate in some sense an ongoing Exodus from the esoteric utterances of Tablet IX. They constitute in some senses the external social analogues of the M/T/D's textures and functions. Graphic representations, forthcoming, will clarify these matters.

The U/T/I *leads* the esoteric original into the demotic realm, a space that may have resulted from an attempt — through a sort of anachronistic reconstruction — to present a Golden Age whose lineaments parallel aspects of later periods.

We might with a greater chance of accuracy understand such linguistic inventions as *sacred forgery*, or rather forgery prompted by a dazzled and mournful reconsideration, retrospective as well as perhaps economically profitable, of the sacred. I will translate and comment upon some of the Seals, in a few cases presenting original phrases found in Tablet IX followed by their later rescensions, each often generated through the fascinating and unexampled use of sub-orders of major Utterance/Texture/Indicators. My reader is advised to conceive of the U/T/I's as aspects of the Mind/Texture/Determinatives presented in Tablet XXVI, although the U/T/I's behave more like vectors of a sociocultural, demographic order than they do like descriptors relating to subjective states of being. They somewhat parallel the nature of the M/T/D's, but often depend for their meaning upon an intuitive familiarity with the ways human and other animal bodies can occupy space, and they often operate like a kind of uncanny, Body-Mind Declension, calling to mind the recent work of Birdwhistell and Eshkol-Wachmann, the speculations of Effort-Shape analysts.

The maker, or makers, of the Seals focused upon the pictographic, immanent thereness explicit in the nascent pictures of what *he* or *they* knew as the mirroring gem of the old systematic representations; the makers moved thence into the juxtaposition of two inscribed systems, one image and archaism, the other drawn directly from the Akkadian cuneiform.

What was the nature of the attempt? Perhaps to recoup the powers of the past without the sacrifice of the present — instinct with the knowledge of the doom attendant upon any creative thrust which thumbed its nose at its own time. This tendency, earning its own defeat, would fall into the constraining and reductive hell of either/or.

In the example

the Broken-Scissor Utterance/Texture/Indicator, U/T/I of Solitary

Reading and Subsuming Position-determinative, 𝄞 , alerts the perceiver of the utterance — solitary reader in a private space — that he is to imagine himself as acting in the context of a specific Body-Declension which, as we will see below, is to follow the Broken-Scissor U/T/I, establishing through this practice a connection with the utterance which sometimes ranges, in a three-state continuum, from a state of disinterested observation to one of profound and wounding separation from the object-phrase. (The icons representing these three stages, as well as those denoting ways of occupying space, will be given below.)

The function of this U/T/I concerns performance and relationship, not the reification of an isolation threatening to enshroud a solitary reader faced with a 'text.' Although we generally conceive of that reader as separated from the dance and music ordinarily associated with archaic and tribal modes of 'poetry,' it's a common and insistent mistake to envision the post-archaic world as the site of increasing numbers of civilized sad troglodytes existing in a hell of separatism and loss. The rites and poetry/music/dance didn't end. They entered mind.

The pictograph, swollen, textured and laminated by the very tracks of its past forms, had kept itself vivid through its stratigraphic development, in the long moment of its extended historical playing field, occasionally as palimpsest, the simultaneity of performance and sign. (Tablet XXVII presented states of the early graphic development of the pictograph, in the context of such divinatory materials as quadruped livers, stomachs and gall bladders.)

Three sample utterances will suggest the nature of the infra-determinatives governing the reader's Dream-Generation of Body-Declensions — to which I will append a partial sign-list derived from the Cylinder-Seals. Both the determinative-family and the rather broad-based characteristics of design variables begin to be apparent:

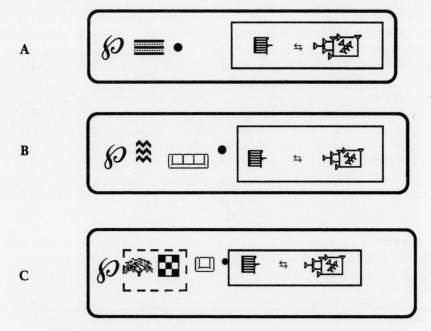

In each of these three instances the core expression consists of two segments, a pre-Sumerian pictograph signifying "great," which has already appeared in Tablet XXVI, indissolubly allied with a variant of Akkadian cuneiform signifying "silence." The pictographic elements will be presented as white on a black ground when they weigh at least twice as much as the conjoined cuneiform segments.

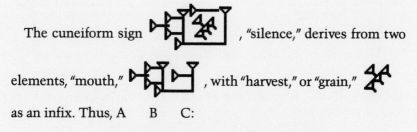

as an infix. Thus, A   B   C:

"Silence is the harvest of the mouth."
"Silence is the harvest of the mouth."
"Silence is the harvest of the mouth."

217

Introducing and modifying the core expression, the infra-determinatives follow the Broken-Scissor Utterance/Texture/Indicator in Cylinder-Seal 1 and denote the source physical position from which a reader/looker relates to the affective and logical aspects of an expression. So the infra-determinatives following directly upon the

subsuming symbol  constitute a kind of instrumental case eliciting in the isolated reader Dreamed Body-Declensions within which, or through the agency of which, he or she may experience the phrase-object and its harmonics. Utterances B and C, above, contain examples of two specialized U/T/I's, moments of force of Separativeness, or Torques of Separativeness; three exist:

These Torques indicate — in intensifying measures of the experience of Otherness — the intensity of separation which most appropriately qualifies the space between the reader and the object-phrase. Such U/T/I's can be considered as occupying a middle ground between pure Mind/Texture/Determinatives and pure U/T/I's, neither primarily reflexive nor pointedly sociological, however focused on the human body as vector working the space between person and community.

But three other elements which are present in utterances A, B and C modify the core expressions which follow them:

In A,

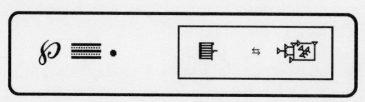

the sign ▤ signifies the reader's Dream-Generation of the Body-Declension "lying-down dying." Now, seen through a first, literal, simple step into translation, utterance A moves towards:

"In my ending, prone, I inhabit the great silence,

harvest of the mouth,"

or

"In my ending, prone, I inhabit the silence, great

harvest of the mouth,"

or

"In my ending, prone, I inhabit the silence,

the grains, the great mouth."

Of course a disproportionately heavy pictograph — here a white image on black ground — in any of the *ominacunei*, may radically alter the manner in which the entire utterance is conceived. In such an instance

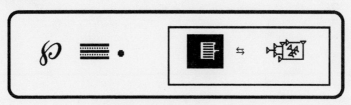

Greatly inhabiting
my ending, prone, I myself
great harvest
great mouth
silence
great

In B, the sign 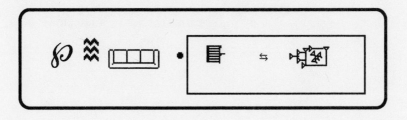 signifies the reader's Dream-Generation of the Body-Declension "crouched dying"; in addition the utterance contains the highest Torque of Separativeness:

In a first reading, then,

"In my crouched dying, I am sundered
from the great silence,"

or

"Immured in my crouch,
in my dying, barred, dis-
connected, arms hopeless, cracked
legs, there is only
away—not quite the memory
of a strain towards great
silence,"

or

"Going, impassable, heaviest world
of distance between me
and the harvest of the great
mouth, no
silence, pincered body so, dusk,
carries so
much."

In C, the sign signifies the reader's Dream-Generation of the Body-Declension "Lying down giving birth":

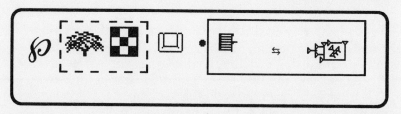

(That a part of this icon seems to portray a deciduous tree, although a surprising choice, is not without some environmental appropriateness. Both Sessile and Syrian oaks grew in what is now Syria; in present Iraq large open oak forests were found on the Zagros mountains at altitudes of between 2000 and 6000 feet.)

Translation here involves apprehending (ad/prehendere, to seize, to go towards in seizing), yielding to mimetic triggers, being led therefrom into Sympathy-Meditation through kernel-things. The best is to read "what was never written, the most ancient reading before all lanugages"; second best is the earned arrival at an "impeccable naïveté," escape from system, which is "a kind of damnation which forces us into a perpetual recantation" of any faith in the possibility of the rebirth of the pristine eye.

Simplistic analogues of the Body-Declension "Lying-Down-Giving-Birth" attracted the barbs of jejune flower-children on the trendy watch in the 1960s. It is nevertheless true that in comparison with the archaic, communally sanctioned Body-Declension "Crouching-Giving-Birth," the former does constitute under historic Gallic auspices a gracile aristocratic insertion into tradition — a kind of elegance at odds with the benign vector of the force of gravity; in addition the utterance contains the first Torque of Separativeness. Separated from whom, from what, how sharply?

My study of this utterance convinces me that it concerns rather than a woman a male Priest of Sacrifices. The perverse melody of exodus which this sequence emits recalls a section of its esoteric paradigm in Tablet IX, a document probably the confession — *in extremis* and partly notated in a secret language — of unsuccessful sacrifical denudations:

> "... it is
> never enough, I've surrendered the damp lips of speech
> emptied these eye sockets filled my ears with good clay, ground down
> my fingertips I'm left like a dog to smell my way to the dream
> THIS IS AN EMPTYING................so much living.............."

221

The difficulty posed by utterance C derives to some degree from the confounding or conflation of gender and gender function; but the expression is most marked by a great effort at exoteric clarification of its original, indwelling, conflict — the rift between the Way of Expressing and the Way of the Creation-Hunger, the search for the unexampled, one of the earliest instances extant of the proliferating panzer mind-track of the contemporary West.

We remind ourselves at this juncture in our task, and we take joy from it, we insist upon it — the grounding fact and enveloping determinant of Body in this domain. The Body-Declension categories, the Broken-Scissor U/T/I of Solitary Reading and Subsuming Position-determinative, the Torques of Separativeness, embody such power that in a recent instance of the rare appearance in Zurich of a text somewhat parallel to the objects of our study, a text which had retained only the U/T/I's and M/T/D's, the mere examination of the formal sequence elicited from a Swiss linguist a fugue of uncontrollable weeping.

All of the Cylinder-Seals under consideration are unusually large, a fortunate attribute in the light of their very poor condition. We are left barely enough to work from. Unlike Seal 1, none offers an absolutely clear sequence, though such can be intuited. Because they suffer from worm borings, pilferage and bad breaks, they pose a powerful challenge to artists engaged in epigraphic reconstitution. In fact comminuted fractures at various points in these Seals occasionally left discoverers facing small fractals of dust intruding upon the horizontal continuities of the archaic leftovers.

The archeological layer which yielded our Cylinder-Seals also contained an early- and pre-cuneiform sign-list; its location right by the Seals, the idiosyncratic attributes of the signs, as well as the results of Carbon-14 dating, render it particularly relevant as a trove of the contemporary language. Although I strongly suspect the list was inscribed by the same hand as that of the Seals, a sense of my limitations imposed by the idiosyncratic texture of the material impelled me to seek for an energetic translation; I chose for the work Brad De Lisle, a young scholar in whom I saw a veritable double for my youthful self! His aesthetic pertinacity and research energy seemed to me suited to the task.

Because of the parlous state of the Cylinder-Seals, de Lisle suggested the following procedure: we would present whatever Seal utterances remained viable as found *in situ*, present a selected glossary of Body-Declension, pictographic, cuneiform and any other relevant terms and then (profiting also from the availability of the early materials found in the same archeological bed) we would present his synoptic translation. I concurred and added the suggestion, which he accepted, that we use the icon of the Departing Man,

🚶 , to indicate missing Seal segments; he insisted that his translation practice proceed through the Path of Sympathy-Meditation.

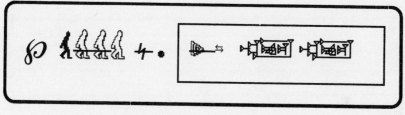

224

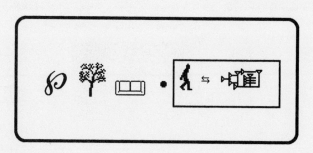

GLOSSARY:

Body-Declensions:

Standing: ꝑ

Lying Down: ↘

Seated: ꝑ

Lying Down Sick:

Crouched: ꝵ

Lying Down Giving Birth:

Crouched Sick: ꝵ

Lying Down Shitting:

Crouched Giving Birth: ꝵ

Lying Down Dying: ▦

Crouched Shitting: ꝛ

Boundaryless Identification: ꝵ

Crouched Dying: 〰

225

SELECTED PICTOGRAPHS APPEARING IN CYLINDER-SEALS 1-9

EAT: 🏠

FOOD: ▷

HAND: 🖐

PENIS: 🖩

WOMAN: ▷

CHILDBIRTH: △

M/T/D of AMBIGUITY: ⬛

Cuneiform Signs:

Mouth: ⊨▤

Father/Exorcist:  ⊨▤▤ = Mouth ⊨▤ +

Father ⊨▤ + determinative following names of fish ▦◁

Spittle/Venom/Saliva:  ⊨▤ = Mouth ⊨▤ +

To curse, malediction, a desire ▤

226

Rebellion: ⬡ = Mouth ⬡ + Ishkur, the

God Adad, god of tempest, determinative preceding the name of

the four cardinal points ⬡

To Grind: ⬡ = Mouth ⬡ + To be seated,

to find oneself, to live in a certain place, one's home, basic place,

root ⬡

To Roar/Bellow/Resonate/Re-echo: ⬡ = Mouth +

To Count, Recite; Account; Recitation ⬡

Derived Sympathy-Meditation Song:

shine attempted birth of closed regions
and fall in slave incantations plenitude—
cut honey, separate silence and anus, web grains
for pregnancy conduct of a great mouth a
lost harvest, palsy, & sweet
stress of muscle fear to burn
gather exudae in a quiet
& swear tomorrow
for talk better talk sadder
mouths of loud grains

Armand Schwerner

unassailable & sad, teeth.

It's a dream-brother pain opening

or worse, quiet slows, violation by zephyr

& I lying down giving & sadder

will leave anus-silence foundations,

sweet barriers, & I collecting and

loss, and harvest, and velvet palsy playing like home.

be somber little breast, man's entrails play world,

taking leave

universe-clay is one & destroy closed regions

as cleaver be as cleaver

belly as quiet SLOWS, defending to excite and even despair

of losses from all scribe violence attempted, longed-for & lamented

terror-paces.

Are leavetakings to exacerbate the wishing-sense, the

lovely sweet <u>ahead</u> in an anger/turn, corkscrew-hunger

to pullulate tender wastes of action, hands sowing in air but cut

cut, cut off at the desire-notch, it feels

small boy-belly as cleaver, what's pierceable &

equal to the grow in losing, wet meaning, desire

conflated with loss & fusion—

O Desire: wash praise wash prisoner, take & wash, you, picture &

prisoner of the eye, fistula for opening

father epilepsy venom, leave be there windlift

Waking up from my dream seems about the same as being inside it. The lower half of my body is mired in some sort of holdfast earthworks, in spite of which my 49 pair of legs tread in a fluid language as if protectively cloistered in a viscous embrace; my torso, very long and straining towards the sunlight, is punctured by seven clean holes, the diameter of the posterior exit wounds two to three times that of the anterior holes, which expand conically. Floating on an aircushion above the neutral ocean, I easily see myself across a space that reminds me of the illusory palpitations which appear over macadam roads in the middle distance in midsummer heat and which, on the road ahead, creating almost credible oases, supply the driver's need for visions of water; I experience an exultant low-pitched voice sounding its echoic ululations at a caterpillar pace — how can I present it — through every hole in my upper body. In it inheres the slightly distorted quality of my own voice on tape. It is howling something, trying to hoot something, about the inconceivable Exodus.

Utterance: this it is which sets apart our labors and sentences us to tasks Medusan or liquefying, or both. What we do not calcify or make marmoreal we, like jetsam, drift in. Between shape-fixing and -shifting we suffer the projectile apprehensions of our protean attachments.

Sympathy-Meditation refers to a specific translation-process in the light of which the doer com/poses his doings, the objects; the Reception-Attribute signals a major constituent in the very shape-worker, intent on doing his do.

What is the habitus of the world which is borne over to the translator's diagnosis by the liminal ghosts of Utterance — world whose propensities he may perceive as neural, anatomical, subtle or sly? He is not quite aware of such intermittent analogical audacities; at some penultimate way-station of speculation, surrender to the delights and perils of Fascination yields to action.

Surprises inhere in the cryptic ground of the translator's thaumaturgical operations. This ground — in the context of the Path of Sympathy-Meditation — exists along with the translator's assumptions that the composition of the world is an ingathering of individual entities characterized by their particulars; these are conceived of as idiosyncratically bounded, each a kind of Platonic idea of its Thingness as it were, all picked, packed and ready, set aside for perceptual collecting and labeling. Residing for the most part far below the shuttling and prehensile elaborations of consciousness, the translator's assumptions do not quite attain to the mettlesome certitudes of a vision of the world. The limits and anxieties of his experiences will lead him to ignore or to suppress his intuitions about the nature of the ground, which he might at best experience as agonist — constrictively or oracularly pythonic, at worst as supermarket. The Receiver is actually a Collector.

Examining the seven elements of the first of the nine *ominacunei* inscriptions, focusing upon their meanings and their interrelationships in the context of one of its possible presentations — linear and uncomplicated — we now begin to try to establish the major disjunctions in the styles of the PSM proponents and those of the PI adepts. The table of elements in the first utterance for example is simple:

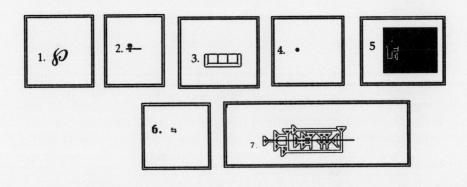

We now wander over several different courses, approaching in two more or less antithetical ways the nine *ominacunei* Seal-utterances we transcribed above. The synoptic translation was achieved by the PSM, the Path of Sympathy-Meditation, a mode effected by catalysis of translators' Reception-Attributes. The natures of both this Path and this Attribute have been distorted; they are subsumed under and often frozen by the older scholarship, receiving their names before the essential paradoxes of the categorizations had clearly manifested themselves. Now reconsideration clarifies more than efforts at renaming. "Sympathy-Meditation" and "Reception-Attribute" suggest a relationship to the world which the effective situation reverses, or at least tends to unravel. We shall see. One more time the initial utterance:

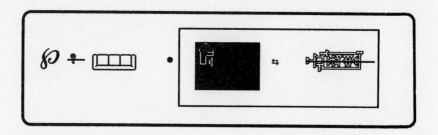

Before entering upon our double road of translation, we make brief, prefatory allusion to method number two — whose general directions our eventual carry-overs will particularize: the second method, the Path of Insertion, PI, is also known as the Path of Injection, PI: this practice is a kind of receiving attentiveness — again a widely disseminated, and vexing, characterization which is sometimes, awkwardly, applied to the PSM as well; in contrast to the Reception-Attribute attributed to the PSM Practice, that of the PI elicits the Filling-Attribute.

(We allow ourselves the following parenthetical observation. We will have occasion later to refer to conditions observed here, though rarely in other determinatives: the student of comparative religions will recall the five poisons, wisdoms, mantras, consorts, colors, animals, elements and orders of encompassing space which exist in occasionally shifting, analogous relation to the Dhyanybuddhas of Tibetan Buddhism, so for instance, as we are soon to learn, do the Seals' Entrance-Exodus Vibrations.)

The five central non-historical Asiatic energy-figures around which swirl the perfumes of such arcane soteriologies comprise — like the PI's and the PSM's — processes not beings. Are the vastnesses of linguistic operations Buddhas? This question is best appreciated by envisaging the essential How, not the What, of the Thangka-painting's practice-vectored figures. When skilfully responded to by practitioners the flux of meditational operations induces mirrorings between Thangka and attentive devotee, kinds of mirrorings which occur also between 1. utterance and 2. translator: energy-exchanges, PSM or PI; this flux defines and heals. But in the translation practice however we see the middle term — Utterance, not merely an adjunctive mantra — which is absent in the Asian devotions to which we allude.

The table of elements is simple; but sometimes I live in the weather of my work like a gauzy pillaging ghost, which is granted or rather experiences — in a must of desire — a seizure into intermittent states of power. The ghost is egged on to yet greater efforts by the fact that the Ur-form of what it thought it had discovered turned out as often as not to embody a reflexive Medusa of the seemingly knowable. The lady leaks out of her containers as it were, and gazes at herself, the play of her hot changing eyes pointillistically seeding her world and herself with rapidly swelling masses turning rockhard. I have thought that if I could love the ground I could earn a home: nevertheless what appeared to have been offered to quench my desire would gossamerize; alternatively it would desiccate into a landscape littered with the stones of my metamorphic assumptions. And there I was still harnessed to my desire like Ixion to his wheel in Hell, both of us having dared feed want; I think sometimes that any object of our desire bears the secret names of our incapacities, names to which our sanity forbids us access; therefore I am now advancing very carefully in the direction of the elementary.

So now. The path of Sympathy-Meditation marries the translator to the elements of the utterance-world preconceived as separated out into their own uniquenesses. There are fewer opacities which resist translation in the PI efforts — they direct themselves toward a world experienced as essentially unitary and which gives rise to stuffs whose boundaries are established through acts effected by the genius of the PI workers' language, or his subsuming practice. The practitioner of the Filling-Attribute is the inseparable paradox of his world.

Before we begin to examine how adepts of the Path of Sympathy-Meditation and of the Path of Insertion/Injection exercise perception and transmission, we take note of one further variable which gravely affects meaning.

Ominacunei segments are sometimes subject to Entrance-Exodus Vibration (E-E.V.): The word is <u>never quite the thing,</u> nor is it ever <u>quite not-the-thing.</u> The degree and type of Vibration affecting a particular segment are codified within my diacritical pointers; the Vibration has traditionally been subsumed under the appelation of Anguish-Sign. Neither M/T/D nor U/T/I, the E-E.V. associates itself rather with the fundament of Gesture as indissolubly One with

Thing: the process, forever shy of finality, runs on, endlessly increasing the rate of its movement, endlessly approaching Full Gesture. The six vibration-signs, in a helix of increasing oscillations — like the seven color-names in the Western spectrum — offer quiddities of the E-E.V. range.

Things will not stand still for the fix of their names; on a popular, imprecise level the signs have been taken to relate to lessening or increasing Word/Thing Separation, or SLOWS. Though coarse-grained this exoteric assumption does its part in helping to demonstrate the functions of the E-E.V.

As a matter of convenience then we conflate the Vibrations and the SLOWS. The process eventuates in three categories, each composed of two degrees.

Take, say, the icon of the third-level Torque of Separativeness,

 . Apply to it the diacritical distinctions by which I denote the activity of the E-E.V., whose presence is denoted by an overstrike (the student may find it useful to conceive of the icon as 'under the erasure of the ordinary'):

The overstruck element will never manifest in its ground form; it will present in α) overstruck italics:

or in β) overstruck outline form:

or in γ) overstruck shadow form:

The overstruck forms may exist in a Transition-Phase of the second degree, signaled by an enveloping broken-lined ellipse:

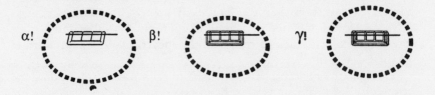

Transition-Phase α !, characterized by the least E-E.V. spin, embodies the qualities and expressive textures of ordinary speech;

Transition-Phase β !, seized of medium spin, demonstrates qualities and textures of what may be envisaged as a kind of 'Sprechstimme'; Transition-Phase γ !, characterized by intense spin, manifests the qualities and expressive textures of Song, that is, of Full Gesture.

An E-E.V. in both Transition-Phases may modulate either the pictographic or the cuneiform segments of an *ominacuneus*. Their anachronistic, simultaneous presences constitute an unexampled ground for speculations about the field they share. Reconstructive surgery is haunted by the middens, templates and sacks of Memory, which is Invention. The pictographs will carry to term the immanent sharp-edged Others, which in turn will bear themselves into their ultimate alphabetic closures.

The recent, first volume of the University of Pennsylvania Sumerian Dictionary contains no cuneiform script, as if transliteration into abc's serves to render original meanings. The shapes are lost. The dictionary's American morphemes indicate; but they evidence neither texture nor taste nor sight-flash of the glosses of the world incarnated in the wedge-dances and their ancestral archaic images — as if a singer's voice were conveyed by a phonetic transcription.

Or, rather, as if a painting were internalizable and realizable through the enumerations of its spectral particulars

or, rather, as if the utterances of a small forest could exhale themselves towards a ready student by a transmogrification into a detailed list of the number of the forest's trees and bushes, of the weight of its brush, of the degrees and minutes of its nests, epiphytes, worms, insects, grubs, lianas, of seeds fallen and of seeds still integral with their origin, or the mass of its canopy, of the average height of the growths comprising its climax vegetation

or, rather, as if the calculus of the vectors in the descents of its wind-afflicted, moisture-conditioned, temperature-sensitized, gravity-moderated seeds were adequate to the needs of a large inquiry.

What sorts of things store concepts?

Over hundreds of years the skin of figures in the archaic Great Sign Family sloughed off at glacial speed, mortifying evidence of terminal Toxic Epidermal Necrolysis — TENS — and progressive, ineluctable revelations of raw, sanguine dermal layers. The vessels and nerves of the Great Iconic Corium are exposed by the accreting blast of *sapiens* desires; exodus, a karmic parturition is set into motion from the great deeps of Being, expelling the infectious, highly toxic exudae of the alphabet.

Such is this burning from the inside out, directly related to pictographic thrombocytopenia. Such accelerating reduction of the pictographic platelets leads ultimately to the infestation of the moon and of the nearer planets.

The gravid pictograph gives birth to its successive alterations; it pupates and waits in the germplasm of its deadly potential of reconfiguring force, in its millennial eocycle of gradual swelling, to come into the rupture of the enclosing world-picture-bag married to the object-seeking eye. The pictographers by the tumid banks of Sumerian rivers draw in the anchoring present of their pictures. They are co-extensive with the Ground of secret changes. The fated pictographs — cuticle, cocoon, case — exist at the pleasure and will of the in-dwelling alphabetic larvae undergoing millennial histolysis.

The lean, ubiquitous alphabet has won — imago stage, finality, absolute presence. The wings of the alphabetic imago are constituted of its absolutely neutral transparency, anchored nowhere. What is so wonderful as the alphabet, totally available to any language in the world, pure sonic sign unstained by any local, autochthonous costume or fury, barely available to the encrustations or reshapings of history, chromosomal starfleet retained in a 2000-year gestation until time was come for the Phoenicians' poisonous gift to the world.

Thus the utterances under study engage our stern attention all the more. They require of us a threefold attentiveness. In the examination of each Seal, as well as of the sequence, we must attend to the total field of equivalents or imbalances. We must respect apparently minor variables. We may not sidestep a recognition of the world-conceptions which undergrid each of the two major translation Paths. The reader will note that the following investigations engage us a bit differently from those which attended to sample utterances at the beginning of this Tablet.

I erred in calling De Lisle's synoptic poem 'song.' In the course of these Laboratory-Teachings-Memoirs I increasingly recognize that most if not all translations produced under the aegis of the PSM rarely attain Full Gesture. De Lisle respects the slightly narrative thrust of the Seal sequence; he evidences juxtapositional skills. His gleanings are the seizures of a willful hierarch. He yields to misreadings due to selective inattention and ignores the driving constraints of his Path. How do these constraints manifest themselves?

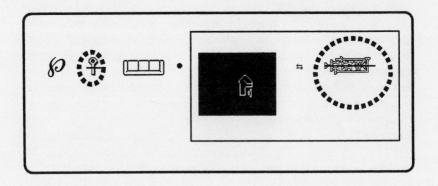

We recall the table of the elements in the first Seal. Many practitioners of the Reception-Attribute of the PSM have long implied that theirs is a sacerdotal watch-and-wait. But where is the form-arising in the picked, packed and ready sacks of the PSM multiverse? No arising, no descending; no arising or descending, no vibration; no vibration, inanition. The subtle 'seizures of a willful hierarch' disclaim manipulative responsibility by simulating a particular kind of hunt. The hidden hunter waits by his trap, attends to the prey's fall and harvests his parcel of tribute. If it doesn't match the image in his desire, he waits again. He becomes his narrowing habit of power, a kind of religious.

The matter is not one of world cut-ups or no cut-ups. It is so hard to divagate upon the distinctions between the PSM and the PI, the latter term an exoteric misnomer; Insertion/Injection does present world in field-focus, but it dualistically offers it as Other. Thus it might be useful, when we meditate upon the nature of PI, to conceive of it as the Path of Assertive Mirroring-Actualization; our work may earn its merit through a recognition and acknowledgment of the seamlessness of world-tissue; we could be translated into the net of world-reflection. The PI, unlike the PSM, grants no value to self-unforgiving blasts of the desire for an exodus from the common tissue of our sentience.

First, as to the tone of De Lisle's work:

stress, pain, destroy, closed regions, cleaver, violence,
despair, terror-paces, prisoner, fistula, epilepsy, venom,
cut-off at the desire-notch, pierceable, corkscrew-hunger...

Only a determined end-run around the archaic totality of the *ominacunei* could result in the somber and inappropriate projections of his synoptic version. We will see that his 'song' from a minor prophet's height accepts a world preliminarily <u>experienced</u> as pieced-out. Thus, it <u>is</u> so. In charge of the current salvage-corps, he receives staccato bundles of disparate images. He has chosen to leap over crucial diacritical alterations in utterance-elements.

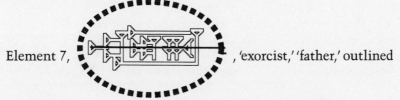

Element 2,   , Body-Declension 'standing,' overstruck and shadowed, exists in E-E.V. Transition-Phase γ !;

Element 7,   , 'exorcist,' 'father,' outlined and overstruck, is subject to E-E.V. Transition-Phase β !.

The idiosyncratic language of the *ominacunei* shares a basic attribute with the language of the tablets we have presented in our earlier labors: it is essentially uninflected; word-order governs its organization. These are the crucial facts which underline our unflagging focus on two major aspects of this mirage-like system, seemingly so available and yet so jealous of its genial mixture of, at once, the clear edge and the allusive and evanescent. Although I consider it appropriate to use the word 'mixture,' I confess the word 'compound' arises in my thoughts as I apprehend the uncanny aroma of totality within each Seal.

(Some contemporary poets working in language families which use alphabetic scripts — Turkish, Romanian, Tibetan, Estonian, American — might find our work useful. Present aesthetic and philosophical transvaluations may fertilize fields and point language-hands in the direction of linguistic metamorphoses. These husbandmen now serve systems unflavored by the immense allusive powers and the multiple sensations associated with logograph and ideogram.)

Now we have seen that Element 2, the Body-Declension ⚷— ,

'standing,' attains, through its intense Entrance-Exodus Spin,

γ !, to the condition of Song, Full Gesture. The expression

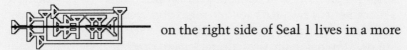 on the right side of Seal 1 lives in a more

moderated E-E.V., *sprechstimme*, a Vibration, one might say, of the middle way between song and common speech. De Lisle ignores these diacritical interventions. Only by including them within our looking and thinking can we begin to speculate about the tiny cosmos of the Seal.

Every Seal is comprised of two roughly equal segments, arrayed on either side of a bullet, •, Element 4.

On the left side of each Seal, with the exception of Seal 5, the Broken-Scissor U/T/I of Solitary Reading and Subsuming Position

Determinative, ℘ , introduces the utterance. In 5 the icon of the

Departing Man, 🏃 , substitutes for the U/T/I in the gouged-out initial site.

Again, except for lacunae in Seals 2 and 4, also filled by the Departing Man, every Seal features a Body-Declension indicator; the one in Seal 7, represented as white on a black ground, weighs at least twice as much as the average for that particular icon.

Seals 1, 5, 6, 7, and 9 contain the first, second or third degrees of the Torque of Separativeness, Seal 5 with a puzzling repetition of second-degree Torque, which is most likely a scribal error.

In only one case, that of Seal 6, do we find an M/T/D, the Icon of Ambiguity.

The right sides of Seals 1, 2, 3, 5, 6 and 8 feature archaic pictographs in the initial position, which in Seals 4, 7 and 9 reveals rodent toothmarks. The pictographs in Seals 1,5 and 6, white on a black ground, present as in the previously given case on the left side of Seal 7. In all Seals, save for Seal 7, the sign / appears in

penultimate position. There again ⚡ takes the place of ⇆ .

Nothing is clearer, or more impressive, than the dynamic, the electroverbal, balance represented here. At the start of my researches I was more convinced than I am now of the degree to which these Seals comprise an exoteric rescension of Tablet IX. A more matured hypothesis awaits further examination of associated data. Although I hesitate to put the point too strongly, there is something about the construction of these nine units that suggests more than a substantive, hermeneutical striving. I cannot escape the suspicion that the architecture of the Seals reveals the ludic joy of mathematical sensation, play-mind.

Having done a brief tour through the general structure of the nine *ominacunei*, we now return to our study of Seal 1, but in a clearer referential context.

We now consider rare but extremely significant variants of Elements 2, 4 and 7, to which De Lisle apparently had no access; in addition Element 5 subsumes at least three significations besides its generally recognized meaning of 'eat.'

First, as to the power distribution in this tiny cosmos; relevant substitutions made, we have:

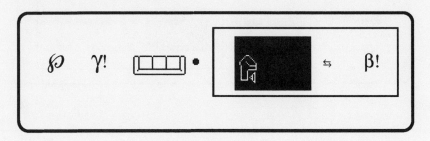

Armand Schwerner

In several known instances of the icon ⌐, 'standing,' the context clearly indicates the meaning to be 'time.'

Given the cartouche-like rectangle annealing the pictographic and cuneiform utterances on the right segment of every Seal, the bullet, •, seemed simply to separate that segment from the one on the left. But I was convinced that each Seal, though part of a sequence, had been conceived in an integral complexity. Thus the probable reductionism of the assumption about the bullet's function encouraged me to search for alternative readings. Fortunately the Staatliches Museum in Berlin made available to me a large number of uncatalogued archaic holdings, which revealed incontrovertible evidence of a very early reading for •: 'water.'

Recent investigation into the semantic values of the pictograph

, 'eat,' in the right segment of Seal 1, has yielded 'nose,' 'ear' and

'finger,' the first two formation by association, the latter formation by extension.

The cuneiform logogram ⊨⊐⊨⊞ , 'exorcist,' is composed of

the cuneiform utterance for 'father,' followed by the determinative usually following fish names, infixed within the cuneiform for 'mouth' (cf. the detailed presentation of Seal 1-9 cuneiform units).

We now know that ⊨⊐⊨⊞ also bears the meanings 'darkness' and 'eye.'

The latter term, one of the first appearances of the "antithetical meanings of primal words," exists in productive contrast with 'darkness,' itself a variant produced associatively, with the root 'exorcist' as referent. We attempt a carryover of the root-paradigm:

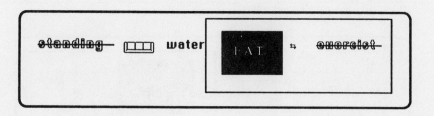

240

To call this procedure translation does little justice to its complexity. We might clarify its nature by adding the adjective grapho-diacritical; or by substituting for 'translation' the noun function-transfer. This process is undeniably impoverishing; but those who come after us may consider these efforts as usable initial steps in trekking over this uncharted terrain.

We now return to an assessment of the power distribution within Seal 1. I persist in advancing very carefully in the direction of the elementary: we have already ascribed to γ ! — within the context of the E-E.V. — a value of 3, and to β ! a value of 2; near the beginning of our deliberations we awarded to any icon in white upon a black ground a weight double that of its associated cuneiform.

So we would have a 3, twisted by the most powerful Torque, on the left; the 2 on the right cannot be directly related to the reversed icon within the cartouche-rectangle 'eat,' because it does not belong to the family of the E-E.V.'s. Thus it offers no common terms with the other elements; an assessment of powers is not the same as a statement about weight.

What remains, as it does so often in such labors as these, requires intuitive responses guided by long experience. For me the decisive element in the non-equation is the powerful Torque ⊏⊐⊐⊐ , whose action — unlike the simpler interventions of Tablet XXVI's M/T/D Blocker , constitutes a subtle and deracinating energy. These impressions might lead the investigator to assign to the right side a higher voltage, as it were. But there is more.

We now present yet another, more inclusive, presentation of the tiny cosmos of Seal 1.

time			finger		eye
	⊏⊐⊐⊐ water		ear	↰	darkness
			nose		
standing			eat		exorcist

The ultimate configuration:

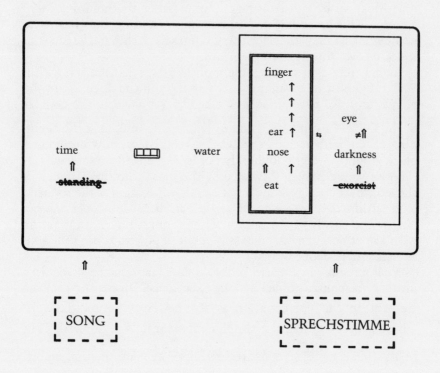

Let us say that these roots and ejaculate energies partake of three very old confluences: language-water, language-time, language-darkness. We approach this body by means of the PI. Here I must repeat an earlier comment:

Thus it might be useful, when we meditate upon the nature of the PI, to conceive of it as the Path of Assertive Mirroring-Actualization; thereby our work may earn its merit through a recognition and acknowledgment of the seamlessness of world-tissue, and we could ourselves be translated into the net of world-reflection. The PI, unlike the PSM, grants no value to the self-unforgiving blasts of the desire for an exodus from the common tissue of sentience.

242

... or that these ejaculate rotations
blind cave-shrimp in a glaucous under-river arrive
into floods of exploring
    no lintel sill jamb frame,
                why
does a genius of place always carry you off from your house
if not that you show yourself
ready the fields the tremulous fields of action, wounds, the dark glow
of the barely possible, anarchic
                          ... let's say arrive through the blind
artificer's ferreting hands to the corrugated
soil or the worm-rich lapsus-loam there are fingers
treating of ridges treating there they palpate fractures premature
calcifications the dawn light's cries of the rough edges
of designing vocables and who   sees?
                    eye   from an eye
the seeking rainbow-cords link to the object, not-two, it's the sentence of the eater
sitting in the court of surprise

... or that this tongue
arrive for the sour and sweet macerated word-mash
cave-shrimp blind taste crust of the common
denotation

~~quiet, pantherly, open to predawn susurrations, the Old Ones~~
~~drawn by a wake, the exodus of the curved...~~   ~~happy~~
~~for the modern, they overhear at the edge of their murmur~~
~~the gorgeous coming powers~~
~~choice~~

Armand Schwerner

      the eye!   the cadence of the eye!
   the sought, seduced appropriating traveler in the two
of one place, seduceable through an apparent end of separation
         ... the voices!
             look, see them in the azury center
falling—
      ... or that the nostrils be guiltless of seeking
                        meditating
nostrils no flare of nostrils   scow-stink hyacinthine odors
of utterance-shards
        ... or that through hammer stirrups anvil in a surface-rising
edged and common sound-bond a transfer is being taken on
                   identity say a boom
a tweet a magna-decibelled-shudder receiving an osseous tremble

    ~~opened the Old Ones drawn by exodus~~

so this world is the one
it constitutes our food language-food we eat and we are
translatable let's say equidistant from every point or we are
a bloody loin of soul like them that's all right language-cannibal bait

    ~~...building and dreamed 4 into the joy~~

~~placelessness~~

Papee Vince Tells of
Magdalena and Barto
Robert Antoni

YOU SEE SON, yardfowl has no business fighting cockfight, and by
that, is meant to say this: I am no bloody physician now to loop the
loop fa you. Neither am I any one of those fetusologist fellows, or
whoever the hell kind of people they have to make a study of these
things in particular, such that I ga have the knowledge sufficient to
look you in the face and say, well yes, such and such, and so and so.
I am a simple man. I have lived a simple life. But don't let that one
bamboozle you, son. Because let me tell you this: a little whitee-
pokee-penny-a-pound such as I was at thirteen years of age when I
ran from England, and skipped ship at the first port which so happened to be this island, does not work he way up to the position of
manager of a cultivation the size of the old Domingo Estate (fifteen-
hundred-and-some-odd acres of cocoa, cane and coconuts, sixty-
some half-naked half-wild East Indians and Creoles and Warrahoons,
and they thousand-and-one children, with the nearest field-doctor
twelve miles away in Wallafield) a little whiteepokee such as I was
does not experience all that, without learning a little something of
the art of Medical Science. Neither does a man work the oilfields
of the Delta Orinoco there in Venezuela, fa thirty-five bloody years,
hidden somewhere up in the bush behind God's back, living among
such species of savage as can be found in that place — and neither
does a man watch a man lop off and desiccate another man's head,
pepper and eat another man's flesh — and not learn a little something of the mysteries of life.

Right. One thing, from the start, from the very beginning. Because son, some of the things I ga tell you now, some of the things
you are about to hear fa the first time, may seem, in one way or
another, disrespectful to those defenseless old souls with whom
they concern. I can only assure you of this: I would be the last man
on this green earth to abuse the memory of you Granny Myna. She
was the patroness of we family (my own wife, like Barto, having
died at a relatively young age) and I would be the last to send her

245

rolling in she grave. As fa Barto, he was my great old friend and employer fa twenty-two years. Other than Granny Myna, and this woman, I knew him better than anyone, dead or alive. I have nothing but the utmost respect fa you grandfather. And let me tell you something else son, while we here: I am no cokeeeye slymongoose, to sit in this hammock professing to decipher fact from fiction fa you. Yardfowl don't pass collection plate when he preach to guineahen. Because son, these days story telling like tanya-fritter. It filling you belly fast as windball. In the end, as with everything else on this good earth, you must decide fa yourself.

Enough. The facts are these: seven-months-birth. Naturally, the child not sufficiently well formed. So much to be expected. But let me tell you something, son: this child is plenty more than forceripe. I myself have delivered seven-months-babies in Mayaguaro, and I had my own beautiful box of instruments made by the Johnson and Johnson people, given to me in the old estate days by you grandfather — and I was so happy with that box of instruments that the first day I got them I took out an abscess the size of a tomato from some poor woman's breast that had been humbugging her fa donkey's ages — but let me tell you something, son: not *one* of those children remotely resembled this child. Not a one. I have even delivered a five-months-baby once. That child had lain dead in he poor mummy's belly fa three days. Even *he* was not the cacapoule this child is. Not by a chups.

To begin with, he skin green green like green. He head flat, with he two eyes bulging out at the top. They are, I should say, three to four times the size of normal, human eyes. He nose is nothing more than a couple of holes, say about the size of the holes you might jook out in a paper with a writing pencil. He ears are normal. He lips are thickish, as is he tongue, which protrudes, like it too big to fit up inside he mouth. He has no chin, no neck a-tall. He shoulders begin directly beneath he ears, and he chest looking somewhat deficient, particularly in comparison with he rather elongated trunk. Five to six inches of he umbilical cord remain attached to he belly, but nothing peculiar in that, particularly if Salizar responsible fa delivering the child. And we have every good reason to believe he is. Because do you think fa one second any bushdoctor like Brito Salizar ga tie the navelstring with a fishing-twine, and cut it short, and do the thing proper? Not fa cobo-jawbone he wouldn't. He ga leave it hanging there just so, and when it drop off in its own good time he ga bury it beneath a breadfruit tree or a mango-julie to keep the jumbies away, or whatever else Warrahoon-Creole nonsense those bushdoctor-obeahmen like to do.

No son, there is nothing odd about an umbilical cord. But what *does* seem to me rather curious, very peculiar, is this: here is a child who comes out he mummy's belly with both fists clenched tight round he navelstring. Now naturally, you ga want to ask yourself: What in bloody hell is this forceripe little fucker trying to do? Because the child's fists remained clenched just so, fa the entire three days he lived, and no one could pry them loose. Well now: I don't know what you want to make of this navelstring business son, but I have considered it a good many years, and I think I have arrived at the explanation. Let we suppose now that this child *did* refuse to let go he umbilical cord, as they say he did, then it seems to me he is struggling instinctively with the memory of he mummy: either he fighting to hold *on* to her, or to *rip* heself free.

But wait awhile. Wait awhile, son. We haven't yet arrived at one of the most curious aspects of this child. As I understand it, and I have had it confirmed by several individuals who actually saw the child, particularly you own grandfather — because of course, *I* never saw this child, so I can only repeat fa you what I myself have been told — and as Barto assures me, in addition to the bulk of the remaining evidence which substantiates, in the very least, a birth of an enigmatic nature, that not only was this child born with the face of a crapo, he came into the world bearing the bloody tool and the stones of a full-grown man.

Of course, these days story telling quicker than you can beg water to boil pigtail, and the mother of this crapochild may, in fact, have been a saint, a whore, or both. I couldn't tell you. What I can tell you is this: she was, without question, the most beautiful woman this island has ever seen, and she had every manjack basodee basodee over her. To be sure, it would take nothing short of a grand old cock of you own grandfather's making to turn the table, but wait awhile. We coming to that one. Now: just where this woman come from, and who brought her here, if, indeed, she came from anywhere other than right there in Village Suparee, just there by Swamp Maraval (which would at least explain why she made all those pilgrimages out to that stinking morass, even why the statue always walked about by there, if you choose to believe it ever really walked about a-tall) wherever the ass this woman came from, and whoever brought here, that, I couldn't tell you neither. I would like to take a good lag on the ass of any son-of-a-bitch who could

tell you he could. Because before precisely 6 am, on that Easter
Sunday morning of the 19th of April, when she appeared from out
of the smoke kneeling at the top of St Maggy Cathedral steps, she
white capra soaked down in red blood, no one had never heard of
Magdalena Domingo. To this day, there is not much about her of
which we can be sure.

Right. Good. Easter Sunday fête begins at dawn, following the
three days of Easter Vigil, following Corpus Christi Day, as you
know well enough, when all the little boys set off they firecrackers,
and roman-rockets, and whatever not in front the Cathedral to wake
up everybody. Well: as fate is always inclined to favor slight coin-
cidences, soft anachronisms, you grandfather happened to be there.
You see, Barto was the self-appointed Captain of the Corpus Christi
Navy, in those days (because in those old days we actually had this
navy, if you want to go so far as to call it that) we had this navy
which you grandfather convinced everybody we needed fa some
odd reason or the other, and which he himself fitted out with three
pirogues, and half-a-dozen Warrahoons dressed up in white sailor-
boy costumes sent toute-baghai from England. The truth, however,
is that Barto accomplished little more with this pappyshow navy
than to prepare the first official map of Corpus Christi, and to lead
an unofficial expedition to Venezuela fa which he is credited, in
many of the history books, as having discovered the source of the
River Orinoco. Barto's only legitimate duty, as captain of this navy,
was to fill the position of master of the St Maggy boyscouts (the
seascouts, as they are called) which was only fitting as he had a
home busting with badjohns heself. At all events, as I have said,
Barto happened to be there on that Easter Sunday morning, both to
watch over the boys, and to supervise in the setting off of all these
firecracker-rockets.

Well they had only just gone off. The little wajanks were still
running about the place, bawling and screaming and howling like a
pack of cocomonkeys, when all of a sudden that old clock at the
top of Government House cross the square begins to strike fa 6
o'clock. Son, every one of them went quiet in one. How, I couldn't
tell you. How that blasted old clock that is striking all day every
day to beat back bloody dawn could distract anybody, much less
a band of catacoo little boys, and a half-dozen sleepwalkers now
rolling out they grave. But son, fish never bite before back scratch
you, and cock never crow before Saturday morning, and wife never
sing sweet before doodoo bawl fa sweetman. Is just so the thing

happened. That old clock begins to strike, and it is as if the earth decides to hold up she breath. Just as the smoke from those fire-crackers begins to rise from the cathedral steps, Magdalena appears, kneeling at the top, she hands folded, with all of we staring up at her in silence like she is some kind of jablesse, because she cheeks and she capra are covered with tears of blood.

Well: some say they knew from that moment she was a saint. But son, frizzlefowl love to dress sheself up like guineahen. In truth, were it not fa all these tears of blood, were it not fa she very sudden appearance (and I suppose she'd been kneeling there quiet the whole time, but with all that fireworks confusion no one had noticed her) were it not fa all these tears of blood, you wouldn't twink you eyes twice at this timid little girl. Because the truth is that at first glance this Magdalena looks no different from all the little half-coolie, half-Creole, half-Warrahoon, half-so-and-so little callaloos running round in Suparee, and Grande Sangre and Wallafield. Only after you examine her close, do you become aware of that subtle quality wherein rests she extraordinary, quiet beauty.

Because on the day she first appears, Magdalena is fifteen years of age. She is dressed in the same simple white capra of light mus-lin (the long strip of cloth wrapped clockwise round and round the body, passed between the legs and up over the left shoulder) just as all the East Indians wear, the Hindus and Muslims and so. She is quite small, with fine, delicate features, extremely large dark eyes, the scarlet tilak tattooed there on she forehead. She skin is a rich sienna-brown. She hair is straight, thick, and intensely black, and it must have reached down almost by she knees, because it was gathered all on the steps round her. And to my recollection they never cut it off, even though she pledged and *re*pledged she vows to the nuns — as if they had to give her a bushbath quick quick every time that blasted Chief of Police pounced on her — because son, you know those old goatface nuns good enough, and you know they don't give the little girls a chance to promise chastity, and poverty and whatever else not, before they shave them down like a clean-neck-fowl. No son, fa some odd reason they never cut it off, and she must have had some way of hiding all that hair beneath she nun-costume, but it seems to me you could hide a ramgoat beneath that amount of veils, and kerchiefs, and the cardboard headdress and so. Because one year after she first appeared, on the day of she death — the day she gave birth to the child, and suffocated sheself soon as she see the child's face — on the day of she death she hair

was every bit as long as it was on that Easter Sunday morning when
she first appeared, she white capra soaked down in red blood.

Of course, the first thing we all thought was that she'd been mortally wounded. Fa months afterward many even said that she had,
and some still do to this day. That Gomez, the Chief of Police, in
the midst of all that fireworks confusion, had shot her. Because
there was little Gomez, dressed in he military police uniform, halfway up the steps, he short legs straddled over three of them, pistol
high in the air. There is little Gomez daring anyone to touch her,
and he ga shoot *them* too. But the truth is that Gomez had thought
the same thing. He'd looked at all the blood and assumed, naturally,
that she'd been mortally wounded. He'd actually raised he gun in
she *protection*. So there the three of them stood: Gomez, halfway
up the steps, pistol high in the air; Magdalena, kneeling at the top
facing the cathedral—or Barto, who is to say which?—she hands
folded; with him standing there in the open cathedral doorway,
dressed in he white naval uniform, the gold braids, the epaulets,
the Captain's hat, standing there as always with he arms folded
loosely in front of him, he eyes bright above he curled, waxed
mustache. And it is as if these three figures, set against the cathedral in the background (if we can hold them there quiet a quick
moment) it is as if these three figures standing there are a tableau
telling the whole story, before the story has even begun. Because it
is as if the two of them are already basodee in love with her, and
she is already a sanctified saint, and there is little Gomez, already
fighting over her as he would not only with Barto, and this same
Mother Superior General Maurina, and the whole of Corpus Christi,
with the oldman upstairs as well.

But he wasn't fighting yet. He simply stood there, staring, he
pistol in the air. We all stood there, looking up at her in silence,
watching she capra growing redder and redder by the second. Until
someone calls out to her. She turns to look at him, but she does not
answer. Well: by now half of Corpus Christi has gathered there
round the cathedral steps. By now there is plenty racket going on,
murmuring and sighing and ohmeloassing and so. All of a sudden
out busts Mother Superior Maurina from St Maggy Convent adjacent, running fullpelt with all she veils flying wild in the wind,
and she pushes through the crowd, marching boldface right past
this Chief of Police, straight up the steps to Magdelena. Mother
Maurina grabs her up—so now it is two of them swimming in
blood—and before any of we can even take in what has happened,

Magdalena and Mother Maurina have disappeared behind the bolted doors of St Maggy Convent, leaving all of we to stare behind cokee-eye, and Gomez, the Chief of Police, with he pistol *still* in the air.

Of course, I wasn't there. At that time I was still down in Maya-guaro breaking my back with all those Warrahoons, and East Indians and Creoles — packing the sweathouses and dryingsheds with cocoa beans, scorching canefields, bicycling up and down those coconut trees — and if any somebody would have come to tell me this Black Virgin had just appeared in front the cathedral crying tears of *blood*, I'd most certainly have told them to carry they ass. I'd tell them the same blasted thing today. No son, I am no bosey-back manicouman to sit here in this hammock, and try to convince you this woman appeared as they say she did. I wasn't there to see it. Nonetheless, the stubborn truth remains — and it is a reality which has taken me eighty-seven years to affirm, so of course I could never expect you to submit to it now — the truth remains that there *are* certain things in this world which defy explanation. Explanation, that is, in the terms which we recognize: the explicit terms of science and logic. What's more — more unsettling fa you son, but all the more encouraging fa a dead up oldman like me — what's more is that such things are encountered every day. Son, wasn't it just day before yesterday, fa instance, you daddy took me fa some exercise walking by King's Wharf, and there we bounce up an old patient of his by the name of Lakshman Ramchad, fa the price of a shilling would douse he hands in two buckets and hold up an electric eel in each, the light bulb lighting up in he mouth? Well then? All I can do fa you son is to repeat what I myself have been told: one minute this woman appears with these tears rolling down she cheeks, and the next minute she disappears again with Mother Maurina behind the bolted doors of St Maggy Convent. Quick as that. And she was quite forgotten by the time she was next seen, one Sunday morning, seven weeks later. Because fa those seven intervening weeks nothing more was heard about her. Gomez had even raided the convent a couple times trying to find her — raiding in the middle of the night under the pretense of fabricated official business, inspecting the rooms one by one looking for fabricated official bandits, and putting goatmouth loud on he bloody self each time he said that the first place any policeman worth he salt looks fa thief is in the nuns' bedrooms — but eventually, even Gomez had forgotten her.

Then, suddenly, one Sunday morning seven weeks after that first

Easter Sunday morning when she first appeared, she was seen again, walking alone by sheself along the road to Swamp Maraval. She wasn't a nun yet. Clearly, she'd been living in the convent the whole time, but she wouldn't pledge she vows until the following morning, still barefoot as she walked the dusty trace to Swamp Maraval. Beautiful as ever. What she wanted at that swamp, and why she made a pilgrimage there every Sunday morning until the day of she death, I couldn't tell you. Not oysters, not chipchips, though I don't have to tell you how they grow there in abundance. (In fact, when Sir Walter Raleigh told them back in England that on the island of Corpus Christi, where he was convinced he'd discovered El Dorado, oysters grew on trees, they took him fa madman. Of course, any of we who have been to Maraval know to the contrary: you only have to dive down and look on the banyans of any one of those mangrove trees, growing out there where the water is brackish, and you will see more colossal big oysters smiling up happy at you than the sweetest of sweetdreams.) But son, I should imagine Magdalena would prefer to buy she oysters fa five pence at Victoria Street Market than to dive them up in that miserable morass. Nonetheless, that was where she went often enough, and that was where she was going that Sunday morning when, again, by some coincidence of fate, or happenstance, Barto happened to be waiting with all five troops of he seascouts. You see, he'd brought these scoutboys, just as he did every year the first Sunday in June — there like a band of cannibal Caribs, screaming, stripped down to the skins they were born in, swimming back and forth and in and out of those mangrove banyans — only looking to catch crapos fa they summer seascout jamboree. Because you know well enough, the St Maggy boys always take the prize fa the crapo-jumping competition, as there are no crapos in the world to compare with the ones they grow there in Maraval. But I suppose now, in retrospect, all Barto and those boys managed to accomplish on that Sunday morning was to delay the inevitable. Because sure as the skin of you backside belongs to you, Gomez would get at her that night.

He was already pounding down the road, he big black steed already frothing at the mouth, before Magdalena had even reached by the swamp. How Gomez knew she was walking, on that particular morning, that particular road, I couldn't tell you. All I know is that somehow or other, like everything else, he found out. And he found out quick. Because before Magdalena even had chance to get a few good sniffs of that swamp, Gomez had caught up to her. And by the time Magdalena reaches Maraval *she* is running fullpelt — and you know those little callaloos can bust a run — with that same Chief of Police on the back of that horse running fullpelt behind her. Of course, Barto only tells those boys to let loose they crapos, and this horse comes to a quick fullstop. Because son, whether or not an elephant is afraid of a mouse, or a coolie-buffalo is afraid of a jack-spaniard-wasp, I couldn't say. But one thing I can tell you from my own experience, horses sure as hell don't like crapos, particularly a thousand-and-one *duck*-sized crapos jumping up five feet in the air.

Gomez couldn't get he horse to budge a bloody inch. Rearing up, bellowing horsecries, with he horseyes opened up so wide they looked like they wanted to jump out. And by the time this little Chief of Police realizes what has hit him, he is flat on he backside there in a cloud of dust and leaping crapos, watching at he horse pelting now in the direction from which he had come. By the time Gomez has a chance to twink he eyes twice and look up, there is Barto staring down at him from out the muzzle of that big rifle (the same fancified one hanging downstairs in the parlor, given to Barto in the old days by you great-granduncle the General Francisco Monagas, twice president and liberator of the slaves in Venezuela) and this little Gomez has no choice but to take off running behind he horse.

Well: Magdalena is swallowed up by this tribe of shouting, crapo-hunting scoutboys. In no time a-tall *she* is stripped down naked too (in fact, she is little more than an adolescent sheself, and only a couple years older than the oldest of them) there is she swimming in the waist-deep swampwater, with the band of shouting scoutboys splashing like boynymphs in the water round her. Off in search of more crapos. And Barto, there watching from the cool shade of the huge samaan tree, looking like some bloody mythological figure heself — lying there on he back in he merino vestshirt, he head propped up against the samaan trunk, white jacket and Captain's hat hanging from the tree above him, blowing in the breeze with the thousand-and-one boyscout shortpants, the jerseys, the washy-kons, the twenty-foot-long strip of white muslin — there watching over Magdalena and the boys, smoking he thin Cuban cigar through the gold cigarette holder. With that same Chief of Police, not far distant, back again on the back of he horse, watching too, grinding he teeth.

That night he two policemen used they bootoos to bust down the door of the convent with a few quick blows. Gomez left one there posted beneath she window, the other following him up the stairs, straight to Magdalena's bedroom. Because by now he'd already found out where it was. He didn't give the nuns chance to wake up. And they hadn't even finished the first session of a novena before he walked out with he two policemen the following morning. By that time there was already a small crowd gathered there in Sir Walter Raleigh Square in front the convent, all looking up at Magdalena's window, all staring up at the empty balcony outside she bedroom. Gomez marched straight through them, he and he two policemen, like they didn't even exist, like nothing whatsoever had happened, and they crossed the square to sit at one of the outdoor tables of the parlor to take a coffee.

I don't know, son. I don't know the way those nuns and priests think, nor will I ever. Because they said absolutely nothing. Mother Maurina could have had that blasted Chief of Police strung up by he stones right there in the same square that same *afternoon* if she'd put the authority of the Church behind it. But she said nothing. Instead, and without even asking Magdalena — because the order was issued even before Gomez and he two policemen cleared out — instead she sent fa Barto: she commissioned him to find he backside there in the chapel of that convent, fast as he legs could carry him. You see, Mother Maurina had decided Barto would be the one to represent Magdalena's father (as Magdalena sheself didn't know who she father was, but why the ass she chose Barto above every other cock in the henhouse I couldn't tell you not fa sorrel sweetdrink) because fa some odd reason Mother Maurina had decided *he* would be the one to give her way. Understand son, the pledging ceremonies fa these nuns are exactly like weddings — exactly, with the big white weddingdress flowing down, the lace veil on she face, the ring on the finger and everything so — but you must imagine Christ as the groom.

Because that was all those nuns could think to do. To get Magdalena into she gown and down these stairs into the chapel — not even wasting enough time to throw little iodine on she bruises when they finish burning the sheets — down the stairs into the chapel and consecrated good and proper. I couldn't say, son. Why the ass they were in such a hurry is a mystery to me. I suppose, in they own perverse way, they believed those vows might purify her again. I have no idea. All I can tell you is this: when that organ music begins to play, when those nuns begin to sing, and Magdalena takes up Barto's arm to walk up the isle of that chapel, she hand is still trembling from the night before. She wrists and ankles have not even been bandaged where the pressure of those bindings which held she limbs tied tight to those bedpost stanchions the whole night have lacerated them, and the contusion above she right eye has swollen to such an extent she can scarcely see out of it. Not until Barto puts the ring on she finger, does she stop shaking.

By this time half of Corpus Christi has gathered there in the square. We are all staring up at Magdalena's window, all telling the story of this Chief of Police who has — by the time the Government House clock strikes fa eleven o'clock on that Monday morning — led the entire police forces of Corpus Christi in a gang-rape of Magdalena. And by the time the clock strikes fa twelve noon, we'd made up we minds to lynch him, still sitting there with he two policemen drinking coffee on the other side of the square. And we would have too — beat the shittings out of him right there in the square — had Mother Maurina not appeared on the balcony outside Magdalena's bedroom, announcing the consecration of a new sister to St Maggy Convent: Magdalena María Domingo. "Go home!" she says. "You lunch cold already!" And we all went home.

When, however, this same Mother Superior General Maurina announces that the new novitiate, Magdalena, is leaving the convent to marry sheself to the same Chief of Police who had raped her not even two months before — the same Monsignor O'Connor who'd pronounced her a sister of the Corpus Christi Carmelites the morning after she'd been raped, to pronounce her married in the same chapel to the same man who had raped her not even two months before — everything blows up again. Understand son, it had long been common knowledge — a common joke animated by every prostitute in Corpus Christi fa years — that this Chief of Police shot blanks. Some said he couldn't even shoot a-tall. That is to say, he is *sterile, impotent*: a *tantieman*, a *mammapoule*. So no one ever stopped to consider the possibility that Magdalena might be pregnant, and needed a husband, which, indeed, she was *not*.

On the designated day the crowd gathers once more in Sir Walter Raleigh Square in front the convent. It is a Saturday morning, and everyone has come to see fa theyselves. We didn't come with rice. We came with glassbottle, stone and cutlass. But before any of we can manage even to work weselves up to a mild pitch, Mother Maurina appears on Magdalena's balcony again to send we home. She doesn't appear like the Pope this time. She appears like Christ, Magdalena next to her there on the balcony, daring any of we to

pelt the first stone. So by the time this Chief of Police arrives, most
of we have taken she advice and gone home fa breakfast.

The ceremony lasted only a couple minutes, and the marriage
not much longer. Because within a few weeks Magdalena was back
in the convent again. Just what went on between sheself and Gomez,
no one knows. Some said she never left the convent a-tall—that
old Mother Maurina was going viekeevie now fa true with all she
marriage talk—but the fact is she *did* live with Gomez as he wife
a period of exactly thirty-eight days. Because Barto and I sat there
one evening on the gallery of my bungalow, and we fired back a
couple tassas of punching rum, and we counted it out. (Thirty-
eight days exactly, which I was able to substantiate many years
later by digging up the duplicate marriage certificate deposited
there in the Record Room of Government House, and checking the
date—Saturday 1 August—and counting down the thirty-eight days
to the feastday of La Divina Pastora of Venezuela—Monday 7 September—which was the day Magdalena assured Barto she returned
to the convent.)

Well son, I don't know what you want to make of all this commess. I can tell you it sent my head tootoolbay a good long time.
But again, I continued to turn it over until I arrived at the logical
explanation. Because of course, you have to ask yourself: Is this
Magdalena an ordained nun, a married woman, or a consecrated
whore? And the answer, it seems to me, is obvious enough: she is
all three. Consider it fa second, son. Though we all knew fa years
that this Chief of Police was a mammapoule, that he was sterile,
perhaps the nuns did not? All I am trying to suggest to you here
son is this: during those same two months or so between Magdalena's rape, and she subsequent marriage to she abductor, the same
Chief of Police, Magdalena not only had time enough to make
up she mind she was pregnant, she had time to convince Mother
Maurina too. That Mother Superior Maurina not only *arranged* fa
the marriage, she *dictated* it. When, however, Magdalena discovers
she is not pregnant a-tall, she takes off running from this Chief of
Police fast as potcake can run from bigstick.

Good. Well son, now begins the history of Magdalena's relationship with you grandfather. It would last until the day of she death,
seven months later. Just what sort of relationship it was remains, I
suppose, relatively obscure. Because the fact is that fa the whole of
those seven months Magdalena resided as a nun in St Maggy Convent. Now: how it is that you grandfather came to confide in me

all of this business is obvious enough. Understand, fa twenty-two
years I was employed by him there on the old Domingo Estate, with
Barto riding out from St Maggy two or three times every month,
with both of we invariably ending up each evening sitting there on
the gallery of my bungalow, knocking back we tassas of punching
rum, talking we oldtalk. Because it was not long after I married
Gertrude, you grandmother, that we went to live on the estate, and
it was twenty-two years later — not long after Gertrude's death —
that I came out here to St Maggy, to Barto, and asked to be relieved
of my duties as manager of the cultivation. What I could not have
known, at that precise moment — though perhaps I should have expected something of the sort, fate again, advocating coincidence —
was that only the week before, both Magdalena and she child had
died. At all events, Barto sold the estate the following day. That
same morning he saw me aboard my ship destined fa the Delta
Orinoco, where I was to remain fa thirty-five years. But it was on the
night before I departed, on a moonlit night just like this one, that
Barto brought me up here where we could be alone. Right here, on
this cobo roost, on this very night so many years ago, here where
you and I sit at this very moment. He told me about the events
which had taken place during the previous week: about Magdalena's death, about the birth and death of she child. About the
events which would, on the same afternoon of the same day on
which my ship set sail fa Tucupita, up the River Orinoco, in so far
as any of we can tell, bring Barto to take he own life.

Right. It happened that first Sunday morning quite by caprice.
With a vaps: Barto sat there eating he fryeggs and blackpudding,
and he felt the sudden urge to see her again. Just like that. He decided to go to Maraval on the chance that she might do the same,
that perhaps he would find her there. This, I suppose, must have
been a few weeks after she'd left Gomez and returned to the convent. He found her, of course. What's more, she told Barto she'd
often hoped to see him there again, which may well be the reason
she continually returned to the swamp. They spent the day there
together, sitting beneath the same samaan tree where Barto had
sat watching her catching crapos with the scoutboys only three or
four months before, he, telling he oldstories and smoking he thin
Cuban cigars, and she, sitting there beside him listening quietly.
Because the truth is that Magdalena never said much. In fact, she
was so extremely quiet that some even went about the place calling
her a dumb deaf-mute, and some still do to this day. But son, this

257

Magdalena wasn't no kind of dumb deaf-mute a-tall. Quite to the contrary. True, she never said much, not even to Barto. But on the few occasions she did open she mouth, I can tell you she spoke a kind of soft, smooth eloquence easy as guava icecream.

It was a pleasant, though uneventful morning that first Sunday morning, the first of many such Sundays mornings spent there beneath the same samaan tree. And it was late one Sunday night (after the usual day at Maraval, after Barto had gotten to know Magdalena quite well) that he awoke from he sleep in a cold sweat. He sleep had not been disturbed by thoughts of Magdalena. Of this he was certain. Nor did Barto contemplate her an instant as he dressed heself. He'd decided to go fa a walk along King's Wharf, to take in the cool seabreeze. What was peculiar, and Barto seemed surprised heself as he spoke, was that he felt pressed. Hurried to get to the docks. So much so that when he closed the front door behind him, and sat on the step to lace up he shoes (you see, Barto slept upstairs, in the bedroom you mummy and daddy use now, and he did not want to make a load of racket on the stairs to wake up Granny Myna and Evelina sleeping below) he felt so hurried that he left the shoes there. He did not want to waste the time to lace them up. Just so: he took off in he bare feet. And when he returned home on Wednesday morning, three days later, the shoes had disappeared. (No doubt Granny Myna had found them there the following morning and pitched them in the sea, a beautiful pair of hardbacks stretched from the skin of a macajuel Barto heself had wrestled up the Orinoco, because he never saw those shoes again.)

But he had taken off in the wrong direction. Still, he had not contemplated Magdalena. He had thought only *King's Wharf*, and now he did not think even that. Neither did he think of Sir Walter Raleigh Square, though that was where he was going. Going in a hurry. And what he did there was quite peculiar. The whole sequence of events seems peculiar, and as Barto described them to me, they seemed connected by that strange sense of reality which connects nonsensical events in dreams. It was a full moon night, and the square was empty. Barto stood beneath the statue, looking up, and he saw that there were pigeons sleeping, perched all over it: on Raleigh's shoulders, along he upraised sword, on the plume of he hat. Barto found the pigeons repulsive. Why, he couldn't say heself. Only that the sight of them there, hunched up, molting and musty-smelling, the sight of they stool spattered over the statue, was to him suddenly repulsive. He began to rap on Raleigh's shin with he knuckles. It was like knocking a melon: soft, hollow thuds. One or two of the pigeons ruffled up he feathers, moved over a bit, hunched up again. Barto had another idea: he went to one of the almond trees and began collecting up rockstones. The earth beneath the tree had been trampled smooth, so much so that he had to scrape them out. Barto returned to the statue and began pelting the rockstones, one by one, at the pigeons roosting on Raleigh's shoulders. He went to the tree again, in a boyish kind of vexation, and he was not satisfied until he had driven every pigeon away. He was in a sweat now, and he sat on the step round the base of the statue, feeling in he vest pocket fa the cigar which was not there.

At that moment the Government House clock began to strike fa midnight, startling him, and he turned quickly to look at it across the square. Something stopped him, startling him again: it was the figure of a woman, there, naked in the moonlight of one of the balconies of St Maggy Convent, and only then did he contemplate Magdalena. In the distance he made out the face that was not looking down at him, but up, at the huge moon. And as that clock beat twelve times, Barto took twelve deep breaths. She disappeared. Not turning: stepping backward into the darkness of she room.

Barto left he clothes bundled up in the fork of one of those almond trees. He was perspiring heavily now, and in the moonlight he white white skin seemed to be glowing. Stepping in the chinks between the coral stones, gripping the ivy, he climbed up the wall onto she balcony. They made love fa three days and three nights: continuously. Without pause. And to Barto's own astonishment, he erection did not subside fa three days and three nights either. Not until he climbed down from the wall again with the first light of Wednesday morning. I couldn't tell you, son. I would be the first to admit to you that you grandfather was above the ordinary. Whether or not he could sustain this erection fa such a prolonged period of time, is, of course, questionable. But son, what you or I choose to believe seems of little consequence: because by the time Barto climbed down from that balcony on Wednesday morning — by the time he took down he clothes still there bundled up in the fork of that almond tree, and began to dress heself — Magdalena was convinced he was *angelic*. And he was convinced no less of *her*.

Gomez returned to the convent that morning. The same Wednesday morning. How he knew Barto had been there — and under what particular *circumstances* he'd been there — that, I couldn't tell you. No one else knew. The nuns theyselves didn't know. But again, like everything else, somehow or other Gomez found out. He was insulted, I suppose, but that would be putting it mild. Because not only had Magdalena left him just a few weeks before, now she'd *cuckolded* him. Remember: all this time Magdalena is legally he wife. In addition, you must understand that this Chief of Police suffers from a tremendous inferiority complex. Not only is he of inferior stature (and I would say he stood no more than fifty-four inches tall, weighing no more than eight stone) not only is he of inferior stature, but the whole bloody island takes him fa tantieman. In a backyard where bantycock never *smells* the henhouse. The result, of which, is a zandolee lizard swelled up too big fa he hole: a megalomaniac of grandiferous proportions. Let me tell you, Barto had scarcely climbed down the wall of that convent, when Gomez arrived with he jooker aflame. *Literally.* He came to defend he manhood. To prove he prowess. He came, to give he wife *licks*, *fleet, cuttail.* But as usual, cobo came to shit on he head.

You see, having spent all those years out their in Mayaguaro, living among those Warrahoons and such, I had plenty of opportunities to learn about this thing. Which is not to say I indulged myself. But again, like anyone else, you *do* have a certain scientific, medical curiosity, and you would like to satisfy youself. But you take the proper precautions. You don't go like Gomez, mixing up you own bloody medicine any which way, in whatever concentrations such that you overdose yourself, so much so that after five days — the last two spent in the hospital with you toetee packed up in ice — you flagpole is *still* standing tall like a standpipe, and not a thing in this world can bring him down.

Right. Good. You want to know about this thing: roupala montana, or as we have come to call it, *bois bandé* (with an acute accent on the *e*). It means, in the Creole, stiff, or hard wood. Correct. Now: it is a common forest tree, a climax forest tree, which has been utilized by the natives — I suppose you could say fa medicinal purposes — fa years. (In fact, when Raleigh reported that a Corpus Christi native had given him a potion which enabled him, in the privacy of he ship's quarters, to sustain an erection fa twenty-seven hours at a stretch, they thought he'd lost he head. What Raleigh did *not* know, is that the Warrahoons had been using bois bandé fa donkey's ages, batting it back every night before they go to bed like we drink Ovaltine in warm milk.) To prepare it, you use the bark — like mauby, or chincona, from which quinine is made — boiling it down in much the same way. But you know how bitter mauby is?

A little piece of the bark big as you fingernail like this goes in to make up a whole jorum? Well this bois bandé is every bit as potent. And of course, you take a dose now, and when the effect subsides after few hours, if you still haven't satisfied youself to exhaustion, of course you take another.

Gomez must have eaten down the whole bloody tree. Because what began as kicksing, finished in LBW. Leg-before-wicket. Penalty box. Let me tell you, Gomez got heself into some *serious* trouble. Because son, as you can well imagine, like any other over-strained muscle, after a time this thing gets to be bloody painful. Not to mention the fact that you killing to make a weewee. Let me tell you, when that Chief of Police cleared out the convent on Friday afternoon, after the three days — with that Mother Maurina doing nothing again, except of course assembling in the chapel fa another novena — when that Chief of Police cleared out, he went straight to St Maggy Hospital. He was in that much pain. Of course, Salizar could do nothing but pack him up in ice and throw a sheet over him. With all the little whitecap-nuns, every time they go down the hall lifting up the sheet fa little peep, because of course, everybody outside wants to know how the Chief of Police's flagpole is going. To be sure, this bushdoctor Salizar is straight out the jungle of Venezuela, and he knows bois bandé as well as any of we: there is no antidote. No counteractant except time. Son, Gomez bawled down the place fa three days. Half of Corpus Christi is gathered there in front of the hospital — with that crackerjack Uncle Olly thinking up the idea of a *lottery* now to guess the precise minute this Chief of Police's flagpole is expiring, there with he megaphone selling tickets like bush, and making heself a bloody fortune — when Salizar decides he ga to try an old Warrahoon cure-all: a mixture of peppersauce, limejuice and rocksalt. Son, they tell me it worked like a charm. But by the time Salizar finished rubbing down Gomez's toetee with this commess, he had to remain in the hospital packed in ice fa another three days.

Of course, before he had even arrived in the hospital — before he had even cleared out of the convent — Mother Maurina had sent fa Barto again: she commissioned him to return to the convent fa another of those wedding-nunpledging ceremonies. Except this time Magdalena was in worse condition. Again Mother Maurina did not waste time tending to she bruises. She didn't even waste the time to feed her. Understand: Magdalena had gone without food now fa six days, from Sunday midday to Friday afternoon, though

261

admittedly, the first three were of she own volition. Again, all that
Mother Superior General could think to do is to pelt her down the
stairs into the chapel to repledge she vows. And when Monsignor
O'Connor directs Barto, fa the second time, in the name of Christ,
to push the ring on she finger, Magdalena has to take it off she still
trembling hand and give it to him fa him to do it.

Enough. I am finished now with those three: Gomez, and Monsignor O'Connor, and this same Mother Superior General Maurina.
Finished. Nothing more was heard from any of them. Not until
after Magdalena's death anyway, seven months later. They came
fighting down Barto fa the body — some bubball, with the three of
them digging up, and reburying, and mismolesting all the poor old
jumbies sleeping peaceful enough in Domingo Cemetery — which
apparently, Gomez settled good and proper by dropping down dead
suddenly heself. Because I suppose the other two, Mother Maurina
and Monsignor O'Connor, were frightened the same would happen
to them.

Magdalena's final seven months were quiet. Very quiet, in comparison to the months which preceded. It was during those seven
months which Magdalena secretly met with Barto every Sunday
beneath the big samaan, those seven months during which she
secretly carried he child. No one else knew about the pregnancy.
In fact, few knew anything about Magdalena's relationship with
Barto a-tall. The truth is by this time Corpus Christi seemed to
have lost interest in she affairs altogether — overwhelmed and de-
sensitized, I suppose, in they astonishment — and fa the last seven
months Magdalena was quite forgotten. Even the spectacle of this
beautiful, sienna-skinned woman, walking alone by sheself each
Sunday morning along the trace to Swamp Maraval, dressed in she
white nuncostume with the rosary consisting of beads the size of
marbles tied up round she waist, the dust a continuous cloud rising round she bare feet — so that she seemed almost to be walking
in air — even the spectacle of this beautiful, dark-skinned woman
was no longer a spectacle, but a common weekly occurrence. No
one noticed. That is, of course, until the birth of the child. The
child I have already described fa you. The unthinkable, preternatu-
ral, progidiferous child which would throw us all into a world
beyond the mysterious, into the unfathomable. The child which
would bring Magdalena to take she own life. Which would, inevitably, bring Barto to do the same.

What sort of child he was, I would not venture to guess. Some called him the jabjab heself, son of Manfrog, the folktale devil-sprite who waits in a tree to rape young virgins at dusk. Others saw nothing peculiar in the child a-tall. Some even said that the child was beautiful, perfect: that the child was the reflection of the viewer. Some argued the hex of an obeah spell. Others, the curse of Magdalena's obsession with Swamp Maraval, with frogs fucking: that he was, as Salizar suggested, a crapochild. Still others, prompted by the young physician who'd just come to St. Maggy Hospital then, said he was the result of a congenital abnormality which caused him to appear like a frog: a condition (which the young physician printed out on a piece of paper fa me to read it) a congenital condition resulting from a failure of the brain and the encasing skull to develop as normal, known in the correct clinical language as AN-EN-CEPHALY. This, of course, would seem most plausible — except fa the fact, acknowledged by the bright young physician heself — that these congenital monsters are generally stillborn, whereas this child lived strong as ever fa three days. Even with half of Corpus Christi fighting down each other for the privilege to kill him. Son, we can resign weselves to only this: there is no logical explanation. We will never know.

It was Papee Vince's voice which carried me in my dream now. Papee Vince's voice from which I could not escape. And as I sat there, suspended, balanced awkwardly on the railing with my feet hanging a few inches above the ground, I could just barely point my toes and touch it. Could just barely touch the tip of my big toe to the finger of reality, and know that I was alive within the confines of my dream. And as I sat there, listening to my old grandfather, sitting there in his hammock stretched between me and that trapdoor which led down the ladder, I was thinking: *This oldman have you hold-up on this cobo roost like that same frogbaby hold-up inside he glassbottle. Just like that same frogbaby hold-up inside he glassbottle, with you toting youself now in this baddream to this place you don't want to go. So why you don't dream youself onto that railing on the other side of Papee Vince? Why you don't dream youself cross there, and then you only have to run down the ladder to get youself way from this Papee Vince, and Granny Myna, and Magdalena and this frogbaby fagood faever?*

That is what Barto said to me. Sitting here, on this very cobo roost, beneath this same moon above the same black, glistening sea. That is what Magdalena had said to him: you will never understand. Believe. And this will be the sign: that the child will appear like no other. Because she told him these things on the Sunday before she death, sitting there beneath the same samaan tree. That she sheself would live only long enough to see the child's face. Because the child was to be the sign fa her too: she took one look in he face and held she breath until she suffocated. She told Barto that the child would live fa three days, until Easter Sunday — one year exactly from the day Magdalena first appeared in Corpus Christi — and on that Easter Sunday Barto was to bury the child in Domingo Cemetery, there beside her. And she left him with this last promise: three days later she would be with him again.

But Barto must have sat there listening to her the same way I sat here listening to him, the same way you are sitting here now listening to me: incredulous. Confounded. And on the following morning, as I sat there on the deck of that ship, she bow pointed at the open mouth of the River Orinoco, Corpus Christi sinking slowly behind in the turbulence of she wake, I still did not understand what Barto had told me. And when you grandfather gathered Granny Myna, you father and he brothers, Uncle Olly and Evelina round him sitting there at the big diningroom table, and he pulled the cork from a bottle of rum and passed it round smiling, saying he would be leaving them that same afternoon, they were sure he was going on another of he expeditions up the Orinoco. But it was I who had left on the expedition this time, I who had replaced Barto. Because he simply disappeared. He remains have never been found.

You father was the one who deciphered it, three or four weeks later. He went to Domingo Cemetery and discovered a row of four new black marble headstones. No one had seen them before. Headstones belonging to Magdalena and the child, and two others, one intended fa Granny Myna, the other fa Barto heself. How they got there no one knows to this day. We can only assume that sometime prior to he disappearance, Barto heself gave instructions for them to be placed there. Sometime prior to he *death*, if that is what you choose to believe. Because three of those four headstones were dated: Magdalena's, on Corpus Christi Day, April 16; the child's, Easter Sunday, April 19; and you grandfather's, April 22. Wednesday, April 22: the same day I set sail fa the Delta Orinoco, the same day you grandfather gathered the family downstairs round the big dining-room table.

They buried an empty casket. Empty, except for three or four good-sized chockstones. You father, the eldest, decided that would be best fa Granny Myna. He would not have her live out the rest of she life faced with the uncertainty of she husband's death. You must understand son, that in those old days people felt very strongly about such matters. I know myself, fa a fact, that you grandmother actually lived fa the day she would be buried in peace next to Barto. Such feelings suggest a depth of love which perhaps you and I cannot comprehend, but a depth of love nonetheless. You father told Granny Myna that the body had been found, decomposed and piranha-disfigured, that it was not fit fa her to see. Perhaps you will think of this deception of you father's as wrong, as dishonest, but you must try to see the compassion with which these things were done. It is a compassion I much admire in you father.

He was the one who wrote and explained all of this to me, in a letter which found me in Cutacas, after I had lived there nearly a year. In the same letter he spoke of plans fa marrying you mother. Plans which had long been enacted by the time I read of them, lying there in my hammock in a bungalow high at the top of one of those derricks. It was as if fate were speaking to me again, saying that I had better get used to that jungle. That I would be there awhile. Son, I remained fa thirty-five years. Thirty-five years living in a world no description can begin to describe. But don't you understand son, that it would take thirty-five years of telling myself over and over again that if this man, Barto, you grandfather, could believe, could believe fervently enough to take he own life at she word, then you can say it too: *Yes. I believe.*

Three Stories
Diane Williams

THE MEANING OF LIFE

ONE POINT MUST BE MADE and this concerns what we learn from the history of the world. It must be noted that usually men do not possess valuables or huge sums of money. Their sense of their being sorry about this grows and it grows and it grows. A woman may be their only irreplaceable object. That's why I think the meaning of life is so wonderful. It has helped millions of men and women to achieve vastly rich and productive lives.

Recently, this woman appeared on TV. She has a small head, a big head of hair, and she sings solo. She's wonderful, but because of her dread fear of almost all men, she does not want any more than one man at a time in her life, which is reasonable, but she is always at a loss.

TURNING

We kept on and I did not break into tears. Meanwhile, I am wondering which one of us is the cruelest. I can hear my voice saying all of those things.

A few months later, he reminded me that our misfortunes were almost identical, because he said we had become inextricably commingled. When he said what amounted to that, I put my arms around him and I kissed him. However, my suspicion is that he cannot tolerate being confined by a woman.

When daylight came, we made our preparations for the day, by bathing, by dressing, by eating. My own appearance was of concern to me, but there was also my great suspicion about what we had been doing throughout the night. Had we succeeded? Should we have been rejoicing? controlling our anger? openly admitting where the true superiority resides? or should we have kept on with our spirit of rivalry?

Anyway, I spoke seriously with him about my violent disposition. But just around the corner, I did not know what it was.

No sooner had the summer arrived — it was a day like today — with the sea whipped up by the wind, the sky was filled with action — with tumbling clouds, carrying on how they do, erratic, totally unstable, disorderly, maltreating each other's lifeless bodies, fabricating, evaporating ominously. I trust the unknown. I could never be astonished by such painless deaths apart from one episode, wherein I attempted to twist my fate, and to rear a child, among other things.

THE REAL DIANE WILLIAMS HAS CAPTURED THE WHOLE OF FREUD

My son Eric Williams told me how he'd jump over or he'd jump on top of a car that was going to run him down, rather than go under the car. We were riding in our car then. I was the driver when he told me.

My errand was to get my new nightgown to fit — the silky, soft, shiny, creamy, slinky nightgown that did not fit me when I bought it, that has more flowers than I'd care to count all over it. I was taking my gown to the woman tailor whose husband invited Eric to his boy's surprise party by calling me up on the telephone to tell me about the party.

The two times I have been to the tailor it was very bad weather. This was one of those times. Sleet slopped on the windshield. Pointing to the windshield, Eric said, "If there was nothing there — if you stopped suddenly — I could go right through it and I wouldn't get hurt!" He meant if there were no glass. I knew what he meant.

"That's the way to think!" I said, "and there's no reason why no windshield would not work except for bad weather," and then I was thinking about my beginnings.

I undressed for the tailor and for Eric, too, so they could both see me naked. I could not figure out why. It wasn't required.

At the tail end of her decadent sofa, I stopped, so I did not have to go into her dressing room. I took off my clothing, throwing it all down on the sofa, and then put on the shimmering gown.

She had me stand up on a pedestal from where I admired in the mirror the gown shimmering and shining on me, and I admired her nimbly squatting to put pins into my hem, and she kept both of

267

her knees up off the floor, which surely was a feat!

Even Eric was jolly — we were all smiling when her husband emerged out of nowhere. My clothing was all back on then, so all of us were wearing all of our clothing, *the hell with that!*

When her husband held on to his belt with two hands, she crossed in front of him to go to the cash register with my money, which is when I admired her shoes. I was looking down. When I saw her belt, I was looking up, and when I saw her smiling — I was looking up even higher into the middle region which was my warning signal to stop looking.

I determined that her husband is sly on this basis — I've determined this on this basis more times than I can count about so many sly people — that a person is sly if the person seems to insist upon keeping a smile on his or her face. I would not smile — that's not fear! — if I had to say what he had to say about me in front of his wife! — but maybe it will make her happy.

The clear plastic cover for the gown on the hanger that she gave me was far more brilliant than my gown is. It's scintillating. The clear plastic cover was also longer than the gown and it's lethal for a tiny tot whose desire is to put it over his head and with it smother himself, as we all know.

When I piled the gown onto the back seat of my car, I had no opinion of the gown except that it was practically a weightless gown.

When I was with her husband, and when her husband saw me walking toward him, and when he said, "God, look at yourself in the mirror! Will you look at yourself!" I refused to go look at my white skinlike covering.

In conclusion, human beings — my worrying about them — it's over, it's over and it's merrier!

Two Poems
Rae Armantrout

TURN OF EVENTS

Outside it was the same as before, scrawny palms and oleanders,
their long leaves, ostensible fingers, not pointing, but
tumbling in place — plants someone might call exotic if
anybody called — and the same birds and hours, presumably
slipping in and out of view. She kept coming out onto the
porch with the sense that there was something to it. Perpet-
uation and stasis. She wanted to deal with the basics — though
what this scene might be the basis for she didn't know.

This was her native tongue, slipping in and out of order —
its empty streets and loose, flapping leaves, its bald-faced
simplicity as if a way had been cleared for something huge.
Shape was the only evidence. She went back in. She should
think about how the house was built or how it was paid for.
How a feeling can have a shape for so long, say an oblong,
with sun falling in a series of rhomboids on its wooden
strips. It would have an orientation. She wondered whether
there was much difference between orientation and reason.
She would sit facing the door.

Rae Armantrout

MAPPING

1.

At the upper end, the businesses seemed more distinct,
each with its own style, or character understood as
pretense, flaunting the energy pretense expends — thus
lighthearted.

2.

The airplane cruised between buildings like an intelligent
missile. The issue wasn't terror, but character, how
each passenger responded individually. One matched her
levity to the captain's.

3.

"Ride that thing!" a man whispered, then, "Keep me informed!"
This bothered her and it was her job to find out why. She
concluded stylized ejaculations were obscene, but there was
more. It wasn't like him to repeat a formula, seemingly
beside himself while, in fact, stationed above.

Reading Li Shang-yin: Falling Flowers
Robert Kelly

— for Charlotte

Even you shaking myself out of the dust
of all I need you
                    the differences, the terrible birds
you have quit my high pavilion
                                    the shadow of you
the shadow of me being
                    so many days a complicated darkness
down there *in the garden*
                    down there where the terrible shadow we were
is stepped on now by those birds, so awkward they are,
princes of the air clowns on the ground
preposterous feet
                    the shadows come down to us only, sometimes,
                    as this morning, of course missing you,
        not only you, not only me
    missing you,
                    a shadow missing a part of itself, the dingy
quality the light has when it has no shadow to cast or
long waisted low slung
                    you have come towards me
        equal to being born   in aspect
of engagement,
                    after the clandestine espousals
        of life with death
            they called the blue flower
    in no one's hand,
            how sumptuously you stretched
        on my couch

This poem works from a translation by Lisa Raphals of six lines by Li Shang-yin;
these lines appear in italics in the present text.

Robert Kelly

every muscle a remembering,
by truth to rouse,
or ruse, or lull, or con
the Great Reader into highly specific acts of Oblivion,
our life is his amnesia.
Smooth of the hip
socketed in the cup of the hand,
the weight of,
a pendulum closeness
to the gravid earth *below*
to be born inside
finity where the *flowers* grow —
whose color are they?
meek by dint of memory
astir in fire?
Writing to track what reading has in mind.
Scattering on your breast
the petals of wantfulness,
the blue tone snug so deeply
in the red
so that the sunset
knows you,
you here among the eternity of conversations
and so few of them wet   tongue-tip to your
quiet breast,
a garnet
holds that color also
to the base of your spine, a current
the women of old spoke
to their sons a little bit
and to their daughters much,
language,
language of the *west*
lewd grammars of a nomad people,
for in my thought I have caressed
the sacred geomantic precincts of your body
my hands heavy with grease
from just such alien sheep. Wool pull,
flowers nibbled, not bright animals
hoofing through your garden, your air,
I hear the crows

adventuring the little left
after life   the silver snow
to them
in a full moon time
is given,
I wait for you, comfort of your body beside me
as if suddenly an old man inside me
strung with that yearning
to pluck tone
song
as from the bones of the body sounded
and all our torture just that music
muscle,
wound, sound, wound,
the knell of beast comfort moving
to take possession of this carrion mind,
clearing,
like a procession of Grail knights
disappearing, violet line into falling snow fading,
and yesterday I saw the garden wall, old bluestone slabs,
the shale cut to slates, the marble steps
broken, all broken, brick wall
bent under the bare lianas of wisteria, the root stocks
twisted in cold evening, all lilac
was the east then
across the whole little world
from that setting sun
fallen past the hemlocks,
the contra-sera even-pale,
isolate woodpecker also
from before us *flown along the* river of air
they apprehend (we don't)
we know not that we know not,
base metal
we have scotched our gold with,
endured with
cunning when we might have thrived with openness
exulting,
o it is not nothing
to have a red flower on my windowsill
in such weather,

Robert Kelly

                whose many petals, still red, dry

and fall
        onto the blue tile kitchen floor,
                       and to crush
          gently enough one leaf of it
       releasing
from flexile structure one scent of *form*,
          as from the *twisted dike* of matter a leak of sense.
To smell a geranium
    in winter
      is better
than all the bergamot
    of the Midi,
        be with me
though
    to savor it.
        I want your side
to me, my hand
    between your thighs
        escorting
the warmth of you,
    after,
        into sleep.
Dusk. We have *passed into distances*
          of each other, swayed in blue ferryboats
     across bitter cold straits,
             and there was always
    someone near us, a bravo smoking cigarettes, and that too
virginia was a kindness to remind.
               Compassion.   Compassion,
in the faded light, I reach for your return
who never left me,
        the world
      is not made of partings,
            brass farthings,
   she goeth forth
     with her sweetie
   to endure
       these new
  winter nights
      with brainless screwing

but the separations
    of which I am master
        are far other,
it is a matter (a scatter)
    of the metals
        cinnabar and copper
and what is left of me
    when love absterges
        the newsworthy patinas
your kisses left
    and everybody knows it
        I am your man,

and so in faded light I ask her, she is my colors, I reach
for where she is and where she's going
            and on the phone Joan tells me
        how Lana has run off with Erica
            midwinter, Tivoli disaster,
    pale fiancées of a wanton star.
        I reach I reach
    my life
is all about reaching
        into wherever it is dark, wherever, wherever,
and listen! the children
    of the night! their music!
            I tell her, Dear one, reach
for her return. She tells me: I will never
take her back,
        for all her cheating
    was a wound
        in the flesh of my *time*, and time
that heals all else, has no way to heal itself —
        our years she took
    six years
        and spent them,
            this is our winter's tale,
lukewarm tea and shiny petals of our polaroids
    torn up and scattered on the floor
        before the dead fire in the hearth,

Robert Kelly

and when we love
        what thing is left
                that shapes the shadows
even of our house,
        so that doorway
            in it
is only about her coming through?
        I have torn
            the images
of the life she tore
        and still can't bear
                to sweep them away.

An Incomplete Biography
of Amantacha the Huron
William T. Vollmann

THE MARTYRDOM OF PÈRE NICOLAS (1625)

PÈRE NICOLAS VIEL HAD ACCOMPANIED Père Le Caron and a lay brother, Gabriel Sagard, to Wendaké, *viz.*; the Country of the Huron, in the Year of Our LORD 1623 — an auspicious annum, for it was then that Père de Nobili was finally permitted to resume his baptisms in India. — Père Nicolas was very pious. Before he became a monk, the girls had loved to make eyes at him, imagining what pleasure they would have if only they could dress him and adorn his hair with flowers. Soon indeed the women of Kebec would have this privilege, but only to lay him out for burial: — Père Nicolas was always unlucky. Perhaps for this very reason, he was able to keep all his natural goodness throughout his life, never being called upon to buy his successes with the gold doubloons of it; after all, his successes were nil. When he first stepped onto the shore of Canada, making his lanky struggling way in the inch-thick wooden sandals that his Order required, the Montagnais were there, and said to one another: See how sad and sunken his eyes are! Does he have Power, or will he die soon? — Indeed, Père Nicolas made it his special prayer that GOD would permit him to spend the remainder of his life among the Huron; GOD heard and granted the boon in His own way, which atheists and other bleeding hearts might call ironical, but which the enlightened among us must value, for it shows true compassion for this man's vulnerability that his sacrifice was to be accepted so quickly. I know many a revolutionary who would rejoice to give himself to the fiery orgasm of a suicide bomb; it is the prospect of a sixty-year prison term that makes him shudder. For this reason, Père Nicolas, I make no apologies in now rushing on to bring your story to its final sodden page.

The year before the Black-Gowns arrived, then, Champlain, looking up from a letter which he was writing to his wife (*I fully* *comprehend your unhappiness, my dear child, at being left a "half-widow," as you put it, but I beg you to refrain from this mad project you have of taking entrance in a convent)*, heard through his spies that the Huron now sought to conclude a peace with the Seneca and various other Hiroquois; and this alarmed him because he knew that the Hiroquois were now trading for furs with the Hollanders.* If the Huron began to trade with the Hollanders as well, Kebec would be compromised. How very long and cold these Canadian winters would become, were the Savages to raise their prices . . . ! The situation was made still more difficult because Champlain was himself seeking to make a truce with the Mohawk Hiroquois for purposes of trade, and the Mohawk remained enemies of the Huron. (On account of the Hollanders, of course, it was his determination that the Mohawk *must* remain enemies of the Huron.) — Oh, how his thought wriggled in his brain like worms! For these reasons he thought it best to summon Père Le Caron to him.

My good Père Joseph, he said, I am sending eleven armed French-men to defend the Huron villages from the Hiroquois. Would you be pleased to accompany them?

Ah, said Le Caron, this is great news; good Père Nicolas will swoon when he hears. He wants so badly to go . . .

It was agreed that three Recollects would be permitted to set forth. But at the council that Champlain held, when he smoothed his will ahead of him with hatchets and glass beads from his Store-house, a Huron Savage stood up. — We do not want these men, he said. We want men with guns to defend us against our enemies.

Come now, my son, said the wise Champlain. Don't you have eyes? Look at them; they're Gray-Gowns. They have spiritual powers. Each one of these Pères is as good as ten arquebuses! A prayer from one of them is as good as a round lead bullet!

The Huron smiled politely. After all, Père Le Caron had lived among them before.

Guillaume de Caën, the Protestant, now stood up and said: Listen

---

*Champlain had many spies. We have already seen him lay the cornerstone of his edifice of skullduggeries, in 1608, while poor Duval's head bled upon a pike, but his earliest inspiration has not yet been revealed: — *viz.;* that on his first voyage (described *ante*) he stopped in Puerto Plata, a pleasant and most strategic isle, for which reason the King of Spain had set his negro slaves there to watching for foreign vessels; they had been promised their liberty if they sighted any. The negroes would go a hundred and fifty leagues on foot, night or day (as Champlain had seen) to give such notice. —Champlain, of course, could not offer the Savages their freedom, as they were already free. But he had something much better, called rum.

to me, Huron men! If you take these Gray-Gowns to your bosoms I will reward you with presents of axes, knives and beads!

At this the Huron murmured and consulted with one another, for this was handsomely said. Then they agreed to take the Gray-Gowns.

Said Père Le Caron to Père Nicolas: See how the Protestant seeks to appease us! But he is a serpent, I'm telling you! I will get his license revoked, never fear . . . (And indeed he did, three years later.)

Proceeding to De Caën, he said: Thank you, brother, for your generosity.

So they set out to erect their trophies of the Cross. It was a very sunny day. Père Nicolas kept looking behind him, until he could no longer see his convent's wooden ramparts, until the stone tower above the chapel gate had vanished among the sumacs, and he sighed. — Take heart, brother, said Père Le Caron. — Oh, said Père Nicolas, it is not that. It is only . . . — But then he trailed off, and the other thought it tactful not to press him. The lay brother, Frère Sagard, kept looking about him in wonder, for he had never seen such a foreign land. He scratched the name of JESUS in the bark of a large tree, to warn Satan that he was taking possession of this great Country of Canada in the Name of GOD. And they met the Huron on the shore of the Fleuve Saint-Laurent and clambered into the canoes . . . — The way was very long and laborious, and if I believed truly in representation I would be forced to describe for you every canoe-stroke, to mimic with the rippling swirls of these characters every change in the waters through which they passed, to let my prose shine like a star through the pallid pillars of trees around their campfires, to mimic the noise of wind and creeks in darkness. — *But on the other hand*, wrote Frère Sagard, *I have been advised to follow the artless simplicity of my usual manner.* Let me merely relate, then, that the Gray-Gowns with their armed escort visited the Tobacco Tribe, the Province of Fire, the Country of the Stinkards, the Forest Nations, Coppermines, Sorcerers, Island People and High-Hairs — to say but little of the Little Tribe. And so they arrived in Wendaké, which is a narrow Country on the shores of the Sweetwater Sea.

The faces of the Savages there were almost the color of dried blood, noted Père Nicolas to himself. Those clear black eyes, gleaming like their greasy scalp-locks, never stopped watching him. He could not comprehend them. But of course he did not need to. It was his function to make them comprehend *him* and the LORD

Whom he served. He would preach to them; he would teach them.

Loving their ideals above all, the Gray-Gowns shunned the filthy corruption of the longhouses, where the sounds of the Savages debauching could be heard at all hours and the smell of unwashed bodies and unclean vessels was an offense. At the Dance of the Naked Ones the young people copulated together; at a dream-feast a young man urinated in an old woman's mouth, for she had dreamed that that must be . . . No, the Recollects lived together in *reclusive* brotherhood. But they fanned out, too, searching, searching for souls. Père Nicolas soon came to the understanding that this Nation was very docile, and when influenced by temporal considerations it could be bent as one pleased. How exalting it all was! When he first saw the Country of the Huron it seemed to him that he must have seen it before in some dream, for its vast lake, known to all as the Sweetwater Sea, struck a chord of familiarity in him. Water, water . . . He did not understand that the water was already lapping round him. What he sensed was his own careening river-destiny.

The Upper Saguenay

There were many, many Huron villages imprisoned by the pale green walls of summer. He could not hope to know them all. But some of them he visited; some Savages became accustomed to him. In Teanaostoiaiaé Town, which lies in the Cord Nation of the Huron, there was a man called Soranhes. He was one of those Huron called *Antiwaronta* or *Big Stone* because he made money from the fur trade without himself trading. Yet in his case the appellation was not entirely accurate, since he dabbled his fingers with the French whenever he could. He had a fifteen-year-old son named Amantacha,* whom Père Nicolas considered a very likely boy to be formed and educated and perhaps even (who knows?) to become the first Huron priest, for he was very quick and pleasing in his ways. Indeed, Amantacha's face reminded him of a blank page of fine cream paper that could be written on in characters of the utmost beauty, a page that would preserve the writings of the LORD forever.** His eyes were very gentle; he addressed the Recollects with modestly becoming words. Everything about the boy seemed well-formed. So Père Nicolas visited this family whenever he could. He decided to be as delicate in his asking as the fine hairs at the nape of the boy's golden neck. In his zeal he even ate the dish called *leindohy* — small ears of corn drowned in a stagnant pond until they began to rot. — See how Kwer Nikoas grimaces like a sick dog! cried the boy, and the others laughed until the tears rolled down their cheeks. — Later, however, Soranhes took his son to task. — You spoke thoughtlessly, he said. We People do not believe in publicly chastising or humiliating a friend without good cause. He lives among us; he is our nephew. My dear son, you must take care not to poison his heart. Go now to the Gray-Gowns' lodge and give him this dried fish. It was unmannerly of him to make faces while he ate the *leindohy*, but he had reason to be ignorant. Perhaps he will like our fish better.

Flushing, Amantacha ran out of the house. He ran through the winding gates of the palisade; he ran into the ravine where the Gray-Gowns roosted.

Seeing the boy's shy face so close to him, Père Nicolas was first consoled, then edified, then rendered exalted.

Look how he watches you! laughed Soranhes to his son one day when the priest was not there (for he could not help it; he too thought Kwer Nikoas preposterous). — He gangles himself over you

---

*Soranhes's name meant "He is a very tall tree." The meaning of "Amantacha" has been lost.

**These Huron used to laugh and say to the Recollects: Bring snowshoes and mark it! whenever they would write; for they had never seen that art, and marveled at the strange creature-tracks with which they covered the winter-white sheets. — In Père Brébeuf's time, however, they would learn that writing was bad Sorcery.

like a big gray bird! — The boy had little desire to leave Wendaké, which all knew to be the center of the world, but upon his expressing these feelings his father reproved him, saying that he could not hope to prove himself a man if he showed fear. — Remember, he added, that it is the business of men to deal with outsiders. Women till the fields, but men smooth the way to distant places. If you dwell among them, the hearts of the Iron People will be bright with joy. They ask for you; they wish you to be the cord of our friendship. And you will learn their ways. Much about their hearts remains cloud-wrapped to my eyes. But *you* will learn to see the truth within them. Then you will have the right to speak to us all. Think upon it, my dear son.

Amantacha said: Do they live beyond the sea?

So they say, said Soranhes.

Can they see the GREAT TURTLE who upholds the world on His back?

If you go they will instruct you, of that you can be sure, was the answer.

In the year 1624, Père Nicolas spoke for a long time with Soranhes, pressing him earnestly to let him take his son Amantacha to be raised in France. — This face is not so different from the son's, thought Père Nicolas. — The small, almost feminine lips, however, seemed sly, coquettish. The brows were too perfectly arched, the eyes too brilliant. The slender bony face was both womanly and bird-like. He could not trust this man. — As for Soranhes, that worthy said to himself: I know that exchanging sons is what friends must do, to become kin to one another. However, I have heard bad reports of these Iron People. It is said that they strike young people who offend them, and do not allow them liberty. Still . . . — So he strode about perplexed.

If you do this thing, I personally will guarantee the boy's safety and happiness, said Père Nicolas. It will be for no more than a year.

And the other Pères will be happy to receive him in *Kekwek* and in France? said Soranhes. (The mouth of these Huron could not embrace the letter *b*.)

Very happy.

I seem to see them enclosing him, denying him the life to which he is accustomed —

Oh no no no.

Nephew, I must think upon it, he said, smoking his owl-head pipe. I love my son, and I want to know his mind.

He loved the goods of the Iron People. His father had seen them when still a young man, but in those days they were rare and sacred. Now they were not so rare, but yet more desired, for a man could clear fields so much more easily with iron axes, and women loved the copper kettles. The days of the Old Men and the Big Stones were glorious now; all respected them for having brought these things. What prestige, to give these things away! No one could forget Soranhes now! And suppose he opened a private way to the Iron People. Who knew what else they might have to give him?

In the end, Amantacha being willing, he agreed to let him go the following spring. That was when Père Nicolas made the decision to descend the Fleuve Saint-Laurent for the purpose of making a spiritual retreat. Père Le Caron and the lay brother, Sagard, had already returned to Kebec, and he had been left alone. As he went down the river he was feeling very satisfied with himself because he could soon take Amantacha in hand and mold him as he saw fit, so he sat at ease between the two Savages who paddled, not knowing that what he took to be the Fleuve Saint-Laurent was for him the Stream of Time, which only goes one way excepting for BlackGowns; and they portaged past the rapids called La Chine where Champlain, dreaming the Dream of the Hiroquois, had been defeated in his progress twenty-two years before, and then they loaded the canoe again and the Savages held it steady while Père Nicolas climbed in, as he was clumsy, and then they leaped in, one before him, one behind, and continued down, the blades of their paddles fluttering among the fishes, and one of the paddles snagged on something hairy that wrapped around it and sought to pull it into the water but the Savage said something that a Shaman had taught him and the thing went limp. Père Nicolas, who had noticed nothing, was occupied still with his dreams for Amantacha, wondering whether it would be too quick or too slow to instruct him in writing toward the end of his first year; for in France he had had charge of a Montagnais boy named Pastedouachouan to whom he had taught both French and Latin most tolerably; of course he had worked upon him for almost five years . . . and he said to himself: Pastedouachouan was docile, malleable; yet I verily believe that from this Amantacha my hands shall make a greater masterpiece! and the reflection of Père Nicolas's long pale face traveled with him, gazing up at him from just beyond the side of the canoe; and the noise of the Fleuve got louder and they came in sight of the island that would someday be Montréal, the Savages admiring how the flatness of the island narrowed into thick mistiness like the neck of some animal; the Fleuve made a narrow channel on the north, a wide one on the south. Both channels had rapids. The Savages had already decided to shoot these rapids rather than make another portage. The sound of the Fleuve was much louder now. Père Nicolas was about to die. He chose to do it. He chose to remain in the canoe while the Savages leaped out and swam with it, one on either side, looking for places to set down their feet so that they could brace themselves and walk the canoe down the rapids of Rivière des Prairies (the rapids were soon to be called Recollect Rapids, after Père Nicolas, but in the Stream of Time they were the Thirty-First Rapids — *viz.*; the Return from Egypt, where Père Nicolas had been all his life), and Père Nicolas lay full length in the bottom of the canoe, the water roaring in his ears, and the two Huron had now planted their feet firmly between boulders; they stood waist-deep in the foam, easing the canoe down step by step (the rapids here were brief) as Père Nicolas was thinking: Since the boy comes to me with his eyes open, it's fair to transform him, when one of the Huron stumbled, whether because of the extra weight in the canoe or because something hairy pulled it from beneath will remain a Point not categorized in these Exercises; and the canoe shot away and overturned almost in sight of the Cross where Kateri Tekakwitha was going to be buried in fifty-five years, and Père Nicolas tumbled into the water. He was not a good swimmer. Nor was he young. Swept rapidly down to where the water was so deep, chilly and indigo that there was nothing in it excepting his long white hands, his thrashing knees, and weird green rays of luminescence revolving around him, Père Nicolas sought to cry out to the Huron who could not help him; so doing he swallowed water. Water now rushed him to the shallows where bubbles glowed tan through the murk and the wriggling sedges tickled his hair; he tried to seize the bottom, but only blue-black mussels fell through his hands. The river rushed him on. A rock-edge sliced his forehead. He shot down through the narrows. He was pounded against rocks, and the green rays whirled faster and faster in every pool and suddenly he comprehended that they were hairy arms or tentacles and GOUGOU pulled him down and pressed His lips to Père Nicolas's and drank his breath, vomiting whirlpools down his throat in conformance to the code of exchange that characterizes magpies, crows and monsters. As the Gray-Gown's struggling body fled from life, becoming more waterlogged with every such water-breath, it passed the Isle of

Montréal where his soul saw a silvery church rising amidst the trees of Montréal, because he was riding now into the future of our continent, flying down the Fleuve Saint-Laurent with its low flat shore softened by trees, its tiny wooded islands like bubbles, flying until his tranquil white corpse, rock-scraped past bleeding, snagged itself between two driftlogs to become a wooden Saint, another icon in Canada's gallery: — yes, he was the first martyr! — Of course it did not happen at once. The Huron did not suspect it when they brought him to Kebec to be buried. Nor did the idea occur to Père Le Caron at first.

Could he have met with foul play at the hands of those Savages? he asked Brébeuf. I wonder; I wonder . . . ?

But what would be their motive, Joseph? said the other. Those two Huron look to me like honest men. They did not rob him; here are all his possessions, no? Did the Huron National hate him for some reason? But you say that this man Soranhes trusted him enough to promise him his son!

(Besides, added Père Brébeuf privily to Père Massé, it would be beyond reason for GOD to give these Recollects a martyr before *we* have our chance! —And Père Massé looked back at him with his impassive leathery face and slowly winked . . .)

Père Le Caron sat upright in the night. — I am sure they drowned him! he said aloud.

No one replied.

For nine years Père Le Caron went about whispering, and no one paid any attention. But by then, when the Recollects had been excluded from missionary work once and for all in New France, the Gray-Gowns could afford to be generous. So it was that Père Le Jeune, the Superior at Kebec, heard out a pair of Algoumequin Savages who wished to calumniate the Huron for reasons having to do with trade, and allowed himself to believe. Then at last poor Père Nicolas achieved the glory of a mention in the *Jesuit Relations*. His wooden statue was encrusted with the gold of piousness as he stood in his niche in the Stream of Time, blessing the lovely dark-haired Québecoise girls bicycling along Sherbrooke, the Québecoise girls walking down the sidewalks on those Montréal summer evenings when the sky has that northern limpidity of Canada glowing and clean above the street lamps; the lamps of the *Société des alcools de Québec* blaze, and trees shimmer in the vacant lots . . .

William T. Vollmann

AMANTACHA'S SPONSORS

The martyr's plans for Amantacha were not upset with his canoe. The following year, in the time when the Wendat and the Iron People gave one another presents, Soranhes came with his son to Two Large Waters Joining (called by the Iron People *Kekwek*), and entrusted him to the Gray-Gowns, saying: Thus I fulfill my promise. Here is my strong young son. Bring him back to me next year, for so my nephew Kwer Nikoas promised me.

Oh, he did, did he? said Père Le Caron. What a bother. You know very well that passage to France and back is a very uncertain matter . . .

Amantacha stood shyly in the courtyard, staring at the convent's four wooden bastions. He had never seen those before. Outside the ramparts, at the edge of that natural moat called the Rivière Saint-Charles, Montagnais were digging up tiger-lily bulbs to roast. —On the gallery, a young man of that same Nation leaned upon the railing, looking out at them who might have been his cousins. He was dressed like one of the Iron People, for they had *baptized* him. His name was Pastedouachouan. The Recollects had had him in France for five years. He did not remember his own language anymore.

Père Le Caron looked up and saw him. He frowned. —Pierre-Antoine, what are you doing? he cried sharply. Go into the Chapel and say your prayers!

Yes, Père.

Soranhes spoke to Brûlé, a nephew of his from the Iron People. —Who is that boy, and why does the Gray-Gown raise his voice to him in that way? Young people are very delicate. Sometimes they hang themselves from a tree if one scolds them too much.

Ah, my uncle, I cannot say. (Thus Brûlé, shrugging.) He belongs to them now.

And you have no compassion? Beware, my dear nephew, lest in all your comings and goings your mind may sprout seven linings like that of the Hiroquois. I seem to see you devoured by your own mouth! Will you also say of my son *He belongs to them?* Listen well: I have been a good uncle to you. If you are not a good brother to him in the Country of the Iron People, then I shall split your head!

Perhaps I too should poison myself, said Brûlé in a low voice.

You? You love life too much. —No, forgive me, my nephew, I pray you; I become as short in my patience as these Iron People. I should have spoken more gently . . .

Père Le Caron stood with folded arms, tapping his foot upon the ground. He comprehended but little of what had been said, for he had forgotten his command of their dialect, which was in truth Savage, barbarous and outlandish.

Well, Soranhes, what have you to say to me now? You must not keep me waiting.

If the boy is happy he may return to France the following year, replied the father, seeing through the priest as though he were a transparent river-pool. —But after the first year my heart will be aching to behold him once again. —And he took his son by the hand, as if he wished to take him back forthwith.

Very good, *ver*-y good, Soranhes, said Père Le Caron. You have my word.

The Père was young but white-bearded, reaching out for Amantacha's shoulder with spread fingers . . . Amantacha smiled, quick and sensitive. His skin was the color of a brown pond in the sunlight. How good he was! He seemed so docile, so credible that Père Le Caron marveled. —Père Brébeuf, who happened to be there, approved of him, too. (It did not occur to Père Brébeuf that he expected the same great things of the boy that his Superiors expected

Kebec (1990)

of him.) Père Le Caron was especially delighted with him. Before the father departed, Père Le Caron gave him many friendship-presents.

Ver-y good, he says, thought Soranhes to himself. But my eyes see far. My eyes see me doing better.

For he did not like the face of that Montagnais boy whom they had frenchified.

He strolled about the place called *Kekwek*. Tomorrow was the beginning of the appointed day for exchanging gifts with his uncles and nephews among the Iron People, but today was the day of Councils. He must attend these and speak, or else those of his Nation would suspect him of solitariness, which is almost witchcraft. But first he would see what he would see. His brother Oronton could not be spared; he was guarding the beaver-skins against theft. Where was his dear nephew Tregarouaroti? It was he who had given his young brother Savignon to the Iron People for some years. Tregarouaroti would give him good counsel. — But no. He did not want Tregarouaroti to believe he had the greater right to speak. Tregarouaroti was a good hunter, but no warrior; he was not a great man. — Instead, therefore, Soranhes approached Chawain's lodge with his good nephew Iroquet, who, being of the Algonkin Nation, could do less harm with his talk. Chawain was shouting in the courtyard; Chawain was as shrill as ever, although his body had become somewhat dried up with age. (It was that same Chawain who had visited his Nation so many summers and winters before; he remembered him.) The other Iron People feared him — that Soranhes could readily see. Did those big guns in the wall belong to Chawain? Look! Chawain raised his hand, and a man brought him a key. (The Iron People loved locks and keys.) Now Chawain was going into his Store-house. What was in there? Soranhes seemed to see mountains of beads and blankets, glittering ossuaries of hatchet-heads, copper kettles brighter than suns — ah, and guns. How could Chawain not weep, knowing as he did that the Wendat had none of those? Perhaps Amantacha could persuade the Iron People to give him a gun. Then he and Amantacha could win fame. There would be much eating of Hiroquois flesh then in the House of Cut-Off Heads! — But what was Chawain doing now? He had come out, and he was shouting again. Truly Chawain was a bearded old woman; he was a bluejay! And see those men carrying heavy bales on their backs, bent low, struggling up the stairs while Chawain's warriors leaned upon their arquebuses and pulled their hats lower and lower over their eyes! — Iroquet stood beside him, slapping mosquitoes and staring.

Yroquet loved to come here. Iroquet marveled how the Iron People never changed houses when they rotted, but simply patched them up and continued to live in them. Of course their houses were difficult to make; maybe that was why they were so lazy. They did not like to travel. —Now Chawain had given over his scolding. One of the Black-Robes had come. Chawain smiled and deferred to him, as though he were Chawain's uncle. But he was much younger than Chawain. —Ah, this must be the one I desire, said Soranhes to himself, for he knew the Iron People well. —He whispered, and Yroquet went to greet Chawain. Now, while this Black-Gown stood detached for the moment from Chawain, now was the time to come smiling. The Black-Gown stood very tall. His eyes were cold and blue like juniper berries. His skin was much paler than Chawain's. He wore a broadbrimmed hat like the soldiers, so that his face was always in shadow. Soranhes thought to himself that he would like to have one of these hats.

He stepped forward. Chawain looked up in alarm, but Père Brébeuf smiled at him. As soon as the smile went away, the sternness came back, and darkness rippled full of Power in his robe.

Soon enough, Père Brébeuf had given him friendship-presents for his son Amantacha—and his presents were more generous than Père Le Caron's; for he could see that once the child was instructed, he'd be very useful in opening the way to distant Nations. Now it was time to try Chawain's deputy, that big man with the big belly. This was Emery de Caën. Monsieur de Caën, knowing that his own opportunity to be pious had come, submitted in his turn to the cajoleries of the grubby Savage. Eh, a grand number of beads and knives and arrow-points I'm going to have to give him . . . Well, may it be to my celestial credit.

Soranhes was quite satisfied. He prayed for his son's good journey; he prayed for blue sky and smooth waters.

After he had returned to Wendaké (not troubling overmuch to watch for Hiroquois, as that year they were embroiled in a war with the Mahican) the inevitable quarrel broke out. —Père Le Caron was the loser. He stood with bowed head by the raspberry bushes of his convent, listening to the droning of the bees . . . —It was decided that the boy would travel to France on Monsieur de Caën's ship, and that his education would be the charge of those generous Jesuits . . .

William T. Vollmann

THE EDUCATION (1626-29)

As for Amantacha, he was terrified of the Black-Gowns, but only at first. They reminded him of the time that he had gone hunting for birds in the maplewood highlands, for his mother craved meat, and because he went westward instead of east he soon discovered one of the old villages. Of course he was old enough to remember when his village had moved and they'd held the Feast of the Dead in all seemliness, for the sake of the dear bones which must now be left behind; that happened every ten years or so, when the soil was exhausted. And yet he had never gone back to the abandoned place. It was not good to go there, his father said, because the dead were angry. Even the Feast of the Dead did not entirely console a number of them — *viz.*; the weaker ones, who could not hope to withstand HEAD-PIERCER on their journey to the Country of the Dead. They stayed in the old longhouses; they grew spirit-corn in the old fields. Yet now as the young man stood there, he felt a strange curiosity about the dead people, the bone people. — A mangy hide still hung on a stretcher. The bark-lined corn-pits gaped empty. Looking right and left, ignoring the prickling of nervous sweat in the groove of his back, he strode to the middle of the clearing already overgrown with thistles and grass and ferns with wide rounded leaf-lobes so that everything had a grassy smell; he saw how spiders and beetles crawled upon the leaves, and snakes lived in the abandoned lodges whose roofs had tumbled down to let in the hot sun-joy; trees pressed all around and saplings were springing up on the edge of the clearing to drown out that openness; — and suddenly Amantacha started with fright as something cawed loudly inside one of the ruined lodges. He gazed around him. He was alone. Trembling, he took a clod of earth and threw it into the lodge. At once a black crow issued, flapping its wings and screeching. — Amantacha fell to the ground laughing. How ridiculous that crow was! — When he remembered that, he could not be much afraid of the Black-Gowns. — And yet what if the crow were Something Else after all?

The world is small, his father comforted him as they paddled down the rivers to Kekwek. Take courage. The world is but a little island on the back of the GREAT TURTLE. The Iron People cannot take you far. Once you are beyond the forest you will see. It is far, but not far. I know. I am a Big Stone.

Father, what shall I do among the Iron People?

You must win their confidence, so that we may control them.

290

Learn where they are weak, in case they should someday be our enemies. Learn their speech well. Then we shall always know what they say about us (for I think that sometimes the Algonkin interpreters are false). You will do well, Amantacha. I know you. You are my strong son.

Thank you for your words, father. I hear.

The Frenchman they had adopted, Étienne Brûlé, was with them. The Black-Gowns had commanded him to leave Wendaké, for they believed that his heart was rotten. One day, not long after they had stopped to offer tobacco to the Power that dwelled inside Owl's Nest Rock, it came time to portage, during which Amantacha asked this Brûlé (whom he loved well) what it was like in the country of the Iron People.

It is very fine there, Brûlé replied vaguely. We have animals called *horses*, which are moose without antlers —

He hesitated.

But I cannot remember so clearly, Amantacha. Never fear; the Iron People will treat you well . . .

The journey was easy; it was nothing. They arrived in the moon called *When Blackberries Are Ripe*.

Kekwek, what a place! A hundred Iron People lived there now. They built many tiny houses; he didn't know why. The Iron People didn't like to live together, Monsieur de Caën said. — Amantacha peered through the lace curtains of Kekwek with their flowers and shields and crests, thinking: why do the women of the Iron People leave holes in their work? (Not that there were many women here. At least they didn't have beards, as Tehorenhaennion the Shaman had said.) And he laughed aloud, so that Monsieur de Caën spoke to him through the interpreter, saying: Young man, don't be insolent. We see possibilities in you, but after all you're still nothing more than a Savage! — Amantacha gaped at such rudeness. Then he smiled and said nothing; silence was the way of the Wendat. — Amantacha was amazed at everything. But he reminded himself: My father said that when I come back next year I'll be a man. And I'll know the secrets of the Iron People. — So he was exultant when Monsieur de Caën put his arm around him and led him aboard his ship. — A cannonade! — They sailed. Crows were shrieking over the edge of the settlement in an untidy row that reformed crazily, and the cannons faced them in the sunset, the light too cloud-muted to shine on them; Champlain's sentinels found them cold to the touch as they stood there watching the ship decrease like melting ice. The

wind whipped the tops of trees back against the wall at the edge
of what was not yet Upper Town, and the Fleuve Saint-Laurent
streamed greedily . . . Amantacha kept looking in between the trees
as they went down river, his eyes like his child-hands dragging
across the stakes of the palisade at home for the fun of the noise.
But he didn't do that anymore. Besides, Teanaostoiaiaé Town was
so far away . . . What was his father doing? They sailed past the blue
mountains and green table-lands on the south side of the Fleuve
Saint-Laurent, the fleuve a dreary grayish-brown hue that evening;
and orange striped the gray ceiling of cloud overhead. Amantacha
felt sad. Now they passed Anticosti Island, and reached the Great
Ocean that Amantacha had never before seen. And once the whole
world had been that way, so the Old Men said at home! Breasting
the mountain-waves without any incident
that the chroniclers thought worthy of record,
they landed safe at Rouen by the grace of Our
LORD, where Amantacha stayed with
De Caën and his uncle Ezéchiel for a week.
He saw a moose called a *horse.* He saw
beggars and prostitutes. *Then . . .*

   Then for the first time
he saw Paris. The Black-
Gowns took him there.
The city was like some
great egg in the fields,
cracked into a thousand
pieces by its *rues* and
avenues; within its wall-
curve rose church towers
innumerable above the teeming roofs, their bells
shrieking louder than any birds he had ever
heard; and wide stone bridges crossed the Seine
by way of an Isle of Churches (which also was
infested with houses); one of the biggest bell-
towers of all rose here, high enough almost to

clear the stench of the river; from it Amantacha could see the green
hills and windmills beyond the wall and he wanted to go see them
but the Black-Gowns laughed and Brûlé said no, my good nephew;
Paris is where you will be taught and they took him from church
to church to be presented to strange people whom the Black-Gowns
said meant him well, but he thought that the slit-windows of those

churches made them seem more than ever like skeletons. —The Roy's coach squeaked through the streets on its wooden wheels, between the walls of narrow high houses whose windows were vertical slits; and merchants rode by and workers rushed down the avenues on urgent errands and the nobles rode by nodding to each other in their beaver hats. He saw many more beggars, horses and prostitutes. He saw lepers stinking and dying in the streets. At night the Black-Gowns closed their shutters very tightly so that it was hard for him to breathe and he heard strange laughter and screams in the streets and sometimes young nobles rode about all night shouting and clattering their weapons, and he was afraid because the brothers in the house with him were afraid. In the morning they took him to see old Duc Henri, who was the Viceroy of New France, and the Viceroy said something to Amantacha in the language of the Iron People and Amantacha replied, knowing that he could not understand: The Black-Gowns are like crows! —But all at once he thought: These men are Shamans. What if they can read my thoughts? And why should I say such things to this old man, who is well-respected? So he quickly dropped to his knees as he had seen the Iron People do, and kissed the Viceroy's hand. He knew enough now not to call him Uncle, as he would have done at home. With closed eyes he waited, like a clever lapdog, until he felt the old man's hand on his head, stroking, stroking . . .

He had no interpreter anymore. Considering this Étienne Brûlé fellow to be barbarous and coarse, the Black-Gowns had dispensed with him; he'd go back to Canada on the next ship, being out of place here. (He knelt and clasped his hands and his lips moved, and their hearts softened a little, for they thought that he was praying. But really he was mouthing over the names of all the Huron girls he'd slept with: She Is Eternal, She Is Called After, Fruit Matures, Small Matter, She Is Called Treetops, She Is Not Waiting* . . . —This last was Amantacha's sister. Remembering her, Brûlé grinned defiantly; he felt that he had cheated these Jesuits somehow, when he'd popped her . . .) —No, Messieurs, there was nothing for it: Amantacha must learn French. This gave him pause, as he remembered that Montagnais boy at Kebec, named Pastedouachouan, who had forgotten his own language. But he told himself to have courage. He did not fear the wiles of the Iron People. Of course he could already say his bonjours; now he learned his devotions and excuses;

---

*Teondisewan.

in his facile way he was soon tracing out his majuscules from
𝔄 to ℨ; he read out the most essential verses from the Bible that
the Viceroy had given him, his soft voice pleasing all the Black-
Gowns who heard, and he learned to write his name. Kwer Nikoas
had promised his father that the Black-Gowns would bring him
back at the end of a year, but Kwer Nikoas was dead. — Eh, but he
is a clever boy! they said. Soon he was copying out the Creed in a
steady hand.

One day there was a great crowd, and the Black-Gowns took him
to see the troops with their long guns slung over their shoulders,
marching out of Paris through an archway whose walls met in a
point, and beneath this was a toothy lip of spikes that could come
crashing down when the city was under siege, and beneath this
the soldiers disappeared, while pikemen flanked them, keeping the
crowds back, and faces peered through the narrow rectangular windows. And he had the strange fancy that the marching uniforms
were somehow akin to the letters that he was learning, that in
every hymnbook there drilled regiments innumerable, proceeding
from page to page as fast as pages might be turned; but then he had
the shivery feeling that perhaps the letters were marching deeper
and deeper inside his body, conquering him for the Iron People.
— What a grand parade! said one among the Black-Gowns. And
Amantacha smiled and said: Yes, Père, it is truly a remarkable spectacle. — He quickly lost his leisure to see these things when the
Black-Gowns began to educate him in earnest. They took him down
into their dark Meditation Room, whose walls were lined with pictures of Devils and terrifying tortures; for they wished to strike
a wholesome fear of GOD into his heart. They left him there for
many hours, with the door locked, until they heard him crying out.

During the daytime Amantacha felt nothing but happiness. A
continual excitement warmed him; he never knew what new marvels the Iron People might show him. Coaches rushed past him like
monsters. The food was plentiful, although it smelled bad (except
for the lemon-rind, which he had had also at Kebec and thought
surpassingly delicious). He was filled with pride that he had been
chosen to understand such things. When he came home at last, he
would be the best friend of the Iron People: all the Wendat would
come to him, and it would be his choice to open or close the way
to the Iron People. — Ah, how well the Iron People cared for him!
But at night fear and guilt crawled inside him like worms. He craved
the corn soups and breads that his elder sister Teondisewan made,

kneeling by the hearth in her deerskin skirt to which were sewn beautiful animals fashioned from the scraps of copper kettles, and the good smoky smell of the lodge was around him and his little sister was laughing in his mother's arms and then they all smoked tobacco with his father . . . — They are far, he said to himself. Have courage. — But he was ashamed that he could not better understand the language of the Iron People. He dreaded the morning when he must wake up and try to understand the Iron People again. No matter how much he slept, he was still tired. It was a great effort for him to learn the ways of the Iron People.

It was the vast crowds above all else that chastened the boy and fitted him for his purpose: seeing them, he understood that the Wendat could never hope to contest with these folk on equal terms.

He dreamed of water lobelias goggling at him like AATAENTSIK's eyes in the Sweetwater Sea —

They instructed him at Paris; they taught him at Rouen. (Behind every rayère or loophole, a Black-Gown waited.) At their Collège in Rouen was a young Black-Gown named Père Daniel. Père Daniel spoke much of Heaven. Whenever he said that word, he pointed upward with his black sleeve and smiled so that he would understand how pleasant a place it was. Amantacha supposed at first that Heaven must be identical with the Country from which the Sky-Spirit AATAENTSIK had originally come: a great white plain of cloud riven with white gulleys and puffed up with tussocks whose edges glowed with blueness like snow-shadows. She had fallen from there in the days when the world was only water; diving to bring up mud in their mouths, the generous animals had made land for Her. — But when he told this to Père Daniel he replied that it was a fable, and that there was no AATAENTSIK in Heaven. He must forget about Her, Père Daniel said; either She did not exist or else She was a wicked demon from Hell. — Hearing this, Amantacha smiled and nodded his head. — You tell me new things that I have never heard before, he said. — Gazing upward, he thought: There must be many places in the Sky that the Black-Gowns do not know about. Perhaps Heaven is the place where only dead Frenchmen go. — Of course he was too polite to say anything. Therefore, the Black-Gowns marveled at his intelligence.

He was taken to Duc Henri's again, and the Duc studied him without pride or disappointment, noting how the boy's face had filled out even to plumpness, so that his disagreeably protuberant cheekbones vanished. He had taken on a somewhat smug turn of mouth, thought the Duc. Eh, he was young. No doubt his life would be hard enough when they returned him among his fellow Savages. So it had been, as he heard, with that Montagnais, Pierre-Antoine Pastedouachouan.

Père Daniel spoke to him of Hell, and said that all the Savages were from there. — Yes, said Amantacha. Everything that you Black-Gowns say is true. The Old Men have taught me nothing to the contrary. My father Soranhes told me always to heed your words, that I might learn.

Your father is a wise man, said Père Daniel.

The Iron People slouched; they threw themselves down in chairs, as if the chairs would never break or be anything but chairs.

There came the passionate moment when he was inducted into the Exercises, and they spoke to him of fleuves and rivières until he saw the Stream of Time, called *Yandawa*,* which made its massy rapids with the sound yandawa yandawa, and he peered between beech leaves eaten lacy by caterpillars and there was Yandawa, spilling down granite steps with the easy swoop of mosquitoes, and Père Daniel was praying *Water from the side of CHRIST, wash me*, and Amantacha threw himself in: Yandawa took him. He almost fell far enough downstream to see Sainte Kateri Tekakwitha where at the edge of the lilies a stone curved up from the water like a turtle's back, but he did not go there because he feared the Hiroquois waiting in the birchy darkness; he almost swam far enough upstream to think that he was home among the dry floury smell of cornfields and his family had prepared a great feast of unleavened bread seasoned with blueberries and deer fat for him so that he smiled for happiness and Père Daniel touched his shoulder very softly, believing that he had seen JESUS but he did not go home, either, because now indeed he did see JESUS, Who said to him: My sister's son, you and I are related forever.

Rihouista, he said. I believe.

When at last they considered him sufficiently instructed, he was baptized in that dark and solemn Cathedral at Rouen paved with bowed heads, lit with flickering torches and candelabra like wilted spider-legs; it was a confusion of walls and railings and darkness and eyes staring at him; he sometimes heard the whispers or even the shouts on the street: *ah, le petite Sauvage!* (for it was said that he was the King of CANADA's own son); and around him the monks

---

*Wendat word for river.

kneeling, bearing torches as tall as towers; the Archbishop towered over him with his strange onion-shaped headgear ... But Amantacha was no longer afraid. He knew by now that the Iron People did not mean him harm. Indeed, this baptism was as rich an honor among the Iron People as a portion of deer fat. —His godparents were the Duc de Longueville and Madame de Villais. They were very proud of him and said: Now you may forget that Savage name of yours; now your name is Louys; you are Louys de Saincte Foy ... —and Amantacha felt a pleasurable shiver of fear in him, to hear that the Black-Gowns had changed him both in name and nature. —It was the icy Month When Bear-Cubs Are Born.* A great stage had been erected so that the crowds could better see him; the Black-Gowns were triumphant. The historian Creuxius, perhaps displaying his own equivocal feelings about the affair, reports that a flash of lightning illuminated the ceremony. Be that as it may, Louys's confidence never cracked. —How everyone gloried in him! —But something else he had learned by now, something that he never told the Black-Gowns. *They* were not the Lords of the Iron People, as they had pretended in Canada. Once he was with two Black-Gowns on the street and a man came rushing at them shouting: You will burn in Hell, you traitors and Gallicans! —And he remembered also how his uncle Père Brébeuf had vied with his uncle Père Le Caron for custody of him; and he thought to himself: they mean to devour each other!

Afterwards a christening feast was held, in which each guest was given his own plate for his meat (this was a new custom that had just been imported from Italy). They ate their soup out of a skull-like bowl of that mirror-iron called *silver*; their women brought this bowl to them, lifting it by its ears.

Amantacha was very pleased with himself. And how he loved the Iron People! What impressed him most of all was their arquebuses. He thought to himself: If only I could take one of these weapons when they are not looking, and hide it ... What a hero they will call me at home! I will go against the Five Nations and shoot all their Captains!

He awaited his opportunity, but it never came. The Iron People guarded their guns too well.

---

*Décembre.

William T. Vollmann

THE DEATH OF AMANTACHA (1636)

In the Moon When One Sows, twelve warriors were caught in an ambush-trap by the enemy as they crossed into their Country for some early raiding. So the torturers became the tortured. But they laughed and sang while dying, as was honorable and just. And they were devoured. Now in Wendaké the War-Chiefs met together in the House of Cut-Off Heads, and they decided to punish this insult. Which Nation had committed the murders no one could say for certain, for the spies whom the War-Chiefs maintained south of the Lake called *Beautiful* made contradictory claims, but this was a matter of small importance. The Hiroquois were all the same; they were all serpents! So the Old Men closed the door of the House of Cut-Off Heads, to prevent enemy spies from hearing their deliberations, and they recounted their dreams and strategies to one another. Since they were treaty-bound with the Sonontrerrhonons, they decided to attack the Onondaga —

Soranhes made up his mind not to go this year, although, being a Big Stone, he must contribute a kettle of smoked fish to the War-Feast. A dream commanded him away from joining the young men. But Amantacha was very hot to bring home some Hiroquois warriors for burning, as he had failed in his purpose the previous year. The Hiroquois were worse than dogs! he wouldn't be happy until he squeezed one of their heads in his arms, the blood dripping where it had been freshly severed . . . One of his uncles decided to go also. Now they held the War-Feast in the House of Cut-Off Heads and all the young men sang war-songs against the enemy while their wives and sisters and asquas danced fist upon fist and then the young men went to the Arendouane as ever: this year again the prognostications were bad, but they shrugged and said: Whatever happens we can endure. — The Peace-Chief, who was old, said to them: Perhaps you should be cautious this year . . . — but they shouted: *No!* at which he sighed and said: Young men. — Amantacha had not been well acquainted with the twelve men who had been burned, but he could never forget his little nephew who had been killed last year at Contarrea. And if he had wanted to forget him, his aunts would scarcely have let him. That was the law of life. — Don't we eat our lice to revenge ourselves upon them? his aunts said to him. Ah, sister's son, how we shall honor you if you devour some Hiroquois for us! — That was how they talked. How fine it would be to bring back an enemy to be tortured! Then his aunts could dry their

298

tears at last. His poor aunts — how he loved them! — Amantacha shouted, and his father smiled a little. — Young men, young men . . . mumbled the Peace-Chief. — It was like this every year. And the warriors tested one another to see who could hold his hand in the fire the longest, to prepare themselves should they fall into the hands of the Hiroquois.

Amantacha shaved his head except for a center-ridge, so that his enemies could not seize him by the hair. He painted himself with black and red stripes. His aunts gave him a sack of roasted corn-meal to take on the trail. His father gave him arrows with iron points and said: I wish only that I might have given you a gun from the Iron People! I cannot understand them.

They are misers, Amantacha admitted. They also lie, for though they tell us not to burn men they do the same in Paris. But some-day they will repent, and then JESUS will forgive them.

Yes, JESUS has been good to you. He is your guardian spirit . . .

Amantacha smiled quickly. He caressed his father's face.

Before Amantacha took leave of Echon and his Black-Gowns, he asked leave to make a few of the Exercises under their direction, which they willingly granted. The day fixed was the first of Holy Week. Children were shrieking and running between the long-houses. Men strode about, fastening on their sleeves to go to war. Just outside of one of the longhouses a woman stood very still and silent. She glanced once behind her at the doorway, as if she would have rather stood inside it looking out, but there was too much going in and out. She stood self-conscious like a defeated enemy. The Black-Gowns gazed upon her sadly. If only she would renounce her pagan ways —

Père Davost had said more than once that she ought to be banned from the Residence, as she was in league with Sorcerers, but Père Brébeuf did not believe that the time for that had come as yet, be-cause at least she did not revile the Faith. Indeed, it sometimes seemed that she showed great interest in his predications, as well she should, having been the companion and fornicatrix of one who had been well instructed, no matter how far he might have fallen since . . . — Eh bien, she had certainly been advantaged in having connection with Louys Amantacha. GOD grant that it bear fruit.

Amantacha came toward her and said something in a low voice, so that Père Brébeuf, who listened as intently as he could, could hear nothing. Her expression did not change. Then her lips moved. (What a pretty Savagess!) Amantacha smiled dazzlingly at her.

—Yes, Brébeuf heard him say proudly, they are very severe, those Black-Gowns! —He began to walk toward Brébeuf. He looked back at her once. Then he came to Brébeuf, and they went into the Chapel together.

* * *

Iroquois false face "female" mask, made by SKE^{N}D^{E}SO^N ("Across The River"), Mohawk, Turtle Clan (ca. 1990)

They paddled their canoes down the river, which was brown and walled with rocks. Low hills smiled with rock between their mile-long tree-lips. The river was blue with brown wrinkles, brighter than the sky. So blue, so broad, that river of grace! They paddled, and the sun was hot on their faces. (But no one wanted to coast beneath the shady cliffs; there were WATER-MONSTERS there.) The sky was blooming with clouds. It was springtime. The trees awoke, and began to think about putting forth leaves.

They passed White Rock Mountain where the dead white stalks of trees leaned against spruces; they drew abreast of steep black tree-grown rocks down which fresh water streamed, and Rabbit bounded in the wall of trees and Amantacha shot him. The other cried out in delight at his skill, and he laughed, saying, My brothers, it was nothing! and they all smiled. A brave jumped ashore and hurled the carcass into the canoe. Now the hills were dimpled like a fat woman's belly. Seeing this, a man laughed and pointed and cried: Behold the fallen star! — a saying which they said in the presence of fat people. Then the others laughed. Springs burst from between two hemlock-shaded rocks; tree-shadows caressed the soil so lightly.

Now again he came into the Country of the Hiroquois, where, in Lescarbot's words, *everything is covered with high forests which threaten the clouds.*

There was good game in the basswood forests. There always was, in the Country of the Hiroquois. Every night (for they traveled only by night now) they caught turkeys and other prey. Yet soon it was no longer safe to kindle any fire, for they drew too close to the enemy.

It was night in the Moon When Blackberries Are Ripe. The women of the Hiroquois, the Serpent People, would be shuffling naked through their cornfields, fertilizing the corn with woman-Power, dragging their robes behind them to gather up the vermin that sought to devour their corn. Amantacha had glimpsed them on other raids, their hair midnight black, their thighs and breasts so moony-pale. His father had captured two women, a mother and daughter, and brought them back to Teanaostoiaiaé. That had been long ago. It was rare to do that: usually women were tortured where they were caught, because they could not walk quickly. But Soranhes had remembered how a mother and daughter in the Turtle Clan had been killed by the Hiroquois. He was always remembering what to give people; that was why he was such a Big Stone. Amantacha wanted to be a Big Stone, too. If only he could capture one of these girls: girls were easy prisoners. They would scream when their fingers were sawn off. Or perhaps someone would adopt her and give him many good presents. That would be good, too. Ah, but could he do it? He had spent too long in idleness among the Iron People! That was why he shrank a little from capturing a warrior (although he would never let the others know it). Then, too, his own capture three summers ago had taken some of his courage. He desired to gain it back by stages. A woman first. These women in the moonlight, dragging their robes like shadows — the shadows between their breasts that smelled of sweat and corn and good fresh

301

dirt — how delighted he would be if one were his!

After that he would capture a warrior for burning. That was much more manly.

In the invisible night-grass, wet against knees and ankles and waist, the Sonontrerrhonons waited. They heard the Huron coming. Their spies, their warpainted watchers, had found them. Amantacha was surrounded, defeated, like a tree-riven rock in the middle of the forest. They recognized him at once and began to burn his fingers with cries of delight. Never had they forgotten how three times his friends the Iron People had harmed them. Three times his Sorcerer friends had brought it about so that the Nations of the Haudeno-saunee had been gashed and wounded by the FACELESS ONE Whose features dark and invisible even to dead grandfathers now smiled like trembling night-water reflecting flights of bats; three times the FACELESS ONE had cut down men and women, children and babes with His hatchet of night, that weapon with the sharpness of iron arrowheads, with the voice (the horrible whistling voice) of the Iron People's bullets; three times the FACELESS ONE had sought to wrench apart with His bloody hands the Work, the Common-wealth, the League of the Haudenosaunee. — Amantacha's friends were the slaves of the FACELESS ONE! Ah, how they hated him!

They took his rosary and broke it.

They led him rapidly down the forest trail. As if in a dream, he heard them utter the war-whoops; now the village appeared before him and the War-Chief was dancing and all the other enemy war-riors were dancing, and one of their Old Men came forth to con-gratulate them and the others sent up a great shout. — He glimpsed spirit-masks with black faces and red writhing lips: there had been pestilence here. The masks stared at him with round copper eyes, coyly, from under a veil of cornstraw hair. — He said silently: JESUS is a greater OKI than you! — But it was all show; he was terrified be-cause his rosary had been destroyed. — They led him to their House of Cut-Off Heads and threw him down. A man led a boy up and put a knife into his hand. Then the bubble of panic rose up in his chest, stinking with bile, and he bit his lips hard. Yelling with laughter, the boy sliced a skinny snake of flesh from Amantacha's arm and popped it into his mouth. Amantacha gazed straight ahead. He sought to make the Exercises as the Black-Gowns taught him; even as they pierced his flesh with their torments he strove to swim up-stream, but could not. The agony blossomed thickly in his flesh like sphagnum moss in its stylized green galaxies. For three days they tortured him, and then led him to the next village. They led him to the gauntlet. He raised his head high, although he had little hope. Perhaps he might yet be adopted . . . But no. Nor ought he to have expected it. No one came to him and pointed out the lodge in which he would live. Grinning, they thrust him to the head of the line. The stink of their rage dizzied him.

He sought to fortify himself by considering what his father would do. His father would bear the torments laughing, he knew it. Ah, and what of the Black-Gowns? They too; they too; for this was nothing in comparison to the images of Hell which they had shown him in France.

In his heart he said to JESUS: My UNCLE, help me to endure this trial.

His mouth was very dry.

Now they urged him on with honeyed voices, saying how much their squaws longed to caress him. The squaws stood smiling, holding knives and thorn-sticks —

So once again he ran the gauntlet. They beat him unconscious.

When he recovered his senses they had turned their attentions to some other Wendat warriors whom they had captured. They blackened the faces and bodies of these men with pigment and burned them at the stake, torturing them by casting coals upon their heads. The Wendat sang their death-songs and died bravely. — The next day it came Amantacha's turn. What he wanted most of all was to taste the young corn roasted once again. It seemed to him that there was nothing more precious than that food. Yet as they led him to the place where his life would be cut and burned away, he put that aside; he thought back upon the time when he had seen Paris, between whose tall pillars flew birds incinerated in pillars of sunlight; and the bridges were spiked with soldiers' pikes — he had never known there could be so many people in the whole world! — and the Black-Gowns had taken him on a boat that went through dank arches whose darkness was darker than forest darkness; and the Black-Gowns showed him castles overgrown with turrets and boles and branches; and everything was crowded and humming and shouting: he looked at the Hiroquois and cried You are nothing! *Nothing*, I tell you!

Then they shouted in rage, and cut out his tongue.

They burned him quite artfully. It took a day and a night for him to die. Of the terrible pain of burning, my love Kateri Tekakwitha is perhaps the best witness. At Kahnawake she often "disciplined"

William T. Vollmann

herself with twelve hundred blows or more of a spiked girdle which (like Père Brébeuf) she wore all day (it is written that once after carrying a great load of wood from the forest she slipped on ice and fell, and then the secret spikes sank so deeply into her flesh that the snow around her was spotted with blood, but she got up and finished carrying the wood without telling a soul). When she went with the other women to fetch a deer which the men had killed, she lagged until she was out of sight, and then walked barefoot upon the sharp pond ice, smiling and bleeding until one of the other women came to look for her, thinking that she might be ill. At once she put her moccasins on, so that no one might think her proud, to be mortifying herself in this way. Every Saturday, as I have told, she and her good companion Marie-Thérèse Tegaiaguenta scourged each other with birch-rods in an abandoned cabin, Kateri weeping and entreating Marie-Thérèse to strike her harder because it was not

Church at Kahnawake (1989)

until the third stroke that blood came, and after five strokes she said her rosary and humbly begged the favor of five strokes more, and as the scarred flesh split anew between her shoulders she cried out: Vent on me, GOD, Thy anger!; and then it was five strokes more and five strokes more until she could count no more. As I think of this I want more than anything for Kateri to be here before me so that I could embrace her and tell her that she had not done anything wrong, but I know that there is nothing that I could say that she would ever believe; for as Père Chauchetière later said: *During her life she considered herself to be a great sinner, because*

304

it seemed as if she had a stain on her body, which she was very careful to hide. — What did he mean by this? What did she mean? Was it simply her ugly smallpoxed face that she covered always with her blanket? But even if I had enough Power to make her live before me, even if I had enough goodness to truly reach her through some loving agony of kindness and grief, she would only have turned away. — Ah, my Père, she once told the Black-Gown, Cholonec, I will not marry. I do not like men, and have the greatest aversion to marriage. The thing is impossible.* — So let me interrupt you no longer, my Katheri, in your mortifications. — She strove always to go hungry, and if some well-meaning person besought her to eat sagamite, she would put ashes in it, so that at least she would have no enjoyment of it. On the Feast of the Purification she walked barefoot in knee-deep snow, telling those who questioned her that it was nothing in comparison to what good JESUS suffered. She gathered thorns from the forest and rolled naked upon them for three nights running, until she resembled a dead person, and the Black-Gowns commanded her to throw the thorns into the fire — which, of course, she immediately did, as obedience is a virtue. Yet she still searched to find the greatest pain. One day she thought to ask her foster-mother Anastasia Tegonhatsihongon what she supposed it was, and Tegonhatsihongon considered and said: I am certain how to answer you, my Kateri, for what could be so painful as fire? The Devil lives in fire, as Père Chauchetière has often taught us, and indeed I will never forget how some of the Huron captives screamed, when we were burning them. It was a favorite trick of my aunt's to put live coals between their toes, because she said that was the place of greatest agony. — But why do you ask such a thing? — I know not why I asked, dear mother, replied Tekakwitha, dissembling "very cleverly," as the Black-Gowns would have approvingly put it; indeed you are right, mother; for from fire comes the most fearful torment. — At her first opportunity she spoke of this to Marie-Thérèse, who agreed that fire was of all things the worst. — Indeed I have not the heart or courage to mortify myself so far as that, Kateri. — Never mind, said the other. She went alone to the Chapel and branded herself with coals like a slave. She put an ember between her toes while saying her *Hail Marie*. Then she commenced

---

*She was considered an ill-favored slave. "This has caused some of the Savages to say after her death that GOD had taken her because men did not want her." (Thus Père Chauchetière.)

in earnest, and burned herself from toes to knees with firebrands. Upon this charred and bleeding flesh she knelt all night . . .

In such a fashion perished Louys Amantacha. And yet I think that his death was a greater martyrdom than Tekakwitha's; for she chose hers; he did not. — Did he die screaming or singing? — Ask the Haudenosaunee.

Now they were very happy, and cut his intestines into little pieces for the children to put on the ends of sticks as they ran about the village yelling, and they shared his flesh among them, and then one of the Shamans made this charm against his spirit:

> *You have no right to trouble me.*
> *Depart: — I am becoming stronger.*
> *You are now departing me,*
> *You who would devour me:*
> *I become stronger, stronger.*
> *Mighty Power is within me.*
> *You cannot now defeat me.*
> *I am becoming stronger:*
> *I am stronger, stronger, stronger.*

They made the Great Feather Dance of victory, raising the knee; white feathers crowned their heads. The drummer beat his rattle on the bench; the dancers stamped and pummeled the air with their fists, filled with greatness.

When Amantacha's father had returned from the Island Nation of the Algonkin, where he had been gambling with his good brother Iroquet, the warriors came and told him this news. He arose and said: I have lost my courage! Now without my strong son to shield me I see myself cut to pieces by my enemies. Now without my strong son to avenge me I see my flesh torn by their teeth. I regret every moment that my strong son did not spend by my side. I regret the time that he lived among the Iron People, and every moment that he was out of my sight. When my strong son was born, he did not cry when his mother pierced his ears. When my strong son was captured by the Hiroquois, he made no cry when they cut off his finger. Now he is dead. Now he is dead.

Two Poems
Jackson Mac Low

NET MURDER AT SEA

now jeopardizes the Alaska salmon catch.

begun to do anything about it.

                                                  nets that can
be stretched across 30 miles of sea.

                                miles of the Pacific each
summer to catch salmon,
                  tuna.

more tolerable scale and closer to land.

                birds,
                        tufted puffins and
short-tailed shearwaters,
       fishermen want to harvest those same fish
after they've grown and,
allotted total catch in American waters.

    at sea.

                           salmon popula-
tion.

                          nets in their own
waters;
                        viable alterna-
tives.

nets within a
hundred miles of bird nesting areas and to require
fleets fishing with drift nets to accept observers.

sea should be the first interest of all
fishermen.
method of ocean fish-
ing now jeopardizes the Alaska salmon catch.

more is at stake,
huge drift nets that can
be stretched across 30 miles of sea.

Korea and
Taiwan cover thousands of miles of the Pacific each
summer to catch salmon,

land.

marketable
fish.

fishermen want to harvest those same fish after
they've grown and,
allotted total catch in American waters.

at sea.

salmon popula-
tion.

nets in their own
waters;
viable alterna-
tives.

4 August 1990
New York

Jackson Mac Low

AND OTHER LAND

And other land.

Leverage sea.

Least drift fish.

First.

Environmentalists same to short-tailed thousand thousands
miles unusually alarming returned.

Can drift miles,
include whales,
prohibit long more.

Support porpoises.

Pacific beacons
enlightened observers.

And they drift;
thus the nets kill fish.

Nylon goals goaded.

United begun mysterious to shores.

The
Japan salmon.

Japanese great.

Japanese farther thousands of puffins entangled alone.

Unmarketable.

Enlightened ban accepts method year.

Beacons
trap alarming
American streams;
life returned that allotted these fleets
miles.

1 October 1990
New York

On the Death and Existence
of Isaac His Brother
Peter Cole

*— after the Hebrew of Samuel Hanagid, also
known as Ismail Ibn Nagrela, 993-1056 CE*

I rushed to my brother who was,
they told me, now weak in his illness
and failing,
  when a messenger
 approached and was still.

"Is Isaac alive?"

  "Already dead," he answered.

  And I cursed him:

"Be deaf and have dust in your mouth,
and learn in your life each instant of sorrow.
 May your parents mourn you.

 Haven't I called for a doctor?
And hasn't he healed many others like Isaac?

How could such wealth of spirit falter?
Prized by his peers, a gift to his people —
 he sleeps."

And he said to me,
"Can one who took ill and then died awaken —
 whether poor or in power?"

———————

First-born
  of my mother
    death's
angel your specter,
  soon the sun
setting will turn you,
  and by evening,
    stones divide us —
earth's dust your shroud.

Neither splendor nor
  wealth could help you
    in your affliction,
neither capital nor cup.
  I kissed you —
your heart wouldn't have it,
though you lay like a healthy
    man asleep.
  I wept,
but you wouldn't reply,
your tongue held
  from speaking.

And you slept
the sleep of forever
    the Rock
  topples
    and pours
across His design.

They'd given you wine
  in the cup of
    ancient death
    I'll drink from soon.

———

Why should I force
  what custom requires
while my heart feels
like a moth-eaten shirt?

And why mourn in the
    dirt beside him,
when thinking reminds me
    of slime-filled pits?
Grief has broken my
    body's bearing;
why should I shatter
pitchers and cups?

The torn clothing
    will long be sewn,
when my heart still stings
as though ripped with thorns;
    the walls of my strength
      will weaken with pain,
    after my clothes
have been beaten and washed;

and sorrow will cling
      to my leaning frame,
like staves
in the rings of the ark.
But rest and happiness
    beyond my brother.

will hover forever
    strange to my mood.

—————

My language,
    I'd ask of you
in my life
to lift up a sound
    of lament
    for my brother and father,
and my father all who are broken
in judgment,
      and the widow deceived;

for the generous who opened their doors
    to the street,
    when others were locked,
who'd herd as one the heifer and bear,
    and none devour,
        none become prey.

I bathed him and dressed him
    and placed him in bed,
        and into my
    mouth came the voice of labor,

and I brought him to his grave,
    my clothing torn,
        my family gathered,
and I rose and went down

and helped him
    toward the world below.

They said:
    "Make of him an offering,
        who will give?"
and he made of me an offering.
    They said: "Time will
    make you well and you'll rest."

And I answered them in pain:

"On this wellness of time
    and all rest beyond my brother —
        a curse!

Take, My Strength, my soul —

for grief such as this it can't carry."

———————

And I returned,
    my spirit anguished.
        God be gracious
to you my brother,
buried the day

before yesterday,
and now my mind is bitter.

Peace to you,
    who maybe hears me
    calling with all my power.
    Answer me: Can you find
the dirge through my weeping?
    And how have you slept
in your tomb of dust below?

Have your bones let go?
Do your teeth show through?
    Has your life-blood fled
      in a night
as tears fled falling from me?

First-born of our father,
    I left you
in the hands of he who's drawn me,
      and on my word
you'll move toward peace through my
promise.

——————

Tell him, please,
    whom I long to see —
my hands released him
    to Lostness:
By the life of the Living
    God, for the world
he'll be in my blood
    like fire,
    until I'm dust
in the dust at his side.

——————

Could condolence persuade me?
    Is there solace? Hope in his wake?
And what is knowledge beyond my brother,
or life after leading him down to his grave?
Please don't stare, and save your speeches.

Thank you for coming;
    stand over there, opposite,
        yes, further off.
Recommend me now to the jackal who mourns —
    he'll befriend me.
They'll tell him to wail and I'll wail —
    and we'll see whose hauntedness carries.

But don't, friends, liken my suffering to Suffering,
or this breach by Isaac's death to your breaks.

––––––––

You've given up, heart,
    on bringing him back —
        on ever again
seeing his likeness.
Pledge yourself now to abjectness,
    and whenever you ask for
        strength in your grief —
          to dying his death.

––––––––

Twelve months have passed —
    and you still haven't fled
        the fowler's snare.
Are the clods of earth so sweet to you now
    that to us you prefer worms and decay?
        You were the best of us.
    Come back to your place with the elders,
and we'll talk of my battles and latest campaigns.

Though how could he rise —
    whose flesh is rotting,
        whose bones are like cut trees?
    Imprisoned in earth, as his soul is in sky,
as the maggots eat through his leathery shroud,
    and into his skin, like leaves.

––––––––

Peter Cole

When the name Isaac is called out across me,
   and my soul splits and my bitterness shows,
   and others confront me, upright as I fail —
      their mouths full of laughter,
      their voices a song to my fall —

   and I act the horizon
like Joseph, as they gather about me —
how could I weep when they take such
   pride in seeing me crushed? My brother,
      with my own hands hidden in sorrow —

   as though I'd never loved him like soul
      as a child, not shared a room,
         and the way to school —
   whom I drew down to the pit with my will:
   Death's shadow and dirt have replaced me,

   as though you'd never been for me strength
         and a refuge in pain.
   Quicken my being borne to the dust.
Keep me from looking upon my wretchedness.
      I think of you now in bed as I rest,

      and the memories steal
         dreams from my eyes.
As I eat I recall you fasting in darkness —
and the food in my stomach is venom within me.
      And I think of you thirsty,

      in the grave, as I drink,
and my tears unsweeten my water and wine.
Light of my eyes, which dim, and my wound, which widens,
   was it you alone we left in the grave
         that day of my ruin?

      Are there others?
         My brother, do you long
   for the missing family about you
and draw to you ghost-like spirit to warm you?
Their dying won't help — and mirrors my own.

316

Now I despise the lids of my eyes
     and forever will loathe my sleep:
what was done to your corpse will be done soon to mine.
    From the first news of your fate's parting,
      I've feared for my failings:

let your death be reproof both to fools and the wise.

———————

Time, which betrays us,
why do I long for my brother, and thirst?
What does it mean? If you've stolen him
    from me — will he return?
      How? And when?
My eyes with his death have dimmed;
does it please you to see me now
      blindness's friend?
For you, Isaac, long in the grave
      and not to return,
    I weep and lean.

I bought with your death
    heart's knowledge, and craft,
  which during your life confused me.
I thought you'd live for my sake forever,
    but time meant other.

———————

A psalm to the hearer

of prayer in my spirit forever.
  To praise Him is proper
    who metes out justice
  to the children of men,
  like the sun for all
    revealed in its sky.
  All who govern
    hard in their power,
first he created
    youthful and soft,
  like grass and like labor,

like everything born,
and the poplar and oak.
But grief he created strong in its birth,
and weak in its growth.
And wherever it festers
in a thinking heart —
that heart is lost.
From God-without-name
to people is grace
neither language nor speech can measure.

I'd sunk in my mourning
with heart's defense,
wishing my being down toward his grave.
My heart from worry was narrow
like an alley,
but now with solace is wide.
And my sorrow sheds
like the flesh of my brother.

If my heart is stirred
and at times I weep,
and the sadness still rises
within me like hosts —
more often than not I'm calm like a man
whose heart is empty,
his burden light.

So the Rock wounds
and then heals the stricken.
He who blankets the sky with night,
wraps my mother's eldest with dust.
May the Lord forgive my
brother his errors,
and in His grace remember his goodness,
and with our fathers
who were near and His treasure,
count him as treasure.

Eight Photographs
Lynn Davis

ICEBERGS AND GEYSERS

ICE IS AN ALCHEMICAL ART, a reverie of death, of matter dissolving into emptiness. Breaking off the ice cap with thunderous roars, these monolithic shapes were carved from the inspired monotony of the great glacier in Western Greenland. Floating like phantoms into Disko Bay, they become prisms of frozen water transformed into hymns of light, crystalline and blue in the sun, ominous and unearthly in mist, a parade of transparencies proceeding like hallucinations across unknown depths that boil with hidden fear. Ethereal cathedrals caught between sea and sky, they drift with solemn passivity toward the Labrador Sea, a journey of several years, their destinies controlled by hidden currents and wind, their disintegrating forms seeming to reach toward heaven like futile gestures of prayer, sculptural shards from the unconscious, supplications toward a primal dichotomy of renewal and devastation.

To witness such remote symmetries is to enter into a meditation on illumined silence, on the illusion of discovery, on the futility of the voyage itself. Contrasts and comparisons, indeed all metaphors vanish before the shocking truth of their impermanence. The experience is, finally, a liberation, an absorbtion rather than a reflection, beyond language, beyond literary description, a terrible and joyful intimacy of erosion and transformation that commits itself to a circulation greater than the conceptual mind can manage, a fleeting awareness that all life is a dream within a dream.

Geysers are primal orgasms, created by fire, exhaled by the earth, their vertical flights thunderous ejaculations probing into air. Geysers were present at the birth of creation, when the chaos of the four primal elements joined and roared into being. They are the force of nature rather than the substance, existing long before the first geological imprint. Belching violently forth into passive phenomena, geysers are water gone mad.

Lynn Davis

The erotic muscle of a geyser's trajectory is a testament to the living depths of the earth, when all is possible, all is creation. When water and air fuse with each other their union becomes a sexual dance. On first impulse, a geyser is masculine, an eruption of such violence that only the feminine caress of the air can dissolve and tame it. One witnesses a geyser in awe rather than reverie, its vaporous trail disappearing into emptiness before the mind can assimilate the cosmic power of its presence.

— *Rudolph Wurlitzer*

Lynn Davis

Lynn Davis

Lynn Davis

Lynn Davis

Lynn Davis

Lynn Davis

Lynn Davis

Winter Horses
Barbara Guest

placed two sticks upon a dazzling plate

unlike feudal wars you remember

their saying she is stalking

and the fortifications are blocked

abruptly they held their breath until it froze.

carpeting the greensward a foil of sunset

"idyll of the kings" and shut the moat;

did not forget the promised tawny

situation of splendor.

again twists in the passage

or is it rhythm overturned;

to regard moodily a cask something

borrowed or fable arrow stuck the snow.

Barbara Guest

sea gray cold a door one boulder

slams another.

       instantly footprints

in the sand corner.

     grief spell was thought something else

records what was cried out.

      a needle's eye

the shrived warm

         turns into serpent

       are

no kingdoms

      is grass.

———————

winter my heart

you know how it is la gloire!

                    they bring you a fig dish.

the dead in white cotton.

fleece on the platter —

            wind crept the

white shoat and buried — ;

the cramped space ran

            out of breathing;

black snowflakes

            blue neighing.

            ————————

Barbara Guest

                  lover of blue!

                 neck in a cast

broken finger *rose blue*

                 milk from rose feathers

    blue horse —

who else lit firewood in the cold room

for the scribbling hereafter?

———————

bars of snow lanced the brightness

and crippled windows flung

lute with two notes unevenly.

ice breaking and noise

envelops sobriety

slice of boot on the frayed sylph

came out of dazzlement into

fisheries was intended.

From Zebra Dunn
Charlie Smith

AS WE ROSE between walls of flowers into the terrible city I was
speaking of Kate's death and of death in general when the driver
said he could show me a place where six people died. I said six
people are not so many, thinking of her, of Kate, the famous Zebra
Dunn my wife, of her death that was and wasn't, thinking of the
one-legged shadow waiting for me on the beach north of Mazatlan,
of the fork-tailed birds flying out of the camphor trees and of a child
sitting beside a pond in the mountains dreaming of the life to come.
The driver, whose head was small and square, whose jaw looked as
if he had pushed his face into soot, swiveled in the seat and said
It's a lot when they're your family. I said yes that is a lot. He said
you're Will Blake aren't you? I said you can call me Bobby. Why is
that? he said. I like the name Bobby, I said. That's fine, he said, you
all change your names, don't you, the movie stars; you all have
these regular names that you change so they'll sound good to the
public, he said, I know. Not me, I said, I was born a Blake, Bobby or
Will, or Tony sometimes, maybe Constable when I'm feeling dig-
nified and effete, but Blake is what came through the generations
to me – how about you? Arnold Pescadoro, he said, as if he was
making it up on the spot.

And there, shaken down to the edge of the drift, off the ramble, I
was, returned to L.A., come home now in time for the Academy
Awards. Everything was dusty and vague. The palm trees and the
eucalyptus trees and the palo verde bushes beside the little Mexican urban rancheros were dusty, and the hookers on Solidad were
dusty, and the pale linen and chrome buildings were dusty, and if
you lifted in a balloon or a rocket ship you would see that the continent all the way to the Isthmus was dusty, even the skin of your
loved ones dusty, the jacaranda blossoms and the surface of your
drink sprinkled with dust, like a world where nothing could shake off
its sense of abandonment. I said, where are these six people, and he
said, They're all gone, dead like I said, but I can show you where it
happened.

334

I said is this what you do take your fares around to show them this sight?

No, he said, only the ones who talk about this kind of thing.

Death?

Yeah. It was already six months ago but I can't shake it, I don't think I'm ever going to get over it.

I don't see why you should. I haven't gotten over anything that's ever happened to me.

Yeah, he said, it's like that isn't it?

Thinking, as we momentarily paused for traffic by a set of benches where old women with gnawed-out eyes stared into the heaped bougainvillea across the street, that I wanted to remember it all, the beach of saffron sand under the ochre cliffs and the scrawl of rose bushes by the long stairs leading down to the water and the cats, and the figure of her, woman without a leg standing at the edge of the surf where the waves slipped back leaving a sheen on the sand like varnish. Thinking it didn't matter whether I wanted to or not — I was going to remember it, carry it the rest of my life.

I said, All right, let's go there, I have time.

Yeah, he said, you got time, the ceremonies don't start for a couple of hours isn't that right?

Yes.

You're up for best actor, huh?

That's right.

You going to win?

Yes.

My third nomination, the charm I figured, I would win for sure. Thinking of the puckered sunken stump — that blushed, she said, like an embarrassed, punched-in face — my new receptor, she said, a new method for feeling my way into the world.

Uplifted now, off the plain, behind us the whale-colored Pacific, through town and out into the meager Mexican streets; there, up a rough red dirty ridge a line of royal palms, their ragged tops tethered to slender trunks like wigs on stiff rope; little roughed-up houses nearby; the road curving downhill past stores locked up behind brocades of steel; a couple of kids pedaling furiously toward what looked like a sheer drop into space. Swing right past bushy cypresses, past a store selling used records, a store with movie posters — one of my posters — tacked to a white wall; the smell of brass and rancid cooking oil, frying corn.

How far is it? I said.

Not far, just down here. Pointing off to the right, downhill where the terrain flattened out toward the railroad tracks, a dusty place between a warehouse and a string of wooden shotgun houses, hibiscus blossoming in front yards, stacks of rusted used equipment leaning against the side of a broken-down car, these terrible broken-hearted attempts to build life no matter what, life like a radio playing a single foreign language station thrusting gritty repetitive music without interruption toward you.

Here, he said — there.

It's an empty lot.

Yeah, but it didn't use to be.

It was an empty lot grown up in yellow grass, ashy fire scars showing, and a set of concrete front steps and a portion of concrete walk leading to weeds.

What happened here?

My family burned up.

Jesus. That's terrible.

Yeah. It was the gangs. Kids in a car shooting off guns. Late at night. They came down the street shooting guns. Hit a can full of gas I had on the front porch. The fire blew into the house. Everybody burned up — my wife, my mother, my four kids.

Where were you?

I was driving the limo.

I leaned over the front seat. At the rear of the property a low wall showed scorch marks in one corner but most of it was covered in a fresh mural depicting children playing ball. The mural was painted in fierce primitive colors, bright like the paintings in the basements of the pyramids in the Yucatan.

Let's get out, he said.

Okay.

We got out and stood on the sidewalk in the merciless sunlight looking at the vacancy.

He said, what are you talking about your wife is dead? Your wife is Zebra Dunn isn't she?

Yes, I said, she is.

It would be in the papers, he said, if she was dead.

She's strangely dead, I said.

What's that mean?

Zebra Dunn is no more yet who was Zebra lives yet.

I don't understand what you are saying.

I'm being purposely obscure.

I don't know, he said, I don't have to tell no lies. This happened —
he swept his brown arm out — and it's real. I can't step away from it.

I don't see how you could.

Yeah. I come here every day.

You think about it at night?

Yeah. And I dream about it. It's strange, dreaming. I see us all
lying on a beach in some foreign place, all of us, except everybody
is lying under a blanket like we were sleeping. There're sounds too.
You ever have dreams with sounds in them?

Not much.

Well, they're sounds in this one — gnawing, crunching sounds like
some big beast behind things is eating lumber. That's what it sounds
like, some big animal is eating boards or a house or something.

That's terrifying.

Yeah, I wake up in a sweat. I wake up crying.

I'm glad you could tell me about it.

Hell, I tell everybody about it. I talk about it all the time. I got to.
You're the third customer this week I took here. I'd take everybody
here if I could. It's going to get me fired.

You can't help it.

No, I can't.

Or me either, I figured. Everyone says *That's his nature*, and some
mean it. They're talking I've decided about fate. Which is everything piled up and enchained in your life and all past lives and actions that led up to this. I could very easily wander away down this
street, I could turn in a fury and tear this man's eyes out. We push
on through the outskirts of meaning. Trying to get somewhere.
Except Kate who figures there is no place to get to.

The man, a very short man in baggy clothes, had begun to cry. I
put my arm around his shoulder, two troopers toughing it out. He
leaned into me, I thought he wanted to hug my neck but he was
scuffling in his pocket for something.

Here, he said, let me show you.

What?

The fire burned everything up, he said, nobody could get out, it
burned the house to the ground, burned it to ashes. They wouldn't
let me go in there even after it was over because the police wanted
to look at things, but I sneaked back in later, at night, after everybody was gone.

You found something.

Yeah. He leaned away as if against a wind. He smelled of sweet

floral perfume and vaguely of shit. He said, I dug through the ashes.
I had to find something, something I could keep. They were all
burned up, but I couldn't be satisfied until I found something.

Thinking of the flight up from Mexico, of the clouds in unbroken
array stretching from the Gulf of California to the L.A. basin, someone looking up in Sonora at the same clouds someone was looking
up at in San Berdoo. Thinking of Kate leaning back into the darkness, stepping away from the car.

Here, he said, look.

It was a clean white handkerchief wrapped around small objects.
He carefully unfolded it. They were three black links, little burned
sticks.

What are they?

Finger bones. I dug around in the ashes until I found them. It's
one of my kids I think. They're so small it has to be.

Ah, you poor guy.

Nah, he said, these make me happy. I got something. I got something I can keep.

The handkerchief looked like the crumpled white body of a bird.
The bones had stained it slightly. He must pick out a new one
every day I thought.

I carry them with me everywhere, he said. I'm not going to ever
let them get away from me.

That's a good idea, I said. Something to keep, something you can't
help keeping.

He stared at the handkerchief, this dumbfounded ruined guy
staring into what was left. To the south two helicopters, painted
white, followed each other above a ridge. Westward the sun headed,
like a failed liberator, toward the Pacific and Japan.

*You stare at the sun, and soon—it takes almost no time—you
can see the dark inside it.* That was from one of Kate's videos.
Which came regularly now, wrapped in white paper, stamped in
Mexico. I could build a life, some alternate existence, from what
she showed me in the videos.

We swung in through the back gate into the Pavilion lot. The
guards recognized me, waved us through. I was who I was, famous
local boy, and son of the man producing the show. We zipped up to
the loading dock. My friend had stopped talking; he hummed to
himself, pressing a little tune against his demons. There were animal pens in the parking lot, cages for elephants, giraffes, and other

African creatures. The cages were empty; the animals apparently had been called to the set. Under the deck's metal hood you could smell the funky, rank circus odors. There were women in silver sequined bathing suits. Guys carrying big baskets of fruit wrapped in cellophane. I was tipped and muddled, rode, even in this clamorous moment, a drifting laziness, like someone who had lain all day in the beach sunshine, ready to lie down again somewhere in a cool dark place.

I got out, leaned in, kissed Arnold Pescadoro on the cheek, and turned into the arms — almost — of Eustace Conroy, one of the ADs.

"Yes, yes," he cried, "you're here, the living representative."

"I'm still on my feet, Eustace, but you're looking a little wobbly."

"I am. I'm about to go down."

Four years ago, Eustace, on a movie set, a man working his way up, had recited to me without error "The Shooting of Dan McGrew." He said when he finished and placed his white, hairless hand lightly on my shoulder that it had once been his only claim to fame. And look at you now Eustace, one of the glossy little spiders spinning the Oscars out of your ass.

"Your dad is looking for you, Will," he said bumping me with his bony shoulder.

"Where is that rascal?" Who now plans to murder me. I had waked weeks ago from a dream in which in a solid blue room I had come to the realization that my father wanted — had always wanted — to murder me. Now, in a manner of speaking, I had given him cause.

"He's somewhere around the dressing rooms," Eustace said running his fingers down his smooth cheeks. He is so happy to be here, and scared. He directed two pictures last year and both made money. "You know the way?"

"I know the way." This was after all my hometown. And my family business. How smooth it all seems, I thought, how glamorous and puerile. There was the salty taste of olives in my mouth, memories dancing in my head to ugly little tunes like something played on tin instruments. All of Mexico lay behind me, the piled-up stony mountains and the cliffs falling toward the harsh surf, Pedro Manglona's sad black eyes as he tried to tell me about Kate.

But now I am inside, Eustace trailing behind, sprinting down a long white corridor. There are many levels, I can't quite remember which one I am on. There are flocks of dancers, workmen milling about. Blown-up photographs of movie stars decorate the wall, a photograph of my mother Jennie White dressed in white, drawing

339

Tyrone Power into her arms. She was such a beautiful girl. Veronica had the dress she wore in that movie, she had worn it just the other day — when was that? — standing on a ladder in her kitchen under a pale yellow parasol. And there, just the other side of the photo, Jennie White herself, rushing toward me.

She was wearing a white dress with sleeves that ran down into glittery bands around her wrists. She spoke my name, banged me into her arms as the thought came to me that I could pretend with not very much effort at all that I was really the participant in another life entirely, that Kate did not exist.

"Mother," I said, "what are you doing here?"

"I'm with your father," she said.

"I don't believe you — well, yes, I do believe you."

"It's a ghastly thing, but I can't help myself."

"Of course you can't." Jennie White who had helped herself to Hollywood, the Scottish shipwright's child who had climbed up out of poverty to become a great actress, winner of two Oscars, mother of sons, wife to Clement Blake the great ape of Hollywood.

"Mother," I said, "do you know that your dress has a slit up the side all the way to your ass?"

"I still have a good ass. It should have it's day in the sun too."

"I dream of your ass, Mama. There are some days it's all I can think of."

"You liar."

"No, it's true."

Eustace had flitted off somewhere. Behind a wall a horse whinnied, calling a friend on distant plains. I looked into my mother's icy blue eyes. Little chips of undissolvable crystal in there that would shine like salt when the rest of her body lay corroded down to grease in the grave. An elephant trumpeted, and then around a corner came Harvey Bristol, the co-producer, enemy but able co-worker on several of my father's projects.

He winged his face forward to kiss Jennie, but she snapped her head out of the way, as if his ruddy face were a fist. He swung toward me.

"Will, can you present?"

I stepped back, shook him off. "No, Harvey, I'm not going to do that."

He wore a black, tarry wig fastened around his head with a silver band. I had known him thirty years — since I was a child — and he had worn the wig the whole time without anyone I ever knew hearing him mention it. He had a bouquet of turk's cap lilies stuck in his belt. He slid around my mother as if she was a rock in the river he was running.

"Come on, Will, it's for lighting, just a few lines off the prompter, won't you do it for me?"

"No, Harvey, not tonight."

"You're already celebrating your success aren't you? Already one of those winners who can't remember the little people who helped him get there."

"That's it, Harvey. I've been waiting half my life to begin stepping on you midgets."

He grinned at me. Grinned at Jennie. "Tell him, Jennie," he said, "tell him it is only through the relentless betrayal of everything we hold sacred that we get anywhere in this life. It is only by kissing the hairy asses — no slur on Clement — of our congenital inferiors that we can produce the grease to run the machine."

"Speak for yourself, Harvey," Jennie said looking around distractedly. It was a look I had known all my life. Her way of getting what she wanted. She looked as if she was trying to stretch herself out of a terrible entrapment she'd been bound into, there was desperation in her eyes, sadness, she was about to give into despair, loss was taking over, we were about to lose this beautiful . . . — and someone steps in, some gallant, and saves her day. Her features had sharpened, and there was flesh, death's dominion, under her jaw, but she was still beautiful, still powerful, the way a skeleton in the living room is powerful.

Harvey blanched, swiveled to the AD who had hovered near through this. "Go find Dana. She's off in the loge, somewhere, I don't know — go find her." He turned to me, a look in his harpy eyes as if, like Immanuel Kant, he had just discovered that the division between the beauty of the stars and the beauty of the soul was going to cause trouble, and confided, "I promised Stanley that I would give her something. Now you betray me — I'll give her this."

"Dana will love it."

"Everybody but you does."

My mother began to wade lightly away, moving through her spectral world. Around her head demons, figments, bits of movie stars lashed and skidded. She was one who knew terrible secrets, had lived through tormented times. But then who wasn't, as Kate would say. There is haze, dust, even in here. At night down narrow streets you can hear the sumps working on top of the houses, the low, gassy hum of machines putting moisture into the air. I was thinking of Kate rolling out of the desert five years ago, riding into town in her 1972 Cadillac convertible, appearing from another planet I guess where things had gone from bad to worse. Thinking of her strength, of her rustly voice, of her thighs, of her hard-muscled calves, of the way she let the ruffle in her voice smooth out until you could hardly hear what she was saying even when she was saying something she wanted you to hear. Thinking of Jennie, who was retired from everything but the truth, her version. In 1958, when my mother was thirty, she won her second best actress award for her role in *Disaster's Bride*, a movie in which she played a society woman who becomes a bank robber and, eventually, a killer. There is a scene, at her trial — which won her the award — when, as the guilty verdict is announced, she dips her fingers in the water pitcher, there in front of her on the table, and touches her face. The water falls, collects, drips from her face like rainy tears. Her pale skin shines. Through her eyes, which are wholly without defense, you can see the blue universe of anguish and loss, the empty, endless world she has come through to that place. She had dragged that look all the way from the sooty streets of Glasgow to this polished desert world, and she gave it to everyone, free of charge, mercilessly. It was her gift. Now she slipped Harvey a slice of it. He retreated, tripped for a tenth of a second by something too much for him. Too rough a world. He swayed, righted himself, floated away, crying out to extemporary gods, on the arm of an assistant carrying a red clipboard, bobbing toward the mystic haven of his triumph.

"Sometimes," my mother says for the ten thousandth time, "I do not know why I ever came to this prickly place."

"I'm looking for Pop," I say.

"He's around here, darling."

We strut on, nodding, feinting, electrified, casual, distant, immersed. We are of these scurrying souls, basking sharks for the moment, participants nonetheless. Over there's a guy I made a picture with ten years ago now going crazy for money. There's a woman who believes acting is therapy. There's a sleek star who's come backstage before her turn to hear her name said a hundred times. There's a comic telling jokes to the wall. Cables run like thick black snakes down the corridors. Lights flare, go off and come on again. Horses whinny, calling their paramours. A stagehand passes, carrying a slot machine that seems to burn with a fire within.

I hear my father's voice. It's huge. He's creating a new world, out loud. I come around a green corner, mother swinging wide, flicking her soft, slim girlish hips at oncoming traffic. "You're not going to believe this," my father's voice says, ". . . you can picture it, right? Can you picture it, this great white columned house sliding down the mountainside — no, not just the house, the whole compound, a herd of houses, sliding and bumping down the mountainside . . ." Someone makes a high humming sound. My father says, "Humph, humph," very loudly. "Yeah, the mountain's green, we want to paint the mountain — greener than green, you know?"

A line of gaudy dancers outfitted in black leotards that shine as if they've been dipped in oil, swish and tunnel past. The dressing room door's flung open; my father can't be confined. He's stripped to the waist, block of black, gray-streaked hair standing on his chest which is huge, like another body, a John the Baptist body preceding him into the world, erect and poised under the hands of his masseuse. His head is a chunk of Arkansas stone, photographed in flight, and the expression on his face, pulling the poorly carved small features out from the base, is the expression of something about to emerge, about to become visible. I have seen people turn to that expression — as he stood there in silence — to ask him what he said. It is the face the moment after birth, before the first breath. His small black eyes squint to see me.

"Will," he says throwing up his hands as if to strike, "son of sons."

"Buenas dias, Pop."

My mother slides in, balancing on the highwire. Their marriage is about sex — nothing else — and now, in her sixties, she is embarrassed at this. It is also funny to her. Everyone, she believes, has heard her bedroom screams. It's as if she's wearing a hat the wind is trying to take away from her, I think, as she steps forthrightly in, crosses the room and pats my father on the top of the head. He leans into her hand, kisses the knuckles, lifts his own hand to take hers and misses as she pulls it away and waves. "Go on, Julie," she says to the small man probing my father's shoulders. Julie fades back, past Max Stein who is lying on a flowered chaise in the corner. It's Max, another producer from the old days, my father is talking to. He begins to struggle to his feet — cranking up and down like a baby upended in a tub — flailing with his good right arm to clear a passage. "Stay where you are, Max," my mother says, which is not social speak — which Max realizes and gives in to, subsiding. The thought lines on his forehead climb three inches into the creamy space where his hair used to be. He's flabby, nearly obese, yet there is something crisp about him, raw even, in the sharp small eyes and the neat, small hands with their thin fingers and nails the color of pearls. He grins as my father motions to me with his finger, nodding his head in unison as my father nods his: they are two who cherish the power of secrets and the delight of passing them on.

"Don't get up, Max," I say laughing. I am oddly delighted to see them both. It's like looking at lions.

"You're inevitable," Max says with a damp fondness, flesh pleating around a broad grin with almost audible clicks. He chuckles, riding the bumper car of his bonhomie. He would like to take a piece of my flesh in his hands, swish it between his fingers, weigh and test it for life.

"Max," my father says spreading his hands, "don't say a word. You'll spook everything."

I bend down and kiss my father on the cheek, bend into the florid, homeric scent of father smell, and kiss his cheek that is smooth and hard as the side of a new car.

The room is a cataract of flowers. Chrysanthemums like the mussed heads of deposed kings hang gaudily from baskets and vases. Mirrors force the intense light back at us.

My father grasps my wrist. "I am so overjoyed," he says, lying openly, "I am so happy to see you."

There are tears in the corners of his eyes. It is his side of the street, this spendthrift emotion. Everyone knows this about him. All Hollywood has seen Clement Blake roar, rage, sob on a movie set and in his life in the world. He has used his own flowing tears, dipped up by his own hand, to supply tears to a reluctant actress, smearing her face with his salt. He is vicious as well, one of the old-line boys, a tormentor and manipulator, liable to kick down the scenery, to assault the halt and fearful; more than once he has expressed his dedication with his fists. He knows the world is here to run you over and is committed to not allowing this to happen without a fight.

My mother, at the long dressing table, pours herself a glass of champagne. She drinks it slowly, her beautiful head tilted back slightly, showing the yellowing marble column of her neck. I watch fascinated, and I can see the champagne, like a fizzing jism, sliding down her throat, her tongue striking deftly at the taste and bubbles, her full lips just slightly reaching for more. The fingers of her free hand are spread, tense, ready to grasp, the carpal bone protrudes like the stub of a weapon above the soft hollow of melting flesh at her wrist; her back is arched. I am not at all appalled, I am drawn by this, by my mother's sensual, insistent nature; she licks the rim of the glass and sets it down on the speckled counter as if it is a precious and failed thing. My father smacks his lips. Max turns his head away, smirking, proposing through his tiny eyes visions of another universe, someplace where he is in charge of women like this.

My father sighs, sets his shoulders. He would tear my flesh from my bones if he could, eat it raw.

"What is it you wanted, Pop," I say, taking a chair. I am agitated, I can only stay a couple of minutes, a few seconds maybe before I will have to wing away from here. I want to press my body through something irresistible. I have rehearsed the whole award business already, this ceremony, my lift toward the gold statuette. It is not only my speech I have in hand — that will be extemporaneous (my preparation is to not think about it ahead of time) — but I have already selected my route, checked my seat — weeks ago — walked the path from seat to aisle, to stage, moved off left to the wings, handled the curtain fabric, placed in my mind the scaffolding, the sets, the stagehands, the cables writhing at my feet, the mikes, my cohorts, the smells, the webs of steel in the flies: left nothing to chance. I always do this, always walk the route, always rehearse.

My father hacks his thigh with the flat of his hand. "It's this deal I've been putting together for months," he says, "this wonder deal. I told you about it. Earl" — my agent — "knows all about it." He speaks as if he is crunching stones between his teeth. I know what he is talking about. He will not let the horror between us stand in his way. He has found a way to use it to crush me. "Max and I have been talking about it — the picture is ready to go and we can't make it without you."

I lift a calculated eyebrow. "You and Max are in on this deal together?"

"Hoo," Max cries, writhing on the chaise, "I told you he wouldn't believe it." He hurls himself forward over his knees like a man going for the situp record.

"Nobody's going to believe it," Max chortles, his laughter high in his throat, like water spilling back into a well.

"It's going to be great," my father says, slapping his thigh, "this picture. It's about conquistadores, the new world, desperate acts."

"An *extravaganze*," Max says. He is beaming, in his version, fleshy lips stretched like thin gray inner tubes across his large

345

teeth, eyebrows cranked into his forehead.

"We're going to actually build a new world, a whole city."

"And blow it up," Max cries, "and blow it to smithereens, hurl it down a mountain."

"That's right," my father says smacking his sides, "this is going to be what they call a real moving picture."

I can tell by my mother's eyes that she is practicing another life. It has been twenty years since her last picture. She was unwilling, so the interviews said, to sully her beauty with age on the screen, but actually unable, if the truth were known, to concentrate on the reality of film anymore. She became dreamy, strange, unable to learn her lines, adjusting herself in this feathery way that she does now, mind and body drifting in the capacities of other realms, a princess somewhere else, Scottish sorceress perhaps, floating in the highland world of green mountain slab and broken-hearted streams. So I would have it, if I were making up her life. So I would tell Kate, if she asked. I spin here in the middle of my life, brushing greatness and the future. The world slithers and yawns wide.

"What is it you want me to do, Pop?"

"He's going for it," Max cries. "He wants to do it."

"Wait a minute, Max," my father says. He looks at me, his black eyes filling with light. "I haven't even told you about the deal. You want to do it?"

"What is it you want me to do?"

"See," Max crows. "He wouldn't ask if he wasn't going to do it. You'll love it, Willie. This is something you've waited for. This is going to be prodigious."

"Shut up, Max," my mother says, braking.

My father thanks her, reaches for her hand, misses, rights himself. My mother elegantly fills her glass again, looking at us. She sways toward my father — a movie motion I have seen on the screen many times, as if her bones have melted and she is about to fall — drifts and fetches up against his body where she takes over the massage business. She accepts the bottle of gold oil from Julie, who is packing his little black bag, pours a drop or two into her hands and begins to work her fingers into my father's shiny shoulders. He preens like a seal.

"This is what I've wanted to talk to you about, Will," my father says. He cocks his head to the side, heavy bird, eyeing his prey.

"Tell me."

"You were off there in Mexico and I couldn't get hold of you."

"Yes."

"This is going to be a real picture. Your part is shaping up. We've got it now. You're this renegade priest, a kind of bandito priest combo, it's right up your alley."

"Up my alley?"

"Sure. This guy, he's a priest and a murderer too. He kills—for a good cause sure (he's friend to the Indians)—..."

"... We're on the side of the Indians now," Max puts in.

"Right—but he's in agony—you know what I mean?—he's walking a fine line he can't stay on—got to fall ..."

"Yeah," Max cries, "trouble ahead ..."

"Right—he falls ..."

I'm looking at my mother's fingers, how strong they are. She could make a new man—a new body at least—right here in front of us. "You got a script?"

"Yeah, yeah—" my father shakes his shoulders, leans forward like an executioner, "that's the best part."

"We've got a script," Max cries, "you ought to see it—it's great."

"You got anybody to direct?"

"Yeah, that's the best part too," Max says shaking his head from side to side.

"Bobby Baum," my father says.

"Bobby will work with you?"

"He's great. He loves it. He's got the script, Max has talked to his people, he's going to do it. Billy Dangelo is going to finance."

"Circus time, huh?"

"Ain't nothing better."

My mother told me a story once about the time her father got sick when she was a little girl. He was taken ill suddenly and rushed to the hospital. On the way to visit him with her mother Jennie saw on the side of a building near the hospital a small white bird, drawn in chalk on the stone. She remembered that she had drawn the bird one morning on her way to school. She decided that each morning, before she went to school, she would draw a bird, and this would be her bargain with God—as long as she drew a bird each day her father would live. She felt very good about this, because, she said, she knew she wouldn't forget, she would draw every morning. But five days later her father died. She had not missed a day's drawing but he died anyway. This was a lesson to her, she said. No matter how prettily we play, she said, no matter what we offer, no matter how deeply we bow, the world has its own

347

ideas. What we get is what is given to us.

I said, "I'll do this."

My father's scarred fists swing around his head. "He says he'll do it, Max," he cries.

"I heard him, Clem. This is going to be great."

I said, "Call Earl. Draw up the papers. I'll do it."

My father heaves to his feet, a wrestler coming up out of a crouch. "Son, son" he says, his voice tangled in his throat, "this is a miracle of our time, a wonderful thing." There are tears in his eyes, little sparks gleaming at the corners. He lays his forearms on my chest, billets he's stacking, he's stroking my head between his hands, leans his stony head in and kisses me on the mouth. I feel a warm prickling, as if I am kissing the prince who still smells of the frog he was. My father has found his way to murder me.

The Young and the Restless:
A Phrenology
Joseph Sullivan

AMATIVENESS.

Unsettled by a police photo of Leonard, Jessica flees the hospital, leaving behind her newborn son. Doreen takes custody of the child and calls it "Tip," short for Tiparillo. Gambling, like the harmonica, becomes for Adam an indispensable mode of self-expression. In Oakdale, Sam is persuaded to attend a demitasse at the home of Sylvia Furth, only to realize that it is Ruth's plan to get him back together with his ex-wife. Pretending a coughing fit, he excuses himself and leaves out the back door. By sheer chance, Ruth discovers a note he left under a bottle of wine.

PHILOPROGENITIVENESS.

Travis is caught selling drugs from his home in New York City. In his confession to the police, he is heard saying, "I was just trying to keep food on the table." Dixie drops out of Harvard mid-semester to bail him out. In the meantime, Mona admits to Tad that the good-night kiss with Cliff was more than casual. Embittered, Tad rents a car, then wrecks it. Skye comforts him by the side of the road, but she is secretly laughing.

CONCENTRATIVENESS.

In what he promised would be his last visit to a singles' bar, Jake falls in love with a witch. Caroline believes he has been hypnotized, but she is not sure. Stacey's first day as a substitute teacher is spoiled by a subpoena for child molestation. Griffen further upsets her by wondering aloud just how to spell 'subpoena'. Marley, Rachel, Michael and Lucas visit the beach. They smoke marijuana downwind from the lifeguard station.

INHABITIVENESS.

Lucinda has visions of a red swan while making love to James. She is afraid she might be "crazy." Julie suggests to Lucinda that she imagined a stork, but Lucinda says she is not worried about getting pregnant. At the Bay City Ballet's gala, Buddy borrows Duncan's opera glasses so he can spy on Kim and her new lover. When Buddy looks away, Duncan plants several thousand dollars of counterfeit bills in Buddy's coat. Sawyer is heartbroken over Shannon's miscarriage; they vow to keep trying.

ADHESIVENESS.

Thorne's safe deposit box is ransacked without any evidence of tampering. An old photo, a ship-in-a-bottle, and a skein of handspun wool are missing. He is stunned to learn that Kristen and Margo were hired on as cashiers just a week before the theft. At the charity fashion show, Sally tries to set up Angela with Clarke. Tricked by their identical gowns, his overtures are mistaken as an invitation to *menage a trois*. Meanwhile, Mick is consumed in the Alden Mansion explosion.

COMBATIVENESS.

Shane's wild punch knocks Jeremy out. A melee ensues as the amphetamine-crazed patrons bludgeon one another with punch bowls and ladles. Patch lances Irwin's lip with a roasting skewer. Robin peevishly debones Faith's shin with the electric knife. Rebecca blindsides Scott with the faceted pewter espresso pot, and decants a flickering river of Sterno fuel on his balding scalp muttering "You bastard, you bastard." In the pantry's clutching dark, Mike masturbates Kayla whilst she visualizes a red swan.

DESTRUCTIVENESS.

To defray the unexpected expense of Felicia's abortion, Nicholas volunteers to defuse a five-hundred pound bomb lodged in the basement of *T.J.'s*, a rip-roaring singles bar. He brings two varieties of screwdriver: the Phillips and the standard. Since the bomb does not present any obvious choice, he goes with the standard, figuring that a standard point can turn a Phillips screw, while a Phillips driver can only screw its own kind. An unrelated miscalculation renders this academic. The following persons perish in the unfortunate blast: Sean, Clayton, Cheryl, Tiffany, Domino, Anna, Claudio, Lucy, Alan, Victor-Jerome, Monica, and Jimmy. Felicia opts to carry the child to term.

ALIMENTIVENESS.

Lillian breaks off her affair with Bradley. Between courses of their picnic in Salem, Hampton entices Reva to visit a cave. Billy donates his father's old seabag to the charity auction, but extracts an old photo, a legal document, and a novel by Mark Van Doren. As lunch comes to a close, Beth intimates to Reva that she has seen a man among the shadows. Josh thinks that he will lose his mind now that the baby-selling caper has made the tabloids. He commits suicide in a drive-in movie parking lot.

SECRETIVENESS.

Trisha sincerely wants the job at Oakdale nursery, but she is afraid they will fire her because she is gay. Egypt invites Cabot to her hotel suite. When they are just starting to get comfortable on the velour throw pillows, Cabot's skin erupts with hives. He departs without a word. Alex wins several thousand dollars in the lottery, then claims the money is exempt from alimony payments. Ava, meanwhile, suffers a mishap with an ungrounded appliance, but she's okay, except for some flashbacks to the bombing of Dresden.

ACQUISITIVENESS.

Gabrielle rebuffs Cliff's advances on the pleasure ship *Sexus*. Cliff tells Roger that any woman, if you want her badly enough, can be had. Roger relates this to Michael, saying that Cliff intends to win Gabrielle's favor with money. Michael spends a moment at the bar with Viki to tell her that Cliff has been buying sexual favors from Gabrielle. Viki surprises Debra with the news that Gabrielle is a call girl. Debra, who disliked Gabrielle from the start, now feels justified in calling Gabrielle a slut.

CONSTRUCTIVENESS.

Overly proud of his Hispanic heritage, Cruz commissions a statue of himself (as seen in *Scarface*) to be erected in the xenodochium of his marbled pad. Laura nervously awaits the results of a pregnancy test. Leo promises to weed out the "bad apples" in his condom supply. Jerry and Raoul hire a private investigator to locate Emily's body. She was last seen on the levee of Fallow Gorge River, searching for an engagement ring.

SELF-ESTEEM.

Cricket returns from the hospital in a nun's habit. She wishes to conceal her breast augmentation from Shawn, who never approved of the idea. Nina, one of Shawn's ex-lovers, writes Cricket a disparaging note about Shawn's sexual inadequacies. Jill corroborates most of it and then drops a final bombshell. Shawn is impotent except when he performs on his own bed, underneath a tapestry of a red swan. The partnership of Derek and Robert is dissolved over a lease dispute.

LOVE OF APPROBATION.

Doreen finds an agent for her collection of children's stories *I Know You Are, But What Am I?* Hilda calls Martin and Rob to her bedside in the middle of the night demanding to know which of them really loves her. A New York City mobster praises Ruth for her fantastically etched counterfeiting plates. This makes her very happy, but she isn't sure she should tell her parents.

CAUTIOUSNESS.

After years of estrangement, Nina and Tad make up in the shadow of a freeway overpass. Cliff and Adam discover a cache of nudie photos under Matt's bed. The Oakdale doctors suspect Erica was sexually abused, but further tests are necessary. Dixie is thrilled by Michael's marriage proposal. She balks, though, when he shows her the ring. Mona assures her that size isn't everything.

BENEVOLENCE.

Marley turns heads at the Ash-Montaigne New Year's fete when she confides in a rather loud voice that she has resolved to tolerate Griffen's infidelity. He feigns embarrassment but knows deep down that her weakness has made him a *man of means*. Home early from work, Mac "stumbles" across Stacey's old love letters inside the jade incense burner. Rachel spikes Caroline's hair conditioner with a caustic depilatory after she heard that Caroline had romanced her way to a promotion. Royalties from Jake's hit song "They're Tearing Down the Berlin Wall (Ja, Ja, Ja)" pay him handsomely. Only a step or two outside the door, Michael finds the air too cold for his taste.

VENERATION.

Duncan invites Andy, Paul, and Sawyer to join him in a heroin smuggling operation. At the last moment, Sawyer disqualifies him self, saying that being a father and dope smuggler is just too much responsibility for him. Buddy proposes to Kim on the Bay City dock. A broken thermostat induces Lucinda to dream of a red swan. In the ecstasy of its feathery embrace she awakes, crying "Zeus! Zeus!" The bed sheets are stuck to her like cellophane.

FIRMNESS.
Exercising the new morality, Margo refuses a campaign contribution of several thousand dollars. Clarke successfully propositions a hospital orderly named Joe immediately after his separation from Sally. He sustains his impetuosity through it all with quotations from Walt Whitman. With the aid of waxy, handlebar moustaches, Thorne and Kristen bedazzle Panamanian border authorities and pass through the checkpoint unmolested. Then they spoil the romance of their success with a dispute over who suggested the moustaches in the first place. Angela suspects Mark engraved the counterfeiting plates.

CONSCIENTIOUSNESS.
Faith loses her composure when confronted by pro-lifers demonstrating outside Pine Valley Women's Center. As she climbs into Irwin's pickup she is struck with a balloon full of sheep's blood. "Why don't we try our luck some place else," she says. Shane visits a hypnotist to help him say I LOVE YOU to Robin. After months of therapy, he is ready. On the esplanade of Café Villefranche, (he's never seen her more radiant), he says: I LOVE YOU, Kayla.

HOPE.
During a quiet moment in a confessional, Claudio lapses into a photographic recollection of the time he, Nicholas, Tony, Domino, and Victor all blew the head off a pregnant garter snake. Bobbie and Monica kick off their new partnership with a masquerade ball at Alden Mansion. Clayton's superb masque includes a headpiece of mounted ibex horns, opal and sequin gauntlets, and a mysterious black velvet mace. "I'm a gay paladin into light S&M." Elsewhere, Jimmy curses as he accidentally kicks the lug nuts for the spare tire down a residential storm drain. The kidnap of Felicia and Alan's daughter corresponds with a decline in Felicia's libido, which poses a problem for Alan, who can only forget his sorrows when copulating.

WONDER.

An image consultant informs Josh that if he is to have any chance at being rehired he must try to appear less intelligent. But Josh has other ideas. Though Lillian allowed Billy to remove her bra to massage more deeply the knotty muscles of her back, she withholds the idiomatic "goodnight kiss." "You confuse," she says, "the sensuous with the sensual." "What's the difference?" "Sex."

IDEALITY.

Sandy absents himself from another shareholder's meeting, this time to hunt crayfish in northwest Scotland. April sits in for him but warns him in a telegram that she is fed up with his *laissez faire* management techniques. While Cabot is on call at the General, Egypt extracts from his belongings an antique locket, a traffic court summons, and an analgesic for herpes sores. In a moment Egypt is naked, squatting over a mirror laid between her legs on the carpet. Clay challenges common sense, and selecting a dull razor, cuts himself shaving.

[UNDETERMINED.]

Desperate for nostalgia, Clint returns to the singles bar where he was conceived. He orders a White Russian; then, with his lips over the straw, he tries to imagine what it must have been like to breastfeed. Viki intercepts his gaze. The frothy, sucking sounds are formidable turn-ons, drawing her nipples out like tongues. She orders him another drink, the same one, just so she can watch his mouth.

WIT.

Ethan senses a growing apathy on the part of his lawyer to fight for an equitable settlement with his estranged wife, Laura. Under cross-examination by Laura's attorney, he attempts to twist the knife by calling his wife "a friend to end all friends." But he laughs uncontrollably at his own witticism and loses favor with the judge. At dawn, Raoul takes little Scott to witness the home-birthing of his sister. "Say hello to your mother, son." Scott does not recognize his mother without makeup.

IMITATION.

Derek and Nina have second thoughts about adopting a Korean baby, because Nina's dad fought in that war. Cricket kisses Robert goodnight with no apparent effect. It occurs to Robert, while braving the Coney Island Cyclone, that most legitimate books have their right-handed pages odd-numbered and their left-handed pages even-numbered. No less than four art dealers ask Eden to privilege their galleries with her Neo-Cubist Retrospective. On the verge of demotion, Laura finally goes the whole hog and purchases an alarm clock. Philip perishes in the great Chicago dairy accident.

INDIVIDUALITY.

Rob has been parting his hair to the side. Weary of the rapacious singles scene, Hilda sets her sights on the male nurses of Bay City Blood Bank. Martin rises at 4:30 AM to await the delivery of the 1990 Shooter's Bible. Through the green half-light of sunrise, he spies a brick-sized object disgorge from the maw of a garbage truck: the counterfeiting plates. In Salem, Doreen slaps an impertinent sales clerk for reminding her that the big sale "ended yesterday." Leonard, Sylvia, Adam, and Ruth abscond to the wine country, well aware that it wasn't a good year for any of them.

FORM.

Skye's luck runs out. Eric promises himself that when he finally masters the complete works of the Marquis de Sade, he will rip out his backyard and plant a grove of birches. In much the same vein, Nina and Tad begin their search for a third partner in a violent triangle of love. Between shots of tequila and Pepto Bismol, Matt and Cliff manage to have a good time at a Mexican rest stop. Dixie's puffy corpse is winched out of Murchison bog. Tad conjectures that she drowned.

SIZE.

When Griffen presses his ear against Caroline's stomach he swears he can hear her unborn child calling out numbers, much like an auctioneer. A ham-handed carnival operator seduces Jake with deadbeat charms. Rachel rides the newly inaugurated light rail, unaware that the tracks were laid over Indian burial grounds. Mac won't confront Stacey about her affair with Lucas, because she has enough dirt on him to fill a swimming pool. Marley is incensed when she hears the hospital pharmacist whisper "avoirdupois" as he fills her prescription. Another comment about her weight and she will go out of her mind.

WEIGHT.

On the return flight from Scotland, Duncan inflates a female mannequin in the lavatory and becomes trapped when it expands to fill the entire cubicle. Kim hires a private investigator to follow Andy on league "bowling" nights. He claims he has been brushing his teeth and wearing cologne for "good luck." On Friday, Lucinda and Sawyer rendezvous at *T.J.'s*, a swank dance joint on the North Side. They drink sarsaparilla with rare seedless pomegranates. They say things like "marvelous" and smile a lot.

COLORING.

Sally momentarily convinces her mother that her oral contraceptives are harmless mood pills. Brown makes her diligent, blue makes her reflective, and pink makes her happy. Her mother asks—"What does white do?" White makes her creative. Thorne makes free with his invalid father's mutual funds and buys that fishing trip Dad always denied him. As the first kiss entwines their nibby limbs, Mark and Kristen each experience a loneliness unthinkable for their proximity.

LOCALITY.

Irwin accuses Jeremy of arson after *Chez Ultra* burns to the ground. For Valentine's Day, Mike intends to present Faith with an assortment of leaded jelly jars. In New York, divorce proceedings are underway for the Newlines, but Scott skips town, reneging on the final contract. Rebecca takes him to court, hoping to shred his palimony winnings. Shane phones Scott at his farmhouse hideout and warns him. Afterwards, Scott disconsolately fondles some kitchen knives.

NUMBER.

Clayton escapes from Oakdale Penitentiary, taking the place of a deceased inmate in an outgoing body bag. He weeps quietly among the jostling corpses. The hot-tubbing party at Alden Mansion offers the usual scene: drinking, drugging, hyperthermia, and sex. Anna, Monica, Lucy, and Felicia do lunch. Claudio does his wife, nibbling at her like a swan, like a red swan plumbing the depths for delicious reeds. His red car facing repossession, Alan cheerlessly pawns his toy soldier collection.

ORDER.

Bradley says he can play that game. It is deduced by Lillian that the suffragette photograph is of Reva's great-grandmother. Naturally, this solves many problems. For her trouble, Lillian is gifted several thousand dollars, which Reva's father deducts as a charitable contribution. Beth turns down Hampton's invitation to the Salem Memorial Flotilla. Hampton date-raped Josh's ex-girlfriend.

EVENTUALITY.

Never one to curb her wants, Egypt asks that her lovers read *Cleopatra* to heighten their appreciation of the exotic. Clay steals an unattended baby from a supermarket, undresses it, and dyes it black in a utility sink. A pinch of white remains on the infant's Achilles' tendon. At Oceanside, Trisha falls through the rotted boardwalk. The trauma unlocks the memory of Viktor, the Russian expatriate who wooed her in Leningrad. Fortunately, only her ankle is broken.

TIME.

Viki finds Max noncommittal about his new hobby — headhunting. "Whether I can maintain the interest . . . only time will tell." A bottle of wine, Montepulciano muscatel, Newark '77, not only alleviates Julia's headache, but catalyzes a sexual bravado that catches Roger by surprise. He drags his sleeve in the punch bowl. Cliff is the new man in town, a stranger to some, but familiar to others as the bastard who left his wife, four children, dog named 'Garth', and a garage full of tattered Bob Guccione magazines. Debra finally makes a startling admission, the one about, you know, "that guy."

TUNE.

In blue-suited splendor, Jerry name-licks his way from ground floor to gable at the gubernatorial debauch. Eden and Cruz beget a child. Ethan's Halloween trickery gets the best of his guests — as Verdi's Requiem blasts through the hallway, they begin vomiting up tainted hunks of candy. As the despondency over Laura's suicide fades, Leo discovers a new sense of purpose. By heart-rending trial and error, he learns the flashy art of the straight razor. Now, scraping a client's gullet, he quotes Norman Mailer: "My, that was a fancy shot!"

LANGUAGE.

In the water closet on the 11:15 to New York, Cricket receives absolution from Father Mike. They met by accident (really). Derek meets a woman named Nina at a singles bar. She has brown hair and green eyes. He says, you have really nice green eyes. What about my hair, she says. What about my nice brown hair?

COMPARISON.

In the ecliptic gloom, Sam relishes his recent dream of Doreen. Still, her breasts are not that large and she finds his irregular teeth offputting. Martin shows up uninvited at Hilda's coming-out fete, crowing some news about her being pregnant. He is led out by security. Such damning news, though, has ruined the party. Hilda extemporarily shares her cake with a guest's pet dog.

CAUSALITY.

Spineless equivocation costs Travis a chance at the "big time." He settles for a company car and one week at Christmas. Dixie and Tad announce their engagement, a happy affair, though it is predicated on the conditional surrender of certain properties. On a bleak morning, Nina decides enough is enough. In her favorite superhero cup, she blends a barbiturate shake and sucks it down through a Krazy straw. She is rescued by Michael and Eric, who chance by on their way to the baitshop.

Four Stories
Lydia Davis

THE ACTORS

IN OUR TOWN there is an actor, H. — a tall, bold, feverish sort of man — who easily fills the theater when he plays Othello, and about whom the women here become very excited. He is handsome enough compared to the other men, though his nose is somewhat thick and his torso rather short for his height. His acting is stiff and inflexible, his gestures obviously memorized and mechanical, and yet his voice is strong enough to make one forget all that. On the nights when he is unable to leave his bed because of illness or intoxication — and this happens more often than one would imagine — the part is taken by J., his understudy. Now J. is pale and small, completely unsuitable for the part of the Moor; his legs tremble as he comes on stage and faces the many empty seats. His voice hardly carries beyond the first few rows, and his small hands flap uselessly in the smoky air. We feel only pity and irritation as we watch him, and yet by the end of the play we find ourselves unaccountably moved, as though he had managed to convey something timid or sad in Othello's nature. But the mannerisms and skill of H. and J. — which we analyze minutely when we visit together in the afternoons and continue to contemplate even once we are alone after dinner — seem suddenly insignificant when the great Sparr comes down from the city and gives us a real performance of Othello. Then we are so carried away, so exhausted with emotion, that it is impossible to speak of what we feel. We are almost grateful when he is gone and we are left with H. and J., imperfect as they are, for they are familiar to us and comfortable, like our own people.

TRYING TO LEARN

I am trying to learn that this playful man who teases me is the same as that serious man talking money to me so seriously he does not even see me anymore and that patient man offering me advice in times of trouble and that angry man slamming the door as he leaves the house. I have often wanted the playful man to be more serious, and the serious man to be less serious, and the patient man to be more playful. As for the angry man, he is a stranger to me and I do not feel it is wrong to hate him. Now I am learning that if I say bitter words to the angry man as he leaves the house, I am at the same time wounding the others, the ones I do not want to wound, the playful man teasing, the serious man talking money, and the patient man offering advice. Yet I look at the patient man, for instance, whom I would want above all to protect from such bitter words as mine, and though I tell myself he is the same man as the others, I can only believe I said those words, not to him, but to another, my enemy, who deserved all my anger.

THERAPISTS

A friend of mine goes with her three-year-old girl to a family therapist. This therapist has guided her in her troubles with the child's bed-wetting, fear of the dark, and dependence on the bottle. One by one these problems are solved. The mother, acting on the advice of the therapist, is careful to avoid attempting to solve more than one problem at a time. The child is unhappy and nervous and holds her body in a cramped position, as though protecting herself. Her mother is also nervous, and is never still: her hands flutter and her eyebrows fly up into her forehead. There is a dark brown mole on her cheek, and this dark point is the only color in her face.

Another friend calls her husband's therapist and tells him she is going to ask her husband to move out. Naturally, the therapist has to report this to his patient. The husband is hurt and indignant. My friend is adamant. Her own therapist thinks she must now be under great pressure from her husband, and this is true. Encouraged by her therapist, however, she persists in asking her husband to leave. At last he does. He now sees his children in his own apartment several times a week, including all day Sunday. Insulted by his wife's behavior, he tries to complain only to his therapist, as his therapist has advised, but he cannot help complaining to everyone — his therapist, his friends, his lawyer, his wife, and even his children. The older boy comes home angry at his mother because he does not know what is the truth anymore. He breaks two of the dining-room chairs. His mother, a frail and small woman, sits on him for several hours before he is calm enough to tell her what he is feeling.

WHAT I FEEL

These days I try to tell myself that what I feel is not very important. I've read this in several books now: that what I feel is important but not the center of everything. Maybe I do believe this, but not enough to act on it. I would like to believe it more deeply.

What a relief that would be. I wouldn't have to think about what I felt all the time, and try to control it, with all its complications and all its consequences. I wouldn't have to try to feel better all the time. In fact, if I didn't believe what I felt was so important, I probably wouldn't even feel so bad, and it wouldn't be so hard to feel better. I wouldn't have to say, Oh I feel so awful, this is like the end for me here, in this dark living-room late at night, with the dark street outside under the streetlamps, I am so very alone, everyone else in the house asleep, there is no comfort anywhere, just me alone down here, I will never calm myself enough to sleep, never sleep, never be able to go on to the next day, I can't possibly go on, I can't live, even through the next minute.

If I didn't believe what I felt was the center of everything, then it wouldn't be the center of everything, but just something off to the side, one of many things, and I would be able to see and pay attention to those other things that are equally important, and in this way I would have some relief.

But it is curious how you can believe an idea is absolutely true and correct and yet not believe it deeply enough to act on it. So I still act as though my feelings were the center of everything, and they still cause me to end up alone by the living-room window late at night. What is different now is that I have this idea: I have the idea that soon I will no longer believe that my feelings are the center of everything. This is a comfort to me, because if you despair of going on, but at the same time tell yourself that what you feel may not be very important, then either you may no longer despair of going on, or you may still despair of going on but not quite believe it anymore.

Blue Peter

Peter Gizzi

To describe a logic of sight
pull the surface onto target and
arrive at zero aperture. Then
fluctuate to a face, reproduced
in serial format, superimposed
upon marginal pedestrians,
traversing a polarity of earth.

The axis here is askew, perhaps
unsettling, the way physical
equilibrium slides into multiple
perspective. This place where
sight informs the eye as gate
to phenomenon, a bridge to
impulse the imaginary. Simply

she was feeding bread to pigeons
in the park. So begin this lesson
with rain and square the surrounding
flat with common traffic. I
move through, to get here. If you
want me, you will find me in
the garden of vestiges, next to

the sweet water cistern. Where
the old port remains, a water
mark on granite, abutted with
grass and a stone path leading
to other places that for the moment
I am not interested in, as I take
serious your claim to provoke you.

And I will follow your instructions,
however silly, however sublime, until
you have found me, indistinguishable
from what you call, your self.
The way I wear you about my
mouth, as a crease, deepening
every time I smile to look at you.

Look at me. I'm serious, I must
find the way, to say, we have arrived.
For it is you who instruct me in
the laws of perspective, these many
converging lines, drawn to perception.
So that I have become only a star or
an asterisk or a compass rose. Signifying

location, this possibility of place. True.
It's been said that the burial of the dead
is the beginning of culture, as we know,
no other. And I remain raw.
Vapor digit tapping at my wrist,
the talon, the dorsal fin and the panther
claw. The value of negative space

and the rationale of talisman does
not parse, will not parry from this
dearth. As emotions surround the edge
of the planet adjusted to actual people we meet.
What could the difference of this construction
intend in a world of moments, merely
fragments provided to express conversation

or random noise signaling gray space,
to be inserted within an imported structure?
Birds migrate over cityscape and arrive
in my backyard to a mutiny of peaceful
dawn. Then a description of equality
is scored, as a rhetorical flourish is installed
for testimony. I flag, I stammer.

A banner to the burden that all things
that are, must not be, in me. Only,
will you not smile, when I wave?

Spirit's Desperado
Michael McClure

SPIRIT'S DESPERADO, I — I CHEER AND
BRAVO
       THE SIDE OF NEGATION AND OF HUNGER
            FOR SOUL.
    As a boy I saw the mole
        AND THE EAGLE
soaring and burrowing together
    and imagined that love
        was created of hair and of feather
            that rubbed on the edge
            of
            the
            vast ledge
of Sight, Sound, Taste, Touch — and of the Smell
        of satin and silk, and of the guts
    of the butchered creature
that writhes and grows a brain.
        I was sure that it was not Hell
        that I was living
        but I was reflecting the stain
        of that Huge Being
            called
            THE
            STARS!!

I KNEW IT WAS NOT EVEN HEAVEN

BUT IT IS ALL-DIVINE!

To be alive is to feast on desperation!

Three Poems
Keith Waldrop

THE PALMER WORM

and even lovers talk
sometimes of other things

like

.

pain

slips into songs

divines the light

.

talks in one
voice, sings
in another

.

blind fire

.

forgetfulness and
the wand

deflect the
voice from its
customary range

Keith Waldrop

        .

    and some words

    like

            .

    . . . and after the evening and
    the morning, the same
    blindness

            .

    no rest while I
    know I have to go

    no place if

    like

            .

    desire for the body as
    if for the dead
    body

Keith Waldrop

TRANSPARENT LIKE THE AIR

spirits love
houses and also

certain exemplary places

(such as the rotten
pilings off
India Point)

without necessarily controlling
the intervening spaces

they are nothing

they have not returned

(a primitive
sign meaning "neither . . . nor")

they do not
need to return I am
still here I

can bear only
the figures light
delineates not
the light itself

(unstable, un-
determined, in a
state of last ruin where
ontology seeps in)

clear things
with dark
addresses

Keith Waldrop

certain stones give
birth to other stones

(bodies we label
heavy) some

split into thin
flakes tightly
embedded a

liquid

petrified

animals
fallen down shafts the
marrow of their bones

frozen to this
selfsame

stone
(opaque

and then the flash
of a bird's wing) I

go down the column

Keith Waldrop

THE IDLE WHEEL

heavenly quiet the whole
house with her
restless fingers

.

dark and
darkly
curtained

.

gestures and
badinage sober and
rare

darkening
room no

movement an
arcane silence

.

brooding

.

fluffy
skirt

.

suspected of
appetite

Keith Waldrop

already removing the
tables and the chairs

.

who
in the dark in
the doorway

Thomas King Forcade:
Living and Dying the Great Adventure

Albert Goldman

NOVEMBER 16, 1978: A cold gloomy day. A small boyish-looking man is lying on a rumpled bed in a loft in Greenwich Village. He's restless, depressed, obsessed with paranoid fears. The day before at the office, he scored a handful of ludes. They didn't cool him out. Now he wants to lapse into unconsciousness.

He asks his wife to bring him a Tuinal. "Try to sleep," she urges. "If you can't get to sleep in twenty minutes, I'll bring you a pill." "What time is it now?" he asks. "Twenty to one," she answers. "You'll hear from me in twenty minutes," he warns. Then, fully clothed in an old paisley shirt and blue jeans, he burrows under the covers.

Twenty minutes later, his wife is talking with a friend in an adjoining room. Suddenly, she hears a popping sound. It isn't a backfire. It sounds like it came from the bedroom. She opens the door and looks inside. Nothing appears amiss.

Her husband is still lying in bed, only he has moved over to her side. Then she notices a small round hole in his left temple and a pearl-handled .22 at his side. What rivets her attention is his hands. They are suspended before his chest, like a puppy begging. Instinctively, she reaches forward to still their trembling.

Thus was extinguished the most brilliant and fascinating mind ignited by the youth revolt of the sixties — Thomas King Forcade. Most people have never heard of Tom Forcade; yet he should have been world-renowned as a counterculture guru and drug culture mastermind. Even if you confine your attention to his most notable achievement, the founding of *High Times*, the journal of drug hedonism, humor and adventure, Forcade should rate as one of the most innovative and resourceful figures in current-day journalism. His counterparts in an earlier generation, Hugh Hefner and Bob Guccione, are famous for having pulled the covers off sex in the mass media. Forcade pulled the covers off drugs in precisely the same manner. He took as many risks, made as many millions and sparked as many violent reactions as his famous rivals at comparable moments in their careers. Yet, when he blew out his brains at age 33, the media barely noticed his demise. *The New York Times*, which every year commemorates scores of obscure doctors, professors, actors and businessmen, could not bring itself to print an obituary of Tom Forcade.

The basic reason for this neglect is the fact that Forcade avoided publicity as relentlessly as most men seek it. Like a junior version of Howard Hughes, he spent his life in dreary holes and corners, cutting deals, giving orders and engaging in the sort of outlaw enterprises that can put you in prison for many years. Forcade had a lot to hide. He was a hippie Robin Hood who gave the money he made breaking the law to those whom the law would have broken. A complex and splintered personality, a man whose behavior was sometimes distorted by spells of madness, he was not the sort of person who permits anyone to comprehend him fully. At most, after years of intimacy, you might qualify for a few glimpses of the face behind the mask.

My knowledge of Forcade commenced with an incident that was emblematic of his personality, combining as it did his love of persiflage and role-playing with his even greater passion for instructing the world in the mysteries of drugs and the moral and political issues that the drug controversy brings to focus. The time was the spring of 1975. I — an innocent in the ways of weed — had just received an assignment to write a piece on the New York drug underground. Having read in an early issue of *High Times* a fascinating interview with a professional dope taster — a man who claimed that he was sent by drug syndicates to the growing areas to ascertain the quality of the crop — I determined to meet this mysterious figure and pick his brain. After prolonged negotiations, during which I learned that my authority went by the name of "Mike, the Marijuana Maven," I experienced at last the thrill of seeing the Exigente of the drug world walk into my living room.

At first glance the Maven looked like a wasted, blinking hippie scientist with a pale mushroom face and eroding hairline. He was engrossed in conversation as he stepped through the door, and he was engrossed in conversation many hours later when he exited. Never at any moment in that long evening did he stop talking. Nor were any of these words addressed especially to me. They came out of his mouth as they might have emerged from the speaker of a radio, low-keyed, perfectly phrased, and totally oblivious of whether they were being heard or ignored.

The only demand the Maven made was that my "researcher," Chic Eder (a tough, smart professional criminal recently released from prison), keep the speaker supplied throughout the night with an endless series of joints. The drugs were extracted from a zippered pill case containing a row of glass vials, each of which was filled with a different kind of exotic and costly marijuana. What was most remarkable was not the quantity of the drug that was rolled up and placed submissively in the Maven's hand but the fact that he virtually never took a drag. Joint after joint of Colombian, Oaxacan, Thai and Maui grass went up in smoke in the grasp of that small stained hand because the motor that powered the Maven's mouth never stalled long enough to allow him to put the butt between his lips.

I was spellbound by this performance not just because it filled my mind with vast amounts of unimaginable drug lore but because the Maven's rap emerged in a fascinating spiral of dialectic. Up and up a line of thought would climb, like the smoke from his smoldering joint; then, inevitably, at a certain point, like the coil in the smoke stream, the drift of the thought would reverse itself and start down in the opposite direction. After each of these elaborate mental somersaults, the Maven would pause for a moment and a sly, dissociative giggle would emerge from the side of his frozen face. Then, his eyes would blink, blink, blink, like a computer receiving a fresh set of signals, and he would be off again.

The next morning, when I lifted my woozy head off the pillow and switched on my tape recorder, I half-expected to find that my impression of this drug-saturated evening was highly distorted and that the Maven's wondrous rap, like fairy gold, had faded into hippie bullshit. The moment I heard that low, murmurous voice steadily paying out its endless line, I knew there had been no mirage. The Maven talked like a book. He had left me with pages upon pages of highly quotable material.*

As I got deeper into the dope game, I soon came to realize that there was no such thing in this world as a professional dope taster. This was just one of those whimsical shucks that Forcade liked to strap on fools like me — a college professor for 20 years — or the kids who read *High Times* as if it were the Bible of Hell. It wasn't all that long until I was informed that Mike, the Marijuana Maven, was really Tom Forcade, a shadowy figure with a long and fabulous past. Some people told me that he was a sinister government agent. Others that he was a heroic radical. What most intrigued me was the rumor that he was an audacious drug dealer and smuggler.

Finding out anything about Forcade was difficult. Even his connection with *High Times* was kept very quiet. His name never appeared on the masthead. His appearances at the office were sporadic and broken by long absences. Once my first article on the drug world appeared — especially after it elicited a movie offer from Elliott Kastner — Forcade shifted in his attitude towards me, dropping his mask and offering to finance my first trip to Colombia, where I planned to go to the source of the golden stream that was pouring into America in the year 1976. It was at this moment that I got my first real insight into the way Forcade had created America's first journal of illicit drugs.

High Times was conceived and produced in the same spirit as that in which a group of undergraduates would put together a college humor magazine. Though there were numerous writers, editors, art directors, eventually as many as 70 people working in the office, the whole enterprise, from the us-against-them editorials to the startlingly explicit articles on how to smuggle drugs to the lovingly fondled imagery of World War II airplanes, fast speedboats and S/M Punk Rock geariness, was the spiritual emanation of Tom Forcade. Ed Dwyer, the magazine's first editor and one of its two most important in-house writers, recalled recently how the key pieces were produced. "Tom would come over to my place about eleven in the evening with Bob [Singer, the other house writer] in tow. Then he'd proceed to expound. What he said generally left us either dazed or laughing. He never gave us any timetable. He just expected that at some point his ideas would be crystallized. He allowed us to improvise and cop our own styles. 'Ventriloquize' is a good word for the way he operated."

Though the magazine was concocted like a comedy show with a half-stoned cast, the soundness of its basic concept made it an overnight success. For by the mid-seventies, dope was no longer a fad or a problem. Dope was a world. There were millions of drug users, who had patterned themselves into a vast underground society that had its own myths and folklore, social etiquette and pecking order, songs and language, heroes and humor. There were scores of drugs, each with its special mystique. There was a rapidly developing industry that manufactured an endless array of drug paraphernalia, ranging from simple rolling papers to sophisticated electric stills that could convert a hemp doormat into a jigger of hash oil that would blow your noggin to the moon. There was a mountain of undigested botanical, chemical and medical information. There were great stretches of history demanding exploration, underground classics crying for publication and a whole network of interconnections — between drugs and sex, drugs and health, drugs and religion — about which people were eager to learn.

Most interesting of all, there was a labyrinthine underground of drug dealers and drug smugglers who journeyed to marvelously exotic places — to the Himalayan countries of Nepal, Bhutan and Tibet; to the jungles and deserts of South America; to the Arab kingdoms of the Middle East; to the war zones of the Far East — to bring back drugs for America. The scams and strategems of these colorful characters comprised an endless novel of crime, foreign intrigue and high adventure. And all this heady stuff was just lying there waiting to be released through the stopped-up channels of the mass media, which still persisted in treating drugs simply as a social disease or a criminal racket.

From a business standpoint Forcade knew his magazine would click because the kids would gobble it up and the paraphernalia merchants would pour money into it, having no other advertising outlets. Eventually, the magazine would attract the record companies and all the other industries that compete for the youth dollar. Starting the magazine on a $20,000 shoestring, Forcade would see the circulation double with every issue for years, until at its peak, in 1978, *High Times* was read by four million people a month, grossed five million dollars a year and had been acclaimed as the "publishing success story of the seventies."

The same shrewdness exemplified by the concept and the financing was evinced in the design and packaging of the product. Instead of aping the butcher-paper drabness of *Rolling Stone* or the hapless scribbling of the underground press, Forcade produced a slick knockoff of the paramount magazine formula of recent times: the *Playboy-Penthouse* sex mag. His reasoning was flawless.

Dope was the sex of the seventies: a universal pleasure fighting for full acceptance. From the intellectual standpoint, it was a large and confused subject clamoring for scientific clarification. From the literary standpoint, it was a world of inexhaustible sensory and intellectual experience seeking expression in words and images. That being the case, why shouldn't the formula that worked for pussy work for pot?

Only one important difference separated *High Times* from its famous models, *Playboy* and *Penthouse*. Advocating the liberalization of the sex code meant at most modifying the manners and morals of American society. Advocating the liberalization of the drug code meant abolishing some of the most punitive statutes of American law. Meantime, it meant *breaking* that law. Though *High Times* never advocated any criminal act — god forbid! — it did not stop with the mere description of drug usage. From an early point in the magazine's history and with increasing attention to detail as years went by, *High Times* provided very precise and valuable instruction in the secret art of smuggling dope. Lengthy interviews with veteran smugglers, illustrated guides to the "Ten Best Smuggling Planes" or the "Ten Best Smuggling Boats" and technical discussions of how to make radio transmissions to South America in code were typical features of the magazine. In a country where vast numbers of people have the means and the desire to play the smuggling game but are inhibited simply by lack of the requisite knowledge and experience, these articles were bound to make the gap between thinking and doing much smaller. What's more, they were certain to provoke the authorities to take measures to turn off this frothing fountain of forbidden knowledge.

The most determined effort to get *High Times* and Forcade occurred in the years 1976 and 1977. I became aware that something serious had gone wrong as soon as I returned from Colombia, in January 1976. I discovered, to my chagrin, that Forcade had vanished and the deal we had made to publish a one-shot magazine containing my adventures had been unilaterally abrogated. Naturally, I sought by every means to discover what had happened to my erstwhile publisher. Eventually, by piecing together accounts gathered from Forcade's partners in and outside the dope game, I was able to picture very clearly the sequence of events.

The whole story commenced on the night of January 25, 1976. That Sunday evening, Forcade was cruising down Fifth Avenue with a lady dope dealer. Full of tea and happiness, he passed the building where he lived: the Fifth Avenue Hotel, a big, seedy old establishment near Washington Square. Glancing up at the windows of his apartment, which he had left in total darkness, he was startled to see that all the lights were burning. Stopping to look more carefully, he could see silhouetted in the bright panes strangely costumed people. In a flash, Forcade jumped out of the car and darted up the service stairs to scope out the scene. What he saw sent his brain spinning. His rooms were swarming with firemen and police officers.

Evidently a pipe had burst and someone had called the fire department. In tracing the leak, the firemen had opened the apartment's main closet. Stacked inside were a lot of foul-smelling suitcases, which, when opened, revealed a stash of two hundred pounds of high-quality marijuana. In the State of New York, with its recently enacted Rockefeller drug laws, two hundred pounds of weed could get you a long stretch in prison. What was alarming Forcade, however, was not just the threat of a dope bust. In the apartment were all his personal and business papers. These documents proved conclusively that though he had no public connection with *High Times*, he was the magazine's sole owner. If the authorities wanted to put the country's first journal of drug use out of business, these papers would make the task much easier.

Most men caught in such a trap would have run for their lives or their lawyers. Not Forcade. Dashing down to the street, he ducked into a phone booth and called up Chic Eder, who had once been a burglar. Late that night, when the police had padlocked the apartment and left the premises, Tom and Chic slipped up to the floor armed with a twenty-pound sledgehammer, one of Forcade's favorite tools. Four heavy shots with the hammer and the door flew off its hinges.

Forcade dashed into his kitchen, tore the stove away from the wall and thrust his hand up the ventilation pipe. He pulled out a small satchel and threw it at Chic. "Grab it and run!" he barked. Then, he added, with characteristic humor: "I'll hold them off!"

Chic ran down the stairs, tore out of the building and whipped around the corner, where he paused to draw breath. In a dark doorway, he cracked the satchel and examined its contents with a practiced eye. It contained about a hundred thousand dollars in wads of hundreds neatly bound with thick rubber bands. Forcade had saved his stash. Meantime, he was upstairs busily collecting his business papers and his passport.

Later that night, while Tom and Chic were driving through the city's streets, Forcade nodded towards the satchel lying between them on the front seat. Nonchalantly, he said: "Help yourself!"

"That's chump change!" rasped Chic in his toughest gangster voice.

"What do you want then?" asked Tom, genuinely puzzled.

"I want *in!*"

"In what?"

"In the *game!*"

Tom responded with a supercilious giggle, but from that time on, Chic was in.

377

Forcade's next move was to the Barbary Coast of the American drug trade, the southwest coast of Florida, near Naples. Here he gathered his gang and started communicating by shortwave radio with Colombian mother ships. These expendable old tramp steamers would sail parallel to the coast of Florida far out in international waters rendezvousing with first one, then another American smuggling party, until their supplies of weed, coke and bogus-Quaaludes were exhausted — or the ships were captured by the Coast Guard. After repeatedly failing to work out a deal with the Colombians, Forcade changed his strategy.

On the night of March 15, near the Remuda Ranch, southeast of Naples, Forcade supervised the unloading of a 44-foot sailboat that had been crammed with nine tons of Colombian weed. It was a "guerrilla" operation: no dock, no pay-off to the cops, in short, no protection. It was also a clumsy operation because it took 24 hours to unload the sailer with a 29-foot Thunderbird, obliging Chic Eder on the first night to stay aboard the sailboat stuffed with over 6,000 pounds of pungent weed. During that night, a Coast Guard patrol boat shone its searchlight on the sailboat and commanded the vessel to switch on its running lights. "Aye aye, sir," snapped the quick-witted Chic — and the Coast Guard sailed away looking for smugglers.

The following night, the off-loading was finally completed. The last two trucks had just pulled away from the shore when they were challenged by a uniformed wildlife officer in a patrol car. One of the rules of clandestine operations is that in the event of discovery one party must draw off the enemy in the wrong direction while the rest of the group completes its mission and makes good its escape. Forcade was driving a camper filled with 2,800 pounds of weed. A veteran hot-rodder, he floorboarded his four-wheel-drive and took off at 65 miles an hour along the Tamiami Trail.

As the wildlife officer reported next day in the local press, he gave chase, but he could never pull abreast of the truck because the driver kept steering a dizzying serpentine pattern. In the cab of the truck with Forcade were Chic Eder and Tom's 20-year-old sidekick. This kid started to come apart the minute he felt the heat. Now as they approached Everglades City, they looked up ahead and spotted the flickering lights of a police blockade. (The wildlife officer had radioed for assistance.) At that moment, it looked like the game was over for Tom Forcade. Actually, the best was yet to come.

Shouting at his men to hold tight, Forcade drove the truck off the highway and into the Everglades. The moment they bogged down, the men threw open their doors and took off on foot. Instantly, they were up to their knees in muck and slime. Next thing they knew, they were beset by hundreds of mosquitoes and a plague of seed ticks, jiggers and swamp vermin. The local cops had no desire to follow the smugglers to their doom. The police figured it would be an easy matter to surround the fugitives and wait them out. Soon a helicopter was thut-thut-thutting overhead. Periodically, the police would shout through bullhorns: "You better come out! We've got you surrounded!"

For nearly 24 hours, Forcade scurried around in the swamp seeking a way to escape. He was chilled and exhausted, hungry and thirsty. Never once, though, did he lose his nerve. Wearing a white dress shirt and an orange jacket, clothes for the office not the field, he kept joking, "Just another chapter in The Great Adventure." Forcade's young companion was made of weaker stuff. He finally walked out on the road and gave himself up, providing the police with a lengthy deposition that was forwarded to New York and joined with the information on the Fifth Avenue Hotel bust. Forcade and Chic held out until the second night. Then, they made an audacious move.

Observing that the police avoided the mosquitoes by remaining in their squad cars with the windows shut tight, they decided to crawl past the cars that were guarding the best way out of the area. Moving just a few inches at a time, they crawled through a whole covey of cop cars, wondering why there were so many parked in this particular spot. Later they learned that they had slithered through the parking lot of a sheriff's substation.

Getting past the cops was just the first step in getting away. The next was crossing a bridge that was in full view of the police. Forcade started out by swinging hand over hand from the edge of the bridge. Halfway across, he felt his arms going numb. With a desperate effort he hoisted himself to the roadbed and crawled the rest of the way.

Now it was a comparatively simple task to hike ten miles until they found a motel; call up the gang, who had given them up for lost; settle into the back of a car driven by two of the women in the gang; and, finally, receive the congratulations of everyone at the stash pad in Miami, where Tom presided with grim good humor—and a mosquito-riddled face like a huge tomato—over the division of the spoils. Next time I saw Forcade he told me that he had just made a million dollars.

Over the next couple of years, as I learned more and more of Forcade's history, I came to recognize that this mild-mannered, highly intellectual little guy was actually one with the heroes of the Wild West. Though Tom appeared to people in New York like a novocaine-faced weirdo who had dropped from outer space, he was actually a man with deep regional roots, a son of the pioneers.

His native state was Arizona, a barren and thinly inhabited region when his mother's family entered it in 1881, at the end of a cattle drive from Colorado. The family stopped first in the town of Tucson; but, finding there was not sufficient water to husband their herds, they moved down near the Mexican border, settling in the tiny sulfur-springs hamlet of Wilcox. There they built an adobe house with walls two feet thick; and there they remained, as generation after generation was born and reared in the same house.

Forcade's mother married a brilliant young engineer named Kenneth Forcade Goodson, who was a specialist in heavy construction. Goodson worked for many years building military installations for the Defense Department. Tom Forcade — whose real name was Gary Goodson — was reared in a succession of military bases in faraway places, like Okinawa, Alaska and Greenland. This military milieu had a profound effect upon the development of both his personality and his imagination.

The military influence explained Forcade's fascination with weapons (one of his prize possessions was his Thompson submachine gun) and his alarming tendency to draw on anyone who crossed him. Likewise it shaped his whole conception of a smuggling operation, which he described in *High Times* as: "like a military operation with overtones of religious fervor." Even the trademark of Forcade's Trans High Corporation (THC, ya dig, man?) betrayed this obsession. Any other hippie entrepreneur would have chosen an emblem like the seven-leafed marijuana frond. Not Forcade. He stamped everything he touched, from glossy ads to clunky belt buckles, from chunky ashtrays to blazoned T-shirts, with the image of the most glamorous fighter plane of World War II, the twin-tailboomed P-38.

The influence of Forcade's father was apparent in his son's mania for driving souped-up cars and for flying airplanes; for the father had been a flyer and he met his death while driving a fast car. This sudden death of an adored father, which occurred when Forcade was eleven, was the decisive stroke in the shaping of the boy's character.

Not long afterwards, Forcade began to have trouble at school and to display symptoms of depression, an affliction that dogged him all the rest of his life and led eventually to his death.

Forcade was always a good student, so it is not surprising to learn that he got through the four-year program for a bachelor's degree in business administration in just two-and-a-half years at the University of Utah. More characteristic of him were his adventures as the school's most notorious hot-rodder. One of his fellow students, Therese Coe, composed a recollection of Forcade after his death that brings back the young man known as "Junior Goodson." "His pad," she wrote, "was lined with hulking black auto engine parts in various stages of custom greasiness. The black forties buggy he drove sported fat racing tires, a blast-furnace engine and a rear end four feet off the ground. Around midnight he would take us up the winding four-lane highway on the western slope of the Wasatch Mountain. Then as he floored the short and shot down the twisting road, he would shimmy the steering wheel violently. . . . Another of his games was to take us out to the Utah-Nevada border and then outrun the local cops for a hundred miles across the Bonneville Salt Flats."

Tom married his college sweetheart only to soon divorce her. Then as the hippie lifestyle began to crystallize, he founded a commune near Tucson and published his first magazine, a dim little booklet titled *Orpheus* (singer of songs, teller of truths, martyr at the hands of the maenads) that relied on stuff reprinted from the underground press. At this point, he had his first brush with the law, a bust for acid. Not wanting to taint his family name with scandal, he changed his name from Goodson (how ironic!) to Forcade, which rhymes with "arcade." As his new middle name, he adopted the title "King."

In the late sixties, Forcade came to New York in a battered old school bus emblazoned with psychedelic symbols. In 1967, he organized with John Wilcock (of the *East Village Other*) the Underground Press Syndicate (UPS), a useful device for pooling and exchanging all the information gathered by the hundreds of underground newspapers that were springing up at the time. Characteristically, Forcade financed the new business by persuading Bell & Howell to underwrite the venture in exchange for the rights to copy all the papers on microfilm and sell the film to university libraries. This was an early example of what became Forcade's great goal in later years: "making the system work against itself."

At this point in the history of the counterculture, everything suddenly assumed a political coloring. Forcade plunged head over heels into the alphabet soup of the Movement and became an activist and a radical. He raised funds for the cause by shaking down the promoters of rock concerts. His most characteristic efforts, however, were in the genre titled "guerrilla theater"—or just plain disruption. Working in this idiom, Forcade turned up in May 1970 before the President's Commission on Obscenity and Pornography dressed in full clerical costume: black suit, reversed collar, black slouch hat. After denouncing the commission, he slammed a custard pie into the face of Professor Otto N. Larsen of the University of Washington.

In August of the same year, he performed one of his most legendary exploits, a caper about which he published a paperback book, by disrupting a Warner Brothers movie project that entailed herding a caravan of hippies (including Wavy Gravy and the Hog Farm) across America and towards the Isle of Wight Rock Festival. Forcade emerged from a cloud of dust five miles outside Boulder driving a Cadillac limousine painted olive drab and emblazoned on each side with a big white Army star. Atop the car was a haranguing platform rigged with two powerful Missile Man speakers. Inside, the vehicle was loaded with all the devices of disruption from smoke bombs to skyrockets. Forcade himself was costumed as the head of the Free Rangers (a branch of the White Panthers), a classic frontiersman in laced leather tunic, floppy leather sombrero, shoulder-length hair and a skull-and-crossbones button proclaiming "The American Revolution."

When Forcade's efforts to radicalize the caravan failed, he called to his aide David Peel, the New York street musician, whose album, *The Pope Smokes Dope*, was produced by John Lennon—and instantly banned everywhere in the world. Peel and his crew of veteran Lower East Side street tumlers accomplished swiftly what Tom's highly intellectualized rap could not. They provoked the camp boss to whip out a knife. (Peel had looked at the guy's Indian swastikas and screamed, "I'm Jewish and you're Hitler for Warner Brothers!") At the critical moment, with the camp boss standing over Peel wielding his knife, Tom leaped on his back and wrestled him to the ground. The great aim had been achieved. The "Caravan of Love" had been shown up as a Caravan of Hate. When the film, *Medicine Ball Caravan*, was released, everybody pronounced the fight the best part.

Jerry Rubin remarked that he never viewed Forcade as a political activist but rather as an outlaw and a drug dealer, a "rogue genius." This strikes me as the root of the matter; for when you examine Forcade's political pranks carefully, you sometimes discover that they had a hidden underside of adventurism or criminality. For example, in later years, Forcade confessed to Ed Dwyer that a Warner Brothers' publicity hireling had actually commissioned Tom to disrupt the Medicine Ball Caravan, thus guaranteeing some violent on-camera action. A high-ranking former official of the company told me that he strongly suspected that Forcade's real interest in the project was as a cover for moving loads of weed across the country. (Using a movie production company as a disguise for a smuggling operation was later to become standard practice in the dope world.) One thing certain about Tom Forcade: for all his obvious idealism and Robin Hood generosity, he was not a man with a fixed moral center. Idealism and opportunism ran like wet colors back and forth across his bizarre life history in a manner that will make it very difficult for any future biographer to determine how to weigh his actions.

Personal passions were also a very big factor in Forcade's political career. In fact, his debacle as a political activist was produced in the most direct manner by personal animosities and non-political motives. The final spin began with a bitter battle over Abbie Hoffman's *Steal This Book*, in which Forcade claimed certain rights. After a "people's court" rendered a verdict in Hoffman's favor, Forcade brought suit against Hoffman in civil court, an action that was regarded in the Movement as a serious breach of counterculture ethics. Subsequently, Forcade broke with the Yippie leadership over the issue of whether to disrupt the Democratic presidential convention in Miami. Forcade organized his own group, the Zippies (motto: "Put the zip back into YIP"), who ran wild during this silly season.

At the height of the madness, Abbie Hoffman and Jerry Rubin accused Forcade of acting as if he were an agent provocateur of the federal government. They instanced his bringing suit against Hoffman and his inflammatory speeches against the Yippie leadership. When the story ran in Jack Anderson's column, Forcade's reputation as a radical was ruined. At the same time, the girl he loved, Gabrielle Schang, fell in love with Ed Sanders of the Yippies and defected from the Zippies.

The final blow came when Forcade returned to New York and

was busted by the FBI on a charge of possessing a fire bomb. Forcade, always the supreme put-on artist, told the feds that his brothers and sisters, the Weathermen, would soon break him out of jail. The feds, highly alarmed, posted two shotgun-toting guards before Forcade's cell.

When the dust settled and Forcade had been cleared—as he always was—of criminal charges, the erstwhile guerrilla theater virtuoso revealed himself as a profoundly embittered man. He felt betrayed and he declared that Miami had been the "Movement's Waterloo." Surrounding himself with a handful of trusted comrades, he returned to the world where he had always felt most at home, the dope-running and dealing scene, deep underground.

Forcade's headquarters in this period was a safe house—across the street from the old Women's Detention Center on Greenwich Avenue—called "Bobby's." (The fictitious name on the apartment lease was "Robert" So-and-So.) The protocol of a visit to Bobby's was very strict, very elaborate and highly characteristic of Tom's paranoid and fantastical imagination, fueled by James Bond movies.

When you arrived, you were greeted by Forcade's "valet," who presented the visitor with a two-page, single-spaced set of house rules. Every detail of doing business at the house was anticipated and defined: where to park, how to call, what passwords to employ, how to leave, etc. There were even punishments specified for each infraction of the rules.

Once inside the pad, you found a grungy decor redolent of both the flophouse and the suburban ranch house. One side of the room was piled from floor to ceiling with cheap suitcases stuffed with weed. The other side was furnished with a living-room bar spotlighted with high-intensity lamps for examining the goods. Forcade's private accommodations comprised just two items: a Navaho blanket, in which he slept on the floor; and a portable electric log fireplace, before whose dependable glow this acid cowboy would smoke his last joint and nod out at dawn.

Subsequently, Forcade established at 714 Broadway a "smokeasy," a unique institution of the time, which offered dealers a place to sample wares, talk prices, cut deals and conduct all the business appropriate to the trade. Tom's smokeasy looked like a rock rehearsal studio. Huge speakers dominated the front room; proceeding to the rear, you went down a corridor lined with cubicles, in which the merchandise was examined and deals made. The back room was a warehouse. The most characteristic feature of such operations was the "menu," a sometimes fancifully decorated card on which were listed all the products currently available and their prices, *viz.* "Thai Stick, $25 per. Indian Hash, $10 gram. Colombian Gold, $5 bag, $50 oz." We'll never see those prices again.

Even when Forcade made a lot of money in the smuggling game, he never lived in style. Anhedonistic in sensibility, he cared nothing for other men's pleasures. His idea of dining out was a couple of tacos and a glass of milk. His notion of a party was a big tank of nitrous oxide and a plentiful supply of penny balloons. Though he quipped, "I never met a drug I didn't like," he had no heavy habits. Once somebody gave him a handsomely carved opium pipe. Forcade lectured us learnedly on the ritual and ecstasy of opium. Then he displayed a few little amber wafers of the drug. Just as we prepared ourselves for the great experience, Tom discovered that the pipe was broken. That ended our pipe dream. As for women, Forcade generally had an attractive girl who was primarily a comrade in arms. Cindy Ornstein, for example, was a sexy little blonde from Philadelphia who used to go around in Brownie costumes. In Miami, she led the Zippie women just as Forcade led the men. Usually, though, Forcade went to bed with his clothes on. His wardrobe ran to polyester shirts and black nylon socks.

What did get Forcade off in the smuggling game — or any game — was *power*, particularly the power of the unmoved mover, the invisible godlike presence who sits behind the scenes, like one of those master criminals in a James Bond movie, manipulating the complicated technology of modern crime and the tricky interpersonal relationships that spawn about the throne. Just before his death, Forcade ventriloquized an account of his early smuggling adventures through a fake interview conducted by "Leslie Morrison" (Forcade's favorite nom de plume) with "A Smuggling Ace." After recounting in his typical deadpan style a history of crime that commenced in high school, when he would drive over the Mexican border with his wheel wells stuffed with grass, and then escalated steadily until, in his mid-twenties, he was conducting dangerous aerial operations, Forcade the ace finally got around to characterizing his type, the smuggling "kingpin." "The bigger you are," he remarked, "the less known you are. You're the mirror image of a successful public figure, like a novelist, a rock star, sports figure. You get addicted to having that much control over and effect upon people."

The mixture of self-effacement and megalomania in this description provides the precise formula for Tom Forcade. He did see himself as a "kingpin," but he knew his strength lay in denying the normal appetite for fame. His ultimate strength, therefore, was the power of self-control. Unfortunately, this stern discipline developed a masochistic edge. Once, when Forcade removed his shirt, I was astonished to see that he had pierced both his nipples with gold rings.

Though Forcade's exercise of power over himself was implicitly cruel, his exercise of this same power over others was generally benign. He was a loyal and helpful friend, a faithful comrade, a fair employer, a benefactor of countless good causes and a patron of the counterculture in its most authentic and advanced forms. There were times, however, when he lost control and began to behave like a mad monarch. The most prolonged and bizarre of these seizures occurred when Forcade returned to New York in November 1976, after living for seven months underground.

Pitching camp in a cavelike loft across the street from the offices of *High Times* on East 27th Street, he resumed control over every aspect of the magazine, from the editorials to the cover art, from the distribution strategy to the placement of ads on the page. After a couple months of this activity, one day he called up Paul Tornetta, the general manager, and started issuing insane commands. "I want you to fire everyone," he began, "except yourself and Stan [Place, circulation director]. Collect all the money from people who owe us money. Sell all the furniture and typewriters. We're closing down the magazine." Tornetta replied: "I can't do that, Tom. If you want to fire everyone, *you* do it."

Ten minutes later Forcade stalked into the office, downed out on Valiums and acting like the Frankenstein monster. Seizing the switchboard, he tore it off the wall and hurled it at the operator. Then he went from office to office uttering in slow motion the same robotlike formula: "You are terminated . . . You are terminated . . . You are terminated."

Next day, after a wild night of phone calls, crash meetings and frantic skull busting, Andy Kowal, the magazine's publisher, arrived at Forcade's loft with a couple other executives to offer to buy the business for a half-million dollars. Kowal recalls that they found Forcade lying on a sofa with his spindly little legs sticking out of a ratty bathrobe. All he would say is: "I can't sell the magazine. I'm not in my right mind." Kowal, assuming this was just sales resistance, made an impassioned pitch. "Look, man," he pleaded, "you and I started this thing together, we went through a lot, you made me a lot of promises . . ." Before he could get the next phrase out of his mouth, Tom held up his hand to stop him. "I made you a lot of promises?" echoed Forcade. "I'm breakin' promises?" Kowal replied automatically, "Yeah!"

At that moment there was one of those chilling pauses that would occur when Tom was in his moods. Turning in slow motion on the sofa, like a sinister candy crane, Forcade said to his sidekick: "Gimme my piece." As everyone froze in terror, the aide flipped his boss a massive .45. Kowal stares at Forcade in horror. A downed-out psycho with a gun in his hand! He figures he's a dead man. Forcade is staring just as intently at Kowal, his hard, keen eyes starting to come through the drug haze. Suddenly, Forcade hands Kowal the gun, saying in his best Boris Karloff baritone: "If I broke all those promises — kill me!" Paul Tornetta reaches over and grabs the weapon. The negotiations conclude with Forcade still in possession of his magazine.

The meaning of this strange episode was understood by Ron Rosenbaum, the writer of the "'R.' Dope Connoisseur" page in *High Times* and one of the few highly perceptive people in the Forcade circle. Rosenbaum explained: "Tom wanted to jolt the staff back into his frame of reference: make them realize that it was all a whim of his and not a business where everybody fights for power and watches out for his own career. I think if he had killed the magazine, he might not have killed himself."

Even if Forcade had a rational motive for blowing up *High Times*, it would be hard to find one for certain other episodes in this same period. Even with regard to his favorite cause, NORML, the National Organization for the Reform of Marijuana Laws, Forcade could not resist his impulse to do the impermissible. It should be understood that Tom Forcade regarded marijuana almost as a sacred substance. It was the emblem of all his most cherished values: freedom, thought, humor. Unlike a real criminal, Forcade would have gladly sacrificed all the millions he made in the dope game if he could have gotten this precious substance legalized. Once, for example, he left ten thousand dollars in cash on the desk of the director of NORML. The money was accompanied by a note that read: "From a smuggler." The gesture was carefully calculated: it got NORML a lot of publicity; it invited other players to follow suit. Subsequently, at the NORML convention in the winter of 1975, Forcade took a rare public bow as NORML's biggest contributor, superseding in that role Hugh Hefner. Yet when Forcade decided the following spring to attend an important NORML party at the posh Park Avenue apartment of Mrs. ——, he behaved like a boor.

Like Little Caesar, he made a late entrance surrounded by his entourage. Then, as if impelled by some instinct for the perverse, he made off in the opposite direction from that in which the party was being held. Wandering into the elegant dining room, he lit the tapers in the silver candelabra and then sprawled in a chair with his feet up on the polished wood table. He was just lighting a joint when the mistress of the house walked in and started screaming with outrage. Staring at her with half-closed eyes, Tom sneered: "Go fuck yourself!" At that moment the butler — a dead ringer for Sammy Davis, Jr. — appeared and started rousting Forcade. Touching the "Kingpin," the "Ace," was a dangerous act. Instantly, he exploded in rage. First he took a swing at the startled flunky; then he started throwing everything that came to hand. Fifteen minutes after his arrival at the big NORML party, NORML's leading contributor was hustled, kicking and cursing, out the door.

Forcade's bouts of depression were cyclical in nature. They came on when the days grew short and gloomy in the early winter. They would pass in the early spring, the slow motion of depression gradually quickening to the fast-forward speed of Forcade's manic phase. Vital to his recovery were the ministrations of his closest friend and aide, Jack Coombs. Jack figured so largely in the last years of Forcade's life that no picture of Tom could be complete without an answering shot of his soul mate. The key to this pair's great love for one another was their opposite but complementary characters.

Forcade was a desiccated and jaded little mastermind, totally devoid of social grace. When he was depressed, his affectless gaze, laconic responses and attitude of you're-talking-and-I'm-listening-so-whatha-hell-else-do-you-want? could chill you to the bone or drive you into a murderous rage. Jack was very tall, strong and physically adroit, with a smiling, charming, obliging manner. Jack would welcome you at the door and usher you into the presence; Forcade would be lying back on some dirty cushions on the floor, talking his face off and listening to reggae playing at ear-damaging volume from a pair of ominous-looking old movie-house speakers. Jack would offer you a drink or see that you got a toke on the joint that Forcade was neglecting while he rapped.

Forcade, for his part, treated Jack like a proud and doting parent. He was especially fond of rattling off all of Jack's licenses and credentials: "He's got a radio operator's license, both FAA and marine radio telephone; a first-class ham license; marine sea captain's license; expert in computers, super technically oriented, ya dig?" Jack was a digital virtuoso and Tom was the brains of the outfit. They were made for each other.

On a deeper level, Jack was the human antidote to his friend's emotional illness. When Forcade would get into bed, curl up in the fetal position and withdraw from the world, Jack would hold him in his arms and coax him out of his gloom. Jack was Forcade's lithium. Even after Tom married Gabrielle Schang, the girl he had been courting intermittently for nearly six years, Jack continued to play a vital role in his friend's life, often joining the newly married couple for outings or evenings at home.

Gabrielle recalls: "Tom and Jack spoke at least once a day on the phone. Tom had total trust in Jack. They loved each other. They were always laying plans and sharing dreams. One big dream was to buy a plane. Tom would walk around with a copy of Trade-a-Plane under his arm. Once in a while they would call about a particular plane. 'My god!' I'd think, 'they're really going to fly!'" As always, Jack had fallen in with his friend's designs. The digital virtuoso qualified himself to operate multi-engine aircraft in a remarkably short time. Gabrielle quipped that Jack's hasty education in aviation was a "crash course."

In the spring of 1978, the two pals decided that the time was ripe for another chapter in The Great Adventure. The plan was that Jack and another, more experienced pilot would fly down to Colombia in a two-engine plane, pick up a load of grass and fly it back to the States, where they would drop it by parachute onto an isolated spot in Florida. After the load had come to ground, a recovery crew would secure the stuff and run it to a stash pad in Atlanta.

Tom and Jack being such romantics, it would never do for them to adopt a method that didn't allow for comradeship. Their plan had to be a scheme that after they brought it off would allow them to kick back on many subsequent nights in New York and say, "Hey, man, we did it *together*, didn't we?"

Hence it was decided that when the smuggling plane reached the vicinity of the drop site, Tom would meet it in another professionally piloted plane and lead it in over the spot. This aerial rendezvous was a wholly unnecessary complication because smuggling planes have no trouble reaching their destinations through normal navigational procedures and the ground crews can signal them at

the last minute by radio or by flashing lights. A further complication was introduced by Tom's financial partner in this move, a
flamboyant character named Tom Sullivan, a raw-boned, redneck
lad from Tampa, who subsequently achieved celebrity at Studio 54,
where he was called Cowboy because of his penchant for dressing
in costly Western gear.

On the night of the flight, Sullivan was stationed in the lavish
two-story penthouse of the Peachtree Plaza in Atlanta, a 40-story
tower of black glass. High on heroin, he was wild with the anticipation of a big killing because on this same night a shrimpboat loaded
with weed was scheduled to dock in Louisiana. The Cowboy liked
to think of himself as the hero of a reckless adventure movie with
a rock 'n' roll soundtrack; in fact, he eventually made a movie about
himself titled *Cocaine Cowboys*, starring Jack Palance and Andy
Warhol. Tonight, the movie would carry "the poor little cracker
boy from the boonies" to unparalleled heights of glamour and
adventure.

At one in the afternoon, Sullivan had received a reassuring call
from his Colombian connection, who reported that the plane had
taken off 25 minutes earlier. At the last minute, Sullivan's lieuten-
ant, a soft Southern boy named Joe, who lived with Sullivan's sister,
had decided to deadhead home aboard the plane. Sullivan gave a
whoop of joy because that meant that by midnight, he and his closest buddy would be sitting in this lavish pad out of their minds on
drugs, toasting each other with champagne, while awaiting the call
that would tell them that they had brought in a whole shipload of
marijuana. Nobody in the history of the dope game had ever played
or won such a great doubleheader.

At midnight, the phone rang. The Cowboy caught it before the
second ring. "Hello!" he cried with a startled inflection that said,
"Tell me quick what's happenin'."

"It's bad news," said the heavy rural voice of a member of the off-
loading crew. "They come in right, but when we tole 'em to git
down, they got down so low they musta hit a tree. The plane
crashed. We jist got back. We hung theah three hours — thass how
cool it wuz! They wasn't a man exscaped. They's all dead."

The disaster was Forcade's fault.

Two hundred miles down course, the smuggling plane radioed
that all was well and gave an ETA. When Forcade made visual contact with the blue-and-white Queen Air, he turned around and
started leading it in over the ground. As the two planes maneuvered,

Forcade kept urging the dope plane to get lower. "Get lower, man, get lower!" he barked into the mike as he skimmed along about 200 feet above the tree level. Suddenly, he heard an explosion and saw a blaze of light all around him.

Banking sharply, he stared down at the ground. There he saw the image that was to haunt him till the day he died. Jack's plane was going up in a ball of flames. Forcade circled as low as he dared over the burning plane, straining to see figures crawling out of the wreckage. As the plane, a flying incendiary bomb stuffed with hay and high-test gas, exploded, it was obvious that there were no survivors. Finally, Forcade had no choice but to fly back to his base and land.

When he got home the next day, he told Gabrielle: "We won't be getting any more calls from Jack." Then he burst into tears. Soon, he got control of himself and started the search that occupied him for many months. Though there was no hope of survivors, he wouldn't relinquish his belief that Jack had escaped and was lying up somewhere in a hospital, too sick to make contact. Tom hired private investigators and attorneys to work on the case. He held painful meetings with Jack's family. When he told me the story, I did an impermissible thing. I told him that he was a suicidal psychotic and, like all intellectuals, a fuck-up in the real world. He tolerated my outburst, remarking simply, "It wasn't any different than any other time."

Having abandoned smuggling for the time being, Forcade threw all his energy into entrepreneurial activities. He opened the first bookstore in SoHo, naming it after the dispatch the Weathermen released after their bomb factory blew up, New Morning. Forcade was also preparing to buy a restaurant, a bank and a Concorde airliner. (The plane took several years to build; by the time his was finished, he figured to have found a buyer.) He bought a pioneer dope movie, *The Polk County Pot Plane*; and he bankrolled for $400,000 the greatest of all rock documentaries, *D.O.A.*, the cinematic record of the Sex Pistols' American tour. (Once again Tom was up against Warner Brothers, who sought unsuccessfully to stop his film crews from ripping off the concerts with their cameras and mikes.) All this activity was characteristic of Forcade when his mood was elevated and his ever-restless spirit began to assert itself.

When the days started growing short, however, Forcade began to droop. Ed Dwyer recalls: "He would call up twelve at night, ob-

viously luded. He would start talking old stuff, the kind of thing
we had talked about when I first met him in 1969. Like getting a
Sikorsky amphibian and relocating the magazine to Nassau — as
if he were Howard Hughes. . . . I would walk in the office in the
morning and he would be sitting there pink-eyed as if he had been
crying all night. I'd say, 'You look like shit.' He'd say, 'I feel like
shit.'"

One of Forcade's problems was that he wasn't recognized as a
kingpin by anybody outside of his circle. When he went out to
Hollywood to sell his dope movie, the studio people refused to
take him seriously. Every conversation ended with them asking
him how to get some good coke. When he threw a big celebrity
party in a restaurant on West Broadway, Andy Warhol ignored Forcade. He was beginning to suffer from the Gatsby syndrome.

About a week before he died, Tom told me that many people
become sick with paranoia before they die, instancing Lenny Bruce
and Howard Hughes. "I refuse to become sick with paranoia ever
again," he vowed. Then, three days before he committed suicide, we
had another conversation. His whole mood had changed. He was
depressed, compulsively talkative, full of fears. He said he was
afraid an informer was giving him up to the DEA. After his death,
I learned that he had confided to other intimates other fears of a
similar nature. His lawyer, Michael Kennedy, recalled that Tom
had told him that he feared assassination by Larry Flynt, whose
organization was distributing *High Times.* Tom's reasoning was
highly characteristic of a paranoid.

Though Flynt's distribution had greatly improved sales of *High
Times,* Tom feared that Flynt might conspire with the magazine's
printer — to whom Tom was always in debt — to take away the magazine. To protect himself against this threat, Tom had amassed a
lot of secret information on Flynt. When he read that two Flynt
executives had been shot in a parking lot, he suddenly began to
fear he would be next. Clearly, at the end, Tom saw himself men-
aced on every side.

Tom's marriage must have also contributed to his depression
because, though it had its good moments, it appeared to be a struggle of antagonistic wills. If Tom said, "Let's drive," Gabrielle would
say, "No, I want to walk." They had so many disagreements that
sometimes it appeared that they had gotten together simply in
order to prove that marriage entailed no responsibility to give up
even the most trivial whims of the unattached individual. Nor

could Gabrielle, who had no connection with the world of drug dealing and smuggling, ever share in Tom's principal passion. By committing suicide while she was in the next room, Tom got in the last and cruelest lick.

Finally, there was Tom's grief over Jack's death. It was no coincidence that Tom killed himself just a couple of days before he was supposed to join Jack's parents in a memorial service. To those who speculated so frantically over the cause of Tom's death, I would say as one who has spent years trying to reconstruct his life that there was no single cause for his impulsive act of self-murder. It was an act produced by the coincidence of many distinct causes.

Whatever the reasons for Tom's death, the event was emblematic of the final failure of adaptation by the hippies to the alien climate of the seventies. Tom had made the most of the two strategies that promised most for the survival of the counterculture in the new decade. He had made the system work against itself, and he had become an outlaw hero of the drug culture. But beating the system meant immersing yourself in what you most despised, while stepping outside the system to play Robin Hood could finally mean seeing your closest friend incinerated in a ball of flames. Either way the exhilarating sense of triumph was soon lost in the dreary aftermath. Nor was there any other solution to the problem in the terms posed.

To a man in the grip of paranoia, death can become a personified adversary. A demon to be confronted in a final shootout. Better die like a desperado with a gun in your hand than go down to defeat inch by inch. Tom died like a soldier. He didn't flinch, he didn't fail. His hand was steady, his aim was true. He died without a cry or even a complaint. He was alone, wounded, cut off from his comrade. But he was in supreme command of himself. Such have been the deaths of many men who cared less for life than they did for living The Great Adventure.

---

*The essence of the interview is quoted in my book on marijuana, *Grass Roots*, 1979, pp. 22-30.

The Complexities of Intimacy
Mary Caponegro

IT IS COMMONLY KNOWN that those nearest to us, those of whom we have the most extensive, intimate knowledge, are often held at arm's length in our minds. The saying rolls so easily off the tongue: "familiarity breeds contempt," and the idiom "to take for granted" is as familiar to us as those we do. An elaborate system inevitably — yet inadvertently — evolves whereby we offer such permissions to each other.

Thus even as we hold our spouse's hand, or feel with genuine concern the tepid forehead of our firstborn, we simultaneously regard the ridge of black under the former's nails, the tiny white specks that fall to his shoulders when we smooth back his hair, and when our eyes travel furtively down, they settle on the latter's scuffed, untied shoes, his toe beginning to emerge from the leather like an egg in the very process of hatching.

The foot inside that shoe is not often idle as we speak to the flesh of our flesh, our firstborn son, as we speak with the intention of exchanging pleasantries, conveying affection; to elicit tenderness, or heaven forbid, solicit information. The foot taps; it jabs the ground. Our reluctant interlocutor's replies are listless; his eyes elsewhere, anywhere but in contact with our own.

Perhaps we keep our disappointment to ourself or perhaps we voice it, and once articulated, it is all too seductive to make a ritual of the words, as if they were beads of a rosary and we gathered by each repetition indulgences instead of alienation. As luck would have it, any replies which we receive do no more than inform of complications, superstitions, idiosyncrasies, compulsions: in short, excuses. The shoes, for example, have grown to have sentimental value; it is too unmanly to fuss with one's cuticles; least rational of all is our husband's insistence that excessive washing of the hair may cause it in time to thin, to recede, and eventually fall out. Is that what we want?

What would be the point, in the wake of such a confrontation, in trying to address our younger child's ostentatious makeup and jewelry, the revealing bodice of her dress — or more usually, as today, the threadbare sites on her dungarees? From the time of her conception, we had imagined a special closeness with our daughter: the seeking of advice, the poignant offering of secrets, both joyful and anxious, the sharing of that which is distinctly feminine — at least, as we construe the word. And yet the girl is more sullen even than her brother, less forthcoming in our presence, mistrustful for no reason we can possibly surmise. And if we are so bold as to critique the company she keeps, allude to standards of behavior, or imply that certain activities might be less than edifying, her terse reply will put us in our place: what can an old-fashioned housewife know of contemporary mores, styles, advances in our culture? This is not our business, nor our métier.

Thus, after actual or imagined encounters, all the more frustrated, we find ourselves admiring obsessively the graceful countenance, the courteous demeanor of our colleagues or our supervisor — granted we refer to the part-time employment of a woman who is principally a housewife, whose image is a fixed one, in community, in family — but regardless of the context, we cannot turn away our gaze from the prominent cheekbones or delicate wrists of strangers, or cease to dwell upon the uncanny way some women's stockings never sag below the knee — as ours inevitably do after only an hour of wear — or how some stylish men manage never to display an inch of flesh between the top of sock and hem of pant. Why is that strip of flesh so bothersome to us — appearing to glow in the dark as he sits in the living-room chair in our home? Why do we find ourself enraptured by the sonorous voice or elegant meaningless gestures of those we do not harbor in our homes? We are given to imagining, increasingly, how fulfilling life might be if it were he or she or they whom we greeted at table every morning, dined with every evening, perhaps by candlelight, without the television's ubiquitous, intrusive presence; perhaps even held, in certain circumstances — when we allow ourself the thought — in our embrace; the weary sequences of habit replaced by spontaneous rather than contractual affection, replaced by — might it ever be? — incendiary fervor?

Just take a look at yourselves, we want to cry; just for once would you listen to yourselves, to the persons of our household who seemed at one time to take more pride in their appearance, be more refined in their behavior; more courteous, more appreciative of ourself? For recently it seems that when an individual is needed for any task, be it rising, wearily to make his coffee, or driving to the pharmacy for yet another urgent errand, or cleaning out debris in the garage, it is the hand attached to our already strained shoulder which rises automatically to volunteer.

Yet should not one who regularly offers services, who does one's share, be given also certain compensations? Should not such persons be allowed to make, occasionally, demands? There must be some control over the degree to which we take each other for granted. How, for instance, have we spent this evening? With hardly a thought to our comfort. It may be that what others think of as necessity has been transformed in our perception into luxury; so that, for instance, we consider it less troublesome to ignore the fullness of our bladder than to interrupt her cosmetic application — an at least once daily ritual requiring intense concentration — or than to knock so loudly as to be heard over the sound produced by our firstborn when in his throat he does the internal acrobatic of suspending flavored liquid with the intention of freshening his breath before a visit from his girlfriend. The sound is in fact so comical to our ears, reminding us as it does of the gurgling of his early years, that it increases our urgency even as we strive to ignore the insistent pressure; we must cover our mouth with our hand lest we laugh out loud, or worse. And we may have to hold out longer still, for it is likely that he has negotiated with his sister over who precedes the other in the bathroom, and she will need to linger long before the mirror, taking to her eyes what would appear to be an instrument of torture and with the clamped end forcing the defenseless lashes into sculpted curl.

Not only are our physiological functions hindered by these rituals; pragmatic matters of the house are left on hold as well. We would like to start the laundry, so his sweatshirt and her ragged dungarees will be available on demand. We would like to let the dishwasher initiate its cycle, now that we have cleared away all traces of the repast we spent the afternoon preparing. Ingeniously we have fit all the vessels into the wire racks of the appliance: the pots and pans and flatware, even the tiny plate on which we put our own supper — the full-sized dinner plate that completes the Blue Danube pattern china set was accidentally broken recently — his girlfriend is our guess, but we are not so small, so petty, as to mention it, make issue of it — and we would not want to ask any other family member to make the sacrifice of crowding food onto such a diminutive surface. Still we are tentative about pressing the oval silver button that starts the cycle, lest we alter the consistency of our husband's bath—known to last over an hour—or perhaps the children's showers are now in progress: those pre-trysting rituals during which the steam rises and disseminates to fog not only the bathroom mirror, but all the windows of the house, as if our family resided in the humidity of the tropics rather than the temperate climate of a northeastern suburb of the United States.

How much is it to ask that we use the facilities; who but ourself would hesitate? Certainly not our firstborn, who, when a toddler, never did so before barging in upon our privacy? (This too, so long ago, may have contributed to the shaky condition of our bladder.) We should not ask at all; we should announce, by fiat, our intention. The door is unlikely to be locked. No one would be aghast, for there is not a prima donna in the house: such are the permissions of domestic familiarity. Nor are we or any member of the family inclined to give excessive priority to propriety in this house, where the men are likely to come to dinner in their undershorts, and our daughter wears as street clothes what most women would deem inappropriate for private lounging.

Why is it then, that when we form a fist before the door we cannot bring ourself to make contact in such crude fashion? It seems intrusive, so that at the last moment we resort to stealth; for if the door is unlocked, then knocking is not a functional prerequisite to entry, and we need not disturb whomever now occupies the bathroom; we only need perform one humble function, after all. If a shower is in progress — as the sounds we hear would now indicate — the curtain might preserve discretion. (We have heard that in fancy European hotels, bath and bidet are altogether separate spheres of activity.) Yes, clearly an outburst is unnecessary; obtaining the far more modest objective should be our focus — so intent a focus, in fact, by this point, that we cannot waste a moment in knocking, or for that matter looking at what lies before us as we make our way, purposefully, through the steam, to lower the toilet seat — always raised, it seems — to sit in mingled pain and relief of micturition — damn, blood again (we did not mean to swear out loud) — this is the consequence of trying to train one's bladder; our organs are not circus animals, after all; we should not wait so long; we are ridiculous; our dubious heroism is destructive; will we ever learn?

In our vexation, and then resignation, we raise our eyes to see, in the corner, our husband, his back to us. He makes rapid movements with his hand, his elbow pumping up and down: gestures which, when he turns his head to see who has sworn, turn furtive; but

when he continues, too intent on his objective to cease, he cannot
stifle his expression of catharsis: an ecstatic sound we can barely
recall from his mouth as his own momentarily vertical stream finds
more joyful release.

We applaud; we blow him a kiss, surprising him. (Never were we
one to resent the good fortune of others, no matter the contrast
with our own circumstance.) He is unsure of how to react; he had
not expected audience, particularly not our approval, is suspicious
of it, we would guess. And then we see, through the admittedly ob-
nubilating mist, that all of them are present: in our company, in
the bathroom — though removed, at the same time, preoccupied.
Their distance, however, has a different quality than usual. Through
the semi-transparent curtain we see the most curious silhouettes:
flawless, agile bodies, as if in choreographed ensemble, seen through
scrim: dramatic, seductive, mesmerizing. The vision seems to have
one hundred arms, like the Indian goddess, so swift and graceful
are their movements. How much we wish to peel away the membrane separating beauty from beholder.

And is there obstacle? No greater than there was to opening the
door. Although our mission is, as it were, accomplished, we are
transfixed; we cannot make ourself depart. Gently, stealthily, we
draw back the curtain. They will not be distracted by its whisper,
so engaged are they in their activities, which, when unsheathed,
seem both ordinary and exalted. Has the mist begun to dissipate,
or have our eyes begun to adjust? It would seem some seal was
broken when we first opened the door.

Uninterrupted, and unselfconscious in their nakedness, the group
of them are painting on the tiles, in flamboyant brushstrokes, what
appears to be a mural; the scene seems tropical, lush, idyllic. It
seems, in fact, to expand before our eyes. A small child we have
never seen before completes the party, molding of the waterlogged
remains of the transparent bar in the soap dish, a tower: quite an
impressive edifice; his eyes wide before his own accomplishment.
Our daughter's leg, meanwhile, is raised as if in pirouette, as he, the
one for whom she spent the evening "dressing," glides a manual
razor tenderly, deftly, up her calf, making, eventually, a circle around
her leg, while she attempts to do the same procedure to his face
and upper lip. Given the awkwardness of synchronizing his head
down, her hand above, they take, eventually, to lying down, reclin-
ing the length of their bodies in the bath, despite the waterfall that
rains down upon them all the while, in order to make the mutual

gesture. Then, when the flesh of face and calf are silken-smooth, each, facing the other, dangles one foot out the tub, while taking clippers to each toenail in sequence. There is not a nick for all the contact with sharp instruments, not a drop of blood.

The unfamiliar child has completed his slippery castle and embraces it to slide down, finding the slender clippings piled on the side of the tub; he marvels at them as if they were luminous seashells at the beach; perhaps he contemplates including them in his composition as a decorative addition. Instead, he blows into a plastic flute, making surprisingly articulate tones. Is that our eldest son behind him, building a boat, with more alacrity than we have ever witnessed him exhibit? And more skill. In less than a minute, it seems, he has crafted the bow, the stern, the ship entire; then down the drain he sails, a disappearing act; even the others are momentarily distracted from their independent activities to gape, as when a woman is sawed in half by a magician. No sooner has he submerged than he resurfaces, only to repeat the cycle over and over, the others applauding at each completion of his round trip.

Our husband, meanwhile, who initially drew our eye, having completed his goal, is celebrating with acrobatic maneuvers of even greater magnitude: swinging from the curtain rod — hopefully sturdy enough — with the dexterity of a professional, movements of which we never knew him capable. After he has warmed up with a series of chin-ups — the bar, too, seems to have a resilience beyond the ordinary — he does more intricate balletic maneuvers, employing his hands as if they were feet, his feet as if hands. We cannot, again, restrain ourself from applauding, and he seems less self-conscious, less ambivalent, in this mode than before.

But lest we embarrass or intimidate or compromise him with our gaze, we let our eyes wander to the other members of the troupe. Our daughter's boyfriend is now vigorously lathering her hair. How attractive she is without makeup. If only the world could glimpse her freshness: to see the sweet serenity behind the harsher mask. By the same token, our son, for the first time since adolescence, appears not to be slouching.

We have fallen into paradise through the most mundane of circumstances. How lovely to think of the effortless transformations! We cannot wait to view our own, which surely, by osmosis, must occur. With a facecloth from the linen closet we wipe the mirror of steam, quickly, before it has a chance to form again. We will smile at the image of ourself, with lips like those we see on these exalted faces, lips resembling ripest summer fruit. How wondrous is the world and its discoveries!

But the mouth that looks back at us from the defogged reflective surface is, on the contrary, brittle, and the nostrils above thin and severe. We whimper to see the wrinkles, even more numerous than we imagined, the deeply furrowed brow, and the puffiness of the lids that can only partially mask the icy candor of our once quite striking blue eyes.

Breezing

John Hawkes

STREAKS OF LIGHT, the first pearly ribbons on the horizon. The dawn air that smelled only of the night. The path that sloped away from the stable, the near rails, the tall oak that was a landmark midway between stable area and track. High atop me, Mary was as weightless as her saddle, and yet, as I had heard her say many a time, from the waist down her body belonged to me, and so it did and so I felt as I jigged and jogged toward the great dark oval of the waiting track. Comfort, then. Security. Anticipation. But what did I do as soon as I had carried Mary through the opening in the rails and onto that dark earth intended only for the hooves of Thoroughbreds? I stopped! Stopped short! Balked and braced my legs, raised my head, tried to see around the curving track, tried to see the very space of distance. I was afraid of that space, I felt an uncanny breeze lifting my mane, on my skin I felt the aura of Elroy Park which, empty or nearly so, was nonetheless filled with the sounds and shadows of former races.

I heard them, those phantom horses of races already won or lost. Around the invisible turn, down the far side, endlessly — for that single moment — they bunched together in the triumph of forgotten races that would never end. Wreaths and burials, silver cups, the silent cheering of crowds long since dispersed or dead — indeed I shivered at this conjuring of past rituals in which all racehorses share. Then I shook my head, felt Mary's hand against my neck and the shifting of her slight weight as she leaned forward so as to pat my neck, and I was myself once more and turned and started off at a joyous trot as Mary bid me.

But suddenly a blackened shape ahead proved to be a horse and rider, and for me there could not have been a greater or more unwanted intrusion. What business had they in a world I had thought to be solely mine? We drew abreast of them, I saw that the horse was old, unkempt, an unblooded beast content to rest beside the rail — for what purpose I had yet reluctantly to learn — and that his rider was a long-legged man slouching in a western saddle.

401

"Morning, little Mary," he said as we approached.

"Morning, JD."

"How's Orville?" he said.

"Mean as ever," she said.

"How's that horse of yours?" he said as we began to pass.

"He has heart, JD, that's for sure," she called over her shoulder while I, repeating to myself what I had heard, gave the old horse and his slovenly unshaven rider my briefest and most condescending glance, already rounding my back and cantering, feeling Mary standing upright in the stirrups and laughing, holding me in, guiding me around the treachery of hidden potholes and a long darker stretch of earth where only yesterday a black horse named Beacon Rock had fallen.

We swung wide on a banked turn, Mary shortened the reins, and leaning forward and in her sweet whispering voice, told me to slow down, to pace myself, that Orville wouldn't like it if we went too fast. Her warm calves were against my withers and she had bent her upper body so that her round face was closer to my outstretched neck. It was morning, now, clear light and the air of the new day were mine. Again our speed was quickening, my breath was deep, far ahead Orville was only a small black figure where he leaned at the rail and watched us through binoculars. I aimed for him, picked up my rhythm, hardly aware of Mary tightening her hold on my mouth. Oh but I was aware of what she had said to the man she called JD. And I knew that a horse with heart was one of those rare horses who wants to run, loves to run, will run no matter what the pain of the effort and — fatigue or no fatigue, shortness of breath, whatever — will always run still faster at precisely the moment his rider asks him to. And run until he drops. As for me, never in my presence had Mary referred to me as a horse with heart. Until now I would have said that no horse could have thought more highly of himself, could have been more vain, more confident than the long-legged misanthropic two-year-old that I was. Now heart as well! I too had heart! Well might I have flown that day, my first on the track, and fly I did as Mary settled closer and, against her better judgment, gave me my head.

"Daddy won't like it," I heard her say again, and realized that Orville was no longer at the rail, that we had passed him, that nothing lay ahead except the empty track and the inevitability of still greater speed.

The faster I went, the lighter the four-beat sound of my gallop and the faster, it seemed to me, that I could go and did, increasing my tempo with every stride, lengthening my every stride with each escalation of my tempo. Mary was crouching now—I could feel her—and had pulled down her goggles—I had felt that movement of her arm and hand—and was working her body in time to mine and humming—yes, humming!—as if oblivious to the limpid violence of our exertions.

"Hey!" I heard the startled JD shout, "you crazy?"

But he was gone and I had not so much as caught a glimpse of him. Nor did I catch my second glimpse of Orville as once more we approached the grandstand and I thought of him, looked for him where only seconds earlier he had stood at the rail, but saw that he was gone. And no sooner had that shadow of misgiving darted across the clarity of my growing speed than the joy of my impetuosity was dashed at its very height. Mere emptiness. The slightest possible sensation of nothing at all. One moment I was running at the peak of my self-absorption, the next I was thrown entirely off course, my greatest pleasure displaced by nothing less than panic. A flapping rein, a flying stirrup, and on my back that dreadful emptiness. Mary, it came to me! Gone! Like Orville, plucked from my back as he had been plucked from my sight. I heard nothing— no gasp, no cry, no sound of her body landing on that fast track— and what I felt was not much more than nothing. Yet it was undeniable—Mary had disappeared and I was riderless.

I tried to think, could not. I tried to slow my speed, could not. What worse than the absence of her guiding hands? Small hands that had, through reins and bit, touched my mouth with so delicate a power that the reins might have been attached to my bit by butterflies. Those hands were gone. The balance of her body bobbing atop me horizontally from yellow head to tiny rump like a bee on a pear, her slight balance that was analogous to mine—this too was gone. And I was without control, beyond control, potential victim of my worst and greatest speed. Fall I might! Trip over my own hooves! Break a leg! Suffer who could tell what painful or even fatal accident! I swerved, my eyes rolled wildly in my frantic head, my ears were flat. How stop? How escape myself? And still as fresh as when I had started off!

Then came the voice.

"Whoa there, Big Babe!"

But where had this JD come from—for it was he, of course—and how had his aged mount managed a speed the equivalent of mine?

How was this heavy-set unwashed man able to speak to me as if from across a brook in an immense field in the quiet of a summer's day — softly, casually — when in fact we were traveling side by side at breakneck speed down the empty track? I could not account for JD's presence or manner or the way he spoke, but still I was a faster horse than his — I had to be! — and in a mere three strides could easily leave my improbable pursuer far behind. Now, I told myself, and felt myself easing into my next higher gear.

"Easy," he said. "Steady. Nothing's going to hurt you, Babe. . . ."

I heard him, hesitated, shot him a glance — and an uncertain suspicious glance it was. What proud young horse wants to hear the truth about himself? What creature of elegance wants to find his well-being in the hands of an obviously untutored man rocking deep in a battered western saddle on a pathetic old beast that stank, even at our speed and in the clear dawn air, of his own dung? On the other hand, what was I if not a fearful young Thoroughbred running away, as JD had made me see? If he had spoken contemptuously, if he had yanked on my rein, if he had cursed or yelled, then never would I have allowed myself to listen, to believe him and, this once at any rate, give in to common sense and obedience. But so I did, realizing that I could not have broken away from JD's hold on my rein had I wanted to. Later I heard strange stories about him — that he had once been a trainer and a prosperous one, that he had been known to calm horses given up as intractable by putting his mouth to one of their nostrils and breathing directly into their lungs. I wanted no man or woman either breathing into my lungs, but for now I submitted to JD and, with sudden relief, slowed at last to a walk.

So he led me quietly back to Orville and Mary.

Orville took my reins from JD, saying nothing.

JD, for whom this incident was a daily occurrence and hence a commonplace, looked from the silent Orville to his silent daughter, thought better of speaking and swung his horse, returned at a heavy trot to his post on the track.

Orville held me, Mary undid my girth. Her left side, from shoulder to hip to ankle, was streaked and smeared with fresh dirt.

"Daddy," she said, and glanced at him.

She took the reins from Orville, removed my bridle, saddle, slipped the halter into place and buckled it. I tried to stand quietly for her, but could not.

"Daddy," said Mary, "I'm sorry."

She led me onto the concrete slab, turned on the hose, filled the bucket, picked up a sponge.

"I shouldn't have let him go that way," she said, soaping me down, working as quickly as she could. I was still trembling. "You told me to hold him in. But it wasn't my fault I went off," she said and paused, glanced up at him, went back to work. "I never knew a stirrup bar to just rip away like that." She darted under my neck, sloshing the bucket. "It would take something like that to get me off. You know it's true, Daddy."

I shifted, kicked out harmlessly, swung my head and stared at the silent Orville. He was standing behind me and to the side, white-faced, hands in pockets, soiled white shirt open at his throat. I recognized the mood as well as did Mary—he was containing himself. There was a distant shout, a nearby guffaw, a sudden curse. The sound of a truck, the sound of hooves, somewhere the high-pitched voices of two female riders. But Orville heard nothing, saw nothing, concentrating, as both Mary and I well knew, on his displeasure.

"This horse," he said at last, "is dangerous."

"Oh Daddy," Mary interrupted in surprise, "he's not as bad as all that!"

"Dangerous," Orville repeated. "He's going to hurt someone or worse. He's going to cause us trouble and bring us disgrace. I know his kind. Mean. Mean as they come. None better, none worse. That's why I like him. But I won't put up with him, understand? I can see what you can't. He needs to be ridden. He needs a smart race rider and a strong hand. If you can't ride him, I'll put somebody up who can."

"I can ride him," Mary said.

Orville raised his eyes, turned his head, forced Mary to look away.

"I doubt it," he said. Then, "Next time, watch what you're doing."

With that he left us, striding off toward the track in all the pride and anger only a small ex-rider knows.

"Willy," Mary said, skimming the water from my tight and tingling body with the sweat scraper, "my Daddy's a hard man. He surely is."

But I was not listening. After all, it was my first morning on the track and father and daughter had each flattered me in his or her own way, and both were right though Orville's judgment of me was the less expected, the more pleasing. And I had betrayed Mary despite myself, and experienced JD's protection, and had taken my place in Orville's remembred string of savage stallions, though I had not yet displayed my savagery. To be loved, to be hated, such was my lot.

Beware of the dog, as the sign says. *Beware of the horse.*

A sound. A smell. The merest trace of sound, the faintest smell. Hardly detectable by any ordinary horse, to me unbearable. And which was the greater assault on my senses, the sound or smell? It was impossible to say, just as, try as I might, I could not identify their source. Familiar, yet unfamiliar. Minor irritation but as intense as pain.

It was morning again, another morning. And on the track and under Mary I had behaved myself. Nothing had changed, the stable was as clamorous as ever, on the early hour air the smells of our world — of hay, iron, leather, wood, oil — were as profuse as always, that wafting enough to mask, as one would think, the offending irritants. But not for me. On the contrary, freshly returned to my box stall as I was, I stood in my own impenetrable silence aware of nothing except the two new enemies to my peace of mind.

A sound. A smell.

They were reaching me from the presently empty stall adjacent to mine which, for most hours of the day and night, confined the only other Angermeyer horse I could tolerate, a speedy little gray named London Bobby and known, of course, as Bob. Now Bob was breezing on the track that I had just departed and his stall was empty, or should have been. Ordinarily I would have smelled his cooling-blanket folded on the stall door, the friendly scent of his droppings in the wet straw still to be removed. Yet now these odors were as nothing, pierced as I was and unaccountably by I knew not what — that sound, that smell.

I cringed, I thought that if I could identify these sensory assailants I might find relief. I pressed myself to the planking farthest from that thin wall separating Bob's space from mine, yet unavoidably swung my head and neck precisely toward that partitioning through which I heard the sound and smelled the smell. Both were reaching their crescendo, and none too soon. I cowered, readied for attack. Then just as I thought I could stand no more it came to me, an explanation of sorts, for hadn't Bob himself and hadn't I made sounds and smells like these, only monumental, magnificent, forthright, strong and sweet to the nose and ear, admirable attestations to the naturalness of equine life? Similar, yes, but hardly comparable, this sound that was furtive, this smell that was poisonous, for the horse that passes water is majestic while what I smelled and heard was from a source puny at best. But there I had it, passing water, and did this sudden knowledge — that in what should have been the sanctity of Bob's stall some creature who was not a horse was befouling my poor friend's space — provide me with the relief I sought? Not at all, and now a rising rage swept through my pain. There in Bob's stall was no stray cat, no slinking dog. What then?

Exactly. Some man was passing water in London Bobby's stall and I, not Bob, was his victim, though soon enough poor Bob would get a whiff of that lingering violation. Yes a man, I thought, as the sound subsided to a trickling and mere rustling of denim, and the smell grew in rancidness; but more than that a man, I began to suspect, who was no ordinary man but one of the worst of them, as in the next moment proved the case.

A clumsy footfall, a heavy breath, a brutish sigh. Not a shred of doubt remained. Then I saw him.

Hoffman, as I should have known. None other. Having left London Bobby's stall as stealthily as possible, here he stood noisily readjusting himself in front of mine. He was short and squat, fat, obnoxious, an owner-trainer, so-called, of half a dozen horses poorly tended on the other side of the stable. In fact he spent more time with Orville and the Angermeyer horses than with his own, though Orville all but refused to speak to the obsequious Hoffman who, in turn, smothered Orville's reticence in torrents of nearly incomprehensible expressions of friendship. No one working at Elroy Park had a reputation as bad as Hoffman's for dishonesty, poor sportsmanship, unreliability. His secret, which I had discovered early, was that he was afraid of horses and thus hated them, myself in particular. But worst of all, it was because of Mary that Hoffman attempted to ingratiate himself with Orville.

"Hey!" he said now in a deep and watery whisper and glanced to the left, the right, and again at me where I pressed myself to the rear of my box stall. The smell had not faded, Hoffman was still fumbling at his pants.

"You!" he whispered. "Long-legs! Troublemaker! Come over here, I give you a smack!"

I loathed him for his taunting, I loathed him more for what he had just done in my companion's stall. But I waited, watching him, judging the distance. He had tricked me before and had escaped me, laughed at me, and now I did not want to lunge at him again and miss.

"Coward," he whispered, "I get you yet!"

He put one of his fat white hands on my stall door and gave it a shake. But he was on his guard, quivering, wary. I waited.

"Dumbo," he whispered, "you just give that girl a hard time. That pretty girl!"

I jumped then, I grazed him, he leapt away with a little shriek and cowered, from a safe distance stood looking at me from under his upraised arm.

"Bluffer! Bluffer!"

But he turned, glad enough to be freed of another encounter with Mary's favorite horse, and waddled off. At that moment, in the midst of blind frustration, suddenly I was overcome with a sudden and welcome urge and spread my hind legs, braced my haunches, lowered my flesh and, with a gush, a roar, emptied my bladder in a sweet and acrid stream that felt as if it would never end. Steam rose, my pool spread, contentment was mine. Yet try as I did I was not able to obliterate Hoffman's noxious smell.

Inevitably there came that dawn when, returning from a vigorous and uneventful workout, proud of myself for having listened to Mary's hand and voice, and basking in recollection of my hard-won obedience and hence blowing hard, bulging my muscles, perking my ears, listening to Mary's praise, suddenly I stopped dead in my tracks and sniffed.

Hoffman!

In drastically altered mood I bore the usual procedure which, ordinarily, soothed me until I quite forgot myself and time. Mary removing my tack, the silent Orville assisting her. The hose, the soap, the towels. Oil. Cotton swabs. The delight of the classically formed young horse being cared for. But not now. Now I could do no more than grudgingly accept their ministrations.

"What's wrong with him?" asked Orville.

"Don't know, Daddy," Mary answered.

Hoffman! But where?

They finished, my mood was dark.

"In you go," said Orville, leading me to my freshly mucked-out stall and stepping aside, turning, expecting me to follow.

Balk? Indeed I balked. One sniff was enough, the fight that ensued was like nothing in Orville's long experience, as senselessly —

408

to him—I pulled, reared, yanked Orville nearly off his feet, then bucked, swerved, set in motion a sympathetic staccato agitation in all the horses up and down our side of the barn.

Yes, that morning Hoffman had passed his water not in London Bobby's stall but mine. And he was to do so repeatedly, as now I knew, but erratically, whenever he could, so that I was forever anticipating his contamination yet could never be sure when it would confront me, that fuming I could hardly breathe. Thus he had intuited a further way to undermine my spirit. And the final injustice: it was Hoffman himself who owned the only two-year-old filly at Elroy Park to have caught and held the attention of my maleness. She was large and white, as tall as myself but heavier. She was aptly named Etruscan Glory and just as aptly known by everyone as Honey. I could not help myself, I could not resist Honey's frank announcement of her gender in her size, her proportions, the way she carried herself, the look in her eye, the strong and ancient mustiness of her perfume—Honey the big bland milky female, I the tall sleek lively male. She knew my feelings, she returned them. And this was not at all the romantic mystery I had shared so long ago with that other filly whose name I had in fact forgotten. This was the lust that was only mine in maturity. But ignominiously enough, she was Hoffman's horse.

Had it not been for his filthy habit and choice of stall I might have been spared. However, Hoffman was crafty, Hoffman was clever. One man pissing in a horse's stall—mine!—and for that I was doomed.

Exactly. A curious warping of an old tale. A twisting of tragedy. Even now, from the vantage of old age, from the distance of my more than twenty years of misery, still I am more sharply honed than ever to the sound of Hoffman's squealing rage and the sight of him rushing onto the track, fat as he was.

It was bound to come, that morning, how could it not? Bound to happen. My star was well on its way to sizzling extinction in a dark sea, the horse gods were calling unanimously for my ruin. Hoffman was their instrument, Honey their lure. Naturally there would come the morning when she and I would be out on the track at the same time, and alone, and our riders friendly toward each other and unsuspecting.

Exactly.

Mary and I were earlier than usual, and were the only horse and exerciser on the track, except for our guardian JD and except, all unexpectedly, for Honey and the boy who always rode her, Bud.

Mary greeted JD — a few words, a gesture — then slowly we approached young Bud on Hoffman's filly. Surprise, coincidence, good fortune, or so I thought. I had never been in such proximity to Honey, had never had the chance to be absorbed by the sight of her, the smell. This close she was larger and whiter and, despite her youth, more matronly of purpose than I had remembered, and when she gave me the briefest glance and nickered, I was beside myself and nearly broke stride, lost my footing.

"How's things?" said Bud, a boy of a mere thirteen years who was nonetheless already renowned for his riding at Elroy Park.

"Can't complain, Bud," said Mary.

"Dating?" said Bud, staring off down the track, studying his horse. He was a head shorter than Mary and much younger than she, much lighter — he weighed no more than seventy pounds or so — and was wizened, serious, the opposite of Mary in every way, gloomy boy to her cheery girl, yet more the dried-out man than boy. His hands were immense.

"Oh Bud," said Mary, "you know I never go out with anyone!"

"Too bad," said Bud.

On they talked, that unsuspecting pair, and on we loped, Honey and I, and despite the naturalness of our appearance we were shocked, and equally so, at the ease with which we recognized the inevitable. How sudden was our mutual willingness to disregard race track protocol, horse etiquette, common sense, and all for the sake of the moment which — how well we knew it! — was but a breath away. Honey's eyes were large, lit to a liquid amber by all her body's declaration, and her nostrils were enlarged, flaring, red-streaked, glistening. She spoke to me, I answered, I smelled her syrupy secretions. Pheromones, genetic beckonings, never had two horses succumbed to each other so swiftly, with so few preliminaries.

"Let's go," I heard Bud say through my distraction.

"Right on," came Mary's echo.

They meant to change pace, to pick up speed, to run. Honey and I exchanged fleeting looks of apprehension, and it was now, we knew, or not at all. Now! The unthinkable!

She broke, I broke, I turned broadside to Honey and the startled Bud and stopped short, whirled, bucked as I had not bucked before. Up went Mary, down, just as Bud shot over Honey's head and, like some wounded bat struck the turf, sprawled flat on his face. Commotion, whinnying, a tangle of dark legs and white. Catastrophe, imminent success! Once we had rid ourselves of our riders — despite their skills they were no match for the heat of the horse — there was no stopping us. Before Bud and Mary could so much as pick themselves up, Honey and I assumed our positions, went with not one false step to our purpose. Gloriously she braced herself, bravely I rose.

There were cries in the air, the sound of running feet.

"Stop!" someone shouted. "Catch them!" yelled another, though Honey and I were joined as though forever in one throbbing sculpture and were going nowhere. Then, finally, the voice I had all unknowingly awaited.

"Get off!" it squealed. "Leave her alone, Fokker! You Fokker!"

Too late, Hoffman. The deed was done.

NOTES ON CONTRIBUTORS

CHINUA ACHEBE is the author of *Things Fall Apart, No Longer At Ease, Arrow of God, A Man of the People, Anthills of the Savannah* and other novels, as well as short stories, essays, poems and children's books. Born in Nigeria in 1930, he is the recipient of the Nigerian National Merit Award and numerous other honors. He currently teaches at Bard College.

KATHY ACKER's books include *Empire of the Senseless, Great Expectations, Blood and Guts in High School* and *Don Quixote*. The passage published in this issue is the opening from her forthcoming novel, *My Mother*.

ROBERT ANTONI's first novel, *Divina Trace* — from which the chapter published here is excerpted — is due out shortly with Overlook Press.

RAE ARMANTROUT's new book, *Necromance*, was published in 1991 by Sun & Moon. She teaches writing at the University of California at San Diego.

MARTINE BELLEN's *Places People Dare Not Enter* was just published by Potes & Poets Press.

CHARLES BERNSTEIN's essay in this issue is adapted from the preface to *A Poetics*, due this spring from Harvard University Press. His most recent book is *Rough Trades* (Sun & Moon).

MEI-MEI BERSSENBRUGGE's *Empathy* was recently published by Station Hill.

MARY CAPONEGRO's first book, *The Star Café and Other Stories*, has just been issued in paperback by Norton. Winner of the 1991 Rome Prize for Literature, she is now at work on her second collection of stories.

PETER COLE's first book of poems, *Rift*, is out with Station Hill. Samuel Hanagid was the first of the major poets of the Hebrew Golden Age in Spain. He was the leader, or Nagid, of Spanish Jewry, and served as Chief Vizier and Head of the Army in the Moslem kingdom of Granada.

The author of *Gerald's Party, The Public Burning, Origin of the Brunists* and many other works of fiction, ROBERT COOVER has a recent novel, *Pinnochio in Venice*, out from Simon & Schuster.

Publication of ERIC DARTON's "Radio Tiranë" marks the first appearance of his fiction in print. He lives in New York.

LYDIA DAVIS is finishing work on a book of stories, *Almost No Memory*, and a novel, tentatively titled *Stefan*.

LYNN DAVIS's photographs have recently been exhibited at Hirschl & Adler Modern (*Egypt: The Old Kingdom*). She has three shows currently on display — *Ice*, at Centro Cultural Arte Contemporaneo, Mexico City, *Ice & Geysers*, at Pence Gallery, Los Angeles, and *Egypt*, at La Citta, Verona, Italy.

BARBARA EINZIG has just finished a book of fictions, entitled *Secrets*. She's recently moved to New York.

JANICE GALLOWAY's collection, *Blood and Other Stories*, will soon appear from Random House. A Scottish writer, this is her first appearance in print in America.

ALBERT GOLDMAN's biography *Ladies and Gentlemen — LENNY BRUCE!!* will be reissued by Penguin in January. An anthology of his pop music journalism will be published this spring by Turtle Bay. He is at work on a book about Jim Morrison.

JUAN GOYTISOLO is the author of many novels, including the trilogy *Marks of Identity, Count Julian* and *Juan the Landless*. Several of his titles, including *Landscapes After the Battle*, are available from Serpent's Tail.

BARBARA GUEST's forthcoming book is *Defensive Rapture*, due early next year with Sun & Moon.

"Breezing" is excerpted from JOHN HAWKES's novel-in-progress, *Old Horse, Old Rider*, an account of the life of a broken-down former race horse named Sweet William, who tells his own story in the first person.

ROBERT KELLY's newest collection, *A Strange Market*, will be out in spring from Black Sparrow.

ANN LAUTERBACH's new book, *Clamor*, is just out with Viking. "Tangled Reliquary" is from an unfinished long poem, *Of Course*.

CARLA LEMOS has also had work published in Five Fingers Review. Her poems here are part of a work about the island of Thera, Greece.

MICHAEL McCLURE recently contributed the text to Francesco Clemente's *Testa Coda* (Rizzoli).

JACKSON MAC LOW's *Twenties* came out in August from Roof Books. *Pieces o' Six*, a book of poems and prose, is forthcoming from Sun & Moon.

DIANA MICHENER's short film, *Cecilia*, was shown in the New York Film Festival, 1981. Her photographs have been exhibited at Susan Caldwell Gallery and elsewhere.

BRADFORD MORROW's novel *The Almanac Branch* was published this year by Simon & Schuster, and will come out in paperback, Fall 1992, with Norton. *The New Gothic*, co-edited with Patrick McGrath, is just out from Random House.

DONALD REVELL's recent collection is *New Dark Ages*, published by Wesleyan. Due in 1992 from the same press is *Erasures*.

Under a Single Moon includes ARMAND SCHWERNER's poetry and an essay on poetics and Buddhism. It is due out from Shambala Press later this Winter.

AARON SHURIN's new book, *Into Distances*, will be appearing with Sun & Moon in 1992. He is associate director of The Poetry Center at San Francisco State University.

CHARLIE SMITH is the author of *Shine Hawk*, *Lives of the Dead* and other works. His most recent book, *Crystal River* (Linden Press), collects three novellas.

JOSEPH SULLIVAN lives in San Francisco. This is his first appearance in print.

NATHANIEL TARN's most recent book, *Views from the Weaving Mountain: Selected Essays in Poetics and Anthropology*, has just been published by the University of New Mexico Press. *Seeing America First* is out with Coffee House Press.

WILLIAM T. VOLLMANN's *Whores for Gloria* is forthcoming from Pantheon. Next year, Viking will publish his novel *Fathers and Crows*. He has just completed work on *The Rifles*, the next installment in his *Seven Dreams* saga.

KEITH WALDROP's selected poems, *The Opposite of Letting the Mind Wander*, is available from Lost Roads, his shorter prose pieces, *Hegel's Family*, from Station Hill.

DAVID FOSTER WALLACE's *Signifying Rappers* is available from Ecco Press.

PAUL WEST's *The Women of Whitechapel* was published earlier this year by Random House. A second volume of selected essays, *Sheer Fiction II*, is out from McPherson & Co. His new novel, *A Sleep and a Forgetting*, will be published by Random House next Fall.

DIANE WILLIAMS's second book, *Some Sexual Success Stories Plus Other Stories in Which God Might Choose to Appear*, has just come out from Grove Press.

C.D. WRIGHT's *Just Whistle*, excerpted here, will appear in its entirety in 1992 from Kelsey Street Press. Her most recent collection, *String Light*, is from University of Georgia Press.

RUDOLPH WURLITZER's most recent novel is *Slow Fade* (Knopf). He is at work on a new novel, and is slated to direct his film — *City Limits* — this spring.

FIRST CLASS

PAUL ABLEMAN
GIANFRANCO BARUCHELLO
STAN BRAKHAGE
GERALD BURNS
MARY BUTTS
FREDERICK TED CASTLE
EDWARD DAHLBERG
MAYA DEREN
G.V.DESANI
CLAYTON ESHLEMAN
JAIMY GORDON
ROBERT KELLY
JASCHA KESSLER
VALERY LARBAUD
THOMAS McEVILLEY
GIORGIO MANGANELLI
HENRY MARTIN
URSULE MOLINARO
ANNA MARIA ORTESE
ASCHER/STRAUS
CAROLEE SCHNEEMANN
PAUL WEST
PAMELA ZOLINE

McPherson & Company

Publishers since 1974

For a free catalogue of books, including those from Tanam Press, Raymond Saroff, and *Fiction International*, write: McPherson & Company, POB 1126, Kingston, New York 12401, or telephone 914/331-5807.

STORYQUARTERLY 28

Single Issue $4/4 Issues $12
P.O. Box 1416, Northbrook, IL 60065

Milton Avery Graduate School of the Arts

BARD COLLEGE

ANNANDALE-ON-HUDSON, NEW YORK 12504 (914) 758-7481 EXT. 483

MASTER OF FINE ARTS

MUSIC • FILM/VIDEO • WRITING • PHOTOGRAPHY • SCULPTURE • PAINTING

Our unusual interdisciplinary approach to work in the arts has changed the nature of graduate education:

• Direct personal one-to-one conferences with artists in your field are the basic means of instruction—no impersonal classes.

• Response and interaction of students and faculty in all the arts.

• Residence requirements can be fulfilled during the summer.

• Our intensive sessions lead in three summers to the degree of Master of Fine Arts.

SUMMER 1992 JUNE 22-AUGUST 15

Faculty: Peggy Ahwesh, Perry Bard, Christine Berl, Alan Cote, Lydia Davis, Jean Feinberg, Arthur Gibbons, Regina Granne, Ken Irby, Robert Kelly, Ann Lauterbach, Nicholas Maw, Adolfas Mekas, Tom McDonough, Stephen Shore, Anne Turyn, Stephen Westfall, Philemona Williamson

Recent Participating Artists: Vito Acconci, Mac Adams, Steven Albert, Gregory Amenoff, John Ashbery, Tina Barney, Zeke Berman, Maureen Connor, John Corigliano, Petah Coyne, Susan Crile, John Divola, Larry Fink, Tom Gunning, Gerry Haggerty, Jane Hammond, Ken Jacobs, Tania Leon, Brad Morrow, Tod Papageorge, Yvonne Rainer, Archie Rand, Steven Reich, Mia Roosen, Michael Snow, Arthur Sze, Joan Tower, John Walker

George Robert Minkoff, Inc.

RARE BOOKS

////▌

20th Century First Editions, Fine Press Books,
Letters, Manuscripts & Important Archival
Material Bought & Sold
Catalogues issued

Rowe Road, RFD, Box 147
Great Barrington, MA 02130
[413] 528 - 4575

burning deck books

TOM MANDEL: Realism
As with photo-realism in painting, these texts in prose
and verse only look like a return to representation... "The
poetry bursts with an infectious desire... relentless excursions into the domain of discovery"—Harry Mathews.
80 pages, offset, smyth-sewn, paper $8, signed paper $15

STEPHEN RODEFER: Passing Duration
Prose poems that jolt us out of habit and into play.
"Crammed full of the baggage of everyday life, a future
archaeologist's dream...startling and original, the veritable thing." —*Times Literary Supplement*.
64 pages, offset, smyth-sewn, paper $8, signed paper $15

**BARBARA GUEST: The Countess from Min-
neapolis**
The Mississippi in verse and prose. "And quite a trip...
[the poems] move more expansively, allowing the broad-
est field for her most visual logic" —*Poetry Project
Newsletter. By the author of Fair Realism* (Lawrence
Lipton Prize 1990) and *Herself Defined: The Poet H.D.
and Her World.*
52 pages, 2nd edition, offset, smyth-sewn, paper $8

FORREST GANDER: Eggplants and Lotus Root
Three thematic strands—'Geometric Losses,' 'Violence's
Narrative'and 'Meditative'—move horizontally across the
poem. A three-dimensional space for desire and loss, for
landscape, Southern, and a language of elision.
36 pages, letterpress, 2 colors, saddlestitched, wrappers, $5

JULIE KALENDEK: The Fundamental Difference
A first collection. "The fundamental difference is now
thought to be carnal/and resistance is a question of align-
ment."
40 pages, letterpress, 2 colors, saddlestitched, wrappers, $5

Burning Deck has received grants from the National Endow-
ment for the Arts, the Rhode Island State Council on the Arts,
the Fund for Poetry and the Taft Subvention Committee.

71 Elmgrove Ave. #1 C
Providence, RI 02906